# THE INSTITUTE OF EDUCATION 1902–2002

# THE INSTITUTE OF EDUCATION
## 1902–2002 A centenary history

Richard Aldrich

INSTITUTE OF
EDUCATION
UNIVERSITY OF LONDON

First published in 2002 by the Institute of Education,
University of London, 20 Bedford Way, London WC1H 0AL

**100 years of excellence in education**

ISBN 0 85473 635 2

Design by Tim McPhee
Typeset by Cambridge Photosetting Services, Cambridge
Production Services by Book Production Consultants plc, Cambridge

Printed by in the United Kingdom by Henry Ling Limited, at the
Dorset Press, Dorchester, DT1 1HD

# Contents

# Acknowledgements

Many people, too numerous to name individually, have contributed to this book; I thank them all most sincerely. Former members of the Institute of Education from around the globe graciously responded to my requests for information and materials. Informal discussions took place with many current members of staff, and with former staff and students at alumni and other gatherings organized by Rajee Rajagopalan. Formal interviews were recorded with Claudia and Anna Clarke, Eric Earle, Iris Forrester, Denis Lawton, Peter Mortimore, Peter Newsam, William Taylor, David Warren and Geoff Whitty.

I owe a particular debt to Jennifer Haynes, the Institute's archivist for the greater part of the period of research and writing, and to Stephen Pickles and his colleagues in the Institute Library. Archives and library staff at the British Library; Central Saint Martins College of Art and Design; Columbia University, New York; London Metropolitan Archives; London School of Economics; North London Collegiate School; Public Record Office; Royal Holloway, University of London; University of Leeds; University of London; and the University of Nottingham were also unfailingly helpful. In addition, Claudia Clarke most kindly granted me unlimited access to the papers of her late father currently in her care.

David Crook, Dennis Dean, Bill Dodd, Eric Earle, Peter Gordon, Peter Gosden, Norman Graves, Denis Lawton, Peter Mortimore, Clive Whitehead, Geoff Whitty and Susan Williams commented upon earlier drafts. Christopher Purday and Robert Lawrence provided valuable assistance with the illustrations; Judy Morrison with the bibliography. Deborah Spring, Brigid Hamilton-Jones and their colleagues in the Institute's Publications Department and Sue Gray and her team at Book Production Consultants PLC saw the book into print.

My chief debt, however, as always, is to Averil Aldrich who has been fully involved at every stage in the research and writing of this book.

Richard Aldrich
Institute of Education
December 2001

# Abbreviations

| | | | |
|---|---|---|---|
| AIMS | Academic Information Management System | EEC | European Economic Community |
| ATO | Area Training Organization | EFL | English as a Foreign Language |
| AUT | Association of University Teachers | EMU | Education Management Unit |
| | | EPC | Education Policies Centre |
| BERA | British Educational Research Association | EPSEN | Educational Psychology and Special Needs |
| CAB | Central Academic Board | ESOL | English for Speakers of Other Languages |
| CATE | Council for the Accreditation of Teacher Education | ESRC | Economic and Social Research Council |
| CDEP | Child Development and Educational Psychology | EU | European Union |
| CDPE | Child Development and Primary Education | FCP | Fellow of the College of Preceptors |
| CHES | Centre for Higher Education Studies | FTE | Full-time equivalent |
| | | HEFCE | Higher Education Funding Council for England |
| CLS | Centre for Longitudinal Studies | HEI | Higher Education Institution |
| CNAA | Council for National Academic Awards | HMI | Her/His Majesty's Inspector |
| | | HMSO | Her/His Majesty's Stationery Office |
| DES | Department of Education and Science | ICRA | International Centre for Research and Assessment |
| DfEE | Department for Education and Employment | IDO | International Development Office |
| DHSS | Department of Health and Social Security | IDU | International Development Unit |
| | | IE | Institute of Education Archives |
| DICE | Department of International and Comparative Education | ILEA | Inner London Education Authority |
| EDC | Education in Developing Countries | INSET | In-service education for teachers |

| | |
|---|---|
| IQ | Intelligence quotient |
| IT | Information technology |
| ITE | Initial teacher education |
| ITT | Initial teacher training |
| LCC | London County Council |
| LDTC | London Day Training College |
| LDTCC | London Day Training College Council |
| LDTCLC | London Day Training College Local Committee |
| LEA | Local Education Authority |
| LINC | Language Information Network Co-ordination |
| LMA | London Metropolitan Archives |
| LMP | Linguistic Minorities Project |
| LSB | London School Board |
| LSE | London School of Economics |
| NALGO | National and Local Government Officers' Association |
| NFER | National Foundation for Educational Research |
| NPQH | National Professional Qualification for Headship |
| NQT | Newly-qualified teacher |
| NUPE | National Union of Public Employees |
| NUT | National Union of Teachers |
| OECD | Organization for Economic Co-operation and Development |
| Ofsted | Office for Standards in Education |
| PFUS | Primary Follow Up Survey |
| PGCE | Postgraduate Certificate in Education |
| PRC | Planning and Resources Committee |
| QAA | Quality Assurance Agency |
| QTS | Qualified teacher status |
| RAE | Research Assessment Exercise |
| RAM | Resource Allocation Model |
| SCITT | School-Centred Initial Teacher Training |
| SENCO | Special Educational Needs Co-ordinator |
| SOAS | School of Oriental and African Studies |
| SRU | Sociological Research Unit |
| SSRC | Social Science Research Council |
| SSRU | Social Science Research Unit |
| TCRU | Thomas Coram Research Unit |
| TEB | Technical Education Board |
| TTA | Teacher Training Agency |
| UCET | Universities Council for the Education of Teachers |
| UDE | University Department of Education |
| UFC | Universities' Funding Council |
| UGC | University Grants Committee |
| ULA | University of London Archives |
| ULIE | University of London Institute of Education |
| ULIESA | University of London Institute of Education Students' Association |
| Unesco | United Nations Educational, Scientific and Cultural Organization |
| UR | Unit of resource |
| UTMU | University Teaching Methods Unit |
| WEA | Workers' Educational Association |

# Chapter 1

# Foundation

## Introduction

In 1952 when the Institute celebrated its jubilee, the Director, Dr George Barker Jeffery, was greatly disappointed by his inability to commission a history of the first 50 years. Jeffery was a forceful figure, yet was advised by his 'historian colleagues' that 'the history I demanded should and would be written. But the writing of history is a slow business and cannot be hurried even at the dictates of directors.'[1] The two hardback volumes to emanate from the celebrations of 1952 were a published version of six *Jubilee Lectures*[2] and *Studies and Impressions, 1902–1952*, which comprised some 20 contributions from current and former staff and students.[3] The only history to date is *The Institute: A personal account of the history of the University of London Institute of Education, 1932–1972*, published in 1986.[4] This was written in retirement by Dr C. Willis Dixon, the Institute's former Secretary. Dixon's history is strong on administrative matters, particularly with reference to the wider Institute, the Area Training Organization (ATO) comprising some 30 colleges established in 1949.

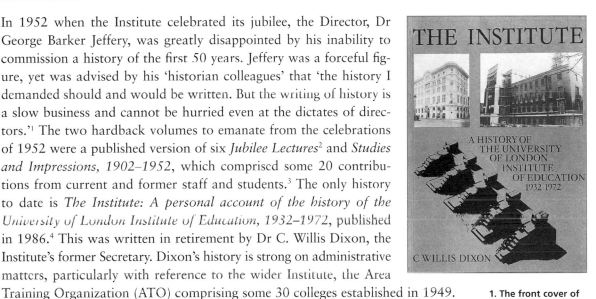

1. The front cover of Willis Dixon's history shows the first two Institute buildings and the design for the third

This volume, therefore, is the first comprehensive history of the Institute and its predecessor, the London Day Training College (LDTC). It is comprehensive in encompassing the first 100 years of the Institute's existence. On the other hand it is clearly impossible to do justice to all the work and influence of the LDTC and the Institute in a single volume. Some of its leading figures have already been the subject of major biographies.[5] Many themes, for example the Institute's role in London or its influence within the Empire and Commonwealth, are worthy of separate studies.

The book is organized chronologically into 11 chapters and demonstrates changes and continuities over time in a variety of settings. Although the basic theme is institutional, the history of the Institute is located within metropolitan, national and international contexts. Brief conclusions are drawn at the end of each chapter, while an extended conclusion to the final chapter provides some analysis of the main themes to emerge in the first century of the Institute's existence and looks forward to the next.

The history of the first 100 years of the Institute of Education falls naturally into four periods. Founded in 1902 by the London County Council in conjunction with the University of London, for the next 30 years it existed as the London Day Training College. Its original purpose was to train teachers for service in London's elementary schools, but in 1909 the LDTC's academic status was confirmed by its admission as a school of the University.[6] By 1932 the majority of students were preparing to teach in secondary schools, while a few were engaged in research for higher degrees. In that year the national and international roles of the LDTC were recognized by its transfer to the University of London. It acquired a new status as a central activity of the University and a new name – the Institute of Education. From 1949 the term Institute of Education was used to describe both the 'central' Institute and a 'wider' Institute, an Area Training Organization that included some 30 associated colleges and departments of education. In 1975 the ATO was formally brought to an end; four years later this decision was fully endorsed in a most practical way when the University of London decided to withdraw its validation of courses in the associated colleges. Thus by 1980 the Institute entered into the fourth stage of its existence, although it was not until 1987 that it received the charter of incorporation which confirmed its status as a school of the University once more.[7]

This chapter examines the foundation of the LDTC. The story begins with London, which in 1902 was widely regarded as being the greatest city in the world.

## London

The greatness of London depended upon several factors. To the west was Westminster, the name synonymous with the mother of parliaments which together with the King Emperor, Edward VII, ruled not only over the inhabitants of the British Isles but also directed the destinies of a vast empire comprising more than 13 million square miles and 300 million inhabitants: an empire upon which the sun never set. At the heart of the city of London lay the undoubted financial capital of the world, the City itself, a term reserved for the original square mile, a mere 677 acres on the north side of the River Thames.[8] To the east was the port of London, its vast network of docks providing safe anchorage and lucrative trading for the world's largest merchant fleet. In the first decade of the twentieth century, London was a dense tangled mass of pedestrians, of horse-drawn traffic, of street sweepers and street sellers, of shops, warehouses, small manufactories, pubs, music halls and theatres. Above the jostling mass of humanity, on the great railway viaducts which traversed the city, trains drawn by steam-powered locomotives daily brought thousands of commuters to and from their work, and other travellers from more distant locations.

Yet there were several dark sides to this city, its inhabitants, and to the nation and empire of which it was a capital. Major rivals, notably Germany and the USA, were challenging British supremacy, both in economic and political terms. In January 1901 its people were stunned by the death of Queen Victoria, whose reign of some 64 years had meant that there were few members of the nation, or indeed of the empire, who could remember a time when she had not ruled over them. The Boer War of 1899–1902 demonstrated the diplomatic isolation of Britain, the inefficiency of British colonial policy and of its military forces, and a regime of callousness and neglect that led to the establishment of the first concentration camps and the deaths within them of some 40,000 women and children. Equally disturbing were the callousness and neglect evident in official attitudes towards the inhabitants of London itself. Crowded together in slum conditions, eking out a desperate existence in the narrow courts and alleys which contrasted so strongly with the elegant terraces of the West End, were a breed of people who bore few of the characteristics associated with an imperial race. The first systematic surveys of child health were to reveal that considerable proportions of the capital's children were undernourished, inadequately clothed, dirty, verminous and suffering from serious physical defects.[9] The same was true for adults, indeed a very high percentage of army volunteers for the Boer War were turned down on physical grounds.

In 1891 Sidney Webb, a trenchant observer of the metropolitan scene and a man who devoted his life to the reform of London, described this dichotomy in a pamphlet entitled *The London Programme*:

By himself the typical Londoner is a frail and sickly unit, cradled in the gutter, housed in a slum, slaving in a sweater's den and dying in the workhouse infirmary. Collectively he is a member of the greatest and most magnificent city the world has known, commanding all the latest resources of civilisation and disposing of almost boundless wealth.[10]

Another observer was Charles Booth, whose *Life and Labour of the People in London* published in 17 volumes between 1889 and 1903, showed that more than 30 per cent of the population were living in real poverty and more than 8 per cent in utter poverty. Booth, a shipowner born in Liverpool in 1840, was a pioneer of the modern social survey. One of his researchers was Beatrice Potter, daughter of an industrial magnate, whose interest in the alleviation of social problems had been aroused by a range of diverse experiences, including rent collecting, friendship with the evolutionary philosopher, Herbert Spencer, and an unrequited passion for the reforming mayor of Birmingham and radical politician, Joseph Chamberlain. Another who exposed the flaws in London society and questioned the political and social foundations upon which the whole edifice of British greatness had been built was the Irish dramatist, essayist, critic and pamphleteer, George Bernard Shaw. In 1885 it was Shaw who introduced Sidney Webb, newly-graduated LLB at the University of London, to the Fabian Society, founded in the previous year to advance the cause of Socialism through the 'inevitability of gradualness'. Within a short period of time Shaw and Webb had become acknowledged leaders of the Fabian cause. Indeed, Socialism was to be defined as 'a great spider with a little Webb at its centre'.[11]

Socialism of various kinds – from municipal to international – was one of the inspirational doctrines of this period; national (and by extension municipal and imperial) efficiency was another. For it was the perception of many reformers, a perception confirmed by revelations as to the widespread poverty of the inhabitants of the empire's greatest city and by the humiliations of the Boer War, that at the beginning of a new century both the nation and the empire were still character-ized by institutions and practices that were medieval in their origins and Byzantine in their obscurantism and operation. Nineteenth-century *ad hoc* solutions to some of London's problems had led to a chaotic administrative situation, not least in respect of education. In consequence, there were at least four London-based bodies with responsibility for education which contributed to the foundation of the LDTC. These were the London School Board (LSB), the London County Council (LCC) and its Technical Education Board (TEB), the University of London, and the Board of Education.

## London School Board

The London School Board, established under the terms of the Elementary Education Act of 1870, was empowered to raise money from rates for the purpose of supplying elementary school places in areas of proven deficiency. Much was expected from the Board. Indeed, in a leading article published on the day of the first election, 29 November 1870, *The Times* declared that 'No equally powerful body will exist in England outside Parliament, if power be measured by influence for good or evil over masses of human beings'.[12] Further legislation of 1880 and 1891 rendered elementary schooling both free and compulsory for those who were not being educated by other means. Nevertheless, in spite of its eminent members – Elizabeth Garrett Anderson, Emily Davies and Thomas Huxley were among those who served on the first board under the chairmanship of no less a personage than John, first Baron Lawrence, a former Viceroy of India – the powers of the LSB were severely circumscribed. Elementary education was its remit, and attempts to supply education of a more advanced kind, as for example at the North London School of Art, led via the Cockerton Judgment of 1901 to the eventual demise of the school boards and their replacement by multi-purpose local education authorities.

One particular problem for the London School Board, as for all boards, was that it was not allowed to establish colleges for the training of teachers. Nevertheless, the Board pursued a vigorous policy of staffing its schools, wherever possible, with teachers who were both trained and certificated. Three initiatives in respect of teacher training may be noted here. The first was the establishment of 12 pupil-teacher centres; the second that for those who sought further training but were unable to proceed to a training college, in 1898 a further scheme was implemented which 'was in effect an illegal training college'.[13] W.T. Goode, head of the Department of Education at Owens College, Manchester, was appointed superintendent of the ex-pupil teachers and, after a brief sojourn in the LSB's own offices in the Embankment, a more permanent headquarters for the new courses was found at Graystoke Place School in the City. Science classes were provided at the Hugh Myddelton School and physical training at the Northampton Institute. Students taught half time in the Board's schools and for the other half of their time were prepared, over a period of two or three years, for the Acting Teacher's Certificate. Some even took a degree of the University of London. Although the Board of Education refused to recognize these teachers as having been college-trained, the London School Board did so from the beginning and in 1904 Graystoke Place became a recognized training college under the control of the London County Council. It continued until 1934, enjoying throughout that period a close relationship with the neighbouring Birkbeck College.[14] The third initiative, and the most pertinent to this story, occurred in July 1899 when the London School Board recommended to the Technical Education Board of the London County Council that a day training college should be established in conjunction with the University of London.[15]

## London County Council

The London County Council was established in 1889. In 1904, following the special London Education Act of 1903 (for London education, with its 2,000 educational institutions, more than 20,000 teachers, a million children and students and annual expenditure of £4 million, was so vast an undertaking that it had been excluded from the Education Act of 1902) it became the educational authority for the metropolis with power to establish elementary and secondary schools, adult and evening institutes and teacher training colleges.[16] Although in 1889 the new county councils were not given jurisdiction over education, they soon began to acquire permissive powers, while finance could be raised under the terms of the Technical Instruction Act of 1889 and the Local Taxation Act on liquor of 1890 (the so-called whisky money). At first the London County Council made little use of these opportunities. In 1892, however, the year of his marriage to Beatrice Potter, Sidney Webb was elected as Progressive member for Deptford and became chairman of a special committee established to investigate the possibility of a scheme for technical education for London. His supporters in this venture included Quintin Hogg, founder of the Regent Street Polytechnic, and Hubert Llewellyn Smith, secretary of the National Association for the Promotion of Technical Education.

Llewellyn Smith's 1892 report on the resources for technical education in the capital 'recommended a policy which combined a generous system of junior and senior scholarships to help elementary school pupils to go on to more advanced courses and institutions, and a programme of grants to support work in the secondary and technical schools and polytechnics'.[17] The report was accepted by the LCC, as was Webb's recommendation that a Technical Education Board should be established, consisting not only of some 20 council members, but also of 15 representatives of other interests. Webb became the TEB's first chairman, and also chaired its Higher Education Sub-Committee. Its first (and only) secretary was Dr William Garnett.[18] Outside bodies represented on the Technical Education Board included the London School Board, London Trades Council and City and Guilds of London Institute (each with three seats) and the National Union of Teachers.

## University of London

The third institution to be considered was the University of London. Its origins and development have been assiduously traced in works by Harte, Thompson and Willson.[19] There is no doubt that it was a curious animal, so much so that in 1888 Henry Wace, Principal of King's College, advised the Royal Commission on Higher Education in London chaired by Lord Selborne that he had only two objections 'to the title of the University of London: one, that it is not a University, and the other that it is not of London'.[20]

The University had developed considerably since its second foundation in 1836 as a body whose powers were limited to matriculating and examining candidates and awarding degrees. After a series of temporary locations, in 1870 it acquired purpose-built accommodation in Burlington Gardens. In 1880 the first women were admitted to degrees, and new colleges for women were established – Westfield in 1882 and Royal Holloway in 1886. The London School of Economics (LSE) was another new foundation, established in 1895 by a group which included the Webbs, with funds from the bequest of Henry Hunt Hutchinson, a Derby solicitor who had committed suicide in the previous year. Yet in spite of these developments, to the great dissatisfaction of many of its affiliated colleges in the London area, the University remained, essentially, what it had always been, an examining body. In the 1890s Richard Haldane, subsequently Viscount Haldane of Cloan, was the leading exponent of the principle that the University of London should become a teaching as well as an examining university. His chief ally in this campaign was Sidney Webb. Their alliance led not only to a reconstituted central university but also supplied the impetus for the creation of further institutions, for example the

London Day Training College in 1902, and, in 1907, by means of an amalgamation of three existing institutions, the Imperial College of Science and Technology. Haldane was also the principal force behind the London University Act of 1898 under whose terms a commission chaired by Lord Davey was established to produce statutes for a reconstituted university.

From 1900 the University of London boasted a new home in the Imperial Institute at South Kensington, an enlarged senate and, most crucially, 24 'schools' of the university located within a radius of some 30 miles. Students of these schools, henceforth designated as 'internal', as opposed to 'external' students from other parts of the nation or indeed of the world, would now be full members of a great metropolitan university. Eight faculties were established and a Board of Studies in Pedagogy set up. Its first chairman was the Revd T.W. Sharpe, Principal of Queen's College, Harley Street and a former chief inspector of schools. The Board had been established following a conference held between representatives from University, King's and Bedford Colleges and the College of Preceptors, which as early as 1878 had recommended to the University 'the institution of a distinctive educational degree'.[21] In 1934 it was renamed the Board of Studies in Education.[22] In 1890 King's College established a training department which took men students for a two-year course of training for teaching in elementary schools.[23] A similar venture begun at University College in 1891 foundered in 1894. A training department for women established in 1892 at Bedford College lasted until 1922.[24]

The reconstitution of 1900 was an essential element in the process which led to the establishment of the London Day Training College. It also helped to secure further recognition of the status of education as a field of study, for at this time there were no professors of education either at King's or at Bedford. As Garnett noted in 1901 in respect of a proposal by the TEB to make a grant of £10,000 to the University:

> it would have been impossible for the Technical Education Board to have made a grant to the London University before its re-constitution as a teaching body.... As soon as the University is responsible for the appointment of professors and for their payment out of its corporate funds ... the University will become an institution actually providing instruction.[25]

## Board of Education

The fourth body to contribute to the founding of the London Day Training College was the Board of Education, London-based, but with national responsibilities. It, too, was newly constituted, having only in 1900 assumed the powers previously exercised by the Education and Science and Art Departments and the educational responsibilities of the Charity Commissioners. Since 1833 central governments had assisted education by a series of grants made to voluntary school bodies. In 1846 a new series of grants was begun which provided assistance for the establishment of a trained and certificated teaching force. By 1890 there were 43 training colleges for teachers: all were voluntary foundations. In May of that year, following a recommendation in the Cross Commission Report of 1888, the government issued Circular 287, which set out regulations under which day training colleges might be established in conjunction with universities and university colleges. The initial intention was that these colleges should supplement existing provision and supply a two-year course for those intending to teach in elementary schools. Very soon, however, some of the new colleges began to provide residential facilities and a variety of courses. These included one-year programmes for those who already held advanced qualifications, and three-year courses (extended to four from 1911) for those who wished to study concurrently for a teaching certificate and for a degree. Though some universities looked askance at education students, with their elementary rather than secondary school connections, the guaranteed funding which they brought was most welcome. By 1902 the central authority had approved the creation of some 20 institutions, providing more than a quarter of the 5,000 students then training for teaching in England and Wales.

### Sidney Webb

Thus by 1900 all the pieces of the jigsaw by which the London Day Training College was to be constructed were at hand. It remained only for them to be put into place. Many individuals contributed to the foundation of the London Day Training College, but the prime mover was Sidney Webb, who was born in

**2. Sidney and Beatrice Webb in the 1890s**

central London, near Leicester Square, in 1859. Although fond of quoting Shelley to the effect that 'Hell is a city much like London', Webb 'to his dying day loved the place with a passion of surprising intensity'.[26] Sidney's energy and devotion to duty were legendary. Unlike Beatrice, his partner in so many enterprises, he had little time for abstract or metaphysical considerations. Shaw described him as 'a unique lump of solid ability, without any complications'.[27]

Webb's educational work has frequently been overlooked.[28] Indeed, Webb has no mention in Dixon's history, although to be fair that volume only begins in earnest in 1932, and only one mention apiece in the *Jubilee Lectures* and *Studies and Impressions*. Nevertheless, the London Day Training College was part of Webb's vision for a postgraduate university in London which would provide an intellectual pre-eminence to complement and reinforce the city's imperial, financial and commercial pre-eminence. As he wrote in an article entitled 'London University: a policy and a forecast', published in the *Nineteenth Century* in June 1902:

> The obvious and imperative duty of a rightly organised and adequately endowed London University is to become the foremost post-graduate centre of the intellectual world. ...
>
> With a highly specialised staff of university professors in each faculty, the London University would attract, not one or two here and there, but a continuous stream of the ablest and most enterprising of young graduates from the colonies and the United States, from every university of Europe and the Far East. ...
>
> But a university is, or ought to be, much more than a mere place for teaching. Its most important function in the State is the advancement of every branch of learning. ...
>
> In the whole range of the physical and biological sciences, in the newer fields of anthropology, archaeology, philology, pedagogy and experimental psychology, in the wide vistas opening out for applied science and the highest technology, in the constantly changing spheres of industrial and commercial relations, administration and political organisation, we may predict with confidence that a rightly organised and adequately endowed London University will take a foremost part in the advancement of learning.[29]

## 1900–1902

Between 1900 and 1902 events moved with considerable speed. In March 1900 the Higher Education Sub-Committee of the Technical Education Board produced a report on the training of teachers which contained four conclusions: that further provision for the training of teachers in London was urgently needed; that the TEB could legally establish or aid the training of teachers and was virtually the only public body in London able to do so; that it was essential that any new training department should be connected with a university institution in order to receive recognition from the Board of Education; that the TEB should provide a further £2,000 a year towards the new department in addition to the £10,000 a year it was already contemplating giving to the University. These recommendations were approved by the TEB. At a subsequent meeting in December 1900 it resolved that: 'The Higher Education Sub-Committee be instructed to draft a scheme for a London University Day Training College, and that the scheme, if approved by the Board, be subsequently submitted to the Senate of the University of London'.[30]

The scheme was duly drawn up and approved. It is important to note that at a time when training for elementary teaching in single-sex colleges or departments was the norm, the proposed college 'would be open to duly qualified students of either sex who were engaged in, or intended to enter, any branch of the teaching profession; or who were making a special study of the theory, history and practice of education'. At its head would be the University of London's first Professor of the Theory, History and Practice of Education, appointed by the Senate at a salary of £800 per annum, who would exercise the office of Principal under the aegis of the College's Council, a body whose members would be nominated by the Technical Education Board, Senate of the University of London, and the London School Board. The College would open in October 1902 with 100 students. A budget of £4,300 per year was envisaged, of which the Technical Education Board would grant £800 to the University for the professor's salary and £2,000 to the College Council for other teaching staff, with a further £1,000 secured from government grants and £500 from students' fees.[31] The innovatory nature of the proposals was 'warmly welcomed' by the Board of Studies in Pedagogy in a report to the University's Academic Council. In turn the Council commented favourably not only on the worth of the proposed institution but also expressed the hope that it might 'initiate a much-needed reform in the mode of training teachers, and set an example for the other Day Training Colleges to follow'.[32]

While the University's Academic Council and Senate both gave general approval to the proposals, some reservations were expressed. These centred upon such issues as the establishment of a 'local committee' to oversee the College, and whether the Professor of Education should shoulder the burden of administering the College or rather whether 'his services should also be available for the teaching of all students in pedagogy within the University sphere of influence'.[33] Financial details also caused some concern, and in November 1901 Sidney Webb was in anxious private communication with the University's Principal, the distinguished physicist, Sir Arthur Rücker, urging him that were the proposed financial arrangements not to be accepted 'You may not quickly get another chance of paying a Professor of Education'.[34]

In January 1902 Sidney Webb chaired a meeting of the Higher Education Sub-Committee of the TEB and representatives of a committee appointed by the Senate. Present on that occasion were A.A. Allen, W. Bousfield, F.W. Verney and

Graham Wallas[35] from the Higher Education Sub-Committee. The University was represented by the Vice-Chancellor, Dr Archibald Robertson, Dr Sophie Bryant, Headmistress of the North London Collegiate School, the Chairman of Convocation, Sir Edward Busk, Professor W.H.H. Hudson, and Sir Philip Magnus, the promoter of London polytechnics and technical education. Since the establishment of a 'local committee' was required by the Board of Education as a condition of aid, it was agreed that such a committee should be established as the College's governing body. Its formal appointment should be by the Technical Education Board, with between 15 and 20 members drawn from the Technical Education Board, the University Senate, the London School Board and other experts. A list of names of members of the first committee was drawn up, which included no fewer than eight of those present: Bousfield, Bryant, Busk, Hudson, Magnus, Robertson, Wallas and Webb himself.

Progress was slow, but in May 1902 Garnett sent a long letter to the Board of Education giving details of the proposed membership of the local committee and outlining general arrangements for the new college. Provision would be made for the appointment of a normal master and mistress, while the bulk of the students would be King's scholars,[36] who would spend one-third of their three-year courses in professional studies and two-thirds preparing for an internal degree of the University of London. Arrangements as to staff, curriculum and buildings were the subject of detailed scrutiny and a 'generally favourable' report from His Majesty's Inspector (HMI) Scott Coward.[37] Nevertheless, although the Technical Education Board expressed its intention ultimately to provide purpose-built accommodation, the London Day Training College was to begin life as a lodger in another of Webb's institutions, the London School of Economics. Only at a Senate meeting held on 25 June was a decision finally taken to approve the scheme for a professor of education. The Senate's continuing concerns were represented in its insistence that the professor 'should be relieved of the secretarial and other business matters which are sometimes associated with the office of Principal'; that he should be 'free to give lectures on Education in other Schools of the University'; and that he should be assisted by 'at least two persons, one of whom should be a lady who should be charged with the tutorial supervision of the students'.[38] Rücker having conveyed this decision to the Board of Education in a letter dated 26 June, on 31 July he received a formal reply from H.F. Pooley which stated 'that the Board of Education are now satisfied that the proposed Day Training College will be "attached to" the University of London within the meaning of Article 112 of the Code'.[39]

The committee established to choose a professor of education consisted of three men – Magnus, Sharpe and Webb – and three women – Sophie Bryant, Miss H. Robertson, Head of the Training Department of Bedford College and Alice Woods, Principal of the Maria Grey Training College – with the Vice-Chancellor in the chair. Appointment of staff and selection of students proceeded apace and on 6 October 1902 the London Day Training College came into existence.

## Conclusion

In 1902 the London Day Training College was established by the London County Council, through the medium of its Technical Education Board, with the support of the London School Board, and the approval of the Board of Education. These bodies were united in the cause of providing well-trained teachers for service in London's elementary schools. Some of the unique and potentially contradictory features of the LDTC that would shape its history over the next 100 years, however, were already apparent.

While all other day training colleges, including those of Bedford and King's, were established in conjunction with a university or university college, the LDTC came ultimately under the control of the LCC. Its relationship to the University of London was ambivalent, and further complicated by the University's federal nature and by the special position accorded to the LDTC's Principal, who was also the University's Professor of the Theory, History and Practice of Education. As such, his major role was to provide intellectual leadership in these fields across the entire University. This concern was consistent with Webb's vision of the reformed University, a postgraduate centre at the heart of the capital, with national, imperial and international responsibilities for the advancement of learning. Over the next 100 years the major challenge for the LDTC and its successor, the Institute of Education, would be fully to discharge both of these responsibilities – to the schools, teachers and children of London on the one hand and to the University, national and international communities on the other.

# Chapter 2

# From Clare Market to Southampton Row
## 1902–1907

### Inaugural

The inaugural meeting of the London Day Training College took place at 4 p.m. on 6 October 1902 at the University Hall of the London School of Economics. Having opened the proceedings Sir John McDougall, Chairman of the London County Council, departed for another engagement and ceded the chair to the University's Vice-Chancellor, Dr Archibald Robertson. Other speeches were made by Sidney Webb, who as Chairman of the Governors of the London School of Economics welcomed the LDTC to its first home, and Sophie Bryant, Chairman of the LDTC's Local Committee, who referred to the long campaign to secure training for secondary school teachers.

These preliminaries having been completed, the expectant audience of students, staff and guests then heard the inaugural lecture of John Adams, the University's first Professor of Education and the LDTC's first Principal. Adams took for his theme the simple title of 'The Training of Teachers'. He began from the proposition that 'The question is not now – *Shall teachers be trained?* but – *How shall teachers be trained?*' In answer to that question Adams declared that teachers should be cultured human beings, educated to graduate level along with other students rather than in isolation, and that wherever possible the professional preparation of teachers should be postgraduate. Such a system would be expensive, but 'There are two ways in which the public can pay for the training of its teachers: it can pay in money or it can pay in children'.

We cannot know which elements in Adams' address, briskly delivered in the compelling Glaswegian brogue that was to become so well known and much imitated over the next 20 years, were of most interest to his audience. The 58 students, some of whom already had considerable teaching experience, might have been most surprised by his remarks about the necessity for teachers to understand the contents of children's minds and the way in which those minds worked. 'The training of the teacher', he declared, 'consists primarily in his acquiring this

knowledge of child-nature and the materials upon which that nature works. ...
The science of education must begin and end with the child.'

Adams' most immediate concern, however, was the need for the LDTC to establish its identity:

> It must be remembered that neither the word *university* nor the word *college*
> fundamentally connotes a building; the essential meaning of each is a group
> of students and teachers. *They* are the university, *they* are the college: so that
> even while the London Day Training College has no home of its own, and
> is, as it were, living in rooms, it has a real identity, a real corporate life, a
> reputation to be made by its students and teachers and an esprit de corps to
> be cultivated by them.[1]

In spite of these brave words the want of a permanent home was to be keenly felt.
Although in the following year the LCC purchased a site in Southampton Row for
£30,000, the new building, which benefited from a 75-per-cent grant of £29,000
from the Board of Education, was not officially opened until 1907.[2] During the
intervening five years the College occupied a number of temporary homes. Classes
were first given in LSE premises at Clare Market, where Margaret Punnett's office
was also located. David Harris, the other deputy, and Adams himself had rooms
in Clement's Inn opposite the Law Courts.[3] With the admission of a further group
of students in October 1903 these arrangements proved to be insufficient both for
administration and for teaching, especially as the London School of Economics
was anxious to assume full use of its own premises.

## John Adams

The first professors of education in a British university had been appointed in
Scotland in 1876: S.S. Laurie at Edinburgh and J.M.D. Meiklejohn at St Andrews.[4]
Not surprisingly, therefore, first choice as the University of London's Professor of
Education was Henry Jones, Professor of Moral Philosophy at the University of
Glasgow. Jones was an outstanding lecturer with an abiding interest in education.
Conscious, however, of his lack of experience as a trainer of teachers, Jones
declined the invitation and recommended instead John Adams, a friend and former
fellow student. Adams was born in 1857 in Glasgow, the third son of a blacksmith
who died when Adams was 11 years old. Educated in local elementary schools,
the young John was indentured as a pupil teacher to a Mr Liddell, headmaster of
the Old Wynd School. Some indication of their relationship is provided by the fact
that Adams was to dedicate his *Exposition and Illustration in Teaching* (1909) to
his early mentor. Adams was the most assiduous of students. Placed fourth in the
Queen's Scholarship Examination for pupil teachers in the whole of Scotland, he
was first amongst the male candidates for entrance to the Glasgow Free Church

3 (Left). Passmore
Edwards Hall at the
London School of
Economics, the LDTC's
first home

Training College, a position he retained throughout his two years of training.[5] Adams also attended classes at Glasgow University, achieving prizes both on the recommendations of his teachers and (according to local custom) on those of his fellow students. He continued university studies while teaching part time at Oatlands School, where Liddell was now the master, taught at the Aberdeen Training College Demonstration School, 1879–81, and two years later completed his Glasgow degree with a first in mental and moral sciences. He was also successful in a course at the Glasgow School of Art for the Art Class Teacher's Certificate. Other studies included at least one summer at the University of Leipzig.

4. John Adams, the University of London's first Professor of Education and the LDTC's first Principal

For the next 19 years Adams moved between teacher training and school teaching in the cities of Aberdeen and Glasgow. In 1883 he was appointed lecturer, and in 1890 Rector of the Aberdeen Free Church Training College. In between these appointments he served as headmaster in Glasgow: at a large elementary establishment, Jean Street School, and a small secondary institution, Campbeltown Grammar School. In 1898 he returned to Glasgow, yet again, as Rector of the Glasgow Free Church Training College, a post which he combined with a lectureship in education at the University of Glasgow.

Though Jones was personally to recommend Adams for the London post, Adams already had some reputation outside his native Scotland. This depended in part upon his book, *The Herbartian Psychology Applied to Education*, published in 1897 during his third spell in Aberdeen. This work, as Robert Rusk observed, 'burst like a new star into the educational firmament, and everything thereafter was different'.[6] Though the name of Herbart, who had died in 1841, appeared in the title of the work, the contents of the book reflected the educational theories of Adams as much as those of Herbart himself. One maxim that was to achieve great fame was Adams' insistence that 'Verbs of teaching take two accusatives, e.g. The master taught John Latin'. In consequence it was important for teachers to know as much about John as about Latin. A second theme was that of interest. Herbart had argued that the educator should not only draw upon the existing interests of the child, but also seek to develop new interests. Adams accepted the importance of interests, but proclaimed that 'the theory of interest does not propose to banish drudgery, but only to make drudgery tolerable by giving it a meaning'.[7] One of Adams' own interests was in writing stories for boys under the pseudonym 'Skelton Kuppord', a name which typified Adams' 'pawky' humour and indicates the more relaxed side of a man whose devotion to study and duty was legendary and who produced more than 160 pieces of published academic and professional work.

An indication of Adams' growing reputation came in 1902 when he was granted leave of absence from Glasgow to accept an invitation from McGill University to inspect educational institutions in Canada. One outcome of this visit was a report, subsequently published as *The Protestant School System in the Province of Quebec*. It would appear that at this time Adams was contemplating a move from Glasgow for he was a candidate for the chair at St Andrews, recently vacated by the death of Meiklejohn. Adams was still returning from Canada when the London invitation arrived. Indeed, it is possible that Agnes Adams, fearing that the St Andrews post would have been '*enterrement de première classe*', accepted the appointment on her husband's behalf.[8] The University post having been accepted, Adams was then appointed Principal of the London Day Training College by the Local Committee. His salary at Glasgow had been £960 per annum. This sum was exceeded when the LCC made an addition of £200 for duties performed as Principal of the LDTC to the £800 that Adams was to receive as Professor of the University.[9]

Although in 1902 John Adams could not rival Henry Jones' reputation as a notable scholar and inspirational teacher who already held a chair at a distinguished university, his experience of teaching and of teacher training was considerable. By most accounts Adams was also a very successful lecturer. Such success was achieved neither by flights of oratory nor by physical presence. He was a short man with a large balding head, soberly attired and brisk in manner. His lectures were meticulously prepared, typed out by a secretary, and carefully placed on the lectern. Rusk wrote that, nevertheless:

> He proceeded as if quite independent of his manuscript. Any topic he treated was presented in the clearest terms; his illustrations were apt and introduced appropriately, witticisms were interspersed throughout, and he appeared as surprised at their occurrence as did the audience. His lectures were finished products, satisfying all the conditions of exposition and illustration which he had formulated in the work with that title.[10]

Some students, however, had other views, and it was noted that

> He made no attempt to simplify his material, which he delivered with wit and pace in a marked Scottish accent, leaving his students puzzling over individual words.... Not a few of his students found his lectures beyond them, and, indeed, questioned their relevance for the practising teacher.'[11]

To many he was a remote figure, confident and caustic. Others, particularly the postgraduate students, who came to know him better, found him kindly and un-assuming. Adams was generally known to the students as 'Uncle John'. Another nickname was 'The White Rabbit', from his habit of pattering briskly into the lecture hall, taking out his big pocket watch, unfastening it from the chain and placing it ceremoniously on the desk in front of him.[12] Such diversities of views did not simply reflect personal perceptions; they also depended upon the two offices which Adams held. As Principal of the LDTC he remained at heart a teacher, always aware of the needs of children and of schools; as the University's Professor of Education he had to overcome considerable prejudice against the subject and to demonstrate his scholarship and erudition, as in his substantial and ambitious study, *The Evolution of Educational Theory* (1912).

### Staff

Adams may be regarded as an heir to those two groups of Scotsmen who had contributed so powerfully to the development of teacher training in England and to the University of London. His principal assistants in the work of managing and teaching the LDTC, however, drew upon experience in England and Wales. In July 1902 Margaret Punnett and David Harris were appointed as mistress and master of method. Punnett, who was 34 years of age, had been educated at South Hampstead High School and the Cambridge Teachers' Training College for Women. She held a certificate from that college, a teacher's diploma from the University of London (both with distinction), together with a London degree in

5. Margaret Punnett, who served as deputy for 31 years, with John Adams (centre) and Percy Nunn

German and mathematics. Her current post was Principal of the Cambridge Training College with a salary of £300 per year together with residence.[13] Prior to her appointment to Cambridge in Easter 1899, Punnett had been a governess and lecturer at Saffron Walden Teachers' Training College.[14] Harris, aged 31, had a similarly distinguished academic and professional record, with first-class passes throughout his teacher's certificate exams at Borough Road College and a first-class degree in mental and moral sciences from St John's College, Cambridge. His previous posts were at Bangor Training College and the Training Department of the University College of Wales, Aberystwyth.[15]

Harris and Punnett each received salaries of £400 per annum. The advertisement for these posts, which attracted 125 applicants of whom four were interviewed by the full TEB, stated that the normal master and mistress[16] would 'have the personal oversight of the men and women students respectively, will give lectures on method and school management, will supervise the attendance of students at practising schools and preside at criticism and model lessons and generally act as tutors and directors'.[17] In 1905 Harris returned to Wales as Principal of Bangor, but Punnett remained in post until her retirement in 1933. Harris was succeeded by Thomas Percy Nunn, who was appointed at a salary of £500 per annum, an increase which led to protests from the Local Committee that Punnett's salary should be raised to the same amount. In 1905 the titles of master and mistress of method were replaced by that of vice-principal.

Adams, Harris and Punnett first met at the Hampstead home of Sophie Bryant in a meeting chaired by William Garnett. Bryant was to play a crucial role in the early years of the LDTC. She chaired its Local Committee, and advanced its cause through her membership of the Senate of the University of London, its Board of Pedagogy and of the LCC's Technical Education Board and Education Committee. The North London Collegiate School of which she was headmistress supplied the LDTC with both students and teaching practice places and a key member of staff in Clotilde von Wyss. As one of the promoters of the Cambridge Training College, Bryant no doubt also knew Punnett before her appointment to the LDTC.[18] Two immediate tasks at this initial meeting were to decide upon the teaching commitments of the permanent staff and to consider the recruitment of part-time specialists. The bulk of the LDTC lecturing was undertaken by Punnett, who assumed responsibility for methods of teaching, and Harris, who provided lectures on the theory and history of education. In his capacity as Professor of Education, Adams delivered lectures three times a week: one at Bedford College, another at the College of Preceptors and a third on Saturday mornings at King's College.

Punnett's role as the first, and for some time only, full-time female member of staff was a crucial one. Her prime duties were to organize and oversee the

6. Sophie Bryant, Headmistress of the North London Collegiate School and Chairman of the LDTC's Local Committee

teaching of the female students and to take overall responsibility for the teaching of arithmetic. She soon added other subjects – for example psychology and scripture – and indeed bore the reputation of being a most efficient lecturer across a wide range of topics. She also assumed a heavy administrative burden, under both Adams and Nunn – 'If owt's been dunn 'ere, Miss Punnett's dunnit' – in the words of a student song. But her principal contribution was to the professional and personal development of countless students. Hers was the ever-open door, and many would have agreed with the judgement of a future Institute Director, G.B. Jeffery, who recorded that:

> She did not *take* an interest in her students; she *was* interested in them and in all their doings. I was one of her students and I married one of her students, and so I know. When our eldest daughter was born, Miss Punnett averred that Janet was the first full-blooded L.D.T.C. baby, made a special journey out to Harrow to inspect the infant, and thereafter kept her framed photograph on her desk in celebration of the event.[19]

She also kept a watchful eye on all the staff, including Adams and Nunn, presided over the teapot in the common room and even interviewed and appointed the College cleaners. On retirement in 1933, Margaret Punnett expressed the hope that she might 'die like a candle being blown out'. On Easter Sunday 1946 she collapsed in church and expired later that day.[20] A tribute in the student magazine declared that she had been the embodiment of the college: 'always on tap from the arrival of the earliest students till late in the evening, and not uncommonly until the early hours of the next morning.... She was a great woman, an academic Martha, active, cheery and eminently sensible.'[21]

One of the first members of staff to be appointed in 1903, albeit initially part-time, was the 32-year-old, Swiss-born Clotilde von Wyss, who taught biology, hygiene, nature study and art. After early schooling in Zürich, von Wyss, like Punnett, was educated at South Hampstead High School. She prepared for teaching at the Maria Grey Training College, and taught at St George's High School, Edinburgh, the North London Collegiate School, and from 1900 at the Cambridge Training College. The extent of von Wyss's magnetic personality and influence upon her charges was apparent at the North London Collegiate School, where Marie Stopes, who herself had previously attended St George's High School, had been one of her favourite pupils. Biographers of Stopes have subjected the passionate letters and intimate relationship between Clotilde and Marie to considerable examination. For example, June Rose has concluded that 'Clotilde's language makes clear that, consciously or unconsciously, she wanted Marie for herself'.[22] In 1926 in *Sex and the Young* Stopes provided a thinly veiled and somewhat disillusioned account of von Wyss's influence at the North London Collegiate School.

A teacher in a large girls' school was most popular with both mistresses and pupils … there was always a long train of girls wanting to walk home with her, eager to hold her hand on excursions or in the playground and to bring her flowers picked in their own gardens or purchased on their way to school. … Each separately deluded girl felt herself pledged to remain all her life in a highfaluting kind of secret Order based on a muddled mixture of mysticism, pseudo-theosophical fantasies of 'purity' and crude physical expressions of personal love and sex feeling.[23]

Throughout her teaching career von Wyss continued to excite admiration. Already well known to Bryant and Punnett, she soon gained the approval of Adams. Her accumulation of artists' materials, animal photographs, collections of plants and introduction of an aquarium brought life and colour into the LDTC.[24]

7. Clotilde von Wyss, 'a rare and very special person'

She remained on the staff until 1936, witty and eloquent, a pioneer of educational broadcasting and film, and overflowing with life, whether in the lecture room or leading a nature excursion to a marsh or muddy pond.[25] Her courage in different situations was widely appreciated, for example in taking over classes of students at a moment's notice or as the first woman to undertake voluntary teaching at Wormwood Scrubs Prison. One of her later colleagues, Dr Percival Gurrey, celebrated her as:

Perhaps the one who was warmest and the most whole-hearted in her praise of first rate teaching, or of anything else that was of high standard. … She was the true artist, responding in every fibre of her mind and body to the beauty of nature, and especially of human nature. She was a rare and very special person, her intense love of beauty and her fearless and irrepressible expression of her wonder and enthusiasm for beautiful things, even quite simple things such as dandelions, which she called 'the glory of the fields', was a privilege to listen to. When she was deeply affected she would say in her soft, almost awed voice: 'You could go down on your knees to it' – to a tree in flower, a picture, a student's lesson.[26]

The most important of the early part-time appointments was that of Thomas Percy Nunn, who also joined the College staff in 1903 and retired, like von Wyss, in 1936. Percy Nunn, the son and grandson of schoolmasters who kept a proprietary school, was born in Bristol in 1870 'with, so to speak, a stick of chalk in his hand'.[27] In 1873 the school moved to Weston-super-Mare, and from an early age Nunn combined his own education with the role of teacher at the school.

Interests from these early years included the writing of plays and the making of scientific instruments. In 1890, on his father's death, Nunn decided not to take over responsibility for the management of the school but to pursue his teaching career elsewhere. By 1895 he had acquired London B.Sc. and BA degrees, followed by an MA and teacher's diploma in 1902. He taught in Halifax, at Bedford Modern, Wilson's Grammar School, Camberwell, and as senior science master and second master at William Ellis School. He also engaged in part-time lecturing at Woolwich Polytechnic and the Shoreditch Technical Institute. From March 1903 Nunn was engaged on a part-time basis to demonstrate methods of teaching mathematics and science, and by the end of the year was also contracted to supervise teaching practice.[28] In November 1905 he succeeded Harris as Vice-Principal.

There are innumerable testimonies to Nunn's abilities as a teacher, to his breadth of knowledge and interests, to his great energy. In spite of his total commitment to the LDTC, Nunn also played significant roles in such bodies as the Aristotelian Society, the British Association, the British Psychological Society, the Mathematical Association and the Training College Association. His achievements and public recognition, however, were combined with approachability, humour, courtesy, kindness, and even diffidence. He took great delight in music and excelled in penning verses and parodies for LDTC concerts. Students naturally appreciated Nunn's participation in the social life of the LDTC, but they also warmed to his 'persuasive rather than didactic manner' of teaching and recorded that he 'made science a delight to us'.[29] Jeffery, having been accepted as an 18-year-old student by Adams in 1909, completed a first-class degree in physics at University College in two years, and arrived at the London Day in 1911 to study in his professional year for the teacher's diploma. Adams, he saw as being remote, but his

> contacts with Nunn were much more intimate and personal, perhaps because we had so much in common. We were both mathematicians with a strong interest in philosophy and music. We were both fundamentally teachers. We both loved a good argument. He had a remarkable power of marshalling facts and arguments in a plain and clear-cut pattern. … So many of the difficulties of the pupil arise from unnecessary complication and obscurity that simplicity and clarity of exposition are one half of the art of teaching. Nunn had the other half too. He never talked down to you. He put himself by your side ready to share your enthusiasms, taking it for granted that you would share his. You were learning and he was learning; you were learning together. The remarkable thing is that it was perfectly true. In teaching you, his vivid and adventurous mind was sure to see some new light and you shared the discovery together.[30]

Nunn's personality and educational philosophy were to exercise a considerable influence over the LDTC and more broadly. An early contribution to the nature of scientific knowledge was *The Aims and Achievements of Scientific Method: An epistemological essay*, published in 1907 and based upon Nunn's London D.Sc. thesis presented in the previous year. Publications of 1912–14 intended for classroom teachers included a co-authored *First Class Book of Chemistry*, and volumes on the teaching of algebra and geometry. He also served as general editor of *Black's Elementary Science Series*.[31] In 1913 the University acknowledged Nunn's academic standing with his appointment as Professor of Education.

In the first year Harris and Punnett of necessity covered a very wide range of teaching and supervision indeed. They frequently repeated lectures, once at Bedford and once at University College, with the prospect of having to do them three times per week when from 1903 some students would be based at King's for their under-graduate work. They also supervised the weekly criticism lessons held on Tuesday afternoons at Prospect Terrace School in Gray's Inn Road, and the students' teaching practices. Some relief was provided from September 1903 when additional full-time staff, Amy Bramwell and Charles Chambers, were engaged at salaries of £300 a year.[32] Bramwell, a London graduate aged 36, had previously been lecturer at Maria Grey College. Chambers, also aged 36, was an Oxford graduate who had been classical tutor and master of method at St John's College, Battersea. Chambers, however, resigned after a term, and was succeeded in January 1904 by the 32-year-old John Hague, one of the previous applicants. Hague had a first-class degree in philosophy and MA from Victoria University, Manchester and a first-class teacher's certificate from the Manchester Day Training College. He had taught English at school and university levels in Prague and from 1901 was assistant superintendent of the training classes of the London School Board at Graystoke Place.[33]

Part-time staff fell into two broad categories. The first were those who gave lectures on particular aspects of the curriculum. Specialist teachers were essential for such subjects as manual instruction, needlework and physical education, which students were required to study under the terms of the Board of Education's regulations. Payments varied. The 'gymnastic instructress', Miss Park, received 10*s*. 6*d*. per hour, while a teacher of French, Miss Pechey, was prepared to work for the lower rate of 7*s*. 6*d*.[34] The second category of part-timers were those recruited to assist with the supervision of teaching practice, since HMI considered that one tutor should not supervise more than eight students. One of the first part-time supervisors was Mrs Platt, who had been a student and member of staff at the Cambridge Training College, a teacher and, before marriage necessitated her retirement, an inspector of elementary schools. Platt was paid at the rate of £5 per week.

Particular problems arose with the supervision of teaching practice in secondary schools. Sophie Bryant and other headmistresses were willing to accept both students and visits from their supervisors, and criticism lessons took place at the North London Collegiate School, which together with the Central Foundation

School, Aske's School, Hatcham and King Alfred's School, Hampstead furnished the first places for school practice. The admission of students and staff to boys' secondary schools for the purposes of teaching practice and supervision, however, was more problematic. There was little tradition of training to teach in such schools. Masters were deemed to be qualified as teachers by virtue of their university degrees, robustness of character and other personal qualities. Particular objection was taken to the prospect of visits from the master of method, the very title so redolent of the elementary school world, and its traditions of inspection and inferior status. Thus the governors of St Dunstan's College, Catford stated that although they were

> anxious to facilitate opportunities of observation and practice in teaching to post-graduate students, they consider it desirable that the students should be placed under the supervising control of the head master; and that the visits of the master of method of the training college should be by arrangement with the head master.[35]

Given the small numbers of men students following the diploma course in the early years, Adams was able to circumvent these problems. Some schools were more accommodating to supervisors from the LDTC; at others, fees were paid to school staff who assumed the responsibility of supervision.

## Students and courses

The original 58 students of the London Day Training College constituted a fairly homogeneous group. All were aged between 18 and 22. Female entrants were in the majority, with 35 women and 23 men. The 1903 intake showed a greater imbalance with 78 females and 33 males. All male, and all but seven of the female, entrants of 1902 had previously attended pupil-teacher centres, with those of Deptford and Finsbury supplying some 20 in total. The great majority had received their first education in Board schools. Two of the men and 11 of the women appear to have spent some time in a secondary school. No fewer than six of these had attended the North London Collegiate School. For their degree work, 15 of the female students were placed at Bedford College; all others, men and women, were at University College. Of the Bedford contingent, two studied for a science degree and 13 for arts. At University College, 21 men and eight women followed science and two men and 12 women arts. Thus overall there were 31 science students (21 men and 10 women) as opposed to 27 arts students (two men and 25 women).

As their educational backgrounds indicated, the early students came from modest homes. The largest single group of occupations was that of skilled labourer. In 1903 the average annual income of the parents of male students was calculated at £155 10s., and of the female students, £174 15s.[36] These figures must be treated with some caution, and it is impossible to make comparisons over time in the financial and social backgrounds of the students as the practice of publishing details of parental occupations and incomes was discontinued in 1904. Nevertheless, in the early years it was clear that for many of the students a place at the LDTC, with the opportunity to qualify as a teacher and to obtain a degree from the University of London into the bargain, held out the prospect of upward social and financial mobility. Students in this category would have included George Allison, whose father was a draper's assistant earning £1 15s. per week, or Herbert Winslow, whose caretaker father received a mere £52 per year. In contrast, it is significant that the highest parental incomes recorded for the 1903 entrants were those for George Smith, whose clergyman/schoolmaster father claimed an income of £700 per year, and the schoolmaster father of Lilian Jackson with a salary of £550 per year. These parents were probably not employed within the elementary school system, but the father of Thomas Keir, a headmaster with the London School Board, earned £350 per year, nearly three times the average of the parents of the male students, while another LSB headmaster, the father of one of the 1904 applicants, Gladys Mortimer, had an annual income of £572.[37] Both Thomas Keir and George Smith had attended Latymer Upper School, before proceeding to pupil-teacher centres in Chelsea and Hammersmith respectively, and both were among the older entrants at 21 years and 7 months and 20 years and 9 months. At the other end of the parental income scale were widows, retired men, and those in employment like the fathers of Allison and Winslow who were attempting to maintain themselves, and their families, on little more than a pound per week. Students from homes such as these often experienced considerable hardship: lacking proper nourishment, walking between the several centres, struggling to find the extra costs of examination re-entry fees, unable to buy books or to participate in social or cultural events.

While the Board of Education paid a grant of £35 and £30 to each male and female King's scholar per annum, respectively, £10 of this went directly to the College, with the balance as a maintenance grant paid in three termly instalments. In 1905, a memorial detailing hardships and requesting an increase in grants was addressed to the Local Committee. Though the memorial, which bore the signatures of 105 women and 68 men, had wide support within the student body, no increase was forthcoming.[38] By 1908, following an initiative from Bryant and support from the Goldsmiths' Company, a hardship fund was established from which interest-free loans could be made to students who found themselves in financial difficulties.

In its *Regulations for the Training of Teachers and for the Examination of Students in Training Colleges*, published in 1904, the Board of Education identified five categories of students in training colleges. One-year courses were provided for certificated teachers who had not received any previous college training. Such courses for 'certificated students', as they were known, 'should be devoted mainly to improving their general education and to such professional training as will best supplement their previous experience'. 'One year students', on the other hand, were those who had already secured a degree or similar qualification and whose courses were principally devoted to professional training. The most common provision, however, was for 'two year students', who received a two-year general education as well as professional training. 'Third year students' were those who, on account of particular merit – for example the passing of a University inter-mediate examination – were allowed a further year of education and training. This third year might be taken 'elsewhere than at the Training College, and, under special conditions abroad'. Finally there were the 'three year students'. This was a new category: the LDTC students of 1902 and 1903 having entered under the old regulations as two-year students whose courses might be extended as third years. These prospective teachers were to undergo courses in 'certain Colleges closely connected with a University and specially approved by the Board as adapted to provide a course of study leading up to and reaching a degree, as well as professional training'.

This was a very substantial programme indeed, and some of the Board's con-cerns about such students were indicated in the following regulation:

> they must be reasonably likely to take a University degree not later than the end of the calendar year in which their training course concludes, and they must enter with the *bona fide* intention of doing so. ...
>
> The Board must be satisfied that the student in each year of his course has made due progress towards his degree; and the medical officer of the Train-ing College must certify as soon as possible after the beginning of each year of the course that the health of each student so admitted is sufficient to allow of his or her continuing in the course without undue strain.

Students who failed to keep up with the pace, either intellectually or physically, would be demoted to the category of two-year students or, if already in the third year, would be required to abandon the degree course and devote themselves principally to professional training.

Many in the first cohorts of LDTC students found difficulty in coping with the University's academic requirements. At the end of the first term Adams reported that 'the university authorities seem to find the training college students badly pre-pared as compared with the ordinary students'.[39] This was hardly surprising, for the great majority of LDTC recruits were products of elementary schools and of pupil-teacher centres. Given that pupil teachers were required to study the subjects in the elementary school curriculum, pedagogical principles, and teach up to 20 hours per week, understandably their academic levels were low in comparison with students who had received a more scholarly education in secondary schools. On the other hand they were considered by LDTC staff to be 'very distinctly above the average, both in tone and in ability and attainments' when compared with students of other training colleges.[40] During the first decade of the twentieth century the balance between academic weakness and professional strength was reversed. By 1907 pupil teachers were being replaced by bursars and student teachers with experience of secondary schooling. Indeed, students who entered the LDTC from 1908 onwards were, upon completion of the three-year course, allowed to teach not only in elementary schools but also in secondary establishments approved by the Board of Education.

Academic failure did not necessarily spell professional disaster. For example, Mabel Barnes from Plumstead began her course at the LDTC in 1903. Her own education had been for ten years at the Bloomfield Road Girls' School followed by three years at the Woolwich Pupil Teacher Centre, with teaching experience for three months at Bloomfield Road and for the remainder of the three years at Earl Street Infants. Mabel was placed at University College to read science but in the intermediate examination of June 1904 she failed in every subject – botany, chemistry, mathematics and physics. Demoted to the two-year course, Mabel completed the certificate in 1906 with a testimonial which described her as 'A student of excellent character with a good deal of quiet force and a patient determination. She has done very good work and shows promise as a teacher.' In August 1906 she began as a class teacher at her former school, Bloomfield Road, but within five weeks was made science mistress, teaching elementary science, botany, hygiene and physiology.[41]

In addition to the rigours of the University's academic courses, the students also faced the professional certificate course, which came under the ultimate control of the Board of Education. HMI not only had the duty to exercise a general supervision over premises, courses and student discipline, but could also examine students on any subject at will and inspect their notebooks. Though these powers were exercised circumspectly in respect of LDTC students, Board of Education regulations as to the subjects of study and the amount of teaching practice to be undertaken had to be followed to the letter. It was for this reason that subjects such as drawing, music, nature study, physical training, voice production, and manual training for men and needlework for women had to be followed by all students. The pattern of professional studies which emerged during the first term of 1902 took up 10 hours a week. Science students spent 1 hour a week in the study of English, and arts students an hour of science. Theory of teaching occupied 3 hours, criticism lessons $1\frac{1}{4}$, voice production, callisthenics and drawing 1 hour apiece, with needlework or manual training a further $1\frac{1}{2}$ hours.[42] A particular problem arose about meeting the Board's requirements for teaching practice, a minimum of three weeks in each year, which in the first two years of the course had to be fitted in during any periods in which the school terms exceeded those of the University, for no interference could be brooked with attendance at academic lectures. Professional studies, therefore, predominated in September, while work in schools took place in University vacations at Christmas and Easter and in July.

Such ferocious application took its toll on both students and staff. Matters came to a head in February 1904 when Adams and Bryant presented a memorandum to the Local Committee which advocated the provision of a two-year course of non-university standard. This could stand in its own right and also be a haven for those who could not keep up with the pace of the three-year course. This proposal was approved. A major factor in this decision must have been a report from Adams that only half of the 58 students then in the second year were expected to proceed into the third. This prediction was correct. Student numbers in October 1904 showed only 10 men and 19 women in the third year, with 32 men and 77 women in the second and 26 men and 69 women in the first. Twenty-five students, all female, had been recruited to the new two-year course and one to a one-year course. Of the three-year students, 57 were attached to Bedford College, 75 to King's College and 101 to University College. Twelve students, three men and nine women, were taking the one-year course of training for teaching in secondary schools.[43]

The most serious academic problem appears to have been with Greek, which was a compulsory subject in the intermediate arts examination until 1907, though optional both in matriculation and finals. In 1904, 18 of the 23 King's College based first-year LDTC students who took Greek failed the intermediate examination. Students at Bedford and University Colleges fared rather better with only 2 failures out of 24. While failure rates in the 1904 intermediate examination in such subjects as physics (3 out of 28) and botany (6 out of 32) were relatively low, mathematics clearly presented problems. Amongst first-year students there were 21 failures (18 of them women) out of 68 entries. Failures amongst second-year students in mathematics in 1903 were also high at 17 (10 men and 7 women) out of 48. Second-year students (the 1902 intake), none of whom attended King's, had fared rather better in Greek in the 1903 intermediate examination, with only 6 failures out of 26.

Academic difficulties were compounded by a lack of social and sports facilities, although the LCC did make premises available for student union meetings, first in a building near Victoria and then in a basement room near Marble Arch.[44] Excessive travel was frequently cited as the greatest problem. As HMI Dr Airy reported in 1904, 'The work of this college is carried on with energy, marked ability and success, under conditions of great and unusual difficulty of which the distances travelled by the students and the dispersal over different educational establishments are the principal'.[45] Casualties soon occurred. Two of the 1903 male entrants, William Kerby and Nahum Makover, were pronounced by Dr Leslie Thorne Thorne to be suffering from organic heart disease and likely to 'break down at any time'.[46] Another of the 1903 intake, Myra Todd, was forced to 'give up attendance on account of heart trouble, aggravated by the amount of travelling and especially going up and down stairs', while one of the original students, Annie Hyslop Atkins, who managed to survive into the second year then withdrew 'on account of a nervous breakdown, caused by the strain of the conditions under which her training has been carried on'.[47] One solution to this problem, canvassed by Adams in 1904, was that of abandoning the concurrent principle and concentrating the degree work in the first two years and professional training in the third. Such rearrangement suggested two further developments – the first a four-year course, the second, a consecutive arrangement whereby three years of study for a degree were followed by a fourth year devoted to postgraduate professional training. The four-year course was achieved in 1911 and Harris was later to argue that 'In bringing this about the London Day Training College played a large and, one might almost say, a decisive part'.[48]

William Ward, one of the original students of 1902, whose widowed mother was a landlady with an income of £100 a year, provided a graphic account of the early days:

The office consisted of two rooms on a first floor in Southampton Row [Street], where every student was interviewed by Professor Adams. We were nearly all, if not quite all, pupil teachers under the London County Council, the qualification on entry being the London Matriculation.

Most of the students of that day were combining the academic training for a degree with the professional training for the Board of Education certificate. To fit in arrangements for the latter work, the degree course had to be selected to leave the times chosen for this work free from university lectures; not a very admirable arrangement, or one fitted to give a liberal view of a university course.

The academic work was taken at one of the Schools of the University. The professional training was sandwiched in between university lectures, sometimes at one's college, but more frequently at odd times and places all over North London. For example I remember a lecture on teaching method and psychology between two science lectures at University College, and another on English literature, squeezed in in the same way.

On Tuesdays, after a morning at U.C. we went to Prospect Terrace School, in Gray's Inn Road, for a criticism lesson and discussion. From there we took a cross-country journey to the Northampton Institute in Clerkenwell, where the men had physical training for an hour before tea, under Herr Oberholzer, who taught us to 'DEVelop' the muscles. I never knew what the women did in this hour, but they were there in the building.

After tea, in the Institute's canteen, we had an hour's 'Art'. My chief recollection of this is learning by heart six drawings, each to fill a blackboard. The examiner had to choose one of these at the Certificate examination, which the victim had to produce on the spot. I can remember only two of these: one a complete crocus plant at which I became very proficient, the other a hideous red, white and blue snake, which, I still believe, never existed on land or sea.

Following this was music, so-called, held in a tiny room in the basement among the motors and dynamos, with a window which gave a good view of the room from the pavement outside. Small boys used to stop and join in or pass scathing comment. The name of Seymour Dicker will be enough to recall these joys to students of 1902–05. I fear the men, at least, regarded this item as comic relief.

At 6.0 or 6.30 our day ended. Naturally we detested Tuesdays and all associated with it. Most of our trekking from place to place had to be done on foot, and travel, when possible by vehicle, was usually by horse tramcars or buses. The journey home in the rush hour on a wet night on top of an open bus was often the end of Tuesday.

On Saturday mornings the men took a handicraft course at the Shoreditch Technical School, while the women, I think, did needlework.

It will thus be seen that we lived, like a pendulum, in a continual state of oscillation between our two lines of study, and naturally enough the two interfered with each other. We inevitably gave them an order of precedence, and always the academic side won, the professional work being regarded as a constant interruption and irritation. We talked of ourselves as the first victims.

Many of the first intake of students left at the end of two years on taking the Teacher's Certificate examination, feeling the game was not worth the candle. However, we must have been a tough group. Counting over my contemporaries, I can recollect only one who did not become a headmaster or headmistress, or occupy some important administrative or tutorial post in the educational world in later years.[49]

This statement as to the priority given to academic work by those who nevertheless proceeded to be teachers is interesting. A more dismissive comment from another student from the first decade revealed that 'We regarded the two or three half-days a week at London Day as a necessary and inevitable price to pay for the opportunity of graduating, seeing that a university course would otherwise have been financially impossible'.[50] In sharp contrast, the value of a permanent base and single purpose was evident amongst the two-year students. These were found a home first at an elementary school in Camden Town and subsequently at the Finsbury Pupil Teachers' Centre, 'two good classrooms and a small teachers' room and a cloakroom for the students being set apart solely for the use of this branch of the training college'.[51] These students appear to have enjoyed their course, appreciating the visits of such eminent scholars and teachers as Nunn, Punnett and von Wyss, and playing hockey in Highbury Fields.[52]

The postgraduate students who took the one-year diploma course similarly had a less frenetic existence. The first course began in January 1903 with six women and two men students. In the early years recruits were few in number, for the principle of training for teaching in secondary schools, particularly for men, was

8. The College of
Preceptors building in
Bloomsbury Square,
home to the LDTC's
postgraduate
students until 1907

still in its infancy. The diploma course was subject to University regulations and included the principles of education, the application of such principles to the teaching of particular subjects, school organization and the history of education including the study of prescribed texts. Adams personally oversaw much of this work, while practical activity in schools was supervised by Harris and Punnett. Given the small numbers, a more individual and tutorial approach was possible and applicants were assured that 'Everything will be done to make the course bear as directly as possible on the future needs of the students'.[53] Until 1907 the post-graduate students took their LDTC lectures at the College of Preceptors building in Bloomsbury Square where a room was set aside for their use, and also attended the appropriate University lectures. Adams, himself, held the qualification of Fellow of the College of Preceptors (FCP), and joined its College Council in 1904.[54] The January entry was determined by the date of the diploma examination, which was held in December. The subsequent addition of a September examination made possible entry in January and September.

Given the very respectful attitudes of the day, one somewhat surprising element which emerges from these early years is the extent to which some students, including Jeffery, a future Director, appear to have had little compunction about 'ragging' certain members of staff. Two particular victims were Seymour Dicker and Dr Henry Hulbert. Both were engaged in 1903, originally to teach 5 and $4\frac{1}{2}$ hours per week respectively.[55] Dicker was an accomplished musician, educated at St Paul's Choir School and Christ's College, Cambridge, who had taught at Brisbane Grammar School, and been musical director and organist at the South Western Polytechnic and Northampton Institute. Dicker became one of the leading characters of the LDTC. He inspired many students and staged annual productions of Gilbert and Sullivan opera in which he occasionally took part himself. But he could be, and was, goaded into furious rages, and was reputed to have sought consolation 'in a time-honoured way after sessions with the unmusical and boisterous'.[56] He retired in 1930.[57] Another target was Dr Hulbert, father of the more famous Claud and Jack, who lectured on voice production and hygiene. Hulbert had been educated at Bath College, Magdalen College, Oxford and St Thomas's Hospital, London. In addition to his Oxford degrees, Hulbert was a Member of the Royal College of Surgeons and a Licentiate of the Royal College of Physicians. An imposing and larger than life figure, immaculately attired in a grey frock coat and grey top hat, with a mellifluous voice, sweeping gestures, the famous Hulbert chin and great powers as a raconteur and mimic, he too suffered from practical jokes, but appears to have been 'equal to all occasions, playing his part with a well-assumed military swagger for an unconventional reception or engaging in urbane conversation with the women until the men became a recognisable part of their class again'.[58] Although the principal baiters were to be found amongst the men, even the two-year female students, on the occasion of a formal visit from Adams to address them and to read out their examination results, supplied 'cheers for those who had achieved bottom place'.[59]

## Southampton Row

In the first five years of its existence the LDTC's major problem was the lack of a building of its own. During the first year, which was spent at the London School of Economics in Clare Market and in Clement's Inn, two options were considered: either the purchase or long lease of an existing building or the acquisition of a building site upon which a purpose-built edifice could be constructed. Whichever option was chosen, however, four major criteria had to be borne in mind. The first was a central location, preferably with easy access to Bedford, University and King's Colleges, the last of these complicated by the separate men's and women's departments in the Strand and Kensington Square. The second was the requirement that any building should satisfy the regulations of the Board of Education in respect of such matters as space per student, heating and ventilation. The third, that it should be capable of accommodating an expanding number of students. Finally, the building should be suitable for academic purposes, with lecture rooms both large and small, sufficient space for a library and some refreshment facilities, and almost above all, a peaceful location, an oasis in which students and staff could drink undisturbed from the fountain of knowledge, with some sense of detachment, however illusory, from the noise and grime of London, its incessant traffic and busy, jostling pavements.

From 1903 the purchase of the Southampton Row site meant that the LCC was committed to a new building. Nevertheless, temporary accommodation would still be required for the intervening period, which proved to be twice as long as originally expected. For the next four years the LDTC was split across three sites. As Harris recorded:

> In its second year the College moved to the Northampton Technical Institute, Finsbury and the College of Preceptors, Bloomsbury. The change had become necessary by the admission of over a hundred students in October 1903, and the fact that the School of Economics itself needed all its accommodation. At the same time offices were provided at 9 10 Southampton Street, W.C.I., for Professor Adams, Miss Punnett and myself. There was also a room for a shorthand typist and a waiting room for the use of the increasing number of Diploma students. The College of Preceptors, just around the corner, provided classroom accommodation for their lectures and discussion groups.[60]

Close connections established in these early years between the LDTC and the College of Preceptors were to continue, not least because of the proximity between Bloomsbury Square and Southampton Row. In 1933, to mark the occasion of the LDTC's recent transmutation into the University's Institute of Education, the College of Preceptors began the Joseph Payne Memorial Lectures which were given in the main lecture theatre of the Southampton Row building. The third and fourth Directors, Fred Clarke and G.B. Jeffery, assisted the College of Preceptors in an advisory capacity, and during the Second World War there was even a proposal that the two bodies 'should be "fused" into one institution'.[61]

The Northampton Institute site had several disadvantages. Described in the LDTC Prospectus of 1904–5 as being 'about five minutes walk from the Angel', it was manifestly located at some distance from the other activities of the LDTC in Southampton Street and Bloomsbury Square. It was also removed from Bedford College, then in Baker Street, and University College in Gower Street, and even more inaccessible from the King's sites. Indeed, the distances were such that there was some relief among members of the Technical Education Board that no major academic classes in science or arts took place at the Northampton Institute, fearing perhaps that students might have been tempted to attend these, rather than travel to the colleges of the University. Even at the Northampton Institute, however, the students could not find a base for social activities. These took place fortnightly, with dances, concerts and occasional dramatic performances, in a hall in Balderton Street hired from the Regent Street Polytechnic.[62]

So it was with great relief that in 1907 the LDTC entered its first purpose-built home. Foundations were laid in August 1905 and erection was carried out by the Works department of the LCC to a design by the Council's architect, W.E. Riley.

9. The ground floor plan of the combined Southampton Row building shows that the LDTC was the junior partner and that even the lecture theatre was shared

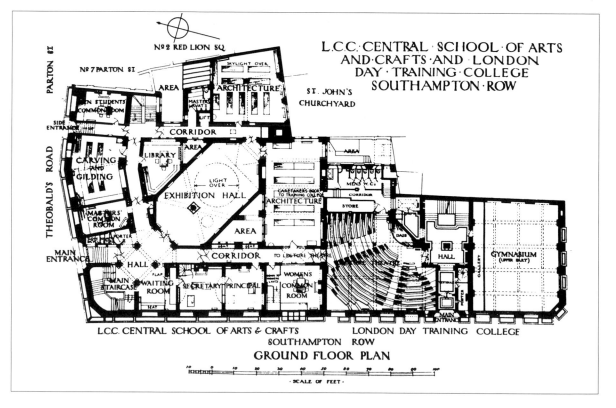

LCC · CENTRAL · SCHOOL · OF ARTS AND · CRAFTS · AND · LONDON DAY · TRAINING · COLLEGE SOUTHAMPTON · ROW

L.C.C. CENTRAL SCHOOL OF ARTS & CRAFTS          LONDON DAY TRAINING COLLEGE
SOUTHAMPTON ROW
GROUND FLOOR PLAN

· SCALE OF FEET ·

The overall block of which the LDTC formed a part, however, was not completed in 1907 and building work continued to the northern side for the LCC's Central School of Arts and Crafts, finished in the following year.[63] In common with many of the Council's buildings from the Edwardian period, Cornish granite and Portland stone were used in the construction. The LDTC building cost some £48,000, in addition to the cost of the site, which had become available as a result

**10. The frontage of the LDTC building in Southampton Row**

of the widening of Southampton Row. The official opening by Lord Rosebery, the University's Chancellor and formerly first chairman of the LCC, took place on Saturday, 2 November 1907.[64] The five-storey building was designed to accommodate 350 students.

The general location of the LDTC's first building had much to recommend it. The College of Preceptors stood literally across the road in Bloomsbury Square, with the London School of Economics and King's College within five minutes walk to the south and University College some ten minutes away to the north-west. But the immediate location was poor, at a busy and particularly noisy crossroads. The disadvantages of the site became greater as horse-drawn vehicles were replaced by motorized transport: 'Outside, in the long tunnel to the Embankment trams roared up and clattered down, cars hooted, buses chugged and stuttered, waiting for their turn at the traffic lights. ... The street was a web of noise and bustle.'[65] Although a special system of double windows and ventilation was incorporated, there was little renewal of air. In 1910 a report from the Board of Education noted that 'the building is admirably appointed though perhaps something more might profitably be expended on cleaning. ... The rumble of the traffic necessitates closing the windows to the outer air; many of the students look jaded and are jaded.'[66]

Nevertheless in 1907 the range of accommodation must have seemed impressive. The basement housed a gymnasium, dressing rooms, bathrooms and cloakrooms, together with a range of storage facilities. The ground floor comprised an entrance hall and large lecture theatre, which had a gallery and rostrum and was fitted out with oak seating. The offices of the Principal, Vice-Principals and Secretary were located on an entresol. Here typewriters clacked unceasingly. Indeed, even before the move to the new building, Adams was having to ask the Local Committee to authorize the purchase of a further 'Barlock', reporting that 'both of the vice-principals have learnt to use the typewriter, but can of course avail themselves of their skill only when Miss Green is engaged at other work'.[67] Male and female students had separate common rooms with fine panelled walls on the first floor, together with a refreshment bar and luncheon room. The second floor housed the library, staff room and one large and two small classrooms. More classrooms and tutorial rooms were on the third floor, together with a manual training room and a museum for the display of students' work and educational appliances. The top floor, which soon became known as von Wyss's particular domain, housed a laboratory with balance room and dark room, two further specialist rooms for art and for nature study, and a kitchen. In 1909 the LCC art inspector, A.H. Christie, reported most favourably upon von Wyss's work in drawing and nature study and commented that 'The large art room is well furnished and equipped; it is well lighted and conveniently planned and presents an attractive business-like appearance'.[68] An attic flight of stairs led to the roof, a suitable site for obtaining a breath of (not so fresh) air, and for observing the proceedings of the Art school. But there was only one staircase, and no lift, so that in between lectures and indeed

11. The single staircase: 'Whenever the student population was on the move it was like Wembley after the Cup Final'

'Whenever the student population was on the move it was like Wembley after the Cup Final'.[69] Characteristically Adams, who felt that the proximity of the Principal's room to the entrance made him too vulnerable to casual callers, had a small, secret staircase made which corkscrewed down to the caretaker's room. When the caretaker spotted an unwelcome visitor he gave a pre-arranged signal 'and while the visitor went up one staircase Adams went down another'.[70] Even the single main staircase, however, had its advantages. Whatever the strengths and weaknesses of the new building, both staff and students must have relished the fact that they now could become a real community, and the staircase, which all had to use, became

A COLLEGE FOR THE ÉLITE.

1. Professor Adams, Principal of the College.    2. The Southampton Row frontage.    3. Men's common room.    4. Women's common room.    5. The library.    6. The lecture hall.
7. Manual labour class room.    8. In class room A.    9. The museum.

THE LONDON DAY TRAINING COLLEGE IN SOUTHAMPTON ROW, WHICH IS TO BE OPENED BY LORD ROSEBERY, TO-DAY. ("Graphic Photo Union.")

453

12. 'A College for the Elite', from the *Daily Graphic* of 2 November 1907. The pictures show: 1. John Adams at his desk, 2. Southampton Row frontage, 3. men's common room, 4. women's common room, 5. library, 6. lecture hall, 7. manual training room, 8. a classroom, 9. museum

the great rendezvous point. Not until the inter-war period, when the building had become shabby and worn, and when the fundamental problem of a lack of natural light had been compounded by the division of rooms and the partitioning of landings, would this close community begin to feel claustrophobic.

## Conclusion

In the first five years of its existence the LDTC struggled to survive. Many of the students were academically ill-equipped to cope with the demands of a combined degree and certificate course. Their problems were compounded by incessant travelling and the lack of a building to call their own. The LDTC was the only day training college under local authority control. Even the Southampton Row building reflected the hybrid and uncertain status of the early staff and students who inhabited it and of the activities in which they were engaged. One newspaper account of the opening was headed 'A College for the Elite'.[71] This was true in comparison with other contemporary LCC colleges such as Avery Hill, Clapham, Graystoke Place and Islington. Nevertheless, in 1906 Avery Hill had begun at Eltham in an elegant mansion and park, former home of the nitrate millionaire, Colonel North.[72] The new building in Southampton Row was grander in conception and design than other LCC buildings 'for technical education',[73] but it was not a mansion, nor did it have the style of a university college. On grounds of economy it was physically joined to, and shared many services with, one of the LCC's schools which had neither university connections nor pretensions. In 1907 the future development of the LDTC was by no means clear.

Chapter 3

# A clash of cultures
## 1907–1922

### Introduction

The years covered by this chapter were amongst the most momentous in modern British history. The election of 1906 had marked a turning point in politics. From 1908, with David Lloyd George as Chancellor of the Exchequer, Liberal governments produced a programme of social and financial reform which led directly to the introduction of old age pensions and national insurance and indirectly to a substantial reduction in the powers of the House of Lords. Under the leadership of a former LCC member, James Ramsay MacDonald, the Labour Party became a recognizable political force. The campaign for women's suffrage achieved a partial success. The Fisher Act of 1918 raised the school-leaving age to 14. Overshadowing all these and other national events, however, was the First World War, which brought death and destruction on an unprecedented scale. Dynasties and empires were overthrown. Events in Russia from 1917 appeared to herald changes at least as substantial as those that had followed the French Revolution of 1789. In comparison with such great matters, events at the London Day Training College might seem to have been of limited importance. Nevertheless, it was in this period that a significant clash of cultures occurred and the identity of the new institution was formed.

### Management and control

The new building, the immediate environment in which staff and students worked, has been described in the previous chapter. But behind the new building lay a complex set of providing and controlling bodies and mechanisms. The most important of these were the LCC, the Board of Education and the University of London. The decisions of these bodies, in respect of such matters as financial allocation, lengths of courses, levels of grants and dates of examinations, impinged upon all the members of the LDTC, staff and students alike. The main burden of trying to steer the best course between their different and at times sharply conflicting priorities, lay with John Adams.

In 1904, the London County Council had finally assumed responsibility for education in the capital. In addition to the former responsibilities of the Technical Education Board, the new authority inherited 521 Board and 438 voluntary schools.[1] In consequence the LDTC was but one (albeit important and distinctive) educational institution among many under LCC control. The Council's Education Committee, which had 50 members and on occasion dealt with some 200 items in meetings of two hours,[2] accordingly established eight sub-committees to oversee various elements of its work.[3] The College's governing body, the London Day Training College Local Committee (LDTCLC), reported directly to the Higher Education Sub-Committee. The College's Local Committee was composed of the Chairman of the LCC and Chairman and Vice-Chairman of its Education Committee, the Chancellor and Vice-Chancellor of the University, together with six further representatives apiece from LCC and University. The Local Committee was required to exercise a general supervision over the College and to make recommendations to the Higher Education Sub-Committee. Its members were to receive an annual report from the Principal of the College. They were also encouraged to take an interest in the College's work and social activities and to pay visits during College hours. Individual members of the Local Committee and subsequent Council did take considerable interest in the work of the College, but with a complement of only 17, of whom five were ex-officio, meetings were often sparsely attended. For example, on 28 January 1907 Sophie Bryant chaired a Local Committee meeting of five members.[4] From 1909 when the Local Committee became the College Council, the Principal and two Vice-Principals were in regular attendance, and indeed, on occasion were in the majority.

From 1904 there were three professional officers who oversaw the LCC's education work – the Clerk to the Council, the Educational Adviser and the Education (Executive) Officer. By 1908, when it had become clear that this division of duties was not working well, Robert Blair, the Education (Executive) Officer, was appointed to the new post of Education Officer with overall responsibility for administering the service, a post he held until his retirement in 1924. Blair, a Scotsman, a former pupil teacher, and graduate of Edinburgh University, had taught in Kelso, London and Cheltenham, and worked as an inspector in Scotland and Ireland. The Education Officer was clerk to the governing bodies of all the LCC's training colleges and Blair's name appears at the bottom of the agenda papers of the College Council and on several important memoranda connected with the work of the College.

Blair faced a multitude of problems: the strong party political element in the LCC; the power of the Finance Committee and frequent calls for retrenchment; the possibility of further administrative reorganization; the critical state of London's antiquated stock of school buildings and overcrowded classrooms; the particular problems associated with the day continuation schools, which Blair with his interest in technical education strongly supported. Given this range of problems, it is perhaps not surprising that Blair believed that 'the business of admin. is to secure the maximum efficiency at the minimum cost',[5] and that the several moves by Adams and his colleagues to loosen LCC control and strengthen ties with the University were viewed askance.

One example of the clash between the priorities of the LCC and of the University occurred in 1909 over the recognition of the LDTC as a school of the University. In April 1908 the LDTC was inspected for this purpose by a committee headed by the University's Principal, Sir Arthur Rücker. This gave general approval, but recommended the withholding of formal recognition until the staff had a representative body with the right to make recommendations to the governing body on academic matters, and staff representation upon the governing body itself.[6] A College Board was duly established. This comprised all full-time members of teaching staff, together with the headteachers of the LDTC's demonstration schools, and was chaired by the Principal. The Board met monthly during the University terms, and had the right to make representations on academic and general management matters to the governing body. Blair, however, strenuously opposed staff representation upon the Local Committee, arguing that this would constitute a breach of Standing Order 271, adopted by the LCC in October 1905, which declared that:

> No officer, teacher, inspector or other person employed by the Council shall be permitted to accept the position of manager or member of a committee of any school or institute aided or maintained by the Council or provided by it under the Education Act, 1902, with or without the county. ... The standing order embodies a fundamental principle of government, that the paid officer shall have no power to vote on his own recommendations.[7]

Nevertheless Blair's advice was over-ruled. Following a conference between representatives of the University and the LCC, in which Sidney Webb and the Chairman of the Education Committee, Cyril Jackson, were to the fore, the LCC agreed to suspend Standing Order 271. Accordingly it was conceded that 'as an exceptional case, the principal and the two vice-principals for the time being of the London Day Training College (Holborn) be *ex-officio* members of the local committee of the college'. Henceforth the Local Committee would 'be designated the London Day Training College Council'.[8] The first meeting of the new Council took place on 22 November 1909.[9]

In 1914, following another University inspection and report, the Senate agreed to extend the LDTC's recognition as a school for a further five years.[10] The report on this occasion advised that any increase in staff numbers would necessitate the addition of elected staff representatives on the College Council, and also argued that 'for work of equal responsibility and importance the payment should be the same to women members of the staff as to men'.[11] Adams reported this latter view to a sympathetic College Council at a meeting in October 1914, but the Higher Education Sub-Committee, arguing that financial matters were the province of the LCC, refused to recommend any changes.[12]

The LDTC's status as a school of the University was widely welcomed, but the potential for conflict in management matters was also increased. One area of dispute concerned the right of the College Council to communicate directly with the Senate of the University, as over the issue of student hostels. Viewed from the standpoint of the LCC, the purpose of the LDTC was to train London students to teach in London schools. No residential accommodation, therefore, was required. Many staff and students, however, believed that hostels would serve to increase the national and international dimensions of the LDTC and to encourage a corporate existence. Matters came to a head in the spring of 1912. The College Council decided to write to the Senate of the University asking for the establishment 'of hostels of which students of the London Day Training College and other colleges could avail themselves', but were over-ruled by the Higher Education Sub-Committee on the grounds that much of the cost of such hostels would no doubt fall upon the LCC.[13] Though in 1912 the College Council had reluctantly to accept the decision of the Higher Education Sub-Committee, the issue did not disappear. By 1920, when recognition of hostels at other colleges had occurred, there were 94 LDTC students living in hostels. Nevertheless, LDTC students could only live in such hostels during the three years of their degree courses, not during the final training year, and Nunn and Punnett argued the case for an LDTC hostel for fourth-year students or, failing that, at least for an LCC officer who could oversee student lodging arrangements. In 1921 Punnett had an interview with the LCC's Assistant Officer for Higher Education, Philippa Fawcett, but no lodgings officer was appointed and the College was advised to refer students to other colleges of the University where lists of suitable lodgings were kept.[14]

The most fundamental questioning of the status and nature of the LDTC in this period, however, arose not from the LCC, as in the case of the LDTC's recognition as a school of the University, nor from the LDTC staff and students, as over the provision of a hostel, but from the University itself. In 1909 a royal commission under the chairmanship of Richard Haldane was appointed 'to inquire into the working of the present organisation of the University of London'. The final report of the Haldane Commission was published in March 1913; its principal proposal was 'that the teaching of the University in its several faculties should be concentrated as far as possible in one place'. In August 1913, the Board of Education established a committee under Sir George Murray to examine the possible implementation of the Haldane recommendations, which included not only concentration around a single site or 'University quarter', but also a smaller Senate, a permanent salaried Vice-Chancellor, and the phasing out of external degrees. Its deliberations were overtaken by the First World War.[15]

Sections 135 and 140 of the report of the Haldane Commission proposed that:

> the London Day Training College might properly be constituted a University Department of Education … since King's College also includes a department for the training of teachers for elementary schools some co-ordination of the work in this department with that done in the London Day Training College would no doubt be desirable if the London County Council consent to place their college under the financial and educational control of the University.

Adams prepared a memorandum welcoming these proposals. Independence from the LCC would mean that:

> the College Council would have the power to do the real work of the College instead of having, as present, to refer every matter, however trifling, to the Higher Education Sub-Committee, which, with its great burden of other work, cannot devote to the affairs of the College the attention they deserve. …
>
> The ideal should be the establishment of a department of the University of London comparable to Teachers' College in the Columbia University, New York. … From every point of view, therefore, it seems highly desirable that such a department should be founded, and the London Day Training College, as the largest institution within the area, should form the centre of the department. By transferring this College to the University the Council would make it possible for the University to organise its educational work in a way that would be otherwise impossible.[16]

This memorandum was adopted by the College Council in April 1914, a meeting of only five members, including Adams, Nunn and Punnett, and forwarded to the Higher Education Sub-Committee.

Nothing, however, came of this attempt to transfer the LDTC to the University. In common with the remainder of the Haldane proposals, it became yet another casualty of the First World War. But it was also a casualty of the confusion that surrounded the possible nature of the new University. If the University of London were to become a single unit with power over all matters financial and educational, then the transfer of the LDTC would raise problems for the LCC. If, on the other hand, the colleges were to remain as the key units of administration, and the educational and financial control of the University were to continue simply in respect of such matters as hours of teaching, minimum salaries for staff, and regulations covering attendance and examination for students, then, providing certain safeguards were met, a transfer of the LDTC to the University could be contemplated. By 1932, when the collegiate nature of the University had been confirmed, and a University quarter had begun to grow upon the Bloomsbury site, the Institute of Education would be at its very centre.

## Staff

One of the most striking features of this period was the continuity of the leading full-time members of staff. Adams, Nunn, Punnett and von Wyss formed the core of the staff in 1922, just as they did in 1907. It would appear that the teaching hours of the Vice-Principals were similar to those of other members of staff, in spite of their additional administrative responsibilities. In 1910, Nunn was teaching for 22 hours a week and Punnett for 20. Von Wyss had the highest total at 25 hours a week, while Hague taught $22\frac{1}{2}$ hours and Miss F.J. Davies, recruited in 1908 from Graystoke Place Day Training College, taught 22.[17] In January 1910, when Adams applied for an extra member of staff, principally to assist von Wyss whose weekly hours of teaching would increase to 30 in the coming session, the request was initially refused. A solution was found in December 1910, when a decision was taken to replace the half-time post in French with a half-time post in drawing and nature study.[18]

Towards the end of 1912, following the ending of two-year students and the introduction of the four-year course, Adams agreed to a reduction in staffing levels by the equivalent of one half-time lecturer for the year 1913–14. The teaching establishment for that year comprised the Principal, two Vice-Principals, three lecturers, three part-time assistant lecturers, plus visiting teachers for physical exercises, domestic subjects, manual training, singing and voice production. The

13. A business training class, probably for the Central School of Arts and Crafts, in the LDTC lecture theatre in 1914

amount of staff time devoted to supervision of teaching practice, which had recently been cut from a total of 72 weeks per year to 47, was further reduced to 42.[19] One benefit of the four-year course, which provided for a single year of post-graduate training as opposed to a concurrent undergraduate and training course, was that it was possible for staff to have longer periods of non-teaching time, particularly in the summer vacation. This 'incidental though important effect' was warmly welcomed by one of the LCC's divisional inspectors, Cloudesley Brereton, who reported in 1911 on 'the need of adequate time for research and preparation in the case of teachers of University rank'.[20]

Evidence as to the quality and competence of the staff in this period is mixed, and at times difficult to evaluate. For example, in 1909 the LCC divisional inspector, F.S. Boas, declared that 'my impression is that the Staff of the College is, as a whole exceptionally able and enthusiastic: but that the students had scarcely risen to the full use and appreciation of the splendid opportunities offered to them'.[21] An HMI report of the following year, however, not only criticized the students, many of whom 'look jaded and are jaded', but also declared unequivocally that 'the distinction and practical ability of the Principal, Vice-Principals, and Miss Von Wyss cannot wholly compensate for the inferiority of some of their colleagues as trainers of teachers'.[22]

On occasion, His Majesty's Inspectors and LCC inspectors clashed directly over the standards of teaching. One notable example of this occurred in 1911 when the Board of Education sent a letter announcing that although the HMI inspection had revealed a generally satisfactory standard in physical exercises among the women students, the standard of the men was so lamentable that 'the Board feel doubtful whether they could regard any of these students as having passed in the subject this year'. No credit for physical exercises would be awarded for men students for the coming year 'unless a considerable improvement takes place'.[23] The member of staff under criticism, Mr Pearce, had the support of the LCC's organizer of drill, T. Chesterton, who queried why, at the 1911 inspection, the Board of Education's inspector had 'made neither a single complaint, remark nor suggestion as to the efficiency of the instructor or the abilities of the pupils, and the whole of the latter passed the examination'.[24] Early in 1913, however, following a second adverse report, Pearce departed to a post at the Strand School. The Board of Education report for 1914 concluded that under the new instructor, F.N. Punchard, there had been 'a great improvement in the work and that the students appear to be taking a more genuine interest in the subject. The instruction is well arranged and the teaching is skilful and stimulating.'[25]

Inspectors, both national and local, invariably complimented the teaching of the full-time members of staff, with Nunn and von Wyss most frequently singled out for praise. A seminar class by Nunn on mathematics, was described by Brereton as 'thoughtful and inspiring',[26] while the LCC art inspector, A.H. Christie, reported most favourably on von Wyss's work in nature study and drawing.[27]

Nunn's prowess and loyalty was much appreciated by Adams who, in October 1912, reported to the College Council that in the previous 18 months the Vice-Principal had received several unsolicited offers of other posts, at salaries in excess of £700 per annum. Nunn's salary, which was £400 on appointment in 1905, rising by increments of £25 to £500, was raised to £600 forthwith. The resultant discrepancy between the salaries of Nunn and Punnett was no doubt one factor which led to the comment in the University report of July 1914 on the desirability of equal pay for equal work. The Academic Council had noted that 'the scale of payment for women teachers is lower than that for men teachers, as is shown in the difference between the salaries of Normal Masters and Normal Mistresses'.[28]

One member of staff who regularly received unfavourable comment was John Hague, who was in charge of work in English. Although Hague was an acknowledged scholar, and noted for his particular enthusiasm for Norse legends, he was widely 'suspected of not appreciating the practical difficulties of classroom work'.[29] In 1909, Boas observed two lectures by Hague: one with a first-year class, the other with a postgraduate group. Although he acknowledged Hague's literary feeling and taste and capacity for improvement, Boas also recorded that he was 'lacking in assurance of manner and the discipline in his class did not seem to me to be perfect'. He concluded that 'Mr Hague is at present scarcely equal, in my opinion, to the responsibilities of the important post he holds'.[30]

Other critical comments at this inspection, comments endorsed by Brereton, were directed at the standard of reading. Boas not only criticized the standard of reading by students in classes conducted by Hague, but even that of students in a second-year class conducted by Punnett. It seems likely that the inspectors were objecting to the students' accents as well as to their powers of enunciation. This was one item raised at a special conference held in 1908 between seven members of the College's Local Committee, headed by Sophie Bryant, and the Board's chief inspector of training colleges, HMI Barnett, accompanied by three other members of the inspectorate. Although Barnett's report on the College's work was broadly favourable, he also drew attention to deficiencies in the students' ability to analyse sounds: 'In his opinion the study of elementary phonetics is extremely important for the teaching of language in any form, and not least in the case of London students'.[31] Board of Education and LCC inspectors clearly saw eye to eye on this issue. In 1909, Brereton duly recommended both the purchase of a gramophone and other phonetic apparatus, and the separation of the sexes, for the teaching of this important subject.[32]

Problems continued, and came to a head in 1913. Brereton maintained that it was 'absolutely indispensable that the future teachers who leave the college should be as far as possible masters or mistresses of the art of clear and correct speech'.[33] In the spring of that year, however, when interviewing College students for appointment to LCC schools, it became apparent that many were still deficient in this regard. Brereton acknowledged that 'indistinctness of speech' was partly the fault of secondary schools and that inducing students to change their ways of speaking was particularly difficult, but threatened that unless improvements were made it would be necessary to appoint 'a definite teacher in elocution'.[34] Accordingly, a hasty reorganization took place. Punnett took over the teaching of phonetics, leaving Hulbert free to concentrate upon general and remedial work in voice production. He would also spend more time supervising students in schools, and oversee 'in a general way the teaching of elocution and singing in all its branches'.[35] Reports on teaching practice at this time were assiduous in drawing attention to deficiencies in the speech of students. Even the future Director, G.B. Jeffery, described as 'a student of brilliant ability', was criticized for 'a slight nasality in his speech … a regrettable defect of which he is trying to cure himself'.[36]

In the early years of the LDTC, members of staff had to cover considerable areas of knowledge. Punnett in mathematics, Nunn in mathematics and science and von Wyss in art and nature study became acknowledged leaders in the teaching of these subjects. Nevertheless, with a mere half dozen full-time members of staff (including the Principal and two Vice-Principals) it was difficult to provide leadership across the several elements of the training college and school curricula. Yet by the time the College entered its second decade, the need for specialist staff was becoming ever more apparent. Such staff would be required to take responsibility for a particular dimension of the curriculum and of professional training within the LDTC and demonstration schools. They would also assume a wider responsibility by means of publications, lectures and leadership within the emerging subject and other professional associations. Such responsibility and specialization would be of particular relevance to the increasing numbers of students seeking posts in secondary schools.

14. A cartoon of James Fairgrieve, pioneer of geography education and tutor to the colonial course

Specialist qualifications in a particular subject of the secondary school curriculum were exemplified in the person of James Fairgrieve, who was appointed in 1912. Fairgrieve was 42 years of age at the time of his appointment, a Scot and the eldest of the six shortlisted candidates. Born in Saltcoats, Fairgrieve had been educated in Glasgow and at Jesus College, Oxford, from where he graduated in 1895 with second-class honours in mathematics. He had also 'starved' his way through the University of Wales at Aberystwyth and acquired a BA pass degree from London and a certificate from the London School of Economics. His geographical studies had been with Mackinder in Oxford and Lyde in London. Fairgrieve had taught mathematics at grammar schools in Kelso and Campbeltown, before founding his own school in Southgate in London in 1899. In 1907 he moved to William Ellis School as senior assistant specialist in geography. At the time of his appointment, Fairgrieve already had a considerable reputation – as a Fellow of the Royal Geographical Society, author of publications on geography, and as an examiner for various bodies in both geography and history. His book, *Geography in Schools*, first published in 1926, would become the bible of geographical education for some 30 years.

Other details of staffing changes in this period are contained under the section dealing with the period of the First World War which, together with the ensuing financial restrictions, delayed further recruitment of subject specialists until the Nunn era.

## Students and courses

Extract books covering the period 1907–18 provide interesting, if somewhat random, details of early life at Southampton Row. Dinner prices were 3*d*. for soup and bread, 6*d*. for hot meat, two vegetables and bread, 5*d*. for cold meat, pickles and bread and 2*d*. for pudding. Ten general instructions on students' conduct in demonstration schools included: the importance of lesson prepara-tion and punctual attendance, the keeping of a diary of lessons and observations in the form of a practice report book, the learning of pupils' names as soon as possible, the opening of windows when a class left a room, and the close observation of 'two individuals of diverse types … care being taken that the children are unaware that special attention is being given to them'. Precise instructions were issued on the drill costume for women students. This was to consist of tunic and knickerbockers (preferably of dark blue serge) with both to reach the knee so that the tunic completely covered the knickerbockers. Corsets were never to be worn at drill lessons, and drill costumes were only to be worn in the gymnasium and adjoin-ing dressing room.[37] Missing library books were a perpetual source of concern (the College's assistant secretary, Miss Grassam, also acted as librarian) and Nunn and Punnett regularly sent a letter to departing students enclosing 'a list of books and pictures which, during the last session, have been removed from the Library and Museum without acknowledgement and have not been returned'.

15. The front cover of the *Londinian*, Lent term 1916, the magazine of the LDTC Students' Union

Student activities flourished and in 1914 the University report on the LDTC noted the College's 'active social life'. Student clubs and societies included badminton, chess, debates, drama, hockey, music, football and tennis – amalgamated into a Union, which received an annual grant of £50 from the LCC. Four-year students paid £1, three-year, 15*s*. and one-year students 10*s*. to belong to the Union. Staff and former students were admitted to membership for 5*s*. per annum.[38] Reports in the student magazine, the *Londinian*, provide details of these activities: a programme of ten socials in the academic year 1910–11, an attendance of 116 students at the Christmas social of 1911; a triumph for the men's soccer team which drew 2–2 with St Bartholomew's Hospital in the final of the University Cup Competition of 1912–13.[39]

Although from 1907 LDTC students had a permanent home, the intensity of the three-year course still caused considerable problems. Results from the final examinations of 1908 indicate the levels of attrition. Of the 43 three-year students who took the Board of Education's certificate examination in July, 26 passed and 17 failed. Fifty-one of the three-year students sat the University's final degree examination in October. Of the 26 men (one arts and 25 science) one was placed in the first class, two in the second, and four in the third. Seven were awarded pass degrees and 12 failed. Of the 25 women students (13 arts and 12 science) three were placed in the first class, two in the second, and two in the third. Eleven were awarded pass degrees and seven failed. In total, therefore, six LDTC students secured the BA at honours level and five at pass, while three failed. Of those taking the B.Sc. eight secured honours and 13 a pass, while no fewer than 16 failed.

These results were undoubtedly disappointing, for some students had neither degree nor certificate to show for three years of strenuous work. The failure rate of LDTC students in finals in 1908 was 37 per cent, as opposed to 33 per cent in 1907, 35 per cent in 1909 and 18 per cent in 1910.[40] Nevertheless, such performances must be placed in context. In commenting on the 1907 results, the LDTC Local Committee noted that even though its students had 'to do all their professional work in addition' their pass rates were higher than those of the average student. In that year, 70 per cent of LDTC students passed the final BA examination as against 65 per cent in the University overall. Similarly, 64.1 per cent of LDTC students passed the B.Sc. examination as opposed to 54 per cent overall.[41]

In 1911 the Board of Education finally acknowledged the enormous burdens faced by the three-year students and made provision for a four-year course. In future virtually the entire first three years would be given to academic studies, at the end of which time students would take their final degree examinations. Professional training would occupy the whole of the fourth year. This development was widely welcomed on academic and professional grounds, although Blair characteristically doubted 'whether many students would be prepared to devote four years to study in preparation for a university degree when they could obtain the Board of Education's certificate after a two years' course'.[42] His doubts appear to have been misplaced. Indeed, three of the four LDTC students who achieved first-class honours degrees in 1912, Simon Rosen in chemistry, Sarah Wechsler in history, and Stephen Whitaker in English, were among those who stayed on into a fourth year. In July 1913 they not only qualified as certificated teachers but also acquired the University's diploma in education, in which Wechsler 'excelled in the written examination'.[43] Described as 'An able and intelligent student and a very promising teacher', Wechsler's first post was at the County School for Girls in Hackney where she taught history and German.[44]

In 1911, the LCC decided that three-year courses should be ended at the LDTC and that although in 1912 some students might exceptionally, on the recommendation of Adams, be admitted under the old regulations, from that date the LDTC would be committed to the four-year course. Under the four- (as opposed to three-)

year regulations, students were still interviewed by Adams, admitted by the LDTC and allocated to a college of the University for their academic studies. During the first three years of the undergraduate course their professional work was limited to half a day per week, on Saturday mornings. In consequence many students became even more attached to their colleges than under the previous system of mixed academic and professional work.

In academic and professional terms the four-year consecutive course represented a distinct improvement upon what had gone before, yet for the next ten years LDTC students faced a particular problem – the date of the University of London's final examination. Although Adams and his colleagues frequently allied themselves with the University of London as against the LCC or even the Board of Education, the issue of the timing of final degree examinations was a notable exception. For three-year students the extended year provided by the autumn date of the University's final examinations might be a boon; for their successors, the four-year students, it was a disaster. For the examinations, which took place at the end of October and beginning of November, seriously disrupted the first term of the fourth year – the year assigned to professional training. Matters were brought to a head by the intervention of the Board of Education. The four-year course required a full academic year of professional training, but a special article, (31(a)), had been introduced into the teacher training regulations to accommodate the unique circumstances created by the autumn date of the London examination. In 1921 the Board declared that while in all other universities in England and Wales the Board's intentions were 'systematically and consistently carried out', the course at the LDTC 'does not fulfil the spirit and the intention of the regulations'.[45] The Board now proposed that postgraduate grants should not be paid until students had completed their final examinations. In consequence, it would be necessary for LDTC students to begin their fourth year in the January following their graduation. This threat had the desired effect. The LCC offered to assist the University in rescheduling finals by lending some 1,000 examination desks and by prevailing upon the polytechnic authorities to make their examination halls available. In January 1922 the Senate resolved that from 1924 final degree examinations should be held in the summer.

In the early years of the LDTC most students proceeded to teach in London elementary schools. Some student destinations were recorded simply as 'other' or 'unknown', but it appears that of the 340 students who qualified as teachers from the LDTC between the years 1904 and 1908, 256 proceeded to posts in the capital's elementary schools and only 16 to secondary schools.[46] In sharp contrast, figures of identified destinations of three- and four-year students who qualified from the LDTC between 1913 and 1917 suggest that 174 proceeded to secondary posts as opposed to 100 to elementary.[47]

Some of the students from this period are known to us only as names in examination or other lists, but one for whom a considerable amount of information is available is Reginald Charles Penfold. Although Penfold should not be considered in any sense as 'typical', he may be taken as representative of the many LDTC students whose lives were dramatically interrupted by war and who, though educated in the elementary system themselves, would spend their teaching careers in secondary schools. Born in 1890 and educated at All Saints School in Fulham and the Wandsworth Technical Institute, Penfold spent a year as a student teacher before entering the LDTC in 1910, being allocated to King's College. In 1913, he achieved a BA degree in French with third-class honours, winning a scholarship to France, and then proceeded to a fourth year. In July 1914 Penfold passed the University's diploma examination, while the Board of Education certificate shows his qualification as a certificated teacher from 1 August of that year. In this latter examination Penfold scored 57 per cent for principles of teaching, 60 for class management and methodology, 72 for physical education and hygiene and 66 for music, an average of 64 which placed him second among the 16 men students. His teaching practices were at the Cromer Street demonstration school, where he taught arithmetic, English, geography and history. The College report describes him as 'A man of the highest character and a capital teacher – enthusiastic, kindly, hardworking, capable'. The teaching practice report, however, also drew attention to 'His one serious defect … a jerky mode of speech that sometimes makes him difficult to follow'. A member of the University's Officer Training Corps while at the LDTC, in November 1914 Penfold enlisted as a lieutenant in the Royal Fusiliers, rising to the rank of major. He served in France from August 1915 until October 1918, twice being wounded and winning the Military Cross with bar. After the war he returned to teaching French at Enfield Grammar School, but the remainder of his career, 1920–55, was spent at the City and County School for Boys in Chester, where he was senior French master and, from 1937, second master. He also served for more than 40 years as secretary and later president of the Chester branch of the Workers' Educational Association, and as a Justice of the Peace. He died in 1970.[48]

16. Reginald Penfold, student 1910–14

Higher degree work developed during the war. The University's Board of Studies in Pedagogy recommended the establishment of MA and D.Lit. degrees in education, arguing that of three recent doctoral theses which might have been presented in education, two had had to be submitted under philosophy and one in history.[49] From 1915 a course of training for the University's MA in Education, to which King's College staff also contributed, was provided over a period of one to two years. Classes took place on Saturday mornings and on one or more evenings per week. Fees were 10 guineas for one year and 15 guineas for two, but teachers within the LCC area received free places on the same terms as students in the secondary department. In 1916 there were 11 students – nine men and two women – following the MA course.[50] The first MA thesis, entitled 'The influence of 1845 on education', was presented by Olive Sinclair in that year.[51]

Finally, mention should be made of the course for those intending to teach in the day continuation schools established under the Education Act of 1918. This was short-lived, as were the schools themselves, but provided another interesting exercise in co-operation, this time with the LSE, where half of the course was taken under the direction of Professor Urwick.[52] Some students acquired varied practical experience. For example, Marjorie Tomson, who took the course in 1920–1, not only did teaching practices at Cromer Street and at the Wild Street Continuation School, but also had a period of residence at the Canning Town Women's Settlement. There she taught in the Working Girls' Club and undertook casework in connection with the Children's Country Holiday Fund and the Metropolitan Association for befriending Young Servants.[53]

## Demonstration schools

One of the most distinctive features of the early years of the LDTC was the demonstration school. During the first five years of peripatetic existence, temporary arrangements were made to use two LCC Islington schools – at Station Road and Thornhill Road – for practice purposes. In these schools the LDTC was responsible for the teaching of a number of subjects in certain classes. For example, in 1906 two standards in the Boys' Department at Thornhill Road were placed at the disposal of LDTC staff for demonstration purposes, and were taught on four mornings per week by the group of postgraduate elementary students. Demonstration and criticism lessons, therefore, took place within a series of meaningful contexts, with staff and students assuming a direct responsibility for the work and progress of these groups of pupils.

During 1907 Nunn and Punnett considered how best to provide for the new situation created by the move to the Southampton Row site. Accordingly, two nearby Holborn schools – St John the Evangelist Church of England School in Red Lion Square and the LCC Princeton Street School – were designated as temporary practising schools. The longer-term aim of the Vice-Principals, however, was 'the establishment of a special practising school in which the teachers are practically members of the college staff'.[54] In 1909–10, in addition to these two practising schools, the LCC assigned Cromer Street School to the LDTC as an official demonstration school.

The essential qualities of a demonstration school, as outlined by the Board of Education's inspector, were three-fold. The first was that the staff of such a school, including the headteacher, should be specially selected and come under the influence of the training college and its principal. The second was that the school should be large and organized into three departments – infants, boys and girls. A third consideration was the size of classes; HMI Barnett considered that in no case should there be more than 40 pupils in a class. Only if such favourable conditions prevailed, could the students be assured of a wide range of opportunities for seeing the very best methods of teaching in operation.[55]

Nunn's view of the value and purpose of demonstration schools was expressed in a report considered by the College Council in February 1910. Nunn identified the first purpose of a demonstration school as being to provide a more effective teaching practice experience than might be obtained in schools outside the control of the College.

> The second function of a Demonstration School is less obvious but in reality more important. It is to form a solid basis for the whole of the professional studies of the college. It is difficult to over-estimate the importance of sound theory in Education. ... But it is no less certain that the theory, unless it remains firmly rooted in professional practice, tends to become a devitalised and useless growth ... the Demonstration School becomes one in which curriculum and method express to a degree beyond that of the ordinary school a conscious and unified educational doctrine.[56]

The third purpose of a demonstration school, in Nunn's judgement, was that it should promote, in a cautious fashion, new theory and practice. Nunn firmly believed that pedagogical experiments were essential. His personal commitment to 'novel courses of instruction' as opposed to 'mechanism and routine' cannot be doubted. Demonstration schools could also serve to promote improved pedagogy amongst existing teachers. In 1912 it was reported that some 1,000 teachers from elementary schools and 250 from secondary schools had attended courses on work done in the demonstration schools or arising immediately out of such work.[57]

Nunn thought it essential that the syllabuses and methods in the demonstration school should express the convictions of the College staff. A copy of the *Syllabuses in use in the College Demonstration Schools* of 1912 began with a prefatory note which appeared over the names of Adams, Nunn and Punnett. The syllabuses, which provided a first-year general course together with others in English, history, geography, science, mathematics, drawing and handwork, constituted a programme which extended over six years for children aged from 8 to 14. The general course was intended to occupy the greater part of the first year's work, together with supplementary instruction in reading, writing and mathematics. The introduction to the general course for the first year clearly indicates the educational philosophy which Adams, and particularly Nunn, espoused:

> The child's instincts and other specific tendencies are an inheritance which gives him his start in life and determines the general character of his activities. ...

Learning by direct experience is, therefore, the key-note of the scheme of
work. ...

Since the earliest stages of industrial and social development embody many
things which appeal to the nature of the child and set him on the road to
understanding the complex life about him, this experience has been selected
as subject matter of the course of instruction in the first year.

A considerable gap existed, however, between the ideals expressed in Nunn's
memorandum of 1910 and the syllabus of 1912 on the one hand, and the realities
of life at that time in the LDTC's principal demonstration school at Cromer Street
on the other. This suffered from a variety of problems – cramped and inadequate
conditions, a limited age and curriculum range, overlarge classes and teachers
who, apart from the headmaster, E.H. Beresford, had been appointed without any
concern for their potential roles as trainers of teachers.

The demonstration school occupied the second and third floors of the Cromer
Street building. There were six classrooms on the second floor, with drawing and
science rooms on the third and a roof playground. Two small teachers' sitting
rooms were located in the mezzanines between the first and second and second
and third floors, but these were barely adequate for the permanent staff, and could
not cope with the 20 or 30 students who taught regularly in the school, and

17. A girls' science
class at Cromer Street
School, 1906

**18. A boys' physical exercise class at Cromer Street School, 1906**

certainly not with 30 or 40 students who attended for half days for the demonstration lessons. There was no separate room for the headteacher, and no areas in which staff could meet students to discuss their work. One solution to these problems would have been for the demonstration school to take over the ground floor of the building, but this was occupied by a special school for 60 'mentally defective' children.

Unlike St John's, which was an all-age school, Cromer Street was a 'senior mixed' elementary school of 290 pupils aged between 10 and 14. In 1912 two of the six classes contained more than 55 pupils and two others more than 50. Cromer Street was fed almost entirely by children, some 100 in number per year, who had passed Standard IV in the neighbouring school in Prospect Terrace. This meant that children entering the school had not been taught along the lines presupposed by the College syllabus. This difficulty could only be overcome by Cromer Street becoming an all-age school or by an extension of the College's syllabus and pedagogy into the Prospect Terrace School. A further problem arose over the teaching of domestic economy and handicraft. No provision in these subjects was made for the 100 younger pupils at Cromer Street, while older pupils attended classes at the separate domestic economy and manual training centres. A final issue concerned the abilities of the Cromer Street teachers. Nunn emphasized the extent to which school staff would need to understand and participate in the development of the new syllabus and assume responsibility for much of the super-

19. Cromer Street
School orchestra,
1906

vision of students. His memorandum of 1910 concluded that the ultimate success of the whole enterprise depended 'upon the efficiency of the support which is given to it by the whole staff'.[58]

Early in 1914 Adams declared himself very satisfied with the work done in the demonstration schools, and was seeking to add another. But his main concern was to extend the principle to the secondary sector. In advocating the closest possible connection between theory and practice, Adams called for 'the supply of two large and thoroughly equipped secondary schools, one for boys and one for girls, placed entirely under the control of the training college authorities in such a way that the staffs of the schools should form an integral part of the staff of the College'.[59]

The call went unheeded as other, and more urgent, matters arose.

## The war years, 1914–1918

The Archduke Francis Ferdinand, heir to the Hapsburg thrones, was assassinated at Sarajevo on 28 June 1914. On 1 August Germany declared war on Russia, and on 3 August on France. On the following day Britain declared war on Germany and on 12 August on Austria-Hungary. The battle of the Marne took place early in September and by the middle of the month trench warfare had begun. In September 1914, the LDTC began the session with a total of 308 students: 113 men and 195 women. In September 1916 there were 211 students: 16 men and

---

# Roll of Honour.

## Staff and Students, Past and Present, L.D.T.C.

### KILLED IN ACTION.

#### STAFF.

J. A. Monkhouse, 2nd Lt., R.A.M.C. (died), late Headmaster of St John's.

John Steel, Lt., R.N.V.R., late Master of Method, Islington Training College.

P. Warner, Royal Fusiliers, late Asst. Master, St. John's School.

#### STUDENTS.

Basswitz, A., Capt., M.C., London Regt. (mentioned in despatches), 1911-14.

Bunting, R. R., 2nd Lt. Essex Regt., 1910-14.

Burrows, A., Capt., Northampton Regt., 1912-13.

Despicht, L. T., Lt., M.C., Bedford Regt. (mentioned in despatches), 1909-12.

Desmond, S. M., Lt., R.A.F., 1913-16.

Draisey, E. R. W., 2nd Lt., Bedford Regt., 1913.

Dunkley, A., 2nd Lt., Worcester Regt., 1910-13.

Fisher, R., 2nd Lt., Staffordshire Regt., 1915.

Garland, J. R., Capt., London Regt., 1911.

Handley, H. E., Lt., London Regt., 1911-14.

Heatley, H. F., Lt , Yorkshire Regt., 1909-12.

Hedgeland, C. S., Lt., M.G.C., 1911-14.

Le Cheriton, G. A.

McCance, F., 2nd Lt., Border Regt., 1914.

March, C. C., Corpl., R.E., 1913.

Moule, A. A., Corpl., R.E., 1913.

Mount, E. A., 2nd Lt., R.F., 1911-14.

Nancarrow, P., Bedfordshire Regt., 1912-15.

Pearson, J. A., 2nd Lt., London Regt., 1908-11.

Plumb, E. S., Lt., Leicester Regt., 1909-12.

Preedy, J. B. K., 2nd Lt., U. of L. O.T.C., 1903-6.

Scannell, M. H., H.A.C., 1912-15.

Simons, L., Capt., M.C., R.E., 1906-9.

Stamp, T. G., Corpl., R.E., 1913.

Tantram, H., 2nd Lt., R. Fusiliers, 1912.

Taylor, W. F., Lt., E. Kent Regt., 1910-14.

Walker, J. A., R.A.M.C., 1905-8.

Whyte, J. D., Capt., Royal Sussex Regt., 1913.

Wilkinson, W. A., 2nd Lt., R.F.A., 1906-9.

Williams, W. A., Dr., R.F.A., 1910-13.

Wisemam, J. M., L.Cpl., London Regt., 1908-11.

Worthy, F., Tpr., Dragoon Guards, 1915.

20. A roll of honour, published in the *Londinian*, 1919–20, records the names of 35 of the 40 past and present members of the LDTC who lost their lives in the First World War

195 women. By this date the only likely male recruits were those pronounced medically unfit for military service.[60]

The First World War brought great suffering and hardship. Millions of lives were lost, and the lives of millions more blighted forever. The names of 40 LDTC members are recorded on the memorial plaque to those who died – three staff and 37 students or former students. The three staff were two members of the St John's demonstration school, J.A. Monkhouse, the headmaster, and P. Warner, and J. Steel, master of method at the Islington Training College which was merged with the LDTC during the war. The four key LDTC staff, Adams, Nunn, Punnett and von Wyss, were not required for military service, and attempts to requisition the LDTC building for war offices were successfully resisted.[61] Indeed, the LDTC provided a refuge for one training college and one training department. The first of these was the Islington Training College, an LCC college for men students opened in 1906. By the summer of 1916, however, there was only one Islington student left and plans were in hand to locate him elsewhere.

In the summer of 1915 the Board of Education decided that on grounds of economy 'the elementary training department of King's College (Strand) should be closed until further notice, and that the students should be transferred to the London Day Training College (Holborn)'.[62] This transfer took effect immediately. Professor John William Adamson, the head of the King's Training Department and Albert Cock, who subsequently became Professor of Education at the University College of Southampton, were added to the LDTC staff.[63] Thus, albeit for a brief period and under wartime conditions, the oft-mooted union between the LDTC and King's took place.

For staff and students still at the College, the war impinged in a variety of ways. There were procedures to be followed in the case of an air raid. The building was increasingly used for meetings of other groups, as on 8 June 1917 when H.A.L. Fisher, the President of the Board of Education, addressed representatives of the country's education committees in the LDTC lecture theatre.[64] As staff shortages in schools grew, the teaching practices of students at the LDTC, in common with those of other training institutions, took on a new significance. Like the pupil teachers of old, students were now often placed in full control of classes. To facilitate this, teaching practices were re-arranged so that half of the students taught in schools from Monday to Wednesday lunchtime, and the other half for the rest of the week. A further development was the recruitment of women to teach in boys' schools. For example, in 1914 Annie Thomas began her teaching career at the County School for Boys, Harrow, and in 1916 Marguerite Grimes took up her first post at the Boys' Grammar School, Hitchin, where she taught chemistry, mathematics and physics.[65]

As the war came to end in November 1918, schemes were devised to enable those students whose courses had been interrupted or deferred by war service to complete their training. In February 1919 Adams reported news of returning students to the College Council and also advised that half a dozen officers from overseas were taking special courses at the College from January to July 'with great advantage to the social and intellectual life of the College'.[66] By the beginning of June some 200 students had already been admitted for September, ensuring that the LDTC, which had been under strength during the years of conflict, would be considerably above its capacity of 350 students. Special courses for ex-servicemen

| Table 1 | Post-war student numbers[67] |
|---------|------|
| 1913–14 | 301 |
| 1918–19 | 199 |
| 1919–20 | 487 |
| 1920–21 | 743 |
| 1921–22 | 913 |

began and finished at different times in the year, and their attendance was frequently arranged on a part- rather than full-time basis. In consequence the post-war years saw a considerable increase in student numbers.

Student memories of this period are mixed. For one ex-serviceman, the experience 'set me on my feet as a normal civilised human being and, I hope, a useful teacher, after being for three years an extremely uncouth troglodyte'. Others, including an ex-serviceman who took a four-year course from 1919 to 1923, felt that 'There was a feeling of now being washed up into a backwater'.[68] A group of 60 Australian schoolteachers awaiting repatriation, together with five from the USA and three from New Zealand, attended regular and additional courses and an extended series of demonstration visits. Their distinctive contributions to the life of the LDTC included a 'Diggers' College Song'.[69]

The Diggers' College Song, first sung at an end of term 'Diggers' night ' in March 1919

---

## THE DIGGERS' COLLEGE SONG
### (First Sung at the Diggers' Night)

We're from the Sunny South,
Australia is our home, sir,
A finer place you'll never face,
No matter where you roam, sir.

Chorus:
Toujours, toujours,
Pour Bacchus et les amours,
Yap, yap, tra-la-la-la-la,
Yap, yap, tra-la-la-la-la,
Pour Bacchus et les amours.

We're now at the London Day,
In midst of Winter's grip, sir,
But to one and all there's a weekly call,
That early morning trip, sir.

Chorus.

The Principal's a man,
He's what you call a trump, sir,

At game and classic fame,
Prof. Adams can give 'em a bump, sir.

Chorus.

Prof. T. Nunn lives
On $H_2SO_4$, sir,
Of graphs and lines and surds and signs
He has a wondrous store, sir.

Chorus.

The ladies of this Coll.
A sample you have here, sir,
With look and smile they do beguile,
Without them we'd be queer, sir.

And now, God bless this Coll.,
Give the County Council prudence
To pay the noblest band on earth
The training College Students!

Adams and Nunn sought additional staff to cope with this increase in student numbers and diversification of activities.[70] Indeed, both seem to have felt the strain of the post-war years most keenly. In a letter of December 1918 Adams apologized for mistakes in examination marks which he attributed to 'attempting to add up figures at the end of a ten hours' Sunday',[71] while early in 1919 Nunn admitted to an error in an examination schedule, pleading 'that I was working at very great pressure at the moment'.[72] In the summer of 1919 Adams even had an interview with Sir Michael Sadler, Vice-Chancellor of the University of Leeds, in connection with the chair of Education there.[73] It clearly was essential for the future standing of the LDTC that the makeshift arrangements of the war years were set aside and that lectures and classes in professional subjects and tutorial guidance in theoretical and practical work should be undertaken by full-time staff. In particular, specialists of the calibre of Fairgrieve were required in each of the subjects of the secondary curriculum.

## Conclusion

In 1907 the London Day Training College was a small, though growing, collection of young students and their teachers, firmly located within the elementary school tradition, who after five years of breathless and somewhat precarious existence had finally found a home. By 1922 the LDTC was a graduate institution whose students were increasingly connected with secondary schools, both as former pupils and as prospective teachers. In that year the first 20 years of the LDTC's existence were celebrated by the inauguration of Foundation Week – a mixture of lectures, reviews, dances and other entertainment. This became an annual event, a demonstration of strong community spirit with full staff and student participation.

From 1909 the LDTC had a new status as a school of the University. Recognition as a school meant that the LDTC was no longer merely 'attached to' the University, nor even simply the training department of a college, as at Bedford or King's, but a nascent university college in its own right. Such recognition brought immediate benefits, for example the establishment of a College Board and staff representation on the governing body. It also strengthened the determination to achieve academic excellence in education and to become a British equivalent of Teachers College, Columbia. Three years later, this ambition was reinforced by the introduction of the four-year course. In future the LDTC would be providing an uninterrupted course of postgraduate professional training for students studying for a University diploma in education.[74]

Academic aspirations and professional excellence went hand in hand. By 1922, when Nunn succeeded Adams as Principal, the LDTC had become the intellectual and professional centre for London's teachers, while Adams himself had become

> We are John Adams's Army,
> His little lambs are we,
> We cannot work, we cannot teach—
> What earthly use are we?

**Early Foundation Week rag song**

their role model. Robert Blair, another Scot and former pupil teacher, who was knighted in 1914, once remarked at a public dinner that 'There are 20,000 teachers in London, and the greatest of them is John Adams'. In an appreciation of Adams, written in 1935, the LCC school inspector and author, P.B. Ballard, commented that this was 'a remark which was not only striking but had the additional merit of being true'.[75] The mantle of being the greatest teacher in London was subsequently assumed by both Nunn and Clarke.

Adams was active in a number of educational causes located in the capital. These included the Child Study Society (London), of which he was a vice-president, and the College of Preceptors, which he served for many years as a vice-president and as an examiner, and even briefly, from 1910 until 1911, as dean. Adams instituted and taught on courses for university lecturers, and contributed to summer courses for teachers, both from Britain and overseas. He also retained his Scottish educational links, and in 1911 was awarded an honorary doctorate by the University of St Andrews, then celebrating its 500th anniversary. In the following year, Adams presided over the Educational Science section of the British Association meeting in Dundee. The theme of his presidential address was 'An Objective Standard in Education'. During the closing months of the war Adams lectured to troops in France, where his contribution was considered to be 'worth more than twenty of the rest of the team'. On one memorable occasion when the electric lights failed at a great evening service 'out of the darkness there came that strangely compelling Glaswegian voice of John Adams preaching a sermon upon the devil which held the soldiers silent and delighted in their seats'.[76]

Adams also promoted the international reputation of the LDTC. In retirement he undertook a long-planned tour of Australia, New Zealand and South Africa, lecturing in universities and to teachers' associations. Indeed, it was while returning from this tour in 1925 that Adams received information about his knighthood. Adams' final years, however, were spent mainly in the USA and in 1923 he took up an appointment at the University of California, at Los Angeles, where he lived until his death in 1934. Nevertheless, Adams still found time to undertake his imperial tour, to teach two summer semesters and four summer schools at Harvard, and to lecture at numerous other American universities. Honours were heaped upon him, including honorary degrees from the University of Southern California in 1930 and from the University of California at Los Angeles in 1934. The University of California also instituted a series of memorial lectures in his honour, as did the University of London.[77] When in the 1960s the Institute acquired residential accommodation, a facility of particular benefit to students from overseas, it was fittingly named John Adams Hall.

# Chapter 4

# From Day Training College to University Institute
## 1922–1932

### Introduction

In the immediate post-war years Britain faced many problems. Influenza epidemics, rampant inflation, strikes in essential services and unemployment in excess of 2 million by the summer of 1921, were complemented by massacre in India and civil war in Ireland. The public debt was virtually incalculable; the prospect of reparations proved illusory. The Burnham Committee, established in 1919, had led to the introduction of national salary scales for teachers, but in education, as in other spheres, 'the inter-war years were dominated by the cry for, and the practice of, economy'.[1] The Geddes 'axe' of 1922 brought cuts of more than £6 million in an Education budget of £50 million, while the May Committee of 1931 added a further 10-per-cent reduction in teachers' salaries on top of the 5 per cent introduced under Geddes. Although in 1918 the school-leaving age had been raised to 14, implementation of the oft-mooted rise to 15 years would be delayed until 1947. The average attendance of pupils in elementary schools in England and Wales declined from 5,182,116 in 1921–2 to 4,526,701 in 1937–8. In contrast, pupil numbers in grant-aided secondary schools rose from 354,956 in 1922 to 470,003 in 1938.[2] Figures such as these reinforced the shift of emphasis from training for the Board of Education's teacher's certificate to preparation for the University's diploma, and from elementary to secondary work. Other features of this period included the growth of research and higher degrees, particularly within the field of psychology of education. Finally, the introduction of a course to prepare students for work in the colonies confirmed the LDTC's international role. These developments provided new challenges. They also led inexorably, though at times painfully, to the transformation of the LDTC into the Institute of Education of the University of London.

21. Percy Nunn, the LDTC's second Principal and the greatest figure in the first century of the Institute's history

## Percy Nunn

Many distinguished teachers, scholars and administrators have served on the staff of the LDTC and the Institute in the first century of its existence, but the greatest of them all was Percy Nunn. By 1922, when Nunn succeeded Adams, his authority and pre-eminence were unquestioned and in the coming years were to be further appreciated by students and staff alike. Marian Arnold was a student at the LDTC in 1927–8. Of the interview by Nunn in 1924 before commencing her degree work she wrote: 'Somehow one knew that one was in the presence of a great man, a brilliant mind, anxious to give of his best to the young folk about him. It is a tribute to his greatness that we all felt this.' This greatness was matched by humility and humour. In 1930, at a Friday morning lecture following the award of his knighthood, Nunn recounted to the students his double discomfiture: first on hearing the words 'Arise, Sir Thomas', since he wished to be known as 'Sir Percy', and secondly on his great difficulty in retiring backwards owing to the entanglement of his sword.[3]

During Nunn's principalship the LDTC staff included people of considerable talent and forceful personality. Nevertheless, as one colleague, Dr Percival Gurrey, lecturer in English, observed:

Over this collection Nunn towered in every way: intellectual ability, force of character, and width of interest and knowledge. There was no doubt about our realisation of his supreme position as a thinker, organiser, mathematician and teacher. The legend of Nunn did not grow after he left us: we saw it growing.[4]

Such judgements have not been diminished by the passage of time. In 1911, following the departure of Michael Sadler to become Vice-Chancellor of the University of Leeds, the School of Education of the University of Manchester tried unsuccessfully to recruit Nunn to a chair. In his centenary history of the School, A.B.

Robertson stated that Nunn 'was to become the most influential educationist of the second quarter of the century'.[5]

Nunn was a great teacher. As one child who had been struggling with map projections remarked, 'My, don't he clean your brain',[6] while Fairgrieve remembered a comment once made to him that 'Nunn could teach the calculus to a class of whelks'.[7] Nunn saw the value of working from concrete forms – he took great delight in designing and making models and instruments, and together with Margaret Punnett assembled a remarkable mathematics and science museum at the LDTC. But he was also a scholar – a scientist, mathematician, philosopher and psychologist of distinction. Such breadth of interest was reflected in his published work. This ranged from textbooks on mathematics and science on the one hand, to the epistemological essay on *The Aims and Achievements of Scientific Method* (1907), a treatise on Einstein's theory entitled *Relativity and Gravitation* (1923), and erudite papers published in the *Proceedings of the Aristotelian Society* on the other. As Selleck has noted, Nunn 'was a man of diverse talents who earned the admiration of such different personalities as William McDougall and Bertrand Russell' and though the corpus of his philosophical writing was small, it exercised, according to J.A. Passmore, 'an influence out of all proportion to its modest dimensions'.[8]

Nevertheless, the most influential of Nunn's books, and surely the most influential single work to have been written by any member of staff (or former student) of the LDTC and the Institute, was *Education: Its data and first principles*, which first appeared in 1920.[9] In his preface, Nunn stated that the book provided a preliminary survey of educational theory and practice and was addressed both to student teachers and to the wider public. Few works on education have been so successful. Between 1920 and 1929 it went through 13 reprints. The second revised edition, expanded 'to take due account of recent advances in knowledge, particularly in psychology', appeared in 1930, with a further eight reprints to 1941. Further revision occurred in the third edition of 1945. Writing in 1936 of English education in the period since 1920, F.A. Cavenagh proclaimed it 'the outstanding book of the period'.[10] For some 40 years Nunn's *Education* served as a 'bible' for educational professionals and public alike.

In the preface to the first edition Nunn declared that the basic theme of *Education* was 'to reassert the claim of Individuality to be regarded as the supreme educational ideal, and to protect that ideal against both the misprision of its critics and the incautious advocacy of its friends'. That claim was to strike a deep chord with prospective and practising teachers who sought to modify the rigidities of an elementary school system which still bore the ethos of standards and payment by results. It also resonated more widely in a country which had recently emerged from the horrors of one world war, only to be plunged some 20 years later into a second, and which viewed with alarm the growth of totalitarian regimes, based upon the ideologies of Bolshevism and Fascism. Published in the year which saw

*When it is*

*all gone*

*There will be*

*Nunn left.*

22. A cartoon in the *Londinian*, Michaelmas term 1924, looks ahead

**23. A be-hatted Percy Nunn with the LDTC soccer team of 1924–5**

the first meeting of the League of Nations, there was a strongly Utopian and idealistic spirit in the book. Indeed, Nunn concluded with a ringing call that:

> though our children cannot build a fairer world on any other foundation than our own, yet they are not bound, unless in our own folly we will have it so, to repeat for ever our failures; that they have in them a creative power which, if wisely encouraged and tolerantly guided, may remould our best into a life far worthier than we have seen or than it has entered into our hearts to conceive.

Not all were convinced by Nunn's arguments and exposition. Some commentators, including his successor Fred Clarke, found his treatment of the social aspects of education inadequate, and argued that he was over-reliant upon biological and psychological data.[11] But many students were inspired. A.R. Moon, a student from 1923, noted the dissatisfactions of many of his contemporary ex-service colleagues at the LDTC. He also noted wryly that the emblem of those days was a dustbin which the students faithfully paraded outside the Albert Hall. Nevertheless, he recalled, 'We melted away to preach the Data and Principles in the hitherto dark land of Cane'.[12]

Nunn's many activities included membership of the Board of Education's Consultative Committee, and he drafted many sections of its reports. These included the chapter on the curriculum of the primary school for the Hadow Report of 1931.[13] He was also an influential witness to the Hadow Committee which reported in 1926, arguing for secondary schooling for all, albeit in three grades of school, with a modern school curriculum in which practical and cultural activities would play substantial parts.[14] Geoffrey Howson has also drawn attention to the extent to which Nunn's thinking pervades the sections on mathematics in the Spens Report of 1938.[15] Nunn served on the Labour Party's advisory committee on education, and was a member of the New Education Fellowship,[16] the Child Guidance Council and Sir Philip Hartog's committee of inquiry into the reliability of examinations.[17]

Nunn's leadership of the LDTC was characterized by his prodigious knowledge and capacity for work, and by his delight in the successes of others, both staff and students. Grace Wacey, who served as Secretary under successive Principals and Directors from 1920 until 1958, remembered him as 'very quiet, gracious and extremely courteous … a very human person'.[18] Nunn's seemingly encyclopaedic knowledge made it possible for him to enter into meaningful discussions with all colleagues about their work. His introduction of a tutorial system provided the opportunity for increased discussions between staff and students. Nunn's inspirational opening and closing addresses at the beginning and end of each academic year were complemented by his leadership of the end of term sing-song, for which he wrote several parodies, including 'Phyllis' and 'Knocked 'em in Southampton Row'.

'Phyllis', one of the favourite pieces written by Nunn for the end of term sing-song

---

### PHYLLIS

'Phyllis was a faire maide
  And she had suitors store',
But love, which other maidens prize,
  To Phyllis seemed a bore;
And so she turned her suitors down
  Despite their high degree.
The one degree that Phyllis craved
  Was Honours B.Sc., the B.Sc., the B.Sc.

Phyllis was a firm maid,
  To college she would go;
And so on fairy foot she sped
  Along Southampton Row.
The Institute she sought – where all,
  Amazed such charms to see,
Exclaimed, 'We must have Phyllis here
  To grace the I. of E., the I. of E., the
    I. of E.'

Phyllis, now a proud maid,
  Postgraduate became,
And as the Union President
  Achieved enormous fame.
Discussion lessons when she taught
  Were queued for like the tea
And soon, to meet the huge demand,
  Broadcast they had to be, they had to be,
    they had to be!

Phyllis was a stern maid
  And when she taught at school
Her pupils, though they worshipped her,
  Yet cowered beneath her rule.
Before her practice days were done
  The staff did all agree
The old headmistress straight must go
  And Phyllis head must be, their head must be,
    their head must be.

Phyllis is a great maid;
  Before her queenly brow
Inspectors doff their haughty mien,
  Directors scrape and bow.
So far her fame has gone abroad
  'Tis sure as sure can be
The Government will send for her
  To rule the B. of E., the B. of E., the B. of E.

Phyllis you're a kind maid
  Whose heart with pity throbs
For all the gallant students here
  Who long for cushy jobs.
If you've a post to give that joins
  With ample £ s. d.,
A life of cultured leisure, please,
  Oh please remember me, remember me,
    remember me!

Nunn's commitment to the LDTC and to the training of teachers was continued through his daughter Elsa, a history graduate from Girton College, Cambridge. Elsa Nunn was a student at the LDTC from 1916 to 1917, teaching history, geography and arithmetic on her practice at Notting Hill High School, and securing a teaching practice mark of B plus and a distinction in the written part of the diploma examination. This 'very able and promising teacher'[19] began her career as a history mistress at Watford Girls' Grammar School, subsequently becoming a lecturer at Furzedown Training College. In 1929 she completed an MA at the LDTC with a thesis entitled 'The subject matter of history in junior schools'. In 1930 Elsa Nunn was appointed Principal of the College of St Matthias at Fishponds, Bristol, so that for a period of six years father and daughter presided simultaneously over institutions for the training of teachers. She retired in 1954.

## Research and Cyril Burt

The introduction of internal MA and Ph.D. degrees in education provided the opportunity for LDTC students to undertake research for the production of theses. Some 50 MA theses were completed between 1916 and 1932. The two theses of 1917 were by Frank Keay on 'Ancient education in India' and Albert Watts on 'The contribution of abnormal psychology to the problems of normal education'. Curriculum topics ranged from 'Teaching pupils how to study with special reference to history' by Samuel Williams in 1918 to 'Vocabulary tests for French' by Ralph Martin in 1932.[20] The range of topics at MA level, however, was in sharp contrast to the singular focus of the majority of the nine Ph.D. completions of this period, as the list in Table 2 shows.

| Table 2    Ph.D. completions, 1925–32[21] | |
| --- | --- |
| 1925 | McRae, C.R., 'Some effects of social and educational opportunities upon mental tests.' Slocombe, Charles S., 'The construction of mental tests.' Strasheim, Johannes J., 'Some aspects of developing intelligence.' |
| 1928 | Hughes, Arthur G., 'An investigation into the comparative intelligence and attainments of Jewish and non-Jewish school children.' |
| 1929 | Wilson, John H., 'A critical evaluation of certain intelligence scales with special reference to the effects of coaching and practice.' |
| 1930 | Shendarkar, D.D., 'An experimental investigation in teaching to solve problems in arithmetic and the light it throws on the doctrine of formal training.' |
| 1931 | Schonell, F.J., 'An investigation into disability in spelling.' Sleight, George F., 'The diagnosis and treatment of the dull and backward child.' |
| 1932 | Entwistle, William H., 'Some aspects of mental work.' |

No doubt these topics reflected, to some extent, the interests of the students who undertook the research. They also represented the research interests of Dr Cyril Burt, the psychologist recruited by Nunn to advance the subject of education in this period. All but one of the Ph.D. theses listed above, together with a further two completed in 1933, and 14 MA theses, were supervised by Burt, who held a part-time appointment at the LDTC from 1924 until 1932.[22]

Burt's later years were clouded with controversy. His views on the constant dimension of an individual's intelligence quotient (IQ) were strongly challenged, particularly in the context of the 11+ examination. Following his death in 1971 more serious charges were raised: that he had fabricated research evidence and invented non-existent collaborators. In contrast, the eight years that Burt spent at the LDTC were in some respects the summit of his career. During this period, as his biographer L.S. Hearnshaw has remarked, Burt was 'at the height of his powers; he was in an environment that suited him admirably; his practical and his academic duties were nicely balanced'.[23]

Burt's appointment represented Nunn's general commitment to the research and higher degree work of the LDTC and his particular concern for educational psychology. But although Nunn had a high regard for Burt and sought his advice on matters to do with London schools and London children, he was unable to secure for him a full-time professorial appointment.[24] The LCC argued that while Nunn's own professorship in 1913 had been fully merited, at a time of financial stringency there was no justification for a second chair and any appointment to replace Adams should be made at lecturer level. In a reply of December 1922, the Academic Council pointed out that the University of Manchester had two professors of education, but that following Adams' retirement there was only Nunn in London, although Adamson at King's who had also reached the retirement age had exceptionally been appointed for another year. Given the introduction of higher degree work in education, the Academic Council endorsed the recommendation of the Board of Studies in Pedagogy that three professors were needed: one in the general philosophy of education, a second in educational history and administration and a third in experimental pedagogy.[25] Nunn's manoeuvrings in 1923 included a suggestion, strongly resisted by the Principal of King's, Dr Ernest Barker, that the King's Training Department should be merged (as it had been during wartime) with the LDTC.

24. Cyril Burt in 1925; his years at the LDTC were in some respects the summit of his career

Cyril Burt was born in London in 1883, the son of a doctor. He won scholarships to Christ's Hospital School and Jesus College, Oxford where, though studying Classics, he took an optional paper in psychology. Burt remained in Oxford to take the teacher's diploma, with teaching practice at Clifton College. He also studied psychology at Würzburg under Oswald Külpe. From 1908 Burt engaged in research and teaching in psychology at the universities of Liverpool and

Cambridge. In 1913 he was appointed to a part-time post as the first psychologist at the LCC, where he was concerned with the testing of delinquent and subnormal elementary school children. Ten years later he was awarded a D.Sc. by the University of Oxford. His several works, including *Mental and Scholastic Tests*, first published in 1921 and reprinted in 1922 and 1927, made a considerable impression on Nunn, who argued that the fact that 'educational psychology is rapidly growing and needs an original and able researcher, indicates that it, rather than history should have the chair'.[26] In 1924 a compromise position was reached whereby Burt, who had gained the full support of Blair, was appointed to a part-time chair at the LDTC while continuing with his LCC work. This arrangement continued until 1932 when Burt succeeded Charles Spearman as Professor of Psychology at University College, London. In 1924, the situation at King's was resolved by the appointment as Adamson's successor of the Shakespearean scholar and former HMI, John Dover Wilson, 'who was able with unfailing charm and delightful humour to apply to the problems of modern pedagogy all that was relevant to them in the writings of the Tudor dramatists'.[27]

The foremost educational psychologist of his day, Burt was a leading member of numerous associations and pressure groups, and became known to a wider audience through his newspaper and magazine articles and radio broadcasts. His work for the LCC gave him an unrivalled knowledge of the capital's 'dull' and 'difficult' children, and in 1925 he published *The Young Delinquent*, an impressive work written in a popular style, which reached a fourth edition in 1944. He was a key adviser to the Board of Education's Consultative Committee and provided important material for the Hadow Reports of 1931 and 1933 on junior and infant schools, and later for the 1938 Spens Report on secondary education.

For a part-time member of staff Burt's influence on the LDTC was considerable. Much of his child guidance work with real 'young deliquates', as the escorting College porter, Mr Low, called them,[28] was now carried out on the LDTC premises, and psychology became a live study. Indeed, Burt's professional advice was even sought when a student, the son of a headmaster, was found to have been systematically stealing items around the College.[29] 'Squirrel Blurt', as he was known from one of the student parodies, was a showman with something to show, and lecture rooms would be crowded long before he was due to begin. 'Students were diverted by the application of intelligence tests, the introduction of actual case histories, or simple tricks of coin spinning to test the reliability of the faculties of perception'.[30] Brian Stanley, an Oxford graduate who later became Professor and Director of the Institute of Education at the University of Durham, resented his year at the LDTC, 1929–30, regarding it 'as a form of slumming'. Nevertheless, even he was mesmerized by Burt, distrusting not only his own watch but even an outside clock, 'because I could not believe that he had really lectured for 50 minutes'. Though now in his forties, Burt entered with zest into the LDTC's social life and Stanley noted that Burt 'used to take the prettiest women students to College concerts'.[31]

The second major appointment for advanced work during this period was that of Herbert Russell Hamley (widely known as HRH) in 1930. Hamley, who was 47 years old at the time of his appointment, was also counted as an educational psychologist, but had a broader approach than that of Burt and as a full-time member of staff could provide some urgently needed organization and overview for advanced studies. In the early years of postgraduate work, students came to the LDTC once or twice a week to hear a talk by Adams, Nunn or Burt who, given their other responsibilities, sometimes found it necessary to cancel these classes. An Australian by birth, Hamley had degrees in mathematics and natural philosophy. His several posts as schoolteacher, college and university lecturer and education inspector in Melbourne had been followed by nine years as Professor of Physics at the University of Bombay in India, and six years as Professor of Education and Principal of the Bombay Secondary Training College. Hamley's considerable experience, coupled with personal interests in metrical psychology, philosophy of education and classroom issues, broadened the remit of research, while his willingness to give talks on such issues as statistical research to colleagues and students in departments other than his own, and to involve other staff in the advanced work, helped to ensure that links were maintained across the increasingly diverse range of LDTC activities. Hamley was initially appointed at reader level but, following Burt's departure in 1932, was given the title of Professor of Education with special reference to experimental pedagogy. By this date he had the firm support of Nunn, who welcomed the fact that Hamley was 'wholly untouched by British class influences' and regarded him as 'indispensable'.[32] Hamley, indeed, became Deputy Director, and deputised for both Nunn and Clarke during their absences through illness, particularly in 1935 and 1937–8.[33]

25. H.R. Hamley, who served as deputy to Percy Nunn and Fred Clarke

Research and advanced work brought new staff of the calibre of Burt and Hamley to the LDTC; they also brought a new group of students – able, experienced and ambitious. One-year courses, whether for certificate or diploma, provided a mere introduction to some of the elements in the ever-expanding field of education. Further study, often at considerable financial and personal cost, for an advanced diploma, MA or Ph.D. could provide both greater intellectual challenge and satisfaction and a passport to promotion. The 'Statement of Policy' of the new Institute of Education drawn up by Nunn, noted that 'In recent years a good many students have passed through the course to important responsibilities: principalships and lectureships in training colleges and training departments of the Universities, inspectorships, headships of secondary schools, etc.'[34] One example of this career path was Elizabeth Williams (née Larby) who in 1914 achieved an upper second-class honours London degree in mathematics at the age of 19. Although continuing at Bedford College for her professional training, Williams took some courses at the LDTC, including the teaching of mathematics under Nunn. As Williams later recorded, 'Nunn was a joy' and when in his capacity as examiner he disagreed with her approach to teaching calculus to a sixth-form group, he invited her to a personal discussion on the following Saturday. This discussion was the beginning of a life-long friendship. In 1922, after teaching at Christ's Hospital and Haberdashers' Aske's Hatcham Girls' School, Williams was obliged to give up her post upon marriage. Nevertheless she and her husband, Richard, became joint principals of a private school in north London, which attracted the interest of Nunn. In 1934 she completed an MA thesis entitled 'The geometrical concepts of children from five to eight years of age'. By this time Elizabeth Williams was a tutor in mathematics education in the Education Department at King's College, and conducting seminars following up Nunn's lectures. In 1935 Williams moved to Goldsmiths' College, subsequently becoming the first Principal of the City of Leicester Teacher Training College, from 1951 Principal of Whitelands College, and a highly respected national and international figure in mathematics education and teacher training.[35]

Another advanced student to achieve international renown was Fred Schonell, whose Ph.D., 'An investigation into disability in spelling', was completed in 1931. Born in Perth, Australia in 1900 and educated there, in 1931 Schonell took up a post as lecturer at Goldsmiths' College. He subsequently occupied chairs in education at the universities of Swansea, Birmingham and Queensland. Schonell, whose diagnostic work was undertaken in the schools of London and Kent, exercised a profound influence on primary schools, not least through his *Essential Spelling Lists* and *Happy Venture* reading books which sold millions of copies. He was knighted in 1962.[36]

## Curriculum subjects

The development of research and higher degrees in education went hand in hand with developments in the teaching of school subjects. Nunn himself embodied this unity and, as Principal, he not only directed the higher degree courses but also gave the core lectures for the diploma and MA and continued to be responsible for tutorial and seminar work in mathematics and science. His work as a curriculum tutor had long been one of the LDTC's strongest drawing cards. Indeed, some tutors of these subjects at Cambridge and Oxford advised their students to proceed to the LDTC so that they could sit at the feet of Percy Nunn.[37] Not until the report of a University of London visitation on 26 January 1925 drew public attention to the size of this burden of work, did Nunn reluctantly agree to reduce his teaching load by giving up responsibility for the teaching of science.[38] His contribution to mathematics education, however, continued. In his history of mathematics education in England, Howson concluded that Nunn:

made gigantic contributions to mathematics education. He was to wield considerable influence within the Mathematical Association, and to write numerous reports and articles … his *Relativity and Gravitation* demonstrates his ability to popularise advanced mathematics; and his three volumes on the teaching of algebra remain unrivalled as a detailed translation of theory into practice within one area of the mathematics curriculum. Notwithstanding all this, his greatest contribution to mathematics education probably resulted from his teaching and the influence this had on future teachers and teacher-trainers such as C.T. Daltry and Elizabeth Williams.[39]

Mention has already been made in the previous section of Nunn's influence on Williams. Daltry achieved a first-class degree in mathematics from East London College, studied at the LDTC under Nunn, 1924–5 and taught at Eltham College and the Roan School. In 1946 he was appointed senior lecturer and head of the Mathematics Department at the Institute. Daltry was greatly honoured to be one of Nunn's successors, and expressed his hope that he might rediscover and reinterpret Nunn's ideas in order that 'the successful apprentice may thus carry on the work of the master'.[40]

During the war years and their immediate aftermath many temporary and part-time appointments were made. The first of the new full-time permanent appointments was that of John Johnston (J.J.) Bell who joined the LDTC in November 1922 as lecturer in methods of the teaching of history. Bell, who was 44 years old at the time of his appointment, had degrees from Liverpool and Oxford and had lectured in history at the universities of Liverpool and Toronto, and in history and teaching methods at Goldsmiths' College, London. As an officer in the Territorial Army Bell was called up on the first day of the war. He worked in military intelligence, and subsequently in the historical records section of the Committee of Imperial Defence. His connection with the LDTC began as a supervisor of school practice from February 1922. During his ten years at the LDTC, Bell served as senior tutor with responsibility for the general supervision and administration of men students.[41] Bell's contribution, entitled 'A tutor in the 1920s', to *Studies and Impressions* is of considerable interest, revealing as it does not only a great deal about Bell himself, but also about the tutorial role that the highly experienced James Fairgrieve adopted towards other staff as well as towards students.[42] It also demonstrates that at this time lecturers in curriculum areas were struggling to develop principles and practice for the more enlightened teaching of their subjects, both in elementary and in secondary schools. Bell's experience of history teaching in higher education seemed irrelevant to his new situation, while his time at Goldsmiths' had convinced him that the majority of history in elementary schools, and indeed in training colleges, was 'of the incoherent, aimless type immortalised in *1066 and All That*'.[43] In consequence, as Bell admitted, 'he thus found himself in what was practically a virgin field, in which there seemed to him to be a great crop of useless weeds. To be frank, he was quite appalled at the task with which he was confronted.'[44]

Bell concentrated not upon the relatively simple task of how to teach school certificate classes in secondary schools, but upon how history could be made meaningful for the ragged and ill-nourished children he came across in the elementary schools of Battersea and Bermondsey, Deptford and Shoreditch. Spurred on by Nunn's repeated question to him, 'What is practical work in history?' and Fairgrieve's own ability to relate the impact of geographical facts upon the lives of children, Bell began to develop his own theory of the contents and methods of school history. This development took place in public. Bell and Fairgrieve attended each other's demonstration lessons and, when the pupils had left, fierce discussions and criticisms would be bandied about between them, an activity in which students and other staff soon entered with gusto. Chastened by these experiences, Bell turned to radical solutions. He dispensed with traditional elements of constitutional and political history which loomed so large in the syllabuses of the time, and turned instead to social and economic dimensions. Bell's philosophy of history

26. 'Hints to student teachers' from the *Londinian*, Michaelmas term 1924

teaching was set down in *History in School*. His many textbooks included such junior titles as *Jimmie's Story Book* and *A History of Homely Things*.

Bell was highly regarded by Nunn and the students. He, on the other hand, was less happy to find that although designated as senior tutor for men students, his varied previous career meant that his salary on appointment was only £470 a year. This was in contrast to the £600 of Fairgrieve and Hague, and Bell was subsequently granted three increments of £15 for war service.[45] In 1932, following unsuccessful applications for posts elsewhere, Bell left the LDTC to become an LCC inspector. His successor was Montagu (M.V.C.) Jeffreys, who additionally assumed responsibility for religious education. Jeffreys, who was 31 years of age at the time of his appointment, had been educated at Wellington College and Hertford College, Oxford, where he gained a first-class degree in history. His teaching experience had been at Oundle School and Armstrong College, Newcastle.

Modern languages was the second curriculum subject to receive a new appointment and an exposure to new methods of teaching and learning. M. Gladys Calthrop had studied at Girton College, Cambridge and been placed in the first class of the medieval and modern language tripos, with distinction in French. Her previous teaching was at St Leonard's School, her own former school, Blackheath High, and at the LCC's Avery Hill Training College. Calthrop was a member of staff for some 30 years following her half-time appointment in 1923. She also strove to make the learning of her subject interesting and exciting for younger children, although facing some opposition from those who wondered whether the essentials of grammar were receiving sufficient attention. Her demonstration lessons attracted much attention, and it is recorded that one of these on a La Fontaine fable drew spontaneous applause from children and students alike.[46]

John Hague, appointed in 1904, was a gentle man and his death in May 1925 from an accident while riding his motor bike came as a shock. L.S. Suggate, a student from 1907–10, remembered him as 'almost too good for this world ... he had a soft voice and a dreamy manner ... I used occasionally to see Mr Hague in a vegetarian restaurant in St Martin's Lane, frequented by Fabians and the like.'[47] An appreciation in the *Londinian* declared that: 'Even when his hair was grey he never grew old. Something there was in him of De Quincy or of Peter Pan. It was part of his exasperating charm that he had an amazed and childlike inability to deal with or understand practical affairs.'[48]

At first the position of lecturer and tutor in methods of teaching English was filled on a supply basis, but in 1926 Dr Percival Gurrey was appointed to a permanent post. Gurrey, who was 36 years of age, had served with distinction both in the Army and in the RAF. He held a University of London first-class degree in English language and literature and a Ph.D., and had taught in four schools. Gurrey also sought to introduce changes in curricula and pedagogy. He approached English grammar 'as part of English usage and not as the bare bones of linguistics which was the heritage of the elementary schools'.[49] 'The English Department was a

**27. A science lesson in the laboratory at the LDTC, undated**

ferment of ideas and enthusiasms'[50] and on one famous occasion in 1935–6 a dispute over whether poetry teaching should concentrate on the meaning of the words or the spirit of the whole even moved Gurrey to announce that he would resign his post if it could be demonstrated that he was in error.

Another appointment of 1926 was that of the 61-year-old Charles Browne as lecturer and tutor in physical sciences, the post recommended by the University report of the previous year to provide some relief to the overstretched Nunn. For the previous 27 years Browne had been senior science master at Christ's Hospital School, including two years when Burt had been a pupil. Browne retired in 1931, to be replaced in the following year by the Belgian-born, 29-year-old Joseph Lauwerys, educated in Brussels and Bournemouth, a London science graduate who had also taught at Christ's Hospital School. Nunn had considerable expectations of Lauwerys, commending him in a letter to Fred Clarke as 'a really valuable young bird … a philosopher, and more than a bit of a genius'.[51]

For many years the teaching of art had been in the capable hands of von Wyss, aided by a succession of assistant, part-time and visiting tutors. The most influential of these was Marion Richardson, one of the most important figures in art education in the twentieth century. Richardson's appointment in 1924 coincided with the establishment of a specialist course at the LDTC for students training to teach art, a course with which her name has always subsequently been connected.[52] Born in 1892 into a large family, Richardson's skill at drawing was soon apparent, and from the age of 16 she studied at the Birmingham School of Arts and Crafts.

Her principal teaching post was as art mistress at the Dudley High School for Girls, but like von Wyss she also taught classes in prison, and in 1926 visited schools and prisons in Russia. Engaged on a rate of 35 shillings a day, Richardson personified the revolution in art teaching. Under the old regulations for art in the teacher's certificate, students had been required to learn by heart six drawings, one of which they had to produce for the examiner on the appointed day. Richardson encouraged students and children to explore new forms, for example by closing their eyes and by painting representations of the consequent mental images. Even the accurate drawing required for school certificate examinations was enlivened by the use of imaginative lighting and the grouping of objects. Richardson's ideas had much in common with those of Franz Cizek, the Austrian painter and art teacher whom she met through her concern for the Save the Children Fund.[53] In 1938 the Nazis closed Cizek's art school in Vienna. In the same year, in the catalogue of an exhibition of LCC children's art Richardson wrote: 'Whenever people are sincere and free art can spring up. … It is not too much to say that unless a relationship amounting to love exists between teacher and children, children's art, as it is now

understood, is impossible.'[54] In common with other colleagues Richardson brought a missionary spirit to her work. In addition to her part-time post at the LDTC, which included the supervision of school practice, she also travelled hundreds of miles each week to fulfil other teaching commitments in Bromley, Dudley and Oxford.

The first course for the training of teachers in art began in 1924. Richardson concentrated upon the teaching of art in relation to secondary and other schools. She was assisted by von Wyss on the relationship of art to education in general and by T.G. Derrick on the work of schools of art and the relationship between art, the individual and the community. The spirit of Richardson, however, prevailed. Henry Clarence Whaite, art master at Alleyn's School and from 1930 Richardson's successor at the LDTC, was a student on the course in 1927–8. He remembered that:

28. A sculpture by Betty Rea of a girl with a paintbrush, a tribute to Marion Richardson from a memorial fund organized by the Society for Education through Art, and now in the Newsam Library

> The department, housed at the top of the Southampton Row building *was* Marion Richardson. Her students were united by their love for her and the crusading spirit which she communicated to them. At a time when there was a revolution in the teaching of art, it was a tremendous inspiration for young art students to be associated with a pioneer of international repute. Marion Richardson was more than a name, however, she was a remarkable and compelling person with a breadth and depth of experience in the worlds of art and education.[55]

On leaving the LDTC in 1930 Richardson, like Bell, proceeded to a post in the LCC inspectorate. In this capacity she organized courses, practical classes and exhibitions of children's work, but still found time to give occasional general lectures on art, open to all. Richardson's publications included *Writing and Writing Patterns* (1935), which achieved international influence and acclaim,[56] and *Art and the Child*, completed in 1946 on the day before her death.[57]

The contribution made in this period by curriculum tutors to the work of the LDTC, and more broadly, was of a pioneering nature. Their zeal for reform, their concern to challenge the worst features of the elementary tradition and to make their subjects interesting and relevant both to teachers and to children marked out Fairgrieve, Bell, Calthrop, Gurrey and Richardson, like Nunn and von Wyss before them, as missionaries in curricular and pedagogical terms. And although, as Selleck has rightly argued, by 1939 these missionaries had not effected the substantial transformation of curricula and teaching methods in schools for which they had hoped, 'they had made a gain vital to any group of reformers – they had become the intellectual orthodoxy'.[58] Some curriculum tutors, like Bell and Richardson, impatient at sending a mere dozen enlightened teachers per year into the system, joined the LCC inspectorate in the hope of taking their message directly into the authority's schools. This strategy was confirmed when Richardson found that 1,500 teachers applied for the 150 places on her first three courses, while an exhibition of children's art work held in County Hall in 1938 was visited by 26,000 people. Others, like Gurrey, who remained at the LDTC, organized conferences for teachers on the Southampton Row site; for example, one in 1934 on the teaching of poetry was attended by 200 teachers.[59]

The slow pace of change in schools was not the only problem to be faced by the curriculum tutors of the inter-war period. The second was their status within the LDTC itself. The appointment of tutors such as Fairgrieve, Bell, Gurrey and Richardson was designed to provide more specialist teaching in the several subjects of the curriculum, but the development of new courses, research and higher degrees meant that their roles were diversified. While some curriculum tutors such as Fairgrieve, who in 1927 became tutor to 'colonial' students,[60] and Lauwerys, who was appointed Professor of Comparative Education in 1947, moved successfully into the new areas of work, others were to be frustrated. As Gurrey recorded in looking back over this period, whereas once all day would be spent helping diploma students, 'discussing their teaching, their essays, their ideas, their futures', now there was less time for individuals and 'the tutorial group, which had been the be-all and end-all almost of our responsibility, now became one of two or three, or even of four major interests and activities'.[61] Brian Simon, one of Gurrey's diploma students in 1937–8, remembered him as 'Gentle, intelligent, consistently encouraging', but also observed that 'He was, I think, overworked – in any case during the entire year he came to see me only twice'.[62]

In the early days, all members of the LDTC staff, including Adams, Nunn and

Punnett, were directly involved in the training of prospective teachers. By 1931–2, however, an incipient hierarchy was emerging both among the staff and the elements of work. In that year the LDTC staff included four appointed teachers of the University – two professors in Nunn and Burt, and two readers, Fairgrieve and Hamley. The status of Burt and Hamley was associated with their work in research and higher degrees, that of Fairgrieve with his responsibility for colonial students. Nunn's annual salary at this time was £1,427 10s.; Burt's half-time salary was £500; Punnett as full-time Vice-Principal received £600. All other full-time members of staff were on the Burnham scale. Punnett, together with Bell, Browne, Calthrop (half-time), Gurrey and von Wyss were described in some documents simply as 'lecturers not appointed by the University'.[63] While these staff at least had the status of 'recognised teachers', the 'part time instructors', Alford (history of art), Bayliss (physical education), Gullan (voice production), Lawson (physical education and school practice supervision), Lofthouse (music), Matthews (needle-work), Minihane (handicraft), and Whaite (art) were specifically designated as 'not recognised' by the University. These staff were paid at an hourly rate of 15s. for men and 12s. 6d. for women, except for Whaite who was engaged at £2 per day and Bayliss who was on loan from the LCC. Of the nine teaching practice super-visors, the four men – Charles, Church, Harrison and Kirkman – were paid at a daily rate of £2, and the five women – Meredith, Pechey, Turnage and Wilshere (together with Lawson) at 35s. In 1932 these salaries were still subject to the two deductions of 5 per cent from 1926 and a further 10 per cent on the remaining salary from 1 October 1931.[64]

## The Colonial Department

In 1902 Sidney Webb had envisaged that London University would become an international centre for postgraduate study. In the first 25 years of its existence, however, only a few overseas students attended the LDTC. For example, in 1905 there were three graduates from the University of Sydney: Percival R. Cole, Thomas I. Roberts and Gertrude A. Roseby. In the following year, Ammenhal Rama Rau from India, was described as being of 'excellent ability and admirable industry'.[65] In 1911–12, when Jeffery himself was taking the diploma course, he noted that the group included 'three men rather older than the rest of us'.[66] These were A.F. Thorpe who was training as a teacher before taking up missionary work in China, F. Hasler, who was on leave from teaching in India, and W.J. Mulholland, who had trained and taught in a teacher training college in Australia.[67] As with the home students, so with those from overseas. Some flourished; others found the going more difficult. For example, the College report on Rajkumari Das from India, who followed the diploma course, 1916–17, stated that 'she has taken her place on quite equal terms with the English students here, has held her own quite admirably in the work, and has taken good places in the College examinations'.[68]

29. Overseas students are to the fore in this undated photograph of a lecture by Nunn. The gallery, much coveted by courting couples, is seen to the top right

In contrast, in 1920–1 Miss N. Ghosh, also from India, though securing a pass in the diploma suffered from poor health throughout her course, and found difficulty in communicating with the children – 'her manner is not lively or energetic enough for them'.[69] Indian students predominated at this time. Although the figures must be treated with caution it appears that of 122 overseas students who took the diploma in the years between 1902 and 1932, no fewer than 84 came from India.[70]

Prior to 1927 most overseas students took the normal diploma course. No provision was made for students intending to teach in other countries. In 1926, however, Margaret Wrong, missionary secretary to the British Student Christian Movement, canvassed support for a separate training course for those intending to teach in the colonies and suggested that it should be located at the LDTC. In her previous post, as travelling secretary for the World Student Christian Federation, the Canadian-born Wrong had undertaken a six-month tour of Africa and become aware of the racism, low levels of literacy and disparity between educational provision for males and females which existed under colonial rule.[71] Additionally, in the same year, Sir Donald Cameron, Governor of Tanganyika, proposed that a scheme of educational training, funded from government sources, should be provided for missionaries before their departure for Africa.

The Colonial Office also envisaged the LDTC as a suitable place for training educators to work in the Empire. In 1923, following the report of the American-sponsored Phelps-Stokes Commission on Education in West and South Africa, a Colonial Office Advisory Committee on Native Education in British Tropical Africa was created. The moving spirit behind this creation was J.H. Oldham, the dynamic secretary of the International Missionary Council. Its successor from 1929, with a much broader title and remit, was the Advisory Committee on Education in the Colonies. Nunn was a member of both of these committees.[72] One of the first products of the Advisory Committee was a White Paper, *Education Policy in British Tropical Africa*, published in 1925.[73] This document envisaged a greater direction of educational policy by central government, the development of a substantial education service staffed by administrators and teachers of high calibre, and an expanded programme of co-operation with the educational work of the various missionary societies. Later that year a further memorandum drew attention to recruitment and training needs and to conditions of service. Recruitment was to be broadened, to include 'probationers', graduates coming straight from university who would receive a year's course to equip them for their roles. Refresher courses would be provided for serving officers, whose superannuation and other rights would be safeguarded. In November 1925 William Ormsby-Gore, Parliamentary Under-Secretary of State for the Colonies and Chairman of the Advisory Committee, expressed the hope that an appropriate course could be in place by the autumn of 1926.

Difficulties arose over the location of the probationers' course. It is interesting to note that although probationers for the Colonial Administrative Service were to be trained at the universities of Cambridge and Oxford, the LDTC was chosen over the Education departments of the two older universities for education officers. There can be little doubt that Nunn's personal standing in the educational world was an important factor in the Colonial Office's choice of the LDTC. Other considerations included London's greater variety in terms of accommodation, opportunities for practice in schools and broader cultural experiences. But the main factor was the quality of training in education provided at this time at the ancient universities. In December 1928 when further courses were under consideration, Hanns Vischer, executive secretary to the Advisory Committee, wrote to Nunn:

I have just been to Cambridge, and found that as far as educational training is concerned they are no better off than at Oxford, and in my opinion rather worse, and I really don't feel that any experiments in post-graduate courses for Malaya and other probationers should be tried at either of these Universities.[74]

Resentment at the LDTC monopoly was particularly felt at Oxford, where the Education Department had made initial preparations for a course by sending a member of staff to examine educational provision in the southern United States. In March 1927, in reply to a complaining letter from M.W. Keatinge, Nunn protested that he had not joined the Advisory Committee 'to secure these people for our College'. On the contrary, he had 'accepted with reluctance any addition to responsibilities which are already sufficiently heavy'.[75] Such caution was understandable. Initial advertisements for the course stated that it would be given under the direction of Nunn himself, assisted by Burt and other teachers of the University.[76] Although student numbers would be small, the probationers would come with considerable expectations and require an intensive course with specialist studies. Ideally, the course should be led by someone with substantial experience of education in the colonies. The LDTC had no such member of staff readily available. Student numbers, moreover, were not guaranteed by the Colonial Office; indeed by 1931 the probationer scheme had virtually collapsed.

James Fairgrieve was the first tutor to oversee the Colonial course, and his account of its origins suggests that it was a somewhat ad hoc affair. As a geographer and educationist of great verve and energy, Fairgrieve regarded Nunn's invitation to him to take charge of the first group of Catholic Fathers, directed to the LDTC as the result of Cameron's initiative, as a challenge and 'the possible beginning of something that could be called big'.[77] But he was, by his own admission:

> quite unfitted for the job. I knew there was a continent called Africa to various parts of which these Fathers were going. I knew something of the land but very little of the people and of the little I knew I found later that I knew a great deal wrong. ...
>
> The first thing to do was to get to know the students, and the second to learn something of the job, so one Wednesday afternoon in the beginning of October, 1927, I met the first group round a table: four White Fathers, two Benedictines and one Franciscan.[78]

Although the Colonial Department was not formally constituted as such within the Institute until 1934, its origins may be traced to this meeting of 1927. The name of the course soon changed from 'African' to 'Colonial', with the arrival of students who were proceeding to posts in Hong Kong and Malaya. In spite of this further challenge to his field of competence, however, James Fairgrieve continued to direct the Colonial courses until his retirement in 1935.

In the following session, 1928–9, a further group of seven missionaries was joined by the first group of seven probationers. Their course consisted of lectures for the diploma, together with teaching practice, tours of rural schools in the company of inspectors, Scout camps, and specialist teaching in such subjects as anthropology, languages and tropical hygiene. In his review of the 1928–9 course Nunn emphasized the need for more experience of work in the classroom, a comment endorsed by the students. The students, however, were more critical, overall, and also raised questions about the value of some of the work in such subjects as physical training, psychology and history of education. One particularly contentious issue was how much time should be given to the learning of indigenous languages.[79] By 1932 those who had taken the course were providing critiques in the light of their experience in the field. For example, in that year a despatch to the Colonial Office from Northern Rhodesia supported the need for preparation in the Bantu language. It also advised that the course was not, as sometimes perceived, overloaded, and should be less focused on English elementary and secondary schooling and more on the African situation.[80]

Strengths of these early courses included the admixture of missionaries and lay people, the pioneering spirit, and the enthusiastic leadership of Fairgrieve. On the debit side, were basic gaps in knowledge about the cultures and contexts to which the students would be going, weaknesses in the teaching of languages, including English as a foreign language and, according to Nunn's report on the course of 1929–30, a lack of quality amongst the 'tail' of the probationers. It would appear that some of the probationers, including recent graduates from Cambridge and Oxford, took a similarly jaundiced view of the LDTC. The very possibility of university studies in London seemed anachronistic in itself, and the crowded and noisy Southampton Row building was a far cry from the cloistered courts in which their undergraduate studies had been pursued. Indeed:

> the whole set up was a profound shock ... class consciousness, public school tradition and Oxford and Cambridge superiority were pretty strong in us ... visiting 'council' schools, meeting 'teachers' – all this kind of thing was not easy for us ... we kept ourselves to ourselves for the most part.[81]

The ultimate indignity was compulsory physical training by order of the Colonial Office. To the great amusement of other students, on one occasion during 1929–30 Bell, who was in charge of fire drill, contrived to turn the 'Colonials' out into the street 'with shorts and bare knees!'[82]

The Colonial course did not flourish in this period. Global economic recession took its toll. Missionary numbers were only three in 1930–1, four in 1931–2, and seven in 1932–3, while probationers fell from 14 in 1930–1 to two in 1931–2 and none in 1932–3. In March 1933 Nunn wrote to Sir Henry Richards at the Board of Education, bemoaning 'the deplorable financial straits in which the Colonial governments find themselves'.[83] Students from overseas remained a rarity. In 1952, A.N. Basu, then Director of the Central Institute of Education in Delhi, recalled that when he took the diploma course in 1930–1 'we were about half-a-dozen oversea students, all Indians. There were no other students from Commonwealth countries.'[84] In 1931–2 there were some 11 overseas students, nine of whom were from India. A further eight students were taking the Colonial course, six of whom were teachers on leave from Africa. In contrast to the 39 MA students, however, only one of whom came from overseas, only two of the seven Ph.D. students were home-based. Four were from New Zealand and one from Australia. An analysis of the first degrees of 280 LDTC students in this year showed that 208 were from London, 18 from Cambridge and 11 from Oxford, together with a further

10 from other British universities and one from Dublin. Twelve were from India, 10 from the Dominions of Australia, Canada and New Zealand, four from the USA and three apiece from China and Germany.[85]

## Institute of Education

In its early days the purpose of the LDTC was to train teachers for service in London's elementary schools. By the later 1920s increasing diversification was apparent. The standard course and qualification was no longer the Board of Education's certificate, but the University's diploma. All students who came to the LDTC with first- or second-class honours degrees (about 80 per cent of the total) were prepared for teaching in secondary schools, and only the remainder for elementary teaching. Although the LDTC retained full use of the three elementary demonstration schools, and the LCC made other central and elementary schools available, most teaching practice now took place 'in public secondary schools ranging from Harrow to Croydon and from Ilford to Uxbridge'.[86] Another development was a course for those wishing to proceed to a career in educational administration. These activities were extensions of the LDTC's original purpose. The LCC, however, would derive less direct benefit from research and higher degree work and the provision of courses for students whose subsequent careers would be conducted overseas. Nor could it be responsible for an institution that would act as a central bureau for educational research and fulfil the role formerly exercised by the Department of Special Inquiries and Reports of the Board of Education. This, however, was Nunn's vision. The Institute of Education that he envisaged 'should aim at becoming a centre of educational thought, inquiry and training for the British Commonwealth'.[87]

By 1930 this aim had widespread and powerful support. Lord Eustace Percy, Sir Charles Grant Robertson and Sir Michael Sadler were named as home authorities who had declared for the cause, while Professor Fred Clarke of Cape Town and Montreal was the most prominent advocate from overseas. Correspondence between Nunn and Clarke indicates the nature and extent of the orchestration of the campaign.[88] For example, in August 1930 *The Spectator* published an article by Clarke entitled 'Empire and Education: the case for a Central Institute'. In the following month *The Spectator* carried a letter from Nunn expressing entire agreement with Clarke's article. Nunn also ordered three dozen copies of the relevant August issue, to be circulated 'among the people who matter most in this connexion'.[89] Meetings of such bodies as the British Association and the British Commonwealth Education Conference provided other important platforms whereby the vision was conveyed to a wider world.[90]

While the overall role for the new Institute might be broadly agreed, academic and constitutional arrangements were more contentious. There were at least three alternatives. The first was that the Institute of Education would stand in a similar relationship to the University of London as the Education Department of King's College. The second was that the new Institute would, both in terms of size and function, be first among equals and would assume an overall co-ordinating role for London's training departments and colleges. The third was that the new Institute would become the University's sole department of education. The solution of 1932 represented an uneasy compromise between the first two alternatives.

Both Adams and Nunn had shown a preference for the third solution. This would mean the abolition of the King's department and its absorption into the LDTC. Indeed, Nunn's memorandum of 22 February 1931 bore the challenging title, 'The University Department of Education'. This bid for a monopoly position placed a further strain on relationships with King's staff who were mindful, no doubt, of the closure of the Bedford Training Department in 1922. Indeed, in 1920 Margaret Tuke, Principal of Bedford College, had contemplated resignation from her position as Chairman of the LDTC's Council on the grounds of conflict of interest.[91] Tuke's position at that time was a delicate one because while rejecting the LDTC's claim to be the University's sole department of education she also opposed the establishment of other day training colleges in London which might threaten Bedford with increased competition. Tuke subsequently attributed the closure of the Bedford department to a number of causes, including 'the policy of the London County Council in the direction of concentrating graduate training at the London Day Training College'.[92] Subsequent chairmen of the Council in this period included Dr Ernest Barker, Principal of King's College, Sir Gregory Foster, Provost of University College and

Sir William Beveridge, Director of the London School of Economics. Beveridge, Foster and Dr William Halliday, who succeeded Barker as Principal of King's in 1928, were all members of the London Day Training College Transfer Committee established in 1931, and Beveridge, Halliday and Nunn comprised its key executive sub-committee.[93]

30. Margaret Tuke, Principal of Bedford College and Chairman of the LDTC's Council

Other developments, for example the establishment of the Training Colleges Delegacy of 1928 which was responsible for syllabuses and examination of students in some 15 training colleges in the London area and for grouping such colleges around schools of the University, foreshadowed the creation of a central institution of university rank with a broad remit.[94] By this date the LDTC was serving as an intercollegiate centre for lectures at diploma level. In 1930 Nunn reported that the LDTC 'on two mornings in the week throws its classes open to graduates from King's College (about 80), Maria Grey College (50), St. Mary's College (10), Goldsmiths' College (10) and Furzedown College (10)'.[95] The only reciprocal elements in these arrangements were Dover Wilson's lectures in history of education which were given throughout the session at the LDTC, and a summer-term course on the teaching of divinity given by Professor Rogers at King's College. Although Nunn abandoned the demand for immediate monopoly, he still envisaged the Institute as the University's centre for advanced work. In 1930 he declared that:

> I judge it to be essential that for all work of the Institute, and particularly for the higher degree courses, the principal teachers of the Training College and the King's College Department should work as a single staff. ... In the proposed building on the Bloomsbury site there should be provision (including a common library) for bringing together all work in Education above the level of Diploma.[96]

While academic and professional issues – students, courses, teaching and research – constituted one contentious and contested area in the transition from LDTC to Institute of Education, constitutional and administrative matters also loomed large. These necessitated lengthy negotiations between the LCC, the Board of Education and the University.

By June 1928 both the LCC and the Senate of the University had given broad approval to the transfer of the LDTC. The four leading participants in the negotiations were Sir Edwin Deller, Sir George Gater and Sir Henry Pelham, chief officers respectively of the University, the LCC's Education Committee and the Board of Education, and Nunn himself.[97] In 1929 new University statutes, including the creation of a Court to control the University's finances, came into operation and the University committed itself to a major programme of building upon the Bloomsbury site, a site which would include accommodation for an Institute of Education. The LCC generously offered a grant of up to £200,000 for new buildings for the Institute and Birkbeck College, of which £150,000 was subsequently allocated by the Court to the Institute. In February 1932 the Lord President consented in writing 'to the transfer of the London Day Training College from the London County Council to the University as from the 1st September 1932'.[98] This was approved by the Education Committee of the LCC at its meeting on 9 March 1932.[99]

The protracted negotiations involving the LCC, University and Board of Education which occupied the years between 1928 and 1932 placed a further heavy burden upon Nunn, who during this period suffered considerably from bronchitis and influenza. For example, in March 1932 Nunn described himself as 'head over heels in business entailed by our transference from the London County Council to the University'.[100] Even an intended restorative ocean cruise in the spring of that year proved to be 'a great failure', and was spent mostly in the ship's hospital. Lord Dawson of Penn, a member of the University's Senate whom Nunn consulted on his return, diagnosed extreme exhaustion and Deller and Gater virtually banned him from setting foot in the LDTC until it should become the Institute of Education. By that date, 1 September 1932, Nunn hoped that, fortified by his new title of 'Director' he, in common with the Institute itself, would be 'stronger and fresher than I have been for years'.[101]

## Conclusion

In 1932 the LDTC was transformed into the Institute of Education. This change of status and role was not inevitable. It had been duly earned. John Adams, as the University's first Professor of Education, had provided a firm foundation. Since 1922 curriculum tutors led by Fairgrieve, Bell, Calthrop, Gurrey and Richardson had pioneered a curricular and pedagogical revolution. Fairgrieve had also played a leading part in the, admittedly stuttering, entry into the colonial field. Burt and Hamley had led the way in educational research with specific reference to psychology. Nunn, the great polymath, had towered over all. The transformation was the cause of much celebration. Even the Board of Education expressed its appreciation 'of the great educational advantages which it hoped to secure by the transfer of the College from the LCC to the University'.[102] There was a widespread feeling that the new Institute, having outgrown its humble origins and ambivalent constitutional position, would now be located at the very heart of the University and flourish as a national and international institution.

Nevertheless, by 1932 two potential problems were also apparent. The first was financial. At a time of general economic depression there was no guarantee that the University Grants Committee (UGC) and the University of London would be able to treat the Institute more generously, or even as generously, as the LCC had dealt with the LDTC. The second problem was a constitutional one. Hitherto the University had championed the cause of greater freedom of action for the LDTC and its staff. The new Institute of Education, however, together with the very subject of Education, was regarded with suspicion in some quarters of the University and found itself subject to a number of constraints. The most important, and in retrospect highly regrettable, decision taken in 1931 was that the new Institute should forego the autonomy and status of a school of the University which it had enjoyed as the LDTC and which had been renewed for three years as recently as 1930. Permanent recognition as a school would be expensive and time-consuming and require a charter and a joint approach to the Privy Council by the University and the LCC. Instead the Senate approved a recommendation that the Institute should become a central activity of the University.

Chapter 5

# New directions
## 1932–1939

### Introduction

The 1930s began in slump and ended in war. Severe unemployment among teachers led to reductions in numbers in training. Even the first stage of the new complex of buildings in Bloomsbury was not completed by the time the University of London celebrated its centenary in 1936. By the following year, when the Institute was still in Southampton Row, it was apparent that there would be insufficient funds to complete the work to Charles Holden's original design.[1]

From 1932 the Institute of Education was a central activity of the University under Statute 39(1) of the 1926 Act, like the Institute of Historical Research. The decision not to seek the status of a school meant that independence from the LCC had been replaced by greater University control. The Institute was now governed by a Delegacy appointed by the University's Senate. Minutes of LDTC Council meetings had been taken by an officer from County Hall. Delegacy minutes were taken by a member of the central staff of the University, not by a member of the Institute's administrative staff.[2] Administrative duties and posts, however, increased. The LDTC office had comprised one secretary, one assistant secretary and a clerk. Grace Wacey now became the chief administrative officer, with the title of Secretary, and specialist posts were created. For example, responsibility for the payment of salaries to staff and grants to students, previously exercised by the LCC, led to the appointment of an Institute accountant.

The Delegacy included five *ex officio* members (including the Director), five members of Senate, five co-opted members and two representatives of the LCC. The most significant change in composition over this period occurred in 1935 when the representation of the Institute's Academic Board, which included all appointed and recognized teachers, was increased from two to four members. Lord Eustace Percy, one of the co-opted members, served as Chairman of the Delegacy from its inception. An outstanding figure, President of the Board of Education from 1924 to 1929, who wanted the Institute to become a truly postgraduate department with an international role, Percy took a keen interest in the work of the Institute. In 1937, however, he resigned from the Delegacy upon returning to his native north-east as Rector of King's College, Newcastle upon Tyne. His successor as Chairman was one of the Senate members, Dr William Reginald Halliday, the influential Principal of King's College, London.

## Change at the top

This period saw the retirement of key figures of long standing: Punnett, Fairgrieve, von Wyss and Nunn. All continued in service until the age of 65. Arrangements made to cover their duties reflected both the range of responsibilities undertaken by these members of the old guard and the new directions of the Institute as opposed to the LDTC. First to go was Margaret Punnett, who retired in the summer of 1933. Punnett served as Vice-Principal throughout the 30-year life of the LDTC and the first year of the Institute. Her invaluable contribution included oversight of the lives and work of women students and of detailed matters of general administration. Nunn envisaged her replacement as a warden and senior tutor for women students who would make arrangements for their teaching practice, act as the 'lady of the house' and 'keep an eye upon the work of the servants and cleaners of the Institute'.[3] He did not believe that this role should be combined with that of deputy. This view prevailed. The Delegacy decided that Hamley 'should succeed Miss Punnett as second in command, and when exercising functions in that capacity should be known as Deputy Director'. Given the ill health of Nunn and his successor, Fred Clarke, however, Hamley's major duty in this role was to 'exercise the functions of the Director in the event of his absence from the Institute'.[4] The post of warden to women students was declined by von Wyss, and a new appointment was made from September 1933 at an initial salary of £500 per annum. Maura Brook Gwynne brought a variety of experience. Prior to her current post as lecturer in English at Bingley Training College, Gwynne had been a postgraduate fellow at Radclyffe College, Harvard, taught in the United States, worked for three years as a factory inspector and served as headmistress of an elementary school in Cheshire.

James Fairgrieve retired in 1935. His successor as tutor in geography was the 27-year-old Neville Vincent Scarfe, an LDTC diploma student, 1927–8. Scarfe had taught at Bemrose School, Derby and was currently lecturer in geography at University College, Nottingham. Scarfe assumed much of the mantle of Fairgrieve, not only in pioneering work in geography education, but also as 'a natural leader for the curriculum departments in discussion about academic policy'.[5] Fairgrieve's role in respect of the Colonial Department was assumed by Dr W. Bryant Mumford, whose appointment in 1934 is considered in a later section of this chapter.

The summer of 1936, which saw the retirements of Percy Nunn and Clotilde von Wyss must have seemed almost as much a watershed as that of 1932. Their long years of service, breadth of interests both in the sciences and in the arts, attractive personalities and reputations as outstanding teachers meant that Nunn and von Wyss, perhaps more than anyone else, personified all that was best about the LDTC and the Institute of Education. Nunn retired to Madeira, where he died in 1944. His gravestone in the British cemetery in Funchal bears the fitting tribute: 'Teacher, Philosopher, Mathematician'.[6] From 1936 work in art continued to be covered by Whaite and other part-time tutors, but a new appointment was made in biology and hygiene. Winifred M. Warden had taught science at a secondary school in Shropshire and at the Lincoln Training College, and biology and education at University College, Nottingham. Since 1933 she had been lecturer in education at the University of Reading.

Nunn's retirement in 1936 had been preceded by considerable discussions about the role of the next Director. As the University's Professor of Education Nunn continued to lecture on the principles of education to students on diploma, MA and Ph.D. courses. He was also responsible for curriculum work in mathematics. The Delegacy noted, somewhat belatedly, that 'If the Institute develops as it is now doing, it is doubtful whether all of these functions can continue to be combined'.[7] From 1936 a full-time appointment in mathematics was made. Max Black, a Cambridge graduate whose research at the University of Göttingen had been published in 1933 as *The Nature of Mathematics*, brought experience as a teacher of mathematics at the Royal Grammar School, Newcastle upon Tyne and as an extra-mural lecturer in philosophy at Armstrong College.

Three possible solutions to the difficulties apparent in attempting to combine the posts of Director and Professor of Education were considered. The first was to create two separate posts: a Director responsible for organization and administration and a Professor to carry out the work of teaching and research. The second was to combine the two offices but to create an administrative chief of staff under the Director who would have few or no teaching responsibilities. The third solution was a modification of the second. The offices of Director and Professor would be combined but another member of the teaching staff would be given the status of Assistant Director and would assume responsibility for all of the work coming under the aegis of the Board of Education, i.e., the courses of teacher training. Unfortunately, none of these solutions was adopted. In 1936 Nunn was succeeded as Director and Professor of Education by Fred Clarke.[8]

Clarke, born in 1880, was educated at a Church of England elementary school where he served as a pupil teacher, at the Oxford Central Municipal Technical School and at the non-collegiate St Catherine's Society and Oxford University Day Training College. There he obtained a first-class honours degree in history. One of his tutors, Ernest Barker, described him as 'perhaps the soundest and steadiest pupil I have ever had to teach'.[9] Clarke also acquired a teacher's certificate and a reputation as the ablest student yet seen at the Day Training College. At the end of September 1903, after a few weeks of school teaching at a higher grade school in north London, Clarke was appointed Master of Method at the York Diocesan Training College. Although unsuccessful in 1905 in his application for the post of Vice-Principal at the LDTC, in March 1906, at the tender age of 25, he became Professor of Education at Hartley College, Southampton. He was Professor of Education at the University of Cape Town from 1911 to 1929 and at McGill University, Montreal from 1929 to 1934.

Clarke, like Nunn, was unassuming, a modest and wise man and a sincere seeker after truth. In announcing Clarke's appointment to the students Nunn described him as 'the wisest man he knew'. Clarke's wisdom had a religious foundation and he was a regular communicant until the day of his death. Clarke was at his best with individuals or small groups, rather than in formal lectures or large social gatherings. In publication terms he was a journalist, always writing, pipe in mouth, notepad on knee. His experiences of education and social and political conditions across three continents made him the ideal Director to develop the international role of the Institute. Clarke's leadership of the Institute was to be characterized by

31. Fred Clarke, who succeeded Percy Nunn as Director in 1936

creativity, humanity and success. Roy Niblett has argued that 'In the ten years from the beginning of the second world war, Clarke perhaps had a greater influence upon the development of education in England and, directly and indirectly, in the Commonwealth than any other one person'.[10]

Clarke's early years as Director, however, were problematic. Though wont to refer to himself as 'Joshua – son of Nunn', Clarke was conscious that he had succeeded a man who had become a legend in his own time. Winifred Warden, the new lecturer in biology, who had also just succeeded another legendary figure, remembered a conversation from the end of 1936:

At the end of the first term he asked how I was enjoying my work and I answered, 'Very much, except that I'm conscious that I am not Miss von Wyss.' He looked out of the window, took the pipe out of his mouth and said, 'Don't worry too much about that; it will pass. You may be surprised to know how often I feel like that too.' I did not know Sir Fred as well then as I did later. But I think this feeling and the death of Sir Edwin Deller did much to contribute to his illness at the end of that year.[11]

Tragedy struck in November 1936, one day before the 100th anniversary of the signing of the charter of the University of London. The Principal of the University, the newly knighted Sir Edwin Deller, was fatally injured while visiting the Senate House building in which the Institute was to be housed.[12] Clarke, who himself spent much time clambering over the building site with Wacey 'following in the rear',[13] was deeply affected by Deller's death.[14] Matters came to a head in the autumn of 1937 and Clarke was granted leave of absence on health grounds from November of that year until October 1938, although he did not return to full duties until January 1939. Hamley assumed the role of Acting Director and some of Clarke's teaching duties, while others were distributed between Institute and King's staff, together with visiting lecturers.

A comparison of the Institute's staffing for the years 1932 and 1938 shows that expansion was achieved by appointments at lecturer level and an increase in the numbers of part-time lecturers and supervisors of teaching practice. Not only did full-time tutors decline as a percentage of the whole, numbers of appointed teachers were reduced.

| | Full-time | | | | Part-time | | | |
|---|---|---|---|---|---|---|---|---|
| | Professors | Readers | Lecturers | Total | Lecturers | TP supervisors | Total | Visiting tutors |
| 1932 | 2 | 1 | 7 | 10 | 3 | 6 | 9 | 10 |
| 1938 | 2 | 0 | 13 | 15 | 8 | 10 | 18 | 10 |

Table 3   Numbers of academic staff, 1932 and 1938[15]

This was a great disappointment. Clarke, whose own lectures as Professor of Education have been described as 'an amalgam of philosophy of education, history of education, comparative education and sociology of education',[16] urged upon the Delegacy that professors should be appointed in each of these subjects and that Dr Susan Isaacs should also be afforded a chair, but in vain. Part-time and one-year contracts continued.

We constitute
The Institute
And may there ever be
For all who feel the call to teach
A place as good within their reach
As I. of E.

**Student rag song of 1936**

## Diploma

Preparation for teaching and for the diploma examination continued to be the largest single activity of the Institute. The general theory element of the course was still based upon 'Principles', but the three 'disciplines' of psychology, history and comparative education also achieved separate status. Curriculum courses in major secondary school subjects formed a second element, complemented by practical subjects ranging from bookbinding to needlecraft, from laboratory arts to speech training. Teaching practice, a minimum of 60 days, consisted of three or four weeks before the start of the University year, followed by two days per week throughout the course. This arrangement was designed to ensure the closest possible fit between theory and practice, but one student from 1937–8 recalled that 'we always seemed to be running round on the outer circle on Mondays, Wednesdays and Fridays and to be hurled unprotected, into the target area on Tuesdays and Thursdays'.[17] Attendance at lectures was not compulsory. A student from 1938–9 remembered that while the Beveridge Hall where the main Education lectures were given on Friday mornings 'looked fairly well-filled to me' and lectures in methods courses were well attended, 'the others (psychology seminars, speech-training, choral speech, practical subjects) were sampled and then dropped according to taste'. Many students found the general lectures and seminars 'an oddly unthought-out miscellany, sometimes interesting in themselves, but disconnected, lacking in overall direction, a ragbag; the course probably stood or fell by the methods courses, for their immediate relevance was obvious to all'.

Student numbers of those training to be teachers rose and fell during this period. Diploma students were generally equally divided between men and women: for example 105 men and 113 women in 1933–4 and 104 men and 102 women in 1938–9. Furzedown, Goldsmiths', Maria Grey and St Mary's comprised the allied colleges, whose postgraduate students attended for parts of the diploma course not provided in their own institutions. The Institute also bore some responsibility for those students, 373 in 1933–4, who were reading for degrees but would proceed to the Institute for the diploma year. Pass rates were high. For example, in July 1939 215 students entered for the diploma examination of whom 203 passed, ten were referred in the written papers and one in practical work, while one failed both in written papers and in practical work. All 15 of the students taking the Art Teacher's course were successful and qualified for the Art Teacher's Diploma.

| Table 4 | Numbers of diploma and associated students, 1933–9[18] | | | |
|---|---|---|---|---|
| | Diploma course | Allied colleges | Occasional students | Art course |
| 1933–4 | 218 | 95 | 23 | 12 |
| 1934–5 | 241 | 89 | 38 | 12 |
| 1935–6 | 244 | 106 | 29 | 12 |
| 1936–7 | 248 | 106 | 35 | 15 |
| 1937–8 | 217 | 115 | 54 | 13 |
| 1938–9 | 206 | 97 | 23 | 15 |

The most popular lecturer in the theory section of the course was Hamley, who taught educational psychology. Erect and distinguished in bearing, courteous in manner, he was 'outstandingly the best lecturer with his quiet charm, clear style and ironic sense of humour which embraced even his own intelligence tests'. Curriculum tutors such as Calthrop and Gurrey were admired, while Jeffreys' preliminary talk on 'Position in Class' and 'how not to be a caged lion, a fidget, a pouncer, a clip twister, or a lady missionary' was often cited as the most useful advice of the year.[19] Although Warden's course on hygiene was popular and practical, the same could not be said of a series of special lectures on 'Sex' by an outside lecturer. These lectures were poorly attended. Some students, indeed, seem to have had a fairly minimal contact with the course. For example Harry Rée, a student of

1936–7 who became Headmaster of Watford Grammar School and Professor of Education at the University of York, confessed that he 'was a most undesirable student. I think I must have cut most lectures, except those of Dr Gurrey, and I took no part in student activities.'

Another student from 1935–6 remembered Gurrey with affection, for his generosity and humility:

> But such humility was very rare at the Institute of those days. I remember with what certainty and pomposity most of the staff pulled us to pieces. In particular many of us never forgave the opening remarks (well meant perhaps but surely psychologically mistaken) 'to throw overboard all we had learnt at college, fancy degrees and highly cultivated thoughts were no use to us now'. There was never a suggestion that a fine intellect might be of advantage to a teacher.

Brian Simon, a student on the diploma course in 1937–8, found the Southampton Row building very different from the Great Court at Trinity 'but a friendly place, full of bustling activity, with staff and students merging most effectively'.[20] Staff who made an impact on the young Simon included Gurrey, Jeffreys, Lauwerys, Scarfe, the director of music, Dr Charles Thornton Lofthouse, and the young German expatriate, Reinhold Schairer. Simon's mixed recollections of the theory lectures, taught to mass audiences on Friday mornings in the newly built Senate House, would no doubt have been generally endorsed. For example, A.C.F. Beales, who lectured on the English Education System, was 'outstanding'.[21] Of Dr Geoffrey Winthrop Young, another of the King's staff, who though losing a leg in the War was still well known as a climber, Simon recorded that 'It did not seem to us that his heart was in it, as it certainly was in mountaineering'.[22] Three books were regarded as essential reading: Cyril Burt, *The Backward Child* (1920), G.A.N. Lowndes, *The Silent Social Revolution* (1937) and Percy Nunn, *Education: Its data and first principles* (1920). Simon's preliminary teaching practice was in a senior school for boys aged between 11 and 14 years, with main teaching practices at the City of London School, where he taught English, and social studies to the sixth form.

Simon also attended lectures outside of the diploma course and attached himself to two other groups. In the spring of 1938 he accompanied the Carnegie Fellows on a trip to Paris led by Schairer – the highlight being a visit to a college for apprentice chefs. He also joined a group concerned with school administration and a fortnight after the end of the diploma course spent a period in Chesterfield under the tutelage of its Director of Education, H.G. Stead. Simon, who as a Cambridge undergraduate had joined the Communist Party in 1935, was doubtless one of the small group of students in the Common Room 'always hotly discussing politics, so that to a visitor we could well have seemed the Institute of Political Education'.[23]

32 (Right). A cartoon from the *Londinian*, Spring term 1936, shows the Institute as 'a friendly place, full of bustling activity'

Simon, indeed, noted that in the event of civil commotion it might be possible for the students to hold the Institute building since 'set at a slight angle near the High Holborn Road crossing, it commanded the whole of Southampton Row to Aldwych to the south, and up to the Euston Road north'.[24] The main concern of most students, however, would doubtless have been whether they could secure a teaching post.[25] Lighter moments included the end of session concerts, which continued even after the departure of Nunn, and the pinning of fake messages on notice boards, announcing, for example, that Mr Shillan urgently needed to see a certain student, or 'the (supposed) forthcoming engagements of various intertwined souls'.[26] Staff changes in this period, other than those noted above, were fairly few. In 1934 a new permanent appointment was made in Classics. F.J. Kinchin Smith was an Oxford graduate, who had taught at Loretto School and the University of Edinburgh. Smith's preference for Greek over Latin extended to taking students on pioneering basic tours of the Greek islands and even to serving the Greek wine, 'Retsina', in the Institute itself.[27]

M.V.C. Jeffreys continued to teach history and religious education until 1939, when he was appointed Professor of Education at Durham. Lauwerys remained responsible for the teaching of physics, while Dr Titley, one of the King's tutors, took over work in chemistry. Gwynne brought some much needed support to Gurrey in the tutoring of students in English, and in 1937 a half-time appointment in the bearded shape of Shillan was made to assist Calthrop in teaching an increased number of students in modern languages. During 1938–9 the Academic Board urged on the Delegacy the need for further appointments to ease the workloads of staff. A School Relations Officer was appointed; the numbers of supervisors were increased. In 1938–9 supervisors were required to attend the Institute for one morning a week for discussions with students and participation in seminars. For this attendance and two days a week of supervision, supervisors were paid a fixed salary, rather than an hourly or daily rate. The Delegacy accepted that although there had not been any major expansion in student numbers at diploma level, curriculum staff workloads had increased as a result of 'the rapid growth in the numbers of advanced students who now resort to the Institute both from Britain and from oversea'. Flexibility of the type seen in the earliest days of the LDTC was urged as a solution to the problem: 'The Delegacy does not favour any rigid departmentalizing of staff'.[28]

## Higher degrees and research

In the early years of higher degree studies there were no organized courses. By the end of the 1920s a dozen or so students came once or twice a week to hear a lecture from one of the three professors: Burt, Dover Wilson or Nunn. The proceedings were informal and the participants 'sat round a large table in armchairs and the lecturer talked. There was no highly-organised course of lectures, no organised timetable, and quite frequently the overworked professors had to be absent.'[29] In contrast Hamley, who in 1932 succeeded Burt as head of the Department of Higher Degrees and Research, organized structured courses and a timetable for both MA and Ph.D. students. For example, new regulations for the MA which came into force in 1937 required degrees to be taken in one of four areas: principles and practice of education; theory and history of educational institutions and administration; pedagogical research; philosophy and history of education. In addition to writing a thesis, candidates were required to complete a written examination which might comprise as many as five papers.

Student numbers in this period, even excluding those listed as 'intercollegiate' or 'occasional', were considerable.

| | MA | | Ph.D. | | All higher degree students | | |
|---|---|---|---|---|---|---|---|
| | Full-time | Part-time | Full-time | Part-time | Male | Female | Total |
| 1933–4 | – | 59 | 5 | 4 | 43 | 25 | 68 |
| 1934–5 | 4 | 59 | 5 | 4 | 52 | 20 | 72 |
| 1935–6 | 2 | 60 | 8 | 5 | 56 | 19 | 75 |
| 1936–7 | 6 | 48 | 6 | 6 | 52 | 14 | 66 |
| 1937–8 | 4 | 64 | 3 | 12 | 57 | 26 | 83 |

Table 5   Numbers of higher degree students, 1933–8[30]

One feature of these figures was the predominance of men students. Another was the high percentage of overseas students among the full-timers. In 1937–8 all seven of the full-time MA and Ph.D. students were men and all but one were in the Oversea Division.

Completion figures for internal students are recorded in Table 6. Although classification of topics is difficult more than 80 per cent of the MA theses completed in this period were in curriculum subjects or psychology. Of the 14 Ph.D. completions, three were concerned with some aspect of mathematics[32] and two apiece with intelligence, personality and behaviour and comparative studies. Other topics included Gestalt psychology, co-education, ancient and modern China, charity schools and backwardness in singing.

| | MA | Ph.D. | Total |
|---|---|---|---|
| 1934 | 8 | – | 8 |
| 1935 | 8 | 1 | 9 |
| 1936 | 11 | 3 | 14 |
| 1937 | 8 | 3 | 11 |
| 1938 | 13 | 3 | 16 |
| 1939 | 3 | 4 | 7 |

Table 6   Higher degree completions, 1934–9[31]

Studies in the history of education still tended to be the preserve of King's College.[33]

Hamley wanted to empower teachers to secure improvements in the curriculum, examinations, methods of teaching and class management. He believed that the Institute of Education was in a position 'to create in this country a body of school teachers who have learned to envisage their problems in a genuinely scientific spirit and are equipped with the means of attacking them scientifically'.[34] He also sought to establish a 'Bureau of Inquiry' which could respond to requests from LEAs and schools for information and advice. One of his first pieces of research was to collaborate with the Director of Education of Wiltshire in developing a Cumulative Record Card. This record of physical and mental qualities of each child would be of use to teachers and to the LEA and would also provide data for further research. One outcome of this research was a co-authored publication entitled *The Educational Guidance of the School Child* (1937). Other projects included an investigation in conjunction with the International Institute Examinations Enquiry into the validity and reliability of essay marks and another into intelligence tests for entry and scholarships to secondary schools for Middlesex County Council and the Great Yarmouth Education Committee. Hamley's appointment as Acting Director during Clarke's illness in 1937–8 brought a temporary halt to his personal involvement in such research.

Advanced courses necessitated the recruitment of further staff. In 1937 these included Dr Charlotte Fleming, a Glasgow graduate who had taught in elementary and secondary schools and lectured at Jordanhill Training College. Her interest in social psychology provided a useful broadening of expertise. Another important appointment was that of Dr Reinhold Schairer, a refugee from Nazi Germany who came as a research assistant and was appointed to a lectureship in 1937–8, thus strengthening the Institute's work in comparative education. Schairer was widely admired by students, who found him 'vigorous', 'enthusiastic', 'inspirational'. His educational tours to the European continent were much appreciated. In 1940, however, 'Dr Schairer went off to the United States on the advice of his friends'.[35]

In his recent biography of T.L. (Blue) Robertson, an Australian Carnegie Fellow at the Institute in 1938–9, Michael White claims that:

> when Schairer was offered a permanent lectureship in 1938, his background was vetted by British intelligence authorities. Their investigations revealed that he was a German spy with high level contacts in the Nazi Party. ... Getting wind of the investigations, Schairer fled to New York and anonymity among the Nazi sympathisers of North America.[36]

White also suggests that Schairer's continental tours were a cover for espionage and that there was speculation among the students 'that Schairer was meeting with high ranking German officers at the dead of night when they reached the German border'.[37] The issues raised by these allegations are too substantial to be considered in depth here. Nevertheless, three points can be made.[38] First, if Schairer's background was being investigated in 1938 it seems strange that he did not leave Britain until two years later. On the other hand it is clear that in 1940 a number of charges were made against Schairer and his Danish wife, Gerda, whose son, Harald, from her first marriage, returned to Denmark shortly before the outbreak of war. These included the Schairers' continual pleas of poverty, when they appeared to be living well – as demonstrated by their generous hospitality, Gerda's acquisition in 1939 of a car for £200 and purchase of some £500 of clothes prior to departure to the

USA. In 1937 Gerda Schairer in association with Egon Jameson visited many coastal towns in the south and east of Britain, talking to coxswains and taking photographs for a book entitled *Heroes of British Lifeboats*, which was published in the following year.[39] It was alleged that the photographs were sent to Germany to be developed. The Schairers' associations with a number of Germans, ranging from two secretaries at the German Embassy to the film actor, Anton Walbrook, were also regarded as suspicious. It was alleged that on the evening of 3 September 1939 the Schairers held a small impromptu supper party in their home in Golders Green to 'celebrate' the outbreak of war.

The Schairers' chief critic appears to have been Arthur Young, who had disbursed sums of money to assist them and had previously been associated with Schairer on secret work for the Foreign Office. During the war Young, an engineer whose peacetime career was spent with British Thomson Houston Company, was Director of the Labour Supply Committee of the Ministry of Labour and National Service. In December 1940 he wrote a confidential letter to Clarke, enclosing a secret memorandum setting out his concerns. Nevertheless, although investigations into the Schairers were clearly being made at this time, in a subsequent letter Young stated that 'I am not suggesting that he is a spy' and 'that his wife is a much more dangerous individual'.[40]

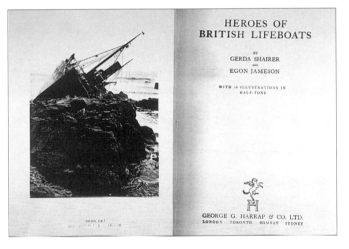

33. The frontispiece of *Heroes of British Lifeboats*, published in 1938, a book which raised suspicions about the activities of Reinhold and Gerda Schairer

White's second charge, that Schairer obtained anonymity among Nazi sympathizers in the USA, is manifestly incorrect. Indeed, Clarke, in common with Young, regretted that Schairer was representing himself too forcibly in the USA as the official spokesman for various bodies, including the Institute of Education, the University of London and the British Committee on Educational Reconstruction.[41] In 1940 Schairer obtained a temporary affiliation with the Institute for Advanced Study, with a grant from the Rockefeller Foundation for salary and travel costs. In the following year he took up a post at New York University and was one of the founders of the United States Committee on Educational Reconstruction. In 1955 he returned to Germany as head of the Karl Duisberg Foundation. As Malcolm Richardson has rightly concluded, 'Schairer's wartime activities are well documented [and] were conducted in association with first-rate American organizations'.[42]

The Schairer episode indicates the atmosphere of suspicion and distrust that existed in 1939–40, the very complex issues confronting Clarke and his colleagues about their most appropriate roles in wartime and the difficulties of conducting historical research into such periods.

## Susan Isaacs and child development

In the 1920s Nunn's recruitment of Burt had determined one direction of research and higher degrees at the LDTC – psychology with particular reference to intelligence and mental measurement. In the following decade his recruitment of Susan Isaacs, again on a half-time basis, established another – that of child development.

The Statement of Policy for the Institute adopted by the Senate in 1931 included a paragraph on the need for 'a department whose aim would be to enlarge and improve the scientific foundations upon which the education of young children should be based'. The case seemed clear. Similar centres already existed in Canada, Switzerland and the USA. In Britain, as the Hadow reports showed, opinion was moving away from an educational system divided upon lines of social class, as represented by the all-age elementary school, to one of growth and development with successive stages of infant, junior and secondary education for all. Such change warranted serious and substantial study and a sound theoretical underpinning. One particular need was to introduce lecturers in training colleges to the most recent knowledge about young children and their intellectual and social development. Difficulties, however, were also apparent. The Institute would not become involved in the initial training of teachers for the primary years. In consequence there would be no basic course with a guaranteed constituency of funded students, nor the opportunity to create a network of practising schools. The existing building in Southampton Row did not lend itself to the provision of an on-site school or classroom. Adequate finance, therefore, would be hard to obtain, and Nunn's attempts to secure outside funding for the new department and for the establishment of a nursery school of the 'laboratory' type where children could be observed under relatively standard conditions were unsuccessful.

In a history such as this which covers the span of a hundred years, it is impossible to do justice to the work and influence of the many outstanding staff (and students) who have been members of the LDTC and of the Institute. Susan Isaacs is one such example, indeed, as Adrian Wooldridge has concluded:

> Susan Isaacs was perhaps the most influential English-born child psychologist of her generation. She published important studies of children's intellectual and social development; founded an experimental school – the Malting House School in Cambridge – and set up a Department of Child Development at the London Institute of Education; acted as a tireless propagandist for the nursery school movement; and, in general presented a difficult subject intelligently and attractively to the general public, lecturing to schoolteachers, writing a weekly problem page in *Nursery World*, and giving evidence to the Consultative Committee of the Board of Education. Above all she did more than anyone else of her generation to introduce educational psychologists to the work of Sigmund Freud, Jean Piaget and Melanie Klein.[43]

Isaacs' own childhood was dominated by the loss of her mother, who died when Susan was only 6. Despite leaving school at 15 she secured entrance to Manchester University, graduating in 1912 with a first-class degree in philosophy. A year's research in psychology at Cambridge was followed by lectureships at the Darlington Training College in 1913–14 and at the University of Manchester in 1914–15. She taught psychology to tutorial classes for the University of London and for the Workers' Educational Association (WEA), and became increasingly interested in Freudian psycho-analysis. In 1922, following the dissolution of her first union, she married one of her former WEA students, Nathan Isaacs, ten years her junior. Between 1924 and 1927 Isaacs was head of the experimental Malting House Garden School in Cambridge. This experience provided data and insights which informed her subse-quent publications, especially *Intellectual Growth in Young Children* (1930), which led to the award of a D.Sc. by Manchester in the following year, and *Social Development in Young Children* (1933). Other impor-tant works from this most fruitful period included *The Nursery Years* (1929), covering the years from birth to 7, and *The Children We Teach* (1932), which dealt with the minds, interests and capacities of children aged from 7 to 11.

Contacts between Nunn and Isaacs were reinforced by her return to London in 1927. In May 1933 Isaacs began work at the Institute on a half time basis, but the hoped-for research assistant and laboratory school were not forthcoming.[44] Indeed, in the Southampton Row building Isaacs and the Child Development Department occupied one room, which served as a study, office and tutorial space. In spite of Isaacs' reputation and publications, Nunn was unable to secure either a chair or a readership for her. She was appointed at £300 per annum, raised to £325 in 1937 with an allowance of £100 for a secretary.[45]

34. Susan Isaacs, 'perhaps the most influential English-born child psychologist of her generation', who established the Child Development Department in 1933

In 1933–4, numbers on the advanced course in Child Development were three full-time students, 12 part-time, four from overseas who attended full-time for one or two terms only, and some 35 others from King's and University Colleges, who attended the intercollegiate course of lectures. The home students comprised teach-ers in nursery and infant schools, two inspectors and a psychologist from the Insti-tute of Medical Psychology, and five training college lecturers.[46] One of the five was Dorothy Gardner, who took the course part-time over two years. In 1933 Gardner, who ten years later would succeed Isaacs as head of the department, was lecturing at Bishop Otter College, where the principal was the ubiquitous former LDTC student, E.T. Bazeley.[47]

Isaacs did much of the teaching in the department. A basic course of lectures on infancy and early childhood ran throughout the academic year, complemented by seminars on such topics as child development, the teaching of child psychology and mental testing, and individual tutorials. Students also attended Nunn's lectures on principles of education and Hamley's on educational psychology. Additional specialist lectures were provided, initially by Professor A.H. Harris of University College on the physiology of children's growth, Dr S. Friel on medical aspects of the early years, and Dr D.W. Winnicott on mental hygiene.[48] Practical work included systematic observation of children in nursery schools in the first term, followed by further observation and some participation in child guidance clinics in the second and third. By February 1939 there were 20 full-time and ten part-time students on the main course, together with three research students working for higher degrees, four engaged in research for other purposes and 70 students attending the intercollegiate lectures.[49] In 1938 the Child Development Department acquired more spacious premises in the new Senate House building. Isaacs' own office, with a fine west-facing window, was a much more appropriate location in which to receive distinguished visitors. A second room was dedicated to student use, while a third was equipped as a play area for six or seven children aged between 2 and 4 who attended for two hours each morning during the university terms.

Isaacs' work and reputation as a lecturer and tutor, guide and friend brought great prestige to the Child Development Department and to the Institute more broadly. Her advice was keenly sought, and unstintingly supplied, not only in the case of students but also of a variety of individuals and institutions from home and overseas. One notable example occurred in the first year of the Department when the father of a 2-year-old child who had fallen from a train was tried for her murder. Isaacs' evidence that the child could have opened the door herself helped to secure his acquittal. Her publications in this period included a series of pamphlets entitled *Concerning Children*, jointly published by the Institute and the Home and School Council, and *The Psychological Aspects of Education*, first published in *The Year Book of Education* for 1935. Isaacs collaborated with Burt in a study of emotional development up to the age of 7 that was published as an appendix to the Board of Education's *Report on Nursery and Infant Schools*. She also assisted Hamley in work on record cards for the Wiltshire Education Committee.[50] From 1935 Isaacs suffered from cancer, and underwent surgery and radium treatment which necessitated two periods of convalescence. With the move to the new building in 1938 came the prospect of a long-overdue expansion of staffing, and of students. Those hopes were dashed by the advent of war, which led to the Department's temporary closure.

## W.B. Mumford and the Colonial Department

In 1931 one of the central arguments in favour of the transmutation of the LDTC into the Institute of Education had been the need for 'The creation in London of a strongly-equipped centre for the continuous discussion and investigation of educational problems that are important to the constituents of the British Commonwealth'.[51] In the same year the Statute of Westminster placed the relationships between the parliaments of the self-governing Dominions and of the Westminster parliament on terms of absolute equality. Between 1932 and 1939 the Institute advanced the cause of imperial and commonwealth education in several ways. The Colonial Department was formally constituted and specialist tutors with experience in education in Africa and other parts of the Empire appointed. Grants from the Carnegie Corporation of New York made possible the establishment of an Oversea Division, the attendance of Carnegie Fellows and the appointment of an 'Adviser to Oversea Students'. Initial omens were poor. From 1934, however, a number of significant developments occurred. These may be grouped around two members of staff appointed in 1934–5 – Mumford and Clarke – and the Colonial Department and Oversea Division of which they were the respective heads. Both Mumford and Clarke had experience of education in Africa and Canada; both also had connections with the USA.

In April 1934, Dr W. Bryant Mumford was appointed lecturer in the education of primitive peoples. Mumford was a controversial character who clearly excited considerable, and sometimes hostile, reactions. Whether such hostility was merited is difficult to determine. In some cases it appears to have been prompted by envy. Mumford and his wealthy American wife, Grace, were clearly not subject to the normal financial constraints. In 1952, the year after Mumford's death, A.S. Harrison, then senior lecturer in education in tropical areas, while praising his 'vigorous and vital personality' and 'friendly and charming manner', described Mumford as having 'the debonair appearance of a man about town who had just dropped in from his club for a chat on colonial affairs'.[52] In his study of the Institute's Colonial Department, Clive Whitehead suggests that Mumford never enjoyed the full support of some Institute colleagues, including Clarke, nor of the Colonial Office.[53]

Nevertheless, Mumford brought a variety of international experience to his post. Educated at St John's College, Cambridge and the LDTC, Mumford served for three years as a superintendent of education in Tanganyika. In 1927 he became headmaster of the Malangali School, and experimented with the adaptation of European education to local African culture. Mumford's work in Tanganyika was interspersed with periods of research and teaching in North America. He gained a Ph.D. from the University of Toronto, where he lectured in psychology and anthropology. In 1934, at the time of his appointment to the Institute, he was Carnegie Research Fellow and instructor in the education of primitive peoples at

Yale. Mumford and his wife brought financial resources to the Institute in the shape of a private trust, the May Esther Bedford Fund. Money from this trust, which amounted to some £1,000 per year, was placed at the disposal of the Colonial Department for travel expenses, the payment of researchers and the establishment of a substantial Colonial Department library. Mumford also obtained a grant from the Carnegie Corporation to support research into the teaching of English to non-European peoples. This work was further sustained by a grant of £1,000 over four years from the Rhodes Trust.[54]

Mumford's numerous activities included overseas visits, lecture tours, the compilation of bibliographies, a range of publications including textbooks for use in colonial schools, and in 1939 the launching of the *Colonial Review*, a quarterly digest of information about all aspects of colonial life including education. But his major contribution was an ability to form networks. Mumford involved virtually all other members of the Institute staff in teaching in the Colonial Department. He strengthened existing ties with the London School of Hygiene and Tropical Medicine and the School of Oriental and African Studies, and also sent students to attend classes by the Polish-born anthropologist, Bronislaw Malinowski, at the London School of Economics. Institute courses were further enriched by the contributions of specialist lecturers, including the secretaries to the Advisory Committee, Hanns Vischer, and Arthur Mayhew.[55] Student numbers grew steadily and in 1938–9 totalled 57. Of these the largest group by far were 40 missionaries, with 27 in training and 13 taking refresher courses. In 1937 the English as a Foreign Language (EFL) course was placed on a regular footing. It comprised lectures on the theory of language teaching, phonetics and speech work, with teaching practice in schools with foreign pupils.[56] Additional part-time staff brought considerable experience of work in the field. One of these was the social anthropologist, Dr Margaret Read. Educated at Roedean and Newnham College, Cambridge, Read had undertaken missionary social work in India in the 1920s and lectured on international affairs in Britain and the USA. Further study with Malinowski led her to pursue ethnographic fieldwork in east central Africa and to the award of a doctorate in 1934. An assistant lecturer at the London School of Economics in the 1930s, in 1940 she was appointed temporary head of the Colonial Department on a half-time basis in succession to Mumford, becoming full-time in the following year.

### Fred Clarke and the Oversea Division

Mumford and the Colonial Department constituted an important element in the life and work of the Institute, but they also formed part of a larger entity, the Oversea Division, and came under the ultimate aegis of the Adviser to Oversea Students, Professor Fred Clarke. The Oversea Division comprised not only those preparing to teach abroad but also all who came from overseas.

Its steady growth is apparent from Table 7.

Students came from many parts of the world. In 1936–7 the largest groups were 27 from India, 13 from Australia and 8 from New Zealand. Those of 1937–8 were drawn from 26 different countries.[58]

Students of the Oversea Division were involved in virtually all aspects of the Institute's work.

| Table 7 | Numbers of students in the Oversea Division, 1935–9[57] | | |
|---|---|---|---|
| | Men | Women | Total |
| 1935–6 | 52 | 31 | 83 |
| 1936–7 | 86 | 22 | 108 |
| 1937–8 | 85 | 32 | 117 |
| 1938–9 | 100 | 40 | 140 |

The Oversea Division was the product of American philanthropy. In 1934 the Carnegie Corporation made a grant of $67,500 to the Institute of Education to establish and support an international centre for three years. This included the recruitment of eight Carnegie Fellows each year from the Dominions and the appointment of an adviser to co-ordinate overseas work.[60]

In the aftermath of the First World War, the vision of a British Commonwealth imbued with a sense of trusteeship whereby subject peoples would be prepared via education for independence was a powerful one. Money for this purpose, however, was in short supply. The Colonial Office made little contribution, and territorial governments were left to provide such programmes as they could from the limited resources at their disposal. Carnegie money was used to support projects in particular parts of the Empire, but there was a further need – a central college for teachers, based in London, that would mirror and match the work of Teachers College, Columbia University.

Fred Clarke, who together with Nunn and Deller played leading roles in securing the Carnegie grant, took up his post as Adviser in January 1935. In May, with the aid of a further Carnegie grant and accompanied by his eldest daughter, Mary, he set forth on a tour of Australia, New Zealand and Western Canada. The 16-week trip, which Clarke undertook with some reluctance, was to serve several purposes.

| Table 8 | Courses of students in the Oversea Division, 1938–9[59] | | |
|---|---|---|---|
| | Men | Women | Total |
| Diploma course (full-time) | 20 | 8 | 28 |
| Colonial course (full-time) | 41 | 2 | 43 |
| Colonial course (part-time and occasional) | 9 | 2 | 11 |
| Art course | – | 1 | 1 |
| MA and Ph.D. courses (full-time) | 10 | 2 | 12 |
| Child Development course (full-time) | – | 4 | 4 |
| Child Development course (part-time) | 1 | 10 | 11 |
| Students taking research work not leading to a degree | 10 | – | 10 |
| Occasional students (school visits and odd courses) | 9 | 11 | 20 |
| Totals | 100 | 40 | 140 |

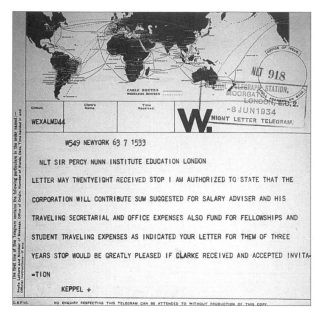

NLT 918

OFFICE OF ISSUE

GENERAL TELEGRAPH STATION,
MOORGATE
LONDON, E.C.2.
−8 JUN 1934
NIGHT LETTER TELEGRAM

W549 NEWYORK 63 7 1533

NLT SIR PERCY NUNN INSTITUTE EDUCATION LONDON

LETTER MAY TWENTYEIGHT RECEIVED STOP I AM AUTHORIZED TO STATE THAT THE

CORPORATION WILL CONTRIBUTE SUM SUGGESTED FOR SALARY ADVISER AND HIS

TRAVELING SECRETARIAL AND OFFICE EXPENSES ALSO FUND FOR FELLOWSHIPS AND

STUDENT TRAVELING EXPENSES AS INDICATED YOUR LETTER FOR THEM OF THREE

YEARS STOP WOULD BE GREATLY PLEASED IF CLARKE RECEIVED AND ACCEPTED INVITA-

=TION

KEPPEL +

NO ENQUIRY RESPECTING THIS TELEGRAM CAN BE ATTENDED TO WITHOUT PRODUCTION OF THIS COPY.

**35. A telegram from Frederick Keppel informing Percy Nunn of the Carnegie Corporation grant**

The first was to equip him with a unique knowledge of the educational systems and leading educationists in the four Dominions.[61] He also had the opportunity to promote and discuss the role of the new Oversea Division, and to meet some of the first Carnegie Fellows for the year 1935–6. In September he arrived back in London in time for the opening of the new academic year.[62]

## Carnegie Fellows

Seven of the first eight Carnegie Fellows, including the only woman, Doris Potter, from Auckland in New Zealand, were aged between 28 and 33. All took Nunn's course on 'Principles of Education', a one-term course on the English Educational System and had a weekly seminar conducted by Clarke. They also engaged in individual studies. Potter's special area of interest was juvenile delinquency, while her compatriot, W.W. Bridgman from Dunedin, followed the diploma course with further work in the teaching of English and dramatics. The two Canadians, C.E. Smith from Toronto and H.A. Weir from Halifax, Nova Scotia, concentrated upon the teaching of science and mathematics and upon the philosophy and psychology of education. T.L. Davis from Salisbury in Southern Rhodesia studied anthropology, psychology and the teaching of English to Africans; C.J.J. Smit from Cape Town undertook further work in the teaching of history and geography and the organization of secondary education. Of the two Australians, F.W. Mitchell from Adelaide (who was to become Clarke's biographer) ranged widely – across maths, psychology, teacher training and films and radio broadcasts. L.W. Phillips from Perth, at 42 by far the oldest of the group, focused upon technical education and juvenile employment.[63]

The Carnegie Fellows were highly selected, highly able and potentially highly critical. Issues rapidly arose about their courses, tutorial support, status and finances. Clarke, who had no higher degrees himself, was opposed to the Fellows spending their year in research for a Ph.D. Nevertheless one Fellow from the first group and two from the second (which also comprised seven men and one woman) engaged in doctoral research during their year at the Institute. One significant change in the scheme was that from 1936 Clarke was combining his role as Adviser with that of Director of the Institute. Some adjustments were made to allow for this and much of the administrative work in the Oversea Division was farmed out to others. The situation became more acute from 1937, following Clarke's breakdown in health.

On the occasion of Deller's death, Frederick Keppel, President of the Carnegie Corporation, wrote to Clarke referring to 'the machinations of an unscrupulous Providence' and observing that 'It would be very disturbing to us, of course, if you should be once more promoted, but perhaps you haven't been about the place long enough to make this likely'.[64] Clarke's sober response included the observation that 'The whole undertaking has now a sanctification which we all increasingly feel'.[65] In May 1937, Keppel confirmed to Clarke that the Corporation would continue the grant for a further three years,[66] but by the summer Clarke's letters to Keppel show that he was under considerable strain – fretting both at his inability to get away from the Institute for a holiday, and at the necessity of postponing certain tasks until they could be done properly.[67]

In April 1938 a formal letter from the Carnegie Fellows, signed by two of their number, I.S. Turner from Australia and R.B. Curry from New Zealand, was sent to Hamley, as Acting Director.[68] The letter was friendly in tone, expressing appreciation for the support they had received and best wishes for Clarke's recovery. Nevertheless, it also suggested that now that Clarke was Director a separate adviser was needed who could provide better (and possibly different?) guidance on choice of courses and support throughout the year. They also objected to the Institute's practice of deducting a flat fee of £30 from each student, regardless of what courses were taken, and asked for an increase in the amount of the Fellowships to £400. Hamley's response to these criticisms and others made by Dr William S. Taylor, a professor of education from Kentucky who had been attached to the Carnegie Fellows, suggests that Hamley and Clarke had disagreed over the appropriate programme for the Fellows.[69] A major reorganization of duties took place, with Hamley and Schairer assuming greater roles in respect of the Fellows.

Two Carnegie Fellows from 1938–9, a year which saw Clarke's recovery of health and the first year in the new building, A.J. van Zyl from South Africa and T.L. Robertson from Australia, contributed accounts of their experience to *Studies and Impressions*, published in the jubilee year of 1952. Van Zyl emphasized the benefits of studying independently and without assessment: 'I worked harder, studied more efficiently, assimilated more and used my time more economically than ever before'.[70] He praised the commitment of Hamley who, though serving as Acting Director, found time to teach him factorial analysis at the weekends. Van Zyl gained a considerable knowledge of the English educational system and of those of Australia, Canada and New Zealand, and adopted a more objective perspective on that of South Africa, which came in for much criticism from the other Fellows. He visited educational institutions in Britain and even, in the company of two other Carnegie Fellows, in Russia. He gave particular praise to the Friday morning lectures in the Beveridge Hall, which 'were very popular with Carnegie Fellows'.[71]

Robertson, who in 1952 was Director of Education in Western Australia, also paid tribute to Hamley, who 'received the Carnegie Fellows one by one and discussed our individual plans and problems with patience and sympathy … and soon became guide, philosopher and personal friend to us all'.[72] Hamley conducted Monday afternoon seminars attended by the eight Carnegie Fellows and some other overseas visitors, and also provided individual tutorials for those engaged in research. Four of the Fellows of 1938–9, indeed, including Robertson, elected to study for the Ph.D.[73] Robertson's educational visits included Denmark, France and Switzerland, and yet a further international perspective when, with war clouds gathering, he returned to Australia via the United States.[74] When the senior common room was opened in the new building, Hamley attended to another of the complaints from the previous year, by securing admission to it for the Carnegie Fellows, who were thus able to mix and discuss with members of staff in their natural habitat.[75] In 1938–9, too, some resolution of the different approaches of Clarke and Hamley to the question of an appropriate course for Carnegie Fellows and other experienced students from overseas was found in the establishment of a new qualification. This was the Associateship of the Institute of Education, which might be granted following a year of full-time study and the submission of a dissertation. In the first year seven candidates were awarded the Associateship. All bar one of these were former Carnegie Fellows, three from 1935–6, one from 1936–7 and two from 1937–8.[76]

The American, Taylor, and the Australian, Hamley, both valued detailed research and the Ph.D. degree. By contrast Clarke and the majority of members of the Delegacy put their faith in a good first degree supplemented by broad cultural experience. In respect of one other issue, however, there was little disagreement. In 1938, Taylor noted that:

> In the first place the Institute of Education seems to be greatly understaffed. Every person connected with it has been gracious and generous, but the work with the large group of students preparing for teaching is so demanding that there is too little time left for students working towards higher degrees, or for groups such as the Carnegie Fellows.[77]

## Lectures and publications

From the LDTC's foundation in 1902, John Adams in his role as Professor of Education had been responsible for providing lectures for a university-wide audience. He and other colleagues also published works that achieved broad acclaim. The Institute of Education, however, provided a more substantial institutional base both for public lectures and for publications. For example, in 1933 the Delegacy approved the institution of an annual lecture to be named the 'Sir John Adams Lecture'. The first, given in October 1933 by Deller with Percy in the chair, was entitled 'Tendencies in University Education'. Adams died in Los Angeles in September 1934 and the second lecture, delivered in December by Sir Michael

Sadler, then Master of University College, Oxford, was fittingly called 'John Adams. A Lecture in his Memory'.

A more substantial series, of two courses of three lectures per year, were the Joseph Payne lectures financed by the College of Preceptors with an annual grant of 50 guineas. Joseph Payne had been appointed the country's first professor of education in 1873 and the several connections between the Preceptors and LDTC have been noted in previous chapters. The Payne lectures provided opportunities to consider educational problems in the Commonwealth and on the European continent. Thus in the second series of 1933–4 Dr E.G. Malherbe, Officer in Charge of the National Bureau of Education in Pretoria, gave a course on 'Some Aspects of South African Education', while Kurt Hahn, the former Director of the Schloss Salem Schools, Baden lectured on the 'Salem System of Education and the Problem of German Youth'. In 1934–5 the courses were given by Sir Philip Hartog, former Registrar of the University of London and a member of the Indian Public Service Commission, on 'Some Aspects of Indian Education, Past, Present and Future' and by Professor Godfrey Thomson of the University of Edinburgh, on 'Salient Differences between the Scottish and English Systems of Education'. Other public lectures in 1934 were given in May by Professor Charlotte Bühler of the University of Vienna, who spoke on the 'Psychological Development of the Pre-School Child' and in June by Clarke, then still Professor of Education at McGill University, Montreal, whose topic was 'South Africa and Quebec: A Study in Cultural Adjustment'. Throughout this period the Joseph Payne lectures continued to attract outstanding speakers. For example in 1938–9 Richard Crossman delivered three lectures on 'Democratic Education: Challenge and Response', and Melanie Klein a further three on 'The Bearing of Psycho-analytic Theory upon some Educational Problems'. Some lectures were published in the Institute series initiated in 1932–3 under the title *Studies and Reports*. The first volume was based upon three lectures given by Professor C.H. Becker on 'Educational Problems in the Far East and Near East', and the second upon a Joseph Payne lecture by Isaac Kandel on 'The Educational Outlook'. By 1939 some dozen volumes had been published, the seventh being Hartog's lectures of 1934–5.

The most important Institute publication of this period, however, was *The Year Book of Education*. This was begun in 1932 by Sir Robert Evans with Lord Eustace Percy as editor-in-chief. The purpose was to represent the educational systems of countries around the world and to provide a forum for discussion of educational problems within the British Empire. The first volume reflected the monumental scale of the enterprise, with more than 1,000 pages. After three years, however, Evans saw the need to draw upon the expertise 'of an organisation for systematic and continuous research, using the YEAR BOOK as its recognised organ'.[78] Agreement was reached between Evans Brothers as publishers and the Institute, and the *Year Book* of 1935 was the first whereby the Institute assumed full editorial responsibility. Nunn and Dover Wilson were associated with Percy in this capacity, but in June 1935 Percy retired from the fray and the *Year Book* of 1936 was published under the authority of an editorial board consisting of Nunn, Clarke, Hamley and Winthrop Young, with Harley V. Usill, who had been associated with the publication from the beginning, as general editor. Usill continued in this role and the *Year Book* of 1939 was edited by a board chaired by Clarke. By this date, as the Institute's annual report for 1938–9 recorded, *The Year Book of Education* had 'an established position and is widely recognized as an international medium for the communication of statements of national policy, records of progress and experiment, movements of opinion, discussion of controversial issues, records of historical investigations, and similar material'.[79]

## The new building

By the mid-1930s the Southampton Row building was totally inadequate. Every nook and cranny had been pressed into service. For example, in 1934 one of the female cloakrooms was converted into a classroom and occupied by Kinchin Smith, the Students' Union was transferred to a store room, while the Conference Room was divided to provide accommodation for Clarke.[80] Thus delays in the completion of the Senate House complex placed increasing strain on staff and students alike.

Major problems also arose in respect of the new building. By 1937 financial difficulties had led to a significant modification of Charles Holden's original 'spinal plan', whereby a grand mass of University buildings in Portland stone (described by George V as 'exactly like a battleship') would have extended in an unbroken line from Montagu Place to Gordon Square.[81] The 'balanced scheme' of that year provided for the completion of the southern end, with the Senate House tower at its centre, and a series of separate buildings in brick to the north end of the site. While the Institute's place in the first phase was not in doubt the LCC, which had generously agreed to meet the cost of the Institute's accommodation, sought a reduction in the total amount, now estimated at £180,000. One proposal was to dispense with a separate library and reading room, and to establish an Education section within the adjacent University Library. This would secure a saving of £16,000. The Delegacy approved this amendment 'provided that suitable arrangements can be made for giving students of the Institute access at suitable hours to the Education section of the Library and to the Education Reading Room'.[82] Such assurances were not forthcoming and in 1938 a compromise solution was reached whereby the main collection of the Institute Library of some 15,000 volumes was housed in the largest classroom of the new building.[83]

In August 1938 the Institute took occupation of its new premises in the north wing of the Senate House complex. Many of the features of the new building attracted favourable comment: the breadth of the corridors, the rapid and silent

36. The north wing of
the Senate House
complex, home to the
Institute from 1938

lifts, the splendid assembly hall, the variety of specialist rooms. The Institute had come to the very heart of the University. The annual report for 1938–9 declared that, 'The spaciousness, the dignity, the convenience, and especially the vastly superior lighting and ventilation of the new home have had a most stimulating effect'.[84] Nevertheless, two major problems existed, problems that were to be replicated 40 years later in the Bedford Way building: inadequate library accommodation and the absence of a refectory.

On the evening of 18 May 1939 the Institute's new premises were formally opened by the Chairman of the LCC, Eveline M. Lowe, in the presence of a distinguished gathering presided over by the Chancellor of the University, the Earl of Athlone. Within the space of four months, however, trenches were being dug in Russell Square, the Institute was evacuated to University College, Nottingham and the new building was peremptorily requisitioned by the Ministry of Information. The era of euphoria was short-lived. One student from 1938–9 remembered the sense of foreboding engendered by 'the shadow of Munich. Though not exactly expecting war, we foresaw the destruction of this barely finished building.'[85] The new building was not destroyed, but 'By the time the Institute returned it had become the Old Building, a change in nomenclature prompted by what some tutors called "depredations by the Ministry" and the totally changed requirements of the Institute'.[86]

## Conclusion

The period between the formation of the Institute of Education in 1932 and the outbreak of the Second World War in 1939 was of great importance. Advanced work was developed, a Commonwealth and broader international role assumed, prestigious lectures and publications initiated, and location within the University finally secured. Such developments, however, without adequate resources, both human and financial, inevitably led to great strains. For most of this period the Institute remained trapped in inadequate premises, and lacking sufficient funds adequately to support staff and students and to make more appointments at professorial level.[87] The Carnegie Fellows received special consideration and had the power to secure some amelioration in their conditions, but by 1936–7 there were more than 100 students who came under the aegis of the Oversea Division. Such students were spread over a range of different courses and interests. Those who came to study at the highest levels, whether from home or overseas, wanted to do so at the feet of the giants of their day – Nunn, Hamley, Clarke – who were already overburdened with other work. Limited expansion and diversification were achieved, but at a high price.

# Chapter 6

# War and reconstruction
## 1939–1949

### Outbreak of war

In August 1939 Clarke was arguing the causes of Christian and democratic education as the best defence against totalitarianism at an international conference at Columbia University, where he was also awarded an honorary degree. On 3 September 1939 Chamberlain declared war on Germany and on the following day a German submarine sank the British liner, the *Athenia*. Accordingly the ship on which Clarke, together with his daughter, Magda, was homeward bound put back into Montreal and then proceeded to Halifax, awaiting the assembling of a convoy. By the time Clarke returned to England the Institute had been relocated in Nottingham.

At the outbreak of war the Ministry of Information gave the Institute one week in which to pack up its belongings and evacuate to University College, Nottingham. In consequence Hamley, assisted by Wacey and the Librarian, Geraldine de Montmorency, who made a hurried selection of key volumes, once more found himself in charge at a crucial time in the Institute's history. The actual removal took place on 11 September.

37. The Ministry of Information at the Senate House

As during the First World War, numbers of male staff and students were much reduced. Gurrey took up a commission in the RAF, Black was recruited to a chair of philosophy at the University of Illinois, while Jeffreys became Professor of Education at Durham. Dr J.W. Jenkins and Dr Sophia Weitzman took over the work in mathematics and history respectively. Both were good appointments. Jenkins, aged 34 and teaching at Harrow Weald County School, had an M.Sc. in mathematics, and a Ph.D. in education from the Institute. Weitzman, aged 43, was a Manchester graduate with MA and Ph.D. degrees in history together with a first-class diploma in teaching. Since 1930 she had lectured in history and the teaching of history at the University of Birmingham. Geography was taught initially by Mrs Scarfe and from 1941 by a former school practice supervisor, Miss Boultwood. In June 1940 Mumford, who had been in Iraq on behalf of the British Council, passed through London on his way to New York 'to carry out work of national importance in connection with the British Library there'.[1] In 1944 Mumford briefly rejoined the Institute, but then resigned his post, returning to New York where he later took up a position with the United Nations. He died in January 1951. With the agreement of the London School of Economics, Dr Margaret Read was appointed acting head of the Colonial Department on a half-time basis.[2] The most serious loss was of Hamley, who in 1940 was seconded for special duties in the Middle East, returning in 1943. During his absence Fleming and Jenkins supervised work in higher degrees and research. Short-term aid came from various quarters. Dr José Castillejo, former Professor of International Law at the University of Madrid, assisted with comparative education, which eventually came under the aegis of Lauwerys. Bishop Neville Talbot supplemented courses in religious education, while one of the Nottingham University College tutors, Mrs Veitch, took charge of music in the absence of Thornton Lofthouse.

Original numbers for the diploma course of 1939–40 (excluding those from allied colleges, colonial courses and occasional students) were 77 men and 92 women, but it is not clear exactly how many of the men joined their units rather than completing the course.[3]

## Nottingham

Make do and mend was the order of the day at Nottingham, whose campus site was shared not only with the staff and students of the host University College, but also with Goldsmiths' College, another London evacuee institution. The Institute contingent comprised some 200 students, together with academic and administrative staff. Space was in short supply: for example Clarke and Wacey occupied a single office, while tutors' rooms might be shared by members of all three institutions. Some 73 women students were housed in the Florence Boot hostel; others were placed in lodgings.[4] Although only one of the eight designated Carnegie Fellows arrived for the 1939–40 session, the new associateship qualification was retrospectively awarded to former overseas students, including four Carnegie Fellows. The Oversea Division boasted 51 registered students. Nineteen of these were taking the Colonial course; nine were diploma students from India. The annual report for 1939–40 noted with satisfaction that conditions at Nottingham had made for a much better 'mingling of four types of students, English, Dominion, Colonial and foreign' and looked forward to the further development of such integration after the war.

There were problems of morale, as students and staff wondered whether they should be playing more active roles in the war effort or sharing the hardships and

38. Students from the Institute and Goldsmiths' are welcomed by the President of the Students' Union of University College, Nottingham in September 1939

dangers of families and friends in bomb-ravaged London, problems which Clarke himself was at great pains to allay by his leadership and lectures. One student remembered that Clarke even asked four of the men to 'circulate among the girls doing what we could to take their minds off the war. This commission – which we possibly interpreted differently from his intention – was accepted with joy, many of the girls of 1939–40 must remember how conscientious we were.'[5] Some tutors commented that the absence of men also affected the level of academic work. For example, Sophia Weitzman reported that the history group of 1940–1 'missed, I think, the stimulus of mixed classes', and that the women students had a tendency 'to be over-serious and worried by the more pedestrian problems of class-room teaching'.[6]

Teaching practice was a particular problem. In the reduced situation at Nottingham where the services of all bar one of the teaching practice supervisors had been dispensed with and secondary schools, in particular, were in short supply, recourse was made to two periods of block practice, students being 'delivered daily by coach like bottles of milk'.[7] During the first practice most students were placed in junior, central and senior schools in Nottingham and the surrounding area, although secondary schools were in the majority for the second practice, including some in London and the Home Counties. The use of these latter schools reflected the pull of London, a phenomenon also increasingly reflected in the habit of students returning home for (sometimes extended and unauthorized) weekends.

On the other hand, the Nottingham sojourn supplied two essential elements hitherto lacking in the history of the LDTC and of the Institute. The first of these was the campus location – with accessible playing fields, fine lawns and lake, rock terraces and caves. There was the opportunity to walk and talk and to hold seminars beneath the trees known as Plato's Grove. Never before had the Institute been so close to nature. In the first year there was a 'solid month of skating in the winter' and 'a long spell of June radiance'.[8] Maura Gwynne, who assumed full responsibility for the teaching of English in the absence of Gurrey, waxed lyrical about this rural idyll:

> Two particularly vivid memories are likely to remain with those who spent their training year there. One, the woods above the opulent and shining Trent where an abundance of bluebells massed under the spring green. It was no uncommon sight to meet students passing through the college on the way home, laden with crab-apple blossom and bunches of cowslips and trailing long-stalked armloads of bluebells. The other, fire-watching at the college on fine summer nights. Beds could be dragged outside and one could sleep on the high terrace where the long view spread across the park and beyond, the magical dark hiding the daytime prospect of Boots' drug factory. It was, in the light of other more sordid associations of the same kind in war years, fire-watching de luxe.[9]

A second benefit was the heightened sense of community. For the first and only time in its history, staff and students were not dispersed across London and the surrounding counties. Not all students lived close to the campus in Nottingham, however. Bicycles were much in evidence and Iris Forrester, a diploma history student in 1940–1, remembered a daily walk of four miles from her 'billet' in each direction. She also recalled the sense of identity, of attending every course that she could – for example in geography and science – taking part in dramatic and musical productions, and serving as president of the Student Christian Movement. Forrester was very appreciative of her tutor, Sophia Weitzman, 'a most understanding woman and a good scholar, she was helpful on school practice too, and she was a great friend of Joe Lauwerys who was my other great star'. She also remembered Clarke's informed but measured lecturing style and how when asking him a question about a book following a lecture 'he became quite a different person, he became alive. ... So good, so thoughtful and he was essentially such a nice person.'[10] Iris Forrester herself was to become an Institute legend. Born in 1905, she obtained an external London degree in history as a student of Portsmouth Municipal College in 1927 and an MA in history from LSE in 1934. On leaving the Institute in 1941 she became a lecturer at Avery Hill College, retiring in 1971 as head of the Education Department. In retirement she completed a BA in humanities at Thames Polytechnic, followed by an Institute MA in history of education in 1988. She was a registered higher degree student and regularly attended research seminars until two weeks before her death in February 2001.[11]

In their individual reports for 1939–40 some tutors remarked on the sense of community and of participation. Lauwerys concluded a wide-ranging report which covered the teaching of science and arrangements made for courses in woodwork, metalwork and laboratory arts, with the observations that 'the students' appetite for lectures is apparently insatiable', and that 'we came into much closer contact than usual with the students, and got to know them very well'. Similarly, Whaite appreciated the 'more than usual opportunity for social contact' and noted that 'the closer contact than usual with nature has been stimulating'.[12]

In sharp contrast, the work of some departments was substantially diminished by the move to Nottingham. For example, the Child Development Department was closed in 1939. Isaacs, herself, led the Cambridge Evacuation Survey, which examined some 850 children evacuated to Cambridge from the London boroughs of Islington and Tottenham, about 200 of whom returned home during the course of the investigation. A class of eight full-time students in the Department of Higher Degrees met in Nottingham throughout the first session; part-time students in and around London were supplied with correspondence, weekend and vacation courses. The Research and Information Section of the Colonial Department initially served as an intelligence resource for the Ministry of Information. Government funding was supplied and four rooms in the Senate House placed at its disposal, but in April 1940 the Section was moved to 1 Thornhaugh Street and from July its activities were much reduced.

Although provisional arrangements were made for the Institute to return to London after one year, the intensive bombing of September 1940 ensured that the Nottingham sojourn continued.[13] Diploma numbers for 1940–1 were 11 men and 82 women, together with a further six from allied colleges and one occasional student. The Department of Higher Degrees had 36 students following MA and Ph.D. courses, all but one of whom were part-time. MA classes were provided both in Nottingham and in London and one energetic teacher whose school had been evacuated to Gloucestershire managed to attend both courses. Clarke, Fleming and Jenkins taught principles, psychology and statistics respectively on both courses, while the London students also received extra lectures from Castillejo on comparative education. Those students unable to attend either class were kept in touch by regular correspondence, and additional two-day intensive courses were provided in London during the Easter and Whitsun holidays.[14]

Of the 36 students in the Oversea Division, 29 were part-time or occasional members of the Colonial course. Some activities took place in Nottingham, but the library and office remained in London, where Margaret Read devoted much of her time to developing the information services and establishing links with Colonial ministries of Allied governments and other organizations. Indeed, two short courses were provided in French in co-operation with the School of Oriental and African Studies for cadets proceeding to posts in the Free French colonies in Africa. Margaret Read's report on the work of the Colonial Department for

1940–1 shows the considerable activity taking place in London. It also reveals that Read herself made only two visits during the year to Nottingham, the first in December to discuss the work of the Colonial students based there and the second in June to deliver a lecture on 'Political and Economic Development in the Colonies with reference to our Educational Policy'.[15]

One important innovation for the diploma students at Nottingham was the Social Services Week, organized by students under the leadership of Vera Netherway, the Union president, in the summer term of 1941.[16] A heightened sense of social responsibility and of the importance of integrating education with a wider range of social services led to this development, which was firmly supported by Clarke and Lauwerys. The week consisted of visits to social service institutions and lectures from outside speakers. One speaker who made a great impression was Dr Karl Mannheim, lecturer in sociology at the London School of Economics. The shared concerns of Clarke and Mannheim about the freedom of the individual in a planned society were demonstrated in two books published in 1940: Clarke's *Education and Social Change* and Mannheim's *Man and Society*. Both men were prominent members of the Moot, a 'think tank' of distinguished clergy, lay people and intellectuals, convened and chaired by J.H. Oldham, which met on 24 occasions for residential weekend discussions in the years between 1938 and 1947.[17] Mannheim was appointed a part-time lecturer in sociology at the Institute in 1941–2, and soon made his mark, both on the higher degree courses and at diploma level. In her report for 1942–3 Weitzman noted of the diploma students that 'whereas before politics and Communism was an all-pervading interest, today religion and sociology are first favourites'.[18]

Other important developments in 1941–2 included the appointment of Lauwerys to a readership – henceforth his energies would be increasingly devoted to comparative education – and notification from the President of the May Esther Bedford Fund that in future it would be impossible to continue the annual grant of £1,000 per annum in support of research and information services in the Colonial Department.[19] There was a second Social Services Week, with students again taking the major responsibility for the arrangements of speakers and visits. By this date many students were devoting their spare time to various forms of voluntary war work – for example, with the Women's Voluntary Service, giving talks to troops, working in canteens and ordnance depots, and helping with youth organizations.

## Portman Square

The session of 1942–3 was the last to be spent at Nottingham. Halliday was succeeded as chairman of the Delegacy by Eveline Lowe, who had herself lectured in the first Social Services Week and who held the post for four critical years. Fittingly, as an LCC member, she presided over the return to London. The sojourn

39. 42 Portman Square, the porticoed house to the left of the picture with cars parked outside, in 1942

in Nottingham had been an interesting episode in many ways. The heightened sense of community had been a gain, but there was also a growing awareness of the dangers of division and depletion. The national responsibilities of some members of the staff required their frequent presence in London, while the Nottingham authorities were showing understandable signs of restlessness at the continuing presence of the evacuees. Clearly the Institute's place was in London. Typically, the house at 42 Portman Square which was destined to be the fourth set of premises occupied by the Institute in a space of six years, was not ready for occupation in September 1943. After one meeting with tutors the diploma students were dispatched for three weeks to their practising schools.

The Portman Square premises were elegant and gracious, with a lofty portal, fine staircase, and more than 30 rooms. But although the main rooms were grand enough, the servants' quarters and back stairs were mean and dark, while the small lift, added at a later date, was of a 'most erratic and obtuse nature'.[20] The town house of the Montefiore family, 42 Portman Square was leased to the Institute for seven years at £900 per annum. Lecture rooms were situated on the ground floor; the library at the head of the main staircase. Lauwerys and science were located in an attic room, Jenkins and maths in 'the back kitchen'. The mews coach house, converted into a studio-workshop for art, was subsequently found to need 'drastic

40. The mews coach house to the rear of 42 Portman Square

repairs'.[21] Boultwood commented on 'the depressing, comfortless gloom of the geography tutorial room' and a lack of basic facilities and equipment.[22]

Numbers at diploma level were much as before, but there were changes. The return to London prompted a greater use of secondary schools for the purpose of teaching practice: 92 compared to 20 elementary schools. Some tutors took advantage of London facilities. For example, Weitzman arranged for some classes to be held at the Institute of Historical Research, now under the direction of Professor Galbraith. Classics flourished and in May 1944 there were full houses for three performances of Kinchin Smith's translation of Euripides' *Trojan Women* at the Tavistock Theatre by a cast of Institute students under the direction of a former English student, Jean Wheelwright.[23]

The desire to attend courses across the whole range of the diploma, begun at Nottingham in part because of the lack of other diversions, continued upon the return to London. This development was generally encouraged both on personal and professional grounds. The prospect of secondary education for all, contained in the Education Act of 1944, seemed to emphasize the need for teachers with well-rounded personalities and several areas of teaching competence. In 1943–4, in addition to main and subsidiary courses in the traditional subjects, together with long-established activities in music and physical training, 'free' courses were provided in arts and crafts, history and principles of science, literature and the arts, mathematical philosophy, religious education and statistics. Interestingly, by this date Mannheim's course and seminars on sociological education had become a required subject. In truth the opportunities for social activity were little greater than they had been in Nottingham. Although Gwynne remembered that 'Life at Portman Square was gay'[24] and a snack bar and student common rooms were established below stairs, Weitzman noted that London cafés were few and over-crowded, the black-out was strictly enforced, and parents and landladies waited anxiously each evening for the students' return.[25] London was still under attack, fire-watching was a constant duty, and in March 1944 incendiary bombs did considerable damage to the roof and upper parts of 42 Portman Square, while one even burnt itself out unnoticed on the concrete floor of the basement. Although 'The classical tutor and two colonial students, Irish Fathers, fought the fire vigorously, ruined their clothes and saved the house',[26] several rooms on the second and third floors were put out of use in this attack and months elapsed before the necessary repair work could be undertaken. During the third term flying bombs fell on London and on 30 June a student, Miss I.N. Rogers, was killed at the Aldwych in one such attack. Understandably, all members of the Institute went about their business with one eye on the sky above. Many lessons on teaching practice were taught in school shelters and at Portman Square increasing recourse was made to the basement.

The annual report for 1943–4 concluded that these difficulties had done little to damage the achievement of the students:

The appointed days for the Diploma Examination coincided with a period of intense activity by the enemy and during the examination alerts were both frequent and lengthy. Yet all the examiners agreed that the work of candidates was distinctly above the average and the number of examinees whose papers gave evidence of serious disturbance was negligible. There may be something here of interest to the psychologist.

This assessment, however, may be contrasted with that of Doris Lee, a diploma student of 1943–4 who subsequently became a member of staff:

The session closed abnormally early, but students were required to take the Diploma examination at King's College at the end of June. No candidate can ever forget Mrs Blackwell's enlightening description of how work could proceed under the desk or in the basement whenever a warning was in progress! Since warnings were many and frequent, it is needless to remark that each examination approached a riot, and more baffled examiners the University has probably never had. After the perpetual strain of the flying bombs, many students were too nervous to achieve much. One member drew each flying bomb as it was heard, and another interspersed this with scrap answers. There must have been many such. On the last day of the examination a flying bomb demolished the entrance to Bush House outside the College. One wondered why the freedom about which so much had been heard had not been used to cut the red tape of the examination. In this session, the power to survive wartime conditions had probably been worth more than the ability to satisfy the examiners for the Teachers' Diploma Examination.[27]

Three departments benefited greatly from the return to London. Although Isaacs was unable to return as head of Child Development (she died of cancer in 1948) Dorothy Gardner, currently working for the Bolton LEA, was appointed from November 1943. Students were few in number, but contacts were re-established with Wiltshire, which offered the Institute the use of one of its rural nursery schools, and negotiations begun for the Institute's direction of the Chelsea Nursery School for the purposes of research and demonstration within the capital itself. Gardner's many activities included the establishment of a research committee, a four-week investigation in Bolton into the effects of using modern infant school methods with children of junior age, and work for such bodies as the Nursery School Association, New Education Fellowship, National Froebel Foundation and the Child Guidance Council.[28]

Hamley returned to London and the Department of Higher Degrees and Research imbued with reforming zeal, and produced a highly critical report for the Delegacy.[29] In 1943–4 there were 25 men and 28 women on the MA and 11 men taking the Ph.D. All were part-time. In Hamley's view, much needed to be done.

Minimum criteria should be established for admission to higher degree classes and universally applied across the Institute and King's. The basic methodology of teaching was a matter for diploma work and should not be admitted for the MA, although the philosophy and psychology of teaching a single school subject would be acceptable. The assessment of the MA should be reviewed, both in respect of the examination and of the thesis, which 'should be regarded as a preparation for research rather than a research in itself'. Library provision was completely inadequate for advanced work. Indeed Hamley declared that overall 'the library is not worthy of the Institute', and remarked that the Institute's library grant was less than a third of that of the Institute of Education in Cairo, which served a much smaller number of students. He also noted the failure of the department to recruit full-time doctoral students who could produce high-quality research work and be prepared for university posts. Of the 19 students awarded Ph.D.s since 1930, all but four had been from overseas. Not one of the home students had been full-time. Hamley's reform proposals included the application of basic entry requirements for admission to higher degrees to all students, the institution of research scholarships to enable home students to study full-time, a reorganization of taught courses under two broad heads – the science of education and the history of education – the appointment of a personal tutor for each student, the introduction of new forms of assessment for the MA and the admission for thesis purposes of research work which formed part of a larger research enterprise. He also recommended the establishment of a single Department of Higher Degrees and Research across the Institute and King's College with a separate office and student facilities and under the general direction of an Academic Board for Higher Degrees. While many of Hamley's academic suggestions had considerable merit, the Delegacy in wartime had no intention of granting separate status to one department within the Institute, nor of undertaking the difficult negotiations with King's College and within the University as a whole that these administrative proposals would require.

The Colonial Department was the third of the major departments to benefit from the relocation in London. Tutorial and seminar work combined with visits, which were considered by Read to be the most appropriate methods of teaching the older and experienced students, could develop once more. Five students successfully completed the diploma course, and a further eight special courses open to outsiders were also provided. Between January and April 1944 Margaret Read was absent in West Africa as a member of the Commission on Higher Education, and A.S. Harrison, formerly of the Education Department of Ceylon who had joined the staff in the previous September, deputized during this period as well as continuing with other duties including the editorship of the *Colonial Review*. Another appointment in the first year at Portman Square, albeit initially part-time, was that of L.J. (John) Lewis. A scientist and former student of the Department, Lewis had nine years' experience in Nigeria at St Andrew's Training College, Oyo and as Principal of the Church Missionary Society Grammar School at Lagos.

Nevertheless, the increasing use of the Colonial Department by colonial officials, missionaries and others as a centre for advice and consultation, coupled with the loss of the May Esther Bedford grant, meant that resources were overstretched. In 1944–5 the Colonial Office grant was increased from £750 to £1,000. At the same time the Colonial Office decided that the best preparation for teaching or other education work overseas would be a normal course of initial training and some experience of teaching in the United Kingdom, followed by an intensive course of some three months' duration prior to service overseas.

## Sociology and Karl Mannheim

Hamley's memorandum drew attention to one of the major problems of the Institute at this time – the shortage of professors and the inadequate provision made for research and higher degrees. Clarke, who in Hamley's absence had been the only professor at the Institute, was fully aware of the difficulties and in a memorandum of 22 October 1942 proposed the establishment of three new chairs: one in history of education, a second in comparative education and a third in educational sociology. In spite of the provision at King's College, Clarke gave priority to history of education and recommended 'the establishment of a school of historical studies in education'. His recommendation of a chair in educational sociology noted that 'The work at present done by Dr Mannheim is on a small scale, but experience has already proved its high relevance and value'.[30]

Mannheim was born in Budapest in 1893. His university education encompassed Budapest, Berlin, Freiburg, Heidelberg and Paris, and in 1918 he was awarded a Ph.D. by the University of Budapest for a thesis on 'The structural analysis of epistemology'. Mannheim was a double refugee: in 1920 from the White Terror in Hungary; in 1933 from the Nazi regime in Germany. A lecturer in sociology at the London School of Economics from 1933, part-time lecturer at the Institute from 1941–2 and professor from January 1946, he died a year later at the age of 53. Mannheim's basic warning, for staff and students, for members of the Moot and for all who would hear him or read his writings was powerfully expressed in *Man and Society*:

> To the Western countries the collapse of liberalism and democracy and the adoption of a totalitarian system seem to be passing symptoms of a crisis which is confined to a few nations, while those who live within the danger zone experience this transition as a change in the very structure of modern society.[31]

According to Mannheim the solution to this problem was to be found in the identification and development of the best ideas and ideals of traditional Western civilization and humanism. But British liberal-capital society of the 1930s and

1940s was very far from ideal. Outside observers such as Mannheim and Clarke, who had spent many years abroad, were conscious of the extent to which British society was shot through with divisions and inequalities based upon class and wealth. The evacuation of urban children during the war demonstrated that education had been a major divisive force in British society. There were some differences between Clarke and Mannheim; Clarke, for example, was a staunch Christian. Mannheim was not, but both challenged Nunn's emphasis upon education as a matter of individual growth and freedom. In their view education must be planned and co-ordinated across society. Clarke dedicated his *Freedom in the Educative Society*, published in 1948, to Mannheim and argued that 'What Karl Mannheim has called "Planning for Freedom" is the first duty of Britain now'.[32] Nor was education simply to be defined in terms of what took place in schools. Clarke and Mannheim both firmly believed that the professional educational world had become divorced from society at large. Mannheim maintained that teachers needed to be aware of a much broader range of issues than hitherto, both pedagogic and sociological. The school should be seen as one social institution among others.

41. Karl Mannheim, 'a devoted scholar, a penetrating critic and a warm-hearted friend'

Mannheim attracted both admirers and critics. His intelligence, missionary zeal and vision of Britain as the bastion of freedom won many hearts. Clarke was a strong supporter, and recommended the appointment of Mannheim to a part-time lectureship because he had the 'profound conviction that Mannheim had something to say that was of urgent importance for the future of English education'. In Clarke's judgement, the success of Mannheim's teaching lay not so much in opening a new world to students as in illuminating the world in which they actually were, and in his manner of doing so.[33] There can be little doubt that many students were inspired by Mannheim. His vision of an essential role for teachers in uniting the nation in time of war and providing a basis for a better society in the years of peace was timely and inspirational. His premature death, after barely a year in post, was keenly felt. Mannheim's knowledge and wisdom, his whimsical smile and gentle humour would be sorely missed. A resolution passed by the Academic Board and endorsed by the Delegacy, referred to him as a 'beloved colleague … a devoted scholar, a penetrating critic and a warm-hearted friend' who 'brought new inspiration to us and to our students'.[34]

On the other hand, some colleagues wondered whether Mannheim's influence was too great and whether the Institute and its students were being diverted from their true purposes. For example, the hard-pressed Gwynne recognized the interest and importance of Mannheim's teaching of diploma students, but she also observed that:

there seems to be a tendency to turn out students who are less able to take a stand on the worth of their subjects and aesthetic subjects as a whole in school and in life, less well-equipped as to theoretical considerations and less alive to the standard of values they must adopt for themselves. In exchange, they might well have better conceptions of the place of the school in the community and broader views of the social responsibility of a teacher. It is a question of which is the cart and which is the horse.[35]

Hamley's views were expressed more forcefully in his report to the Delegacy for 1943–4. Clearly dismayed by what had been going on in his absence, Hamley inveighed against what he saw as the uninformed use of such terminology as 'social theory' and 'political re-orientation'. Higher degree students seemed to have abandoned the writing of theses 'having any direct relation to school work or involving even a modest knowledge of statistical methods'. Instead they wanted to produce surveys: 'social surveys, surveys of youth organizations, of girls' clubs, of out-of-school activities, of reading habits, of cultural amenities, of friendships, of public opinion, of religious opinion'. There was little doubt as to what, or even who was to blame. Hamley reported that 'Even students of science have admitted to me that they ceased to be interested in science (and the teaching of science) when they became interested in sociology'.

## National Foundation for Educational Research

One of the key elements envisaged for the new Institute of Education as established in 1932 was the creation of a Bureau of Educational Enquiries and Research. Such a bureau was seen as exercising a co-ordinating function in respect of educational research throughout the country. Nunn's several initiatives came to nothing, but when the International Examinations Enquiry in which Clarke and Sir Philip Hartog had taken part was wound up, the Carnegie Corporation of New York, which had financed that enquiry, undertook to provide a sum of up to $10,000 if matching amounts could be raised within England.[36] The Leverhulme Trust duly offered £1,000 and the Institute accepted £2,000 to establish a Foundation for Educational Research on the understanding that neither it nor the University would be responsible for any expenditure above this figure. An Advisory Council was formed with Clarke as chairman and Burt, Fleming, Hamley and Jenkins among its members. At its first meeting in January 1943 the Council urged the Institute to assume responsibility for the early stages of what should become a major national body. This proposal, which had the approval of the Board of Education, was accepted by the Delegacy, and the Foundation for Educational Research flourished, with further grants including some from the teachers' associations. In 1943–4, for example, the National Union of Teachers made a grant of £1,000, the Joint Four £250 and the Association of Teachers in

Colleges and Departments of Education £100. Institute staff, including Fleming, Jenkins and Kinchin Smith, were among those who benefited from Foundation grants. A full-time secretary, Lea Perkins, was appointed in March 1944. Following a conference in December 1945 at which formal proposals for the establishment of a National Foundation for Educational Research (NFER) were approved, an Interim Executive was appointed with Clarke as Chairman, Will Griffith of the National Union of Teachers as Vice-Chairman and Dr William Alexander, General Secretary of the Association of Education Committees as Treasurer.

By 1945 the offices of the Foundation had been transferred from Portman Square to more suitable accommodation at 17 Manchester Square. A further move to 79 Wimpole Street, made possible by a generous loan from the National Union of Teachers, took place in December 1946, and on 31 March 1947 the Institute ceased to be responsible for the financial and other administration of the Foundation. With the Minister of Education as its president and 'the active support of the National Union of Teachers and of local education authorities throughout the country'[37] the NFER was poised to become an independent national body. Nevertheless, as the historian of the NFER, Jeff Griffiths, has acknowledged, 'the Foundation is very much a progeny of the University of London Institute of Education'.[38] Throughout its early years Fred Clarke played the leading role and a bronze plaque in the reception foyer at The Mere, the Foundation's headquarters in Berkshire, records his services: Chairman of the Interim Committee, 1943–7, Chairman of the Executive Committee, 1947–9, Vice-President 1949–52. It declares him to have been 'A Founder and Faithful Friend'. Obituary notices in the Foundation's annual reports paid warm tributes both to Clarke and to Hamley who 'had for years before its inception been one of the most consistent and ardent advocates of the national need for an institution with the functions of the Foundation'. Close connections between the Institute and the NFER continued. In 1949 Jeffery (now Director) succeeded Clarke as Chairman of the Executive Committee, while the next Institute Director, H.L. Elvin, served on the NFER's Executive Committee and on the Finance and General Purposes Committee. In 1968 Professor William Wall, who had been Director of the NFER since 1956 and in whose time the NFER moved from its central London location to Slough, was appointed Dean of the Institute.[39]

## The McNair Report

In January 1943 Clarke's services to education were recognized in the New Year's Honours List by the title of Knight Bachelor, an accolade which Clarke modestly accepted 'not so much for any personal merit he might possess, but rather for the institutions he served and the profession he represented'.[40] Only Nunn and Clarke amongst Institute directors have been knighted while in office and there can be no doubt that in both cases the honour was richly deserved. For, by 1943, in addition to directing the Institute and serving as the University's Professor of Education, Clarke was playing a leading role in the teaching of diploma and higher degree students, a prominent member of such bodies as the Moot and the All Souls Group, first convened in June 1941, active in the committees of the British Council and the New Education Fellowship, a member of the Goldsmiths' College Delegacy and of the Schools Broadcasting Executive Committee, and a member of the Advisory Committee on Education in the Colonies from 1937, with service on the Colonial Universities Commission from July 1943. But perhaps the most important of Clarke's public services in this period, and certainly the one which would have most ramifications for the work of the Institute, was his membership of the McNair Committee, established in 1942 'To investigate the present sources of supply and the methods of recruitment and training of teachers and youth leaders and to report what principles should guide the Board in these matters in the future'.[41]

Chairman of the Committee was Dr Arnold McNair, a former lawyer and civil servant, currently Vice-Chancellor of the University of Liverpool, who like Clarke was knighted in 1943. Many of the recommendations of the Report, which was published in 1944, were widely welcomed: an end to the 'pledge',[42] the abolition of the ban on married women teachers, a single Burnham committee for all teachers in primary and secondary schools and a substantial increase in salaries, a minimum training course of three years from age 18, followed by a year's probation. But the Committee was divided over the best means of organizing and administering the training of teachers. Five members of the Committee, including Clarke and S.H. Wood, a former LDTC student, head of the Teachers' Branch at the Board of Education who also acted as the Committee's secretary, wanted all universities to establish schools of education.[43] This proposal was known as Scheme A. McNair and four other members of the Committee, including Mary Stocks, Principal of Westfield College, London, supported Scheme B, which recommended the establishment of a Central Training Council to reorganize the existing Joint Boards.[44] Stocks believed that it would be impossible to raise the training colleges and their students to university status; they were different entities with different origins and different functions. Although the McNair Committee was equally divided on the issue, responses from training institutions, teachers' associations, LEAs and other interested bodies were overwhelmingly in favour of Scheme A. Vice-Chancellors, however, fearing that universities might be swamped by the new schools of education, were less enthusiastic and produced a Scheme C by which such schools would be incorporated as separate bodies, but outside the universities.[45]

Clarke wanted to place the determination and monitoring of academic and professional standards of teachers firmly in the hands of the universities. For 15 years the universities, through the Joint Boards, had exercised major responsibility for the determination of syllabuses and conduct of examinations for students in training colleges. Nevertheless, Board of Education representatives had attended meetings of the University of London's Training Colleges Delegacy for the purpose of ensuring that regulations and qualifications were acceptable to the Board for professional purposes.[46] The Board also continued to examine practical teaching and other practical subjects. Clarke feared that the Ministry of Education established under the 1944 Act might seek to play a more active role. In May 1944, in a speech to the Council of Principals shortly after the publication of the McNair Report, he warned that 'this country might have to meet the problem of strongly developing totalitarian tendencies. Under such a regime the teaching profession was the first that the promoters sought to capture.'[47] Given Clarke's anxieties about over-mighty central government it was somewhat ironic, although also a further indication of his reputation and standing, that R.A. Butler was to appoint Clarke to the chairmanship of the Central Advisory Council established under the 1944 Act.

The London Joint Board scheme, established in May 1928, which consisted of 20 colleges initially organized into six groups, had not been a great success. Niblett *et al.* have argued that 'the working of the London Joint Board Scheme in the first few years proved cumbersome and time-consuming, and some of the leading university figures tended to lose the limited initial sympathy they had for it'.[48] In 1937 Gurrey, in his capacity as moderator for the London Joint Board Examination, described the system as 'a particularly cumbersome piece of machinery for failing a small proportion of students and awarding a decoration to a proportion almost equally small'.[49]

Some 30 institutions were involved in the training of teachers within the London area. These would constitute a very large, and possibly unwieldy, school of education indeed. In contrast to many other areas, moreover, there was no single university department of education. King's College and the Institute were clearly of university rank, while the anomalous position of Goldsmiths' College provided a further complication.[50] Clarke's commitment to Scheme A was well known and widely supported within the Institute. Indeed, in the summer of 1944 Professor H.C. Barnard of the University of Reading, one of the few professors of education to support Scheme B, noted in his diary that Clarke was particularly active in 'throwing his weight about' in favour of Scheme A.[51] Within the University of London as a whole, however, there was little initial enthusiasm for Scheme A. Halliday, the Principal of King's, member of the Institute's Delegacy and its former chairman, argued that the training colleges needed greater independence, not yet further connections with the universities. In November 1944 he expressed his objections at a conference of university bodies concerned with teacher training:

In King's College, the Department of Education is one department and not the most important in the College. So that we look at the matter … from the point of view of the University rather than that of the teachers. Our view is that though in the past the training of graduate teachers has happened to fall upon the University, the training for the professions is not primarily a University business. ... The universities are going to be asked more and more to do jobs which we do not regard as university jobs, and quite frankly we would rather see the training of teachers go out of the University altogether than the training of teachers coming within the purview of the universities.[52]

## G.B. Jeffery

The name of George Barker Jeffery has already appeared in previous chapters: as an able but not particularly assiduous LDTC student in 1911–12 with a slight nasality of speech, tormentor of Dicker and Hulbert, and admirer of Nunn. Born in Lambeth in 1891, in 1944 Jeffery was Astor Professor of Mathematics at University College, London, a post he had held for 20 years. Even as an LDTC student Jeffery was 'involved in some mathematical research and attending some MA lectures on the quiet'.[53] But Jeffery also remembered the LDTC year as 'a turning-point in his life'[54] and in addition to his university roles, as Dean of the Faculty of Science, Deputy Chairman of Convocation and member of Senate, was involved with schools and teacher training in an administrative capacity. For example, he served as Chairman of the Matriculation and Schools Examinations Council, as a university visitor and examiner of training colleges under the Joint Board Scheme, as a member of the University's Training Colleges Delegacy established in May 1928 and from 1935 as a member of the Institute's Delegacy.

42. G.B. Jeffery, who succeeded Fred Clarke as Director in 1945 and who 'always spent, amazingly, a lot of time socially with students, especially those from overseas'

Jeffery was a firm supporter of Scheme A. His main concern at this time was the promotion of greater co-operation between the University and local authorities. In the autumn of 1944 he

> invited to dinner at the Athenaeum two old friends who were in a position to influence the course of events, Graham Savage and Harold Claughton. ... After Savage had gone home, Claughton said: 'You know, this is all rather funny, because I have been deputed to ask whether you would take on Fred Clarke's job when he retires at the end of the session'.[55]

In the course of a lone midnight walk in St James's Park Jeffery, who had never imagined himself as Clarke's successor, resolved on two things: the first to persuade the University to accept Scheme A; the second to secure its implementation from 1945 in his capacity as the next Director of the Institute of Education.

Although R.A. Butler, as Minister of Education, favoured Scheme A, each university was approached separately, the University of London in November 1944. Jeffery took the lead in producing a draft Scheme A proposal for London. According to his own account, in response to criticisms that the University was being asked to adopt a vague and undefined responsibility:

> I replied that, if the committee would appoint a drafting sub-committee and adjourn for a week, it would have a complete scheme. That was on a Friday. I spent Saturday and Sunday at the Athenaeum writing hard, assisted by a volunteer typist who called at the club every few hours for fresh copy. Six carbon copies of the complete scheme were ready when the sub-committee met on Monday morning. With only a few changes, this scheme was that which was afterwards adopted by the Senate and is now in operation.[56]

In December 1944 Jeffery sent a personal letter from his home address to the principals of training colleges and departments in the London area, seeking their support for his scheme and assuring them that they would be genuine partners within it. He wrote, he advised, not in his capacity as Director-elect 'but as a man to the men and women whom he hopes will be his personal friends and collaborators in a great undertaking'. His 'vision of the Training Colleges and the University working together in a great unified effort to lay the foundation on which the future of our schools must be built', was widely welcomed.[57] Understandably, Jeffery was the main proponent of the Draft Scheme in the protracted and often heated debates that took place within the University. In 1945 the argument moved to the Academic Council and Senate. The chief opponents of the Draft Scheme were Halliday and Lillian Penson, Professor of History at Bedford College and the first woman to serve as the University's Vice-Chancellor, from 1948 to 1951.[58] Nevertheless, Jeffery's Senate motion that the University should accept responsibility for the training of teachers in the London area was carried with a large majority. Jeffery had wisely included a statement that 'in any scheme which may be agreed the sphere of responsibility of the University should be precisely defined and that within that sphere the decisions of the University should not be subject to the confirmation or consent of any other authority'. University autonomy was a principle upon which all could agree! A further four years, however, were to elapse before the new Institute, which embodied Jeffery's scheme, was inaugurated in 1949.

In the meantime, on 1 October 1945, Jeffery assumed the responsibilities of Director of the Institute. The dual role of Director and Professor of Education was brought to an end and Mannheim was appointed to Clarke's professorial chair. Clarke, although 65 years of age, continued to hold numerous appointments within the world of education. In 1948 he even returned to the Institute, to his former position as Adviser to Oversea Students, a position he held until his death. He died, unexpectedly, at his home on Sunday 6 January 1952, having attended communion at St Pancras Church earlier that morning. It fell to Jeffery, who 'always spent, amazingly, a lot of time socially with students, especially those from overseas',[59] to deliver the Jubilee Lecture on 'The Institute and Oversea Students' in his place.[60]

Dr Jeffery, as he became on relinquishing his chair at University College, was a new type of Director. Adams, Nunn and Clarke had all been teachers. Although Clarke's experience of school teaching had been very brief indeed, all three had deserved reputations among teachers and as teachers of teachers. Frank Mitchell, indeed, subtitled his book on Clarke, 'master-teacher'. Professor A.V. Judges, Head of the Education Department of King's College at the time of Clarke's death, recorded that although Clarke spent many years abroad, upon his return he 'became the *doyen* of pedagogic leaders in his own country'.[61] In contrast, Jeffery's undoubted prowess as a mathematician and scientist had been exercised in a university context. He brought many attributes to the post of Director – a formidable figure within the University of London and with numerous contacts in the world outside. He was an experienced administrator, a renowned committee chairman and the very author of the new Institute which came into being from 1949. Jeffery had many admirers and supporters. For example, David Shorney has commented that Dr Frances Consitt, Principal of Avery Hill College where a new hall of residence was named after Jeffery, 'was captivated by the Director's vision of the Institute as an organization from which all teachers in the London area, not simply the training colleges, would derive strength, illumination and purpose'.[62] But although Jeffery was widely respected and displayed many of the kindly attributes associated with membership of the Society of Friends, some people were dismayed by his forceful style, mordant wit and 'London' accent, which they contrasted with the gentler manner and mellow tones of Clarke. Geoffrey Barnard recalls a memo from Jeffery pinned to the Senior Common Room notice board deploring the fact that the lectures of some staff were inaudible beyond the front two rows.[63] Dixon recounts how when a College Principal expressed doubts about the relationship between the central and wider Institutes Jeffery 'glared down the table and said: "Reverend Mother, if you can understand the Holy Trinity, a three-in-one, surely you can understand a two-in-one"'.[64]

## Malet Street

By January 1946 the Institute was back in the Senate House. The homecoming, however, was marred by two major disappointments. The Central Office of Information continued to occupy the ground floor and basement throughout the 1945–6 session. They had arrived in days, but took months to depart. The second problem was the condition of the building, so pristine and fine in September 1939,

but now battered and shabby beyond belief. During the war the Institute's pride in its new building had been grimly confirmed by the knowledge that had Adolf Hitler been victorious his headquarters in Britain would have been the Senate House complex, including the Institute's wing. Some damage was the result of enemy bombing, but much harm had also been inflicted upon the building by its British occupants. Open cloisters had been enclosed to create extra rooms, so that while the capacity had been increased, the premises seemed to have shrunk in size and grown darker. Vandalism had taken place. As Gwynne lamented, some of the tenants 'one

**43. The cloisters which were enclosed to provide extra rooms**

might be apt to think were related to Saracen hordes. It is strange but true that there must have been during those years eminent VIPs or their minions, who sported with ink upon the marble walls, or dribbled it playfully upon the carpets.'[65]

Pressure of staff and student numbers prevented a return to the pre-war situation. The bomb-damaged first floor was reconstructed with a central corridor to provide rooms on both sides. Attics under the roof were made habitable. Two pre-fabricated huts were erected in the quadrangle, with a further hut on the east side of the building. The Institute's development policy for the Quinquennium for 1947–52 proposed an extension of the existing building to provide: an adequate library; at least 60 additional rooms for the academic staff; further staff and student common rooms; conference and committee facilities; two or three larger lecture rooms to seat 150–200, and some small rooms suitable for discussion groups of 20; alternative centres for the expanding Colonial Department and Department of Child Development; a visual education centre; workshops for the teaching of additional crafts.[66]

Not surprisingly, a library was placed first in this list. Although in 1952 the Librarian, Geraldine de Montmorency, declared that 'the Library starts its second half-century well established and on a sound basis',[67] her assessment was decidedly optimistic. There were some bright spots, notably the May Esther Bedford Library of the Colonial Department, a comparative education library begun in 1937 with Clarke's own books as a nucleus, and an English as a foreign language library brought together by Gurrey. Four specialist collections had been recognized in the compromise agreement with the University Library – those of higher degrees and research, child development, colonial studies and education in the dominions – and these continued to receive favourable treatment, but overall the Institute Library was small in size and poorly housed. Much depended upon the benefactions of staff. Indeed de Montmorency, who was only appointed on a full-time basis in 1940, calculated that by the time he retired Nunn, who had been involved with the Library from the beginning, had donated about a quarter of the entire stock. In September 1938 the Library of some 15,000 volumes had been installed in the largest classroom of the new building. This was designated as a 'working-reading room', which served not only as the Library office, equipped with telephone and typewriter, but also as the place where students prepared lessons. As accessions increased, some pre-1920 material was consigned to a basement storeroom while corridors were lined with bookshelves. By the end of 1946 the prospect of a much-enlarged role for the Institute's Library was causing additional concerns. The Quinquennium proposals advised that 'It will be the first duty of the Institute under the area training scheme to offer the facilities of a first-class Educational Library to the members of the staff of its associated training colleges'.[68] The information supplied for the University Visitation of 1950, by which date the general and departmental libraries contained 40,653 volumes and 537 periodicals, included the comment that 'In no respect is the accommodation more notably inadequate than in the Library'.[69] The Visitors concurred: 'the housing of the Library is hopelessly inadequate'.[70]

Another longstanding problem was the lack of halls of residence, particularly for overseas students. In 1944 Jeffery had promoted a new type of student residence at University College, known as 'College rooms', when three houses had been leased in Gower Street. In 1946 four houses were leased by the Institute at 12–15 Bedford Way, and renovated to provide a dining room, kitchen and study bedrooms for some 54 women students. The first students came into residence in December 1946 under the wardenship of Miss A.M. (Marian) Stephenson. Svelte and composed, dealing admirably with crises caused by the shortage of coal or the ingress of water through the roof, Stephenson was described by one of her first charges, J.M. Ritchie, as 'something between a Russian ballerina and Lady Macbeth'. About half of the hostel places were reserved for overseas students, and Ritchie remembered conversations with students from the Gold Coast and 'a Turkish girl, who seemed much more volatile than most English women'. She was also fascinated by Child Development students, one of whom asked all the residents whether they had been fed naturally or on the bottle, attributing 'all peculiarities

**44. A student group from 1947–8, with Marian Stephenson, the warden of the Bedford Way hostel and a cross 'between a Russian ballerina and Lady Macbeth', seated in the centre of the second row, seventh from the left**

and peccadilloes since' of the latter group to this particular cause.[71] Further houses were leased in 1947 – one in Gower Street and two in Coram Street – for 49 men students, who took their main meals in Bedford Way.[72]

## Expansion

The most notable feature of the return to Malet Street was the explosion in student numbers. This ensured that the Institute of 1949 was very different from that of 1939, even without the additional role consequent upon the creation of the wider Institute. The Delegacy's memorandum of 28 November 1946 outlining the development policy for the Quinquennium showed that full-time student numbers had more than doubled from 302 in 1938–9 to 658 in 1946–7. They might easily treble within the next five years and limits should be imposed in order to preserve a balance between the various activities. Part-time numbers were also rapidly increasing, especially at MA and Ph.D. levels.[73]

Explosion in student numbers reflected two main factors. The first was the pent-up demand from students prevented by war from training as teachers or following other courses. The second was the 1944 Education Act with its promise of secondary education for all, and the raising of the school-leaving age to 15 in 1947. Although, as in the immediate aftermath of the previous war, there were fluctuations in numbers, by 1948–9 something of a steady state had been achieved. Significant differences in distribution by sex were now apparent. The 371 diploma students comprised 133 men and 238 women; the 205 MA and Ph.D. students 141 men and 64 women.[74]

One immediate result of the increase in numbers of diploma students was the appointment in March 1946 of George Baron, a former teacher of modern languages who had served in the Education Corps during the war, as a full-time school relations officer with particular responsibility for arrangements for teaching practice and other visits to schools. In June 1947 Baron organized a conference with the headteachers of teaching practice schools which 'provided the occasion for a frank discussion of the relative part of staffs of the schools and the Institute in the practical training of students'.[75] Baron's research into educational administration subsequently led him to transfer to an academic role, and he was appointed professor in 1971.

Increased student numbers justified that additional staffing, particularly at the more senior levels, which the formation of the Institute in 1932 had presaged. In 1938–9 there had been 28 members of academic staff; in 1946–7 there would be a maximum of 49, with a proposed total of 77 during the quinquennial period, 1947–52. Table 9 shows the distribution among grades.

Increased numbers on the diploma course facilitated the creation of teams of curriculum tutors with a senior lecturer at the head. This was in sharp contrast to some other smaller institutions where 'method' work in one or more subjects was the province of a single tutor, destined to remain forever at lecturer level. Thus, in art, Whaite was appointed to a senior lectureship in 1945, and Olive Gabriel, a former half-time lecturer, to a full-time post in 1948. Fifty-four students took the Art Teacher's course in 1947–8. Similarly, following the departure of Black and the tragic death of Jenkins in August 1945 in an aeroplane accident while returning from a Forces lecture tour in the Mediterranean,

| Table 9 | Numbers of academic staff, 1938–52[76] | | |
|---|---|---|---|
| | 1938–9 | 1946–7 | Proposed |
| Director and professor | 1 | – | – |
| Professors | 1 | 3 | 5 |
| Readers | – | 4 | 5 |
| Senior lecturers | 10 | 15 | 20 |
| Lecturers | 3 | 11 | 44 |
| Lecturers, part-time | 1 | 3 | – |
| Assistant tutors | – | 8 | – |
| Assistant tutors, part-time | 6 | 4 | – |
| Research fellows and assistants | – | 1 | 3 |
| Totals | 28 | 49 | 77 |

in April 1946 C.T. Daltry was appointed to a senior lectureship and head of department in mathematics. Two further full-time appointments were made in mathematics in September 1948. One was of Dr C. Gattegno, assistant tutor from 1946; the other of Doris Lee, like Daltry another former Institute student with a first-class degree, who had taught at Roedean and was currently lecturer in mathematics at Goldsmiths' College. Gattegno and Lee were independent and forceful characters and 'Daltry had to put up with many a joke in the Senior Common Room about how to keep his department in order'.[77] The History Department, currently in the charge of Phyllis Wilshere in the absence of Weitzman, also secured a pair of appointments in 1948. W. Hedley Burston was a traditionalist with experience in independent schools and a background in philosophy and economics; James L. Henderson an internationalist and devotee of Jung, who had taught at Bedales and worked in student and social services. Gurrey was confirmed as head of department both for English and English as a Foreign Language (EFL). Appointed to a readership in 1946, in the following year he was also named as Senior Tutor and Adviser to Oversea Students. Nancy Martin and Edith Moore were appointed to full-time posts in English in 1946, and F.S. Whitehead in 1948. Nevertheless, in 1948 Gurrey was passed over when Dr Bruce Pattison, a lecturer in English at University College London, was appointed to a chair with special responsibility for the teaching of English as a Foreign Language. Pattison was also appointed head of a Language Division which included English, Classics and modern languages. Gurrey, a member of staff for 22 years, departed to become Professor of English at the University College of the Gold Coast.

Mannheim's chair proved difficult to fill, sociologists of education being in short supply. The eventual replacement, W.O. Lester Smith, a former Director of Education in Manchester, was a stop-gap appointment, serving from 1949 until 1953.[78] In contrast, Lauwerys was appointed Professor of Comparative Education in 1947 and served until his retirement in 1970. Lester Smith's age and experience meant that he emerged as a natural deputy for Jeffery, particularly during the Director's absences in West Africa. Lauwerys himself was frequently abroad, too frequently for Jeffery's liking, but his lively mind and unbounded energy made him a welcome sparring partner for the Director, and behind their banter and arguments lay a considerable mutual respect. Another internal promotion was that of Margaret Read, Head of the Colonial Department and a reader from 1945, who was appointed to a chair in 1949. A fifth professorial appointment of this period, in 1947, was in philosophy of education. Professor Louis Arnaud Reid came from the chair of mental and moral philosophy at Armstrong College, Newcastle upon Tyne. Reid, a graduate of Edinburgh, was a distinguished philosopher, a former lecturer at Aberystwyth and Liverpool and visiting professor at Stanford.

Hamley's final years at the Institute were difficult and contentious. The rapid increase in numbers of higher degree students placed considerable strains upon him and his department. Greater support was clearly needed. Fleming was promoted to a readership in 1946 and H.E.O. James, currently lecturer in psychology at Manchester University, appointed at readership level in 1947. In the 1930s Hamley had been instrumental in securing special facilities and privileges for the Carnegie Fellows, but his attempts to uphold the claims of the higher degree students of the 1940s to club rooms and other facilities for their exclusive use put him on a collision course with the Director.

Jeffery already viewed the semi-autonomous status of the Colonial Department with considerable concern, although the ending of the Colonial Office's annual grant of £1,000 per annum in 1947 meant that it was no longer necessary for separate accounts to be kept. He was determined to prevent Higher Degrees and Research from treading the same path and, in so doing, encouraging others such as Child Development to do likewise. In his view the very concept of a separate department for higher degrees and research needed to be challenged. It was the product of a period in the Institute's history when there had been only one or two professors and a very limited number of higher degree students. Jeffery argued that in the Institute of the later 1940s all professors and readers should pursue research and create around them a body of higher degree students. Academic staff should concentrate upon academic matters and leave administrative matters such as the registration of students to a central registry. Jeffery was firmly opposed to the emergence of a rigid departmental system which would produce 'a set of autonomous institutions under one roof – an arrangement which discourages co-operation, leads to unnecessary academic duplication – and, worst of all, turns the best professors into administrators who have no time to profess'.[79] By this time Hamley's health was a cause of general concern. He died in June 1949, after many years of unstinting service to the Institute and within three months of his retirement. His successor from October 1949 was Dr Philip Vernon, a Cambridge graduate and Fellow of St John's College, who had been head of psychology at Jordanhill College and the University of Glasgow. Vernon was an outstanding psychologist, much admired by Burt, who commended him to Jeffery as 'beyond any doubt the most brilliant research worker'.[80]

Thus by 1949 the Institute had six professors in Lauwerys, Lester Smith, Pattison, Read, Reid and Vernon. Four of the five 'foundation' disciplines – those of comparative education, sociology of education, philosophy of education and psychology of education – were provided for; history of education was not. This still came under the aegis of King's College, where A.V. Judges, a former lecturer and reader in economic history at the London School of Economics, was appointed Professor and Head of Department in 1948.

In the post-war years appointments at professorial and reader levels considerably strengthened the capacity of the Institute to conduct research, to cater for higher degree students and to make a substantial and unique contribution to the delineation and development of the discipline of education in Britain. This situation has continued to the present day and by way of contrast it may be noted that by the time the University of Oxford appointed its first professor of education in 1989, the Institute had appointed 49.[81] One corollary of such appointments and of the increasing numbers of higher degree students, however, was that the initial training of students occupied a less central place than hitherto. It also meant that those preparing to be teachers in schools were sometimes exposed to professorial members of staff whose lecturing techniques, unlike those of their predecessors – Adams, Burt, Clarke, Hamley, Nunn and Mannheim – were regularly called into question. For example, many diploma students of this period were less than enthusiastic about the Friday morning lectures of Reid and Vernon as delivered to the mass audience in the University's Beveridge Hall, and doubted their relevance to the course of professional training in which they were engaged.

## A wider Institute

The purpose of this section is to summarize the events of the period between June 1945, when the Vice-Chancellor forwarded the Senate's approval of Scheme A together with a copy of Jeffery's amended Draft Scheme to the Ministry of Education, and the implementation of the wider Institute from September 1949.

The General Election of July 1945 brought the sweeping victory of Clement Attlee and the Labour party. Ellen Wilkinson, 'Red Ellen' in many eyes, a former pupil teacher, union organizer, member of the Communist Party, and firm supporter of working people both in Britain and abroad, was appointed Minister of Education. Her principal aims included the raising of the school-leaving age to 15, not achieved until 1947, the year of her untimely death, and the introduction of genuine secondary schooling for all children. Although her predecessor, Butler, had been broadly in favour of Scheme A, Wilkinson wished to reconsider matters afresh. Her guiding principles were that as far as possible there should be one basic scheme governing the relationships between universities and training colleges throughout the country, and that the new Ministry of Education should play a more significant role in the training of teachers than the Board of Education had done in recent years.[82] Substantial discussion with her officials, including the new Permanent Secretary, Sir John Maud, led to delay and considerable frustration for those who wished to press on with the new schools of education. In November 1945 Jeffery wrote to Wilkinson, pointing out that in London:

> The long delay is having disastrous effects. The enthusiasm of the training colleges is seeping away. … Within the University the opposing minority has every opportunity to point out that the sense of urgency with which some of us urged the matter is apparently not shared by His Majesty's Government.[83]

Two years of protracted negotiations ensued and by the summer of 1947 even Jeffery was contemplating the withdrawal of the Institute from the initial training of teachers and concentration upon higher degree work and research. One crucial issue was the Ministry's right to inspect courses and examinations for teachers within the University itself. In July 1947 a compromise formula was reached whereby an inspector was not precluded:

> from attending by agreement a lecture or tutorial class for the purpose of elucidating any point that may have arisen in the course of his consultations

with the University authorities, but not for the purpose of reporting on the work of an individual teacher of the University.[84]

This was a most important decision and indicated the changes that had occurred since HMI reported directly upon the work of LDTC staff. The compromise was to hold until the 1980s, when the establishment of the Council for the Accreditation of Teacher Education (CATE) signalled central government's intention to regain control of teacher education courses and qualifications.[85]

In October 1947 the Vice-Chancellor was informed that the University's proposals had been accepted by the government; in February 1948 the Senate approved the scheme for a new University of London Institute of Education to serve as the training body for the London area.

Further discussions occurred over the relationship between the Institute of Education as it currently existed and the new Institute. While Institute staff were keen to take a leading role in the new venture, most believed 'That the Institute should go into the scheme as a unit, retaining its name, its separate administration and its own assets and funds … the Institute should assume no general responsibility for the administration of the School as a whole.'[86] On the other hand Jeffery proposed that 'the present Institute should not remain as a separate institution under its own Delegacy, but that its work should be continued as part of the activities of the "School" as a whole'.[87]

This proposal aroused considerable opposition – not least from within the Institute itself – and Jeffery was forced to concede. The Final Scheme included provision for two separate governing bodies. The Council of the wider Institute would have a wide representation comprising the Vice-Chancellor, Chairman of Convocation, the Principal, the Director of the Institute, and 52 members appointed annually by the Senate, including 10 principals of constituent colleges or departments, 10 teachers of the Institute, eight representatives of local education authorities, six persons representing the views of practising teachers, four representatives of voluntary bodies concerned with teacher training, two persons appointed by the Minister of Education, and 12 other persons of whom four would be nominated by the Academic Council and three by the Collegiate Council. The Council's duties would include giving advice to Senate and exercising executive powers delegated to it by Senate in respect of such matters as admission of colleges and departments to the Institute, admission of students, regulation of courses of study and their examination, and the recommendation to the Ministry of Education of students of the Institute for Qualified Teacher Status. First degree courses, the teacher's diploma and higher degree courses in education, however, continued to come under the aegis of the University's Board of Studies in Education. The Committee of Management, established to oversee the work of the Central Institute, would exercise the powers of the former Delegacy and comprise the Vice-Chancellor, the Principal, the Director of the Institute, together with 20 other persons appointed by Senate. Of these eight should be members of the 12 'other persons' of the Council, four Council members drawn from other categories, and four members of the Central Academic Board.

Other bodies established under the Scheme included a Committee of Principals, consisting of the Director of the Institute and the principals or other heads and representatives of each of the constituent colleges. The Director would not chair this committee. The Institute Academic Board would comprise the Director of the Institute, the Chairman of the Committee of Principals, the Chairman of the Conference of Local Authorities (which the Director was required to convene at least once in each academic year), all professors and readers, 30 elected representatives chosen from among the 555 teachers of the Institute and not more than six co-opted members. The Academic Board, which in 1949 had 17 standing sub-committees, would advise the Council on academic issues. Additionally, there would be a Central Academic Board responsible for advising the Academic Board on matters relating to the Institute's central activity. A new body was formed to represent students within the wider Institute, known from 1949 as the University of London Institute of Education Students' Association (ULIESA).

This Final Scheme, adopted in 1948 and implemented from 1949, did not escape criticism, principally on the grounds that the former Institute, the new 'Central Activity', had too much power. The Education Department of King's College and the Training Department of Goldsmiths' College, together with the 28 other colleges which constituted the wider Institute, were understandably wary of the position of the new Central Activity, which involved 'The development of the work formerly undertaken by the Institute of Education as constituted prior to the coming into force of this scheme'. Such wariness was increased by the fact that General Sir Ronald Forbes Adam, Chairman of the Institute Delegacy from 1946, became Chairman both of the Council and of the Committee of Management, that Jeffery, the Director of the former Institute and current Central Activity, was Director of the wider University of London Institute of Education, and that the offices and officers of both were housed in the former Institute's building in Senate House. There was a feeling that the University had retained direct control over the Central Institute, while the members of the Central Institute were seeking to exercise authority over what they saw as their new empire of the wider Institute. There was also concern that while Institute staff might be experts in the preparation of teachers for selective secondary schools, their experience of non-grammar secondary and of primary schools was much less.

Jeffery's response to such criticisms, and particularly to the charge that the term 'Institute' was now ambiguous, was that the Institute of Education was essentially one and indivisible. As Dixon noted, Jeffery refused to employ the common term of 'Area Training Organization' to denote the wider Institute, and 'organized one Registry, one Accounts Office and one Examinations Department for both ATO and Central Institute'.[88] Niblett *et al.* also commented that, notwithstanding the amendments to Jeffery's original scheme, the University of London's enlarged Institute, 'went much farther in the direction of merging the UDE in the ATO than did the constitution of any other Institute'.[89] Doubts and doubters, however, were set aside in the general mood of optimism. The inauguration of the new Institute on 19 December 1949 was a splendid affair, attended by a host of dignitaries including the Chancellor, the Earl of Athlone, HRH Princess Alice, Professor Penson, now Vice-Chancellor, Wilkinson's successor as Minister of Education, George Tomlinson, and representatives of staff and students from each of the constituent colleges. Nevertheless, while Penson and other former opponents were prepared to give the new Institute their blessing and support, and first degrees in education would be introduced by the 1960s, the school of education as envisaged by Jeffery was not achieved.

## Conclusion

Thus, under Clarke's inspirational leadership, the Institute survived the dangers and dislocation of war and emerged with its reputation enhanced. During the next four years, with Jeffery at the helm, expansion occurred in terms of professorial and other staff appointments and of higher degree work and research. Such expansion provided a belated fulfilment of the expectations generated by the transition from LDTC to Institute in 1932. There would be little time for consolidation and reflection, however, for by 1949 the Institute was already entering upon the third phase of its existence – as an ATO.

# Chapter 7

# New identities
## 1949–1963

### Introduction

Jeffery saw the new Institute of Education as being one and indivisible. It included both the institution that had begun life as the London Day Training College and the larger entity referred to by the Ministry of Education as an Area Training Organization.[1] In his history of the years 1932–72, published in 1986, Dixon used the terms 'Central Institute' and 'Wider Institute' to distinguish between the two, devoting two chapters apiece to the 'central' and 'wider' dimensions between 1944 and 1972.[2] As an administrator Dixon was much interested in the scale and complexities of the larger body. In this centenary history, however, which takes a longer perspective in encompassing both the LDTC years and the demise of the ATO, the Institute as ATO occupies a lesser role.

The immediate post-war years were characterized by food rationing, acute shortages of many goods, and by make-do-and-mend. Large parts of London, including many schools, were still scarred by bomb damage. The bitter winter of 1947 had brought fuel shortages and power cuts, and the country was ravaged by blizzards in February and widespread flooding in March. Many individuals still bore the physical and mental scars of war, immediate experiences too close for comfortable indulgence in reminiscence or nostalgia. John Cameron, a teacher's diploma student in the Colonial Department 1946–7 who later became a member of Institute staff, remembered that 'The demure woman student sitting next to you in a lecture might well have … fired shells in an anti-aircraft battery near London … or even piloted new RAF bombers across the Atlantic from American factories. If she had, she would not have bothered to tell you.'[3] By 1949, in spite of continuing austerity (two eggs and one shilling's worth of meat per person per week) 'London was learning to relax again'. Some students, tiring of drinking powdery cocoa or treacly bottled Camp coffee in their spartan rooms, ventured to Platoni's near Russell Square tube station to experience the new wonder of 'something called an Expresso which served mainly froth', or 'danced in Tottenham Court

Road, perhaps without knowing it to the trombone of the young Peter Sellers'.[4] The students of 1946–7 were earnest and dedicated, keen to build a better future and proud to be members of the prestigious University of London and of its Institute of Education. Nevertheless, as Cameron noted, 'There was still an air of improvisation about the whole place'.[5] By 1949 student attitudes were much the same, but improvisation had been replaced by innovation – in terms of structures, knowledge and international role.

In a structural sense, within London and the surrounding area the power and influence of the Central Institute was much increased by the creation of the wider Institute, an edifice of which Jeffery was the acknowledged architect and builder. At national level, Central Institute staff, led by the professoriate, assumed the lead in redefining and developing the old 'Principles' into a new discipline or disciplines of education. Finally, the Institute's international role was revitalized and revolutionized by the demise of the British Empire and the emergence of a Commonwealth of independent states.

## The wider Institute

The wider Institute was a very substantial enterprise. Nearly a quarter of all students training to teach in England and Wales did so under its aegis. The first major task was the admission and subsequent visitation of constituent colleges. The 28 training colleges which in 1948 applied to the Provisional Council for admission fell into three broad groups. Seventeen institutions already associated with the University under the Training Colleges Delegacy and Maria Grey, which was associated with the University as an 'institution having Recognised Teachers', were admitted for three years in the first instance. Three further specialist colleges, Chelsea, Dartford and Nonington, recognized by the University for the purposes of the extension diploma in the theory and practice of physical education, were admitted for one year and to be inspected in 1948–9. A committee was appointed to recommend procedures for the inspection prior to admission of seven 'other colleges' which had not yet come under the aegis of the University of London.[6] By 1952, the wider Institute comprised 34 training colleges, as well as the Education departments of King's College and Goldsmiths' and the Central Institute itself. Although the number of colleges did not increase, there was a steady rise in student and staff numbers.

The finance and maintenance of colleges rested with their providing bodies – many of them local authorities or religious communions. The Institute's role was confined to the colleges' educational activities, both academic and professional. Nevertheless conflict could arise, as soon happened in respect of the proposed relocation of St Gabriel's College from its cramped site and bomb-damaged premises. In February 1949 the Provisional Council informed the Ministry of Education that it was 'unable on educational grounds to recommend the proposal that St Gabriel's College should move from Camberwell to Crowborough'. Instead consideration should be given to 'the development of St Gabriel's College in its present neighbourhood'.[7] Cramped conditions, coupled with government demands for expansion, caused many colleges to seek new sites. Some, like Shoreditch Training College, which re-located to Englefield Green in Surrey, Coloma College, which moved to West Wickham in Kent, and Clapham and Streatham Hill Training College, which not only acquired new premises in south London but also a new identity as Philippa Fawcett College, remained within the ATO. In contrast, in 1959 Westminster College left the ATO on moving to a 40-acre site at North Hinksey, Oxford.[8]

A second responsibility exercised by the Council was to recommend to the Senate the granting of the status of 'teacher of the Institute'. Professors and readers were automatically included in this category, but a new title was created, that of 'lecturer in the Institute of Education'. Successful applicants were required to hold a permanent and full-time appointment in one of the colleges or departments of the Institute, to 'possess high academic or other professional qualifications appropriate to the particular post', and to 'have had successful experience in teaching or some other relevant field of educational work'.[9] These requirements, however, were interpreted in a generous spirit. Indeed, of the 555 teachers of the Institute in 1949, while 328 were graduates and a further 36 had qualifications in art or music, 191 were non-graduates.[10] The recognition of so many non-graduates confirmed the concerns of those who saw the wider Institute as a threat to the academic standing of the University and to the Central Institute itself.

Syllabuses and examinations constituted another main area of responsibility for the wider Institute. On 1 September 1949 the Council of the wider Institute assumed the responsibilities previously exercised by the Training Colleges Delegacy.[11] New regulations for the teacher's certificate were introduced and colleges were organized into six groups for the purposes of examination. In 1956 the government announced that from 1960 the two-year certificate course would be extended to three years. This would result in a dearth of new teachers in 1962, especially in primary and secondary modern schools. The longer course provided an opportunity for an increase in content, the raising of examination standards and an extension of teaching practice. This latter, however, was problematic, given the pressure on school placements. Four-fifths of the college students were preparing for posts in primary schools, and it was estimated that in 1963–4 some 6,000 primary places would be required, compared with only 3,350 in 1960–1.[12] In consequence teaching practice was extended from the existing 12 weeks only to 15 weeks.

Jeffery, who died in 1957, was an unswerving champion of the wider Institute. His successor, H.L. (Lionel) Elvin, was also assiduous in maintaining the Institute's independence and role in the face of perceived threats from the Ministry of Education and other quarters. Yet the many problems of the wider Institute were also apparent by this time. In 1960 W.R. (Roy) Niblett was appointed Professor of Education and Dean in order to provide Elvin with some relief in his dual role. Niblett, who was charged with strengthening links between the colleges and the Central Institute, brought considerable experience to this role, having previously served as Director of the University of Leeds Institute of Education.

Some of the problems noted by Niblett were peculiar to London. The wider Institute with more than 30 colleges and 10,000 students was simply too widely spread. Too much time and money was spent on travelling. Many college staff, moreover, did not want more contact with staff of the Central Institute. Those staff in the colleges who were teaching subjects such as history or physics as main academic subjects wanted links with leading historians and physicists, 'real professors', at such colleges as King's and University.[13] Similarly, education staff in the colleges were mainly concerned with preparing teachers for work in primary schools. Although the Child Development Department under Dorothy Gardner had considerable status and support, the main expertise of Institute staff lay in the secondary field.

45. W.R. Niblett, appointed Dean of the Institute in 1960 with special responsibility for strengthening links between the colleges and the Central Institute

Two other difficulties were of a more general nature. The first was the abolition from 1952 of separate grants for ATOs.[14] Thereafter ATO money was subsumed into the general University grant and came under close scrutiny. Questions were raised, for example, about the value of paying the travelling expenses of countless teachers of the Institute to attend 50 committee meetings a term at Senate House. Growing University disenchantment with the ATOs was matched by that of the Ministry of Education and its successor from 1964, the Department of Education and Science (DES). Thus, in 1958, in planning for expansion, the Ministry communicated directly with the governing bodies of the colleges, rather than with the ATO or Elvin.[15]

## Lionel Elvin

Jeffery died as dramatically as he had lived, suffering a heart attack at the wheel of his car in April 1957. The funeral took place at Jordans – a simple Quaker meeting on a beautiful spring day. Clarence Whaite of the Art Department gave the main address.[16] In the previous year Jeffery had reached the normal retirement age of 65, but had readily accepted the Committee of Management's invitation to serve as Director for a further three years. That invitation was based upon the Committee's 'opinion that Dr Jeffery retains his remarkable mental energy and vigour and that his experience and guidance would be particularly required in the coming years'.[17] Professor E.H. Warmington, a member of the Committee of Management and of the Council, Professor of Classics and Acting Master of

Birkbeck College during the Vice-Chancellorship of Dr Lockwood, served as the Institute's Acting Director for 17 months until a permanent appointment could be made.[18] Warmington was 'Mild in manner with a benevolent smile. ... As a confirmed bird-watcher, he looked rather sleepy at times as though he had been up early scrutinizing the ponds, but that appearance was deceptive.'[19]

Jeffery's unexpected and untimely demise was one reason for the delay in appointing a successor. Another was the real problem of filling the shoes of a man who had created the very institution that he directed with such force and energy. Grace Wacey, who from 1920 was Secretary under five Principals and Directors, declared him to be 'one of the hardest workers I have known and, when he is set on anything and is sure in his mind that he his right, he will go on until he reaches his goal'.[20] Dixon, who succeeded Wacey as Secretary in 1958, noted that Jeffery 'could be a thundering giant ... his paternal authority was everywhere'.[21] One indication of Jeffery's sheer physical presence, 'his massive head and shoulders', was the decision to commission a bust by Sir Jacob Epstein, rather than a portrait, in his memory.[22] In many ways Lionel Elvin was a complete contrast to Jeffery. Spare of frame, as an undergraduate at Trinity Hall, Cambridge he won an athletics blue in the half mile, and was turning out with the Ruskin College soccer team at the age of 44. His style of leadership was more conciliatory and consensual; as Dixon noted, 'He was prepared to win agreement where Jeffery had sometimes insisted upon it'.[23]

46. Lionel Elvin, appointed Director in 1958, following the unexpected death of Jeffery in the previous year

Elvin was born in 1905 in Buckhurst Hill, Essex, and educated in elementary schools and at Southend High School. In 1930 he was elected the first Fellow of English at Trinity Hall. He was a radical, 'a non-Christian',[24] a man of the Left, active in the Workers' Educational Association and a friend of R.H. Tawney, many of whose ideas he shared. Between 1944 and 1950 he served as Principal of Ruskin College, Oxford, established in 1899 as a residential college where members of the working classes could study subjects 'essential for working-class leadership'.[25] While at Ruskin, Elvin's knowledge of the educational world was increased by his appointment to such bodies as the National Advisory Council for Education, the Secondary School Examinations Council, and the University Grants Committee. Elvin's early international experience had found a particular focus in the United States and during the war he was employed in the American division of the Ministry of Information. He was

Director of the Department of Education of the United Nations Educational, Scientific and Cultural Organization (Unesco) in Paris from 1950 to 1956, and became a frequent visitor both to developed and developing countries.[26]

In 1956 Elvin joined the Institute as Professor of Education in Tropical Areas.[27] His inaugural lecture, delivered in December 1956, at the time of the Suez invasion, was appropriately called 'Education and the End of Empire'. In it he noted the very short period of time during which the British overseas had pursued 'a general policy for education defensible in terms of principle and of the values expressed in the Universal Declaration of Human Rights'.[28] Two years later, in September 1958, Elvin took up the post of Director and reverted to the title of Mr. An austere man of great principle, he even declined to accept the proffered knighthood that had eluded his predecessor.[29]

Elvin's appointment represented the Committee of Management's preference for a person of wide experience and good contacts. Nevertheless, he had never taught in a school, and unlike Jeffery had not even trained as a teacher. Some members of the Central Institute were concerned, interpreting this appointment as giving precedence to the priorities of the wider Institute, for Elvin had only recently joined the Institute staff and his previous connections with the Institute were tenuous in the extreme. He lacked the school and Institute experience of a great teacher and charismatic (albeit occasionally 'mercurial and infuriating') professor such as Lauwerys, whose academic qualifications and international credentials were considered by many, including Lauwerys himself, to be superior.[30] These concerns were to continue. Rapid changes in national policy required Elvin to devote considerable attention to ATO business.

## Foundation disciplines and research

In this period many University Departments of Education (UDEs) were small in size, with one professor and a handful of other tutors, the majority of whom were engaged in curriculum work. Elvin believed that the Institute was the only UDE in the country 'large enough to provide the specialized knowledge and skills that a multidisciplinary study like education needs if it is to have a proper level of academic and professional responsibility'.[31] Indeed, he advocated restricting the number of UDEs to some five or six of a proper size, located in universities which gave them full support. Elvin deplored the attitude of Oxford and Cambridge towards their UDEs: 'They did not believe in them seriously and have kept them underdeveloped'.[32]

As Professor of Philosophy of Education between 1947 and 1962, Louis Arnaud Reid sought to transform the philosophy of education from a study of the great educators of the past into 'sustained philosophical questioning and reasoning about education aims and values and the activities of teaching'.[33] Paul Hirst, indeed, has argued that Reid 'launched philosophy of education as an academic

47. Louis Arnaud Reid, appointed Professor in 1947, who sought to transform the philosophy of education from a study of the great educators of the past

48. Philip Vernon, appointed Professor in 1949, who argued that IQ was not constant

discipline',[34] by mapping out the terrain and emphasizing the importance of such themes as discipline and freedom. Reid believed that staff and advanced students of the Institute, together with schoolteachers, should have the opportunity of engaging with the ideas of leading philosophers. To this end he established the annual residential Easter School of Philosophy. He was also instrumental in founding the residential Staff Weekend. When in 1962 Reid gave a valedictory lecture, entitled 'Philosophy and the Theory and Practice of Education', 'on the excuse that I never gave an inaugural one', he expressed his 'hopes that philosophy of education is going to develop considerably before very long'.[35] These hopes were soon to be fulfilled. His successor, Richard Peters, recruited from a readership in philosophy at Birkbeck College, established the subject as a key discipline of education, not only in advanced courses but also in those of initial training.

For many years psychology had occupied a central place in the Institute's research and higher degree work, as exemplified in the contributions of Burt and Hamley. Thus in 1949, when Philip Vernon took up his appointment as Professor of Psychology, there were already two readers in the subject, Dr Charlotte Fleming and H.E.O. James. Given Vernon's commitment to research and his frequent absences overseas, Fleming often acted as head of department, in addition to the role of adviser to advanced students which she assumed in 1950. Much of Fleming's work, for example the popular paperback, *Teaching: A psychological analysis*, first published in 1958 and reprinted four times in the next ten years, was specifically aimed at teachers. She retired in 1961. Vernon was also concerned with teachers, but concentrated upon exposing what he considered to be the fatal flaws in the field of mental measurement. In pursuing this goal Vernon was clearly frustrated by attitudes towards research which he encountered at the Institute. Indeed, he once caustically remarked to Elvin that at the Institute research was 'what you did in the August of the years in which you did not take a holiday'.[36] Although appointed to a research professorship in 1964, four years later Vernon resigned to take up a post at the University of Calgary.

Vernon's treatment in the Dixon history is rather critical,[37] but the importance of his research is without question. In the 1940s and 1950s theories of a general and fixed intelligence quotient (IQ) still held sway, and provided the justification for selection for secondary schools by means of the 11+ examination. Vernon, however, argued that IQ was not constant; nor could it be accurately measured. Indeed, he demonstrated that simple instruction in the techniques of taking tests could increase IQ scores by some 14 points. In the autumn term of 1954 Vernon concluded a public lecture at the Institute by arguing that there was little point in wasting further effort on refining such tests. Instead 'it would be better to modify the system which forces them to be used in an artificial, competitive atmosphere. Perhaps then we might have time to develop better diagnostic instruments for use in genuine educational and vocational guidance.'[38] An even more significant contribution occurred in 1957 when Vernon prepared an inquiry into secondary school selection on behalf of the British Psychological Society. The ensuing report, *Secondary School Selection*, not only provided a profound critique of the existing selection system, but also argued that on psychological grounds there was more to be said in favour of comprehensive schools than against. This report, which was hailed as the final blow to the 11+ examination, was followed three years later by *Intelligence and Attainment Tests*, in which Vernon concluded 'that there should probably be less rather than more streaming within secondary, and even less within primary schools'.[39]

Lester Smith's retirement in 1953 provided the opportunity for the Institute to recruit a distinguished sociologist, but once again the post proved difficult to fill. Accordingly, Jean Floud, lecturer in sociology at the LSE, was appointed at senior lecturer level. Promoted to reader in 1958, four years later she resigned to take up a post at Oxford. One of Floud's first tasks was to direct a funded research project into the social characteristics and status of the teaching profession in England. Her principal interest, however, was in the relationship between the educational system and social class. There was growing concern that the percentage of children from working-class homes achieving places in grammar schools was far below that from middle-class homes. Floud's major co-authored work, *Social Class and Educational Opportunity*, published in 1956, showed the extent of this disparity and prompted further research into 'the integration of school and home environment at all social levels in such a way as to minimize the educational disadvantages of both and to turn their educational advantages to full account'.[40] Floud's successor, Basil Bernstein, appointed at senior lecturer level in January

1963, was no less successful in obtaining funding to pursue research. Indeed, the Ministry of Education provided a grant of £31,950 over four years in support of the Sociological Research Unit (SRU). The topic for investigation was 'inter-relationships between language usage in working-class family environment and responsiveness to education in school'. This secured an extension of work begun with an earlier grant of £3,455 from the Council for Scientific and Industrial Research. In January 1963 Denis Lawton was seconded from his school teaching post to SRU for a year to work as a researcher on this project.[41] The contributions of Bernstein and Lawton to the development of the sociology of education and to the wider history of the Institute are treated in subsequent chapters.

49. Joseph Lauwerys, appointed Professor in 1947, Dean of the Faculty and Chairman of the Board of Educational Studies

The fourth 'discipline' of education to be considered in this section, that of comparative education, was at this time intimately bound up with the work of Joseph Lauwerys, the Institute's first Professor of Comparative Education, 1947–70.[42] Lauwerys had innumerable international contacts and during the Second World War played a leading role in the work of the Committee of Allied Ministers of Education in London. He was also one of the founders of Unesco and one of its first two consultants.[43] Lauwerys worked for many years for the Organization for Economic Co-operation and Development (OECD), was Vice-Chairman of the New Education Fellowship and in 1961 was one of the founders, and subsequently first President, of the Comparative Education Society in Europe.

Within the Institute Lauwerys was prominent in advanced studies work as a whole, especially after the retirement of Hamley. In 1950 he was elected first Chairman of the Standing Sub-Committee for Advanced Studies, which oversaw the admissions and courses for all advanced work. He was also elected Dean of the Faculty of Education, and served for some 15 years as Chairman of the Board of Educational Studies. His major commitment, however, was as co-editor of *The World Year Book of Education* from 1948 until his retirement. Indeed, in his submission for the Visitation of the Institute carried out in 1950 by R.G. Allen, W.R. Niblett and Godfrey Thomson, Lauwerys noted the following weekly commitments: six or seven lectures, 12 hours supervision of research students, six hours as chairman of the Board of Studies, 18 hours as editor of the *Year Book*. Lauwerys worked first with Nicholas Hans of King's College. From 1953, the year in which Brian Holmes was appointed assistant editor, an arrangement was made between the Institute and Teachers College, Columbia, which ensured a succession of joint editors. The annual volumes provided 'a world-wide forum in which major governmental educational policies, designed to resolve particular problems, could be analysed by scholars and educational policy-makers'.

They also played a significant role 'in the establishment of comparative education as an academic field'.[44]

A second important dimension of comparative education work at the Institute was the programme of overseas tours organized by Lauwerys. These brought Institute staff and students into immediate contact with educators and educational institutions and practices in other countries. For example, at Easter 1960 comparative education tours took place to Austria, Denmark, France, Germany, the Netherlands and Russia. Some 109 students from the Central Institute, together with 11 from King's and 64 from Bristol, Oxford and Reading, took part.[45] A third dimension was the Comparative Education Library. In 1938 when the Institute moved into Senate House, the growing collection of books, journals and reports was kept in the Overseas Students Common Room under the control of Kathleen Usher Smith, secretary to the Oversea Division, who had received some training as a librarian. Lauwerys took a keen interest in the collection, supplementing it with materials acquired on his extensive travels, and encouraging colleagues to do the same. In 1969, when the Institute Library was moved to a converted office block in Ridgmount Street, the whole of the top floor was devoted to comparative education. The opportunity was taken to include the collection of the former Colonial Department Library. From 1954 the Comparative collection was under the care and control of Thelma Bristow, who also played a full role in the academic and pastoral work of the department.[46]

One final indication of the influence of Lauwerys and of comparative education in this period was the number of Institute staff who completed higher degrees under its aegis. These included the doctorates in 1956 of C. Willis Dixon, then Deputy Secretary, and James Henderson of the History Department, Brian Holmes of Comparative in 1962, and Norman Graves in 1963, the year in which he joined the staff of the Geography Department.

Disciplinary studies were complemented by research and advanced work in other departments and units, both old and new. For example, in 1945 courses in child development were recognized by the Ministry of Education for grant purposes and there was a substantial increase in numbers of students (a peak of 214 in 1947) and hence in numbers of staff.[47] In 1948 a Research and Training Centre was

50. In March 1954 students assemble outside the Institute for a month's comparative education expedition to Yugoslavia under the leadership of Brian Holmes …

51. … where they visit schools, are impressed by the enthusiasm and friendliness of teachers, but also encounter some travelling problems

established in Coram Fields under the joint supervision of the Institute of Education and the University's Institute of Child Health. This centre provided 'for systematic research on the health and psychology of young children and the promotion of advanced courses of training in the field of Child Care'.[48] One major project of 1951, begun in pilot form in 1949, involved a longitudinal study of the physical and mental development of children from birth to adolescence. There was some concern that the centre was absorbing too much of the Institute's research energy and resources and in 1959 a major review of its activities was conducted by Dr W.D. (Bill) Wall of the NFER.

Reading research began in 1953, when the Institute received a tax-free gift of £300 a year for seven years from the Simplified Spelling Society to promote research into the influence of spelling in learning to read. Sir James Pitman, Deputy Chairman of the Institute's Committee of Management and Chairman of its Finance Sub-Committee, had a personal interest in this area, and the work rapidly developed. Further grants were received: £16,750 from Sir Isaac Pitman and Sons Ltd; £4,000 from the Howard Samuel Settlement; £14,000 from the Nuffield Foundation.[49] Dr John Downing was appointed to head this burgeoning enterprise, which produced materials in the new Initial Teaching Alphabet (i.t.a.) and investigated their usage and outcomes. Further grants of $31,000 from the USA and £4,326 from the Ministry of Education were made in 1962–3.[50]

In 1960 a Ford Foundation grant of $65,000 over five years led to the establishment of an Economics and Administration of Education Research Unit. This was headed by John Vaizey, author of *The Costs of Education*, published in 1958. In this work Vaizey demonstrated the considerable variation in educational expenditure per child across different parts of the United Kingdom and in different types of educational establishment. For example, he noted that 'a grammar school child receives 70 per cent more per year in expenditure than a child in a secondary modern school and nearly double per school life'.[51] Vaizey was an original and pioneering thinker. Disappointed, however, by his failure to convince Elvin that he merited at least the status of a reader, Vaizey returned to Oxford in 1962. He subsequently became a professor at Brunel University and was raised to the peerage. Dixon recorded that 'the Director, in one of the wittiest speeches ever made in the SCR, took the opportunity on his farewell to introduce him to most of his colleagues'.[52] Vaizey's successor was Dr Mark Blaug, appointed reader in 1965. Further research grants were secured, and the unit also became a teaching department.

Research and publications in the four disciplines of philosophy, psychology, sociology and comparative, and in other areas, set the Institute apart. In this period the intellectual leadership of the subject of education was secured at national level. Outside funding was essential in providing the opportunities for sustained research. As the *Annual Report* for 1962–3 concluded, 'altogether this has been a good year for the furtherance of research. The Institute's activities now seem set for expansion, so long delayed by the paucity of our own resources.'[53]

## Overseas

Comparative education provided one dimension of the Institute's relationship with the wider world. A second was the longer tradition that had existed in the shape of the Colonial Department, and which now needed to be urgently rethought. Two immediate contexts were apparent. The first was the end of empire, symbolized most graphically in 1947 in the independence of India, an event which led to the political division of the subcontinent.[54] The second was the particular responsibility exercised by the University of London for overseas work. For example, Bruce Pattison was a pioneer of the so-called 'Special Relations' programme whereby higher education institutions in other countries prepared students for the external degrees and other qualifications of the University of London. Pattison's support for this programme extended to his spending much time in Africa and in the West Indies.[55] Pattison's principal concern within the Institute was with EFL. The first examination for the Diploma in the Teaching of English as a Foreign Language was held in June 1950. Teaching practice was originally undertaken in Caernarvonshire in North Wales, where Welsh was still the first language. By 1970, however, students were sent to practise in Malta.

Jeffery was also committed to this even wider sense of Institute responsibility. In January and February 1950, at the invitation of the Secretary of State for the Colonies, he visited West Africa to advise on the establishment of a West African Schools Examination Council. In the following year Jeffery chaired a group appointed by the Secretary of State for the Colonies to undertake a general survey of education in West Africa. Jeffery, Lauwerys, and Pattison were all involved with the establishment of a diploma of education for students of the new Institute of Education of the University College of the Gold Coast to serve the four British territories in West Africa.[56]

The third professor with particular responsibility for overseas work in 1949 was Margaret Read, appointed Professor of Education with special reference to Colonial Areas in that year. She was supported by two senior lecturers in T R Batten and A S Harrison, five other lecturing staff and a host of visiting and seconded appointments. Elvin succeeded Read in 1956 and in 1958 was in turn succeeded by Lewis. A former member of the Institute staff, Lewis had served as Professor of Education and Director of the Institute of Education of the University College of Ghana. Just as Elvin had welcomed the change in professorial and departmental title from 'Colonial' to 'Tropical Areas'[57] so Lewis in his inaugural lecture, entitled 'Partnership in Oversea Education' looked forward to a further transmutation into 'Education in Developing Countries'.[58] Lewis, who bore the reputation of a 'hard-headed (and hard-drinking) educational planner' was a teacher and organizer rather than a scholar. His influence was considerable. A former Institute student and colleague, Hugh Hawes, commented that:

**52. The Nigerian group of 1947–8. Margaret Read is in the centre of the front row with John Lewis next to her, fifth from the left. T.R. Batten is second from the left in the back row**

As colonies achieved independence the emphasis of the department gradually changed, though the majority of its students, throughout the 15 years that he headed it, from 1958 to 1973, remained from African nations. Many of those who left the department rose to the highest levels of leadership in their own countries. Several became Vice-Chancellors, Permanent Secretaries and Ministers of Education, and one even became a prime minister.[59]

Further connections were established through the African-Anglo-American programme, which was funded by the Carnegie Trust. An exchange agreement led to lecturers from the department being seconded on an annual basis to Teachers College, Columbia, where they taught on a variety of programmes including orientation courses for the Peace Corps.

Some 314 overseas students were registered for the session 1949–50; more than half were taking advanced or special courses. Senior figures included four Carnegie Fellows and eight Imperial Relations Trust Fellows from the Dominions. Two other notable features were the range of countries from which students came, some 57 in 1950–1, and the continuing popularity of the Associateship course, which was taken by more than 40 students in that year. Concerns were expressed that the ending of empire would mean a decline in student numbers, but this did not occur. The period witnessed a modest rise overall which contained a significant change in the balance between men and women. For example, the overseas students of 1950–1 comprised 223 men and 98 women. In contrast, in 1959–60 there were 212 men to 194 women.[60] The *Annual Report* for 1957–8 welcomed this trend which it saw as representing a response to 'the great need for more and better education for girls in the countries concerned'.[61]

## Students and courses

Numbers of students rose steadily in this period, both in the wider and Central Institutes.[62] In 1949–50 a grand total of 6,877 students was recorded for the wider Institute of whom 6,477 were full-time, with 6,163 following initial courses of training primarily designed for teaching within the United Kingdom. Some three-quarters of these, 4,615, were women. Six colleges trained men; 22 women. Only the Institute, King's and Goldsmiths' provided initial training for both men and women.[63] Colleges joining the ATO after 1949 – Brighton College of Art and Crafts, Garnett College, Hornsey College of Art and Crafts and Trent Park Training College – would also be mixed. By 1962–3 there were 12,290 full-time students, including 11,747 who were following initial courses of training. The Ministry of Education was urging yet further expansion, to be achieved principally by a more intensive use of existing premises.[64] Suggestions included a four-term year, extended day, and 'Box and Cox' schemes whereby one third of the students would always be on teaching practice. The situation was further complicated by Ministry directives about the balance of training, away from secondary schools towards a new 'bulge' in infant schools. One significant result of this expansion was an increase in size of the colleges. In 1949–50 only three of the 28 colleges of the ATO – Avery Hill, Froebel and Furzedown – had more than 300 students registered for courses of initial training. By 1962–3, the number had risen to 15 colleges out of 34.[65]

In 1949–50 full-time students at the Central Institute numbered 331 men and 328 women, with a further 163 men and 210 women part-time and occasional – a total of 1,032.[66] Figures for 1962–3 were 478 men and 457 women full-time and 250 men and 104 women part-time, a total of 1,289.[67] Two comments may be made upon these figures, when compared with those of the ATO overall. One reason for the greater equality between sexes was that the largest group of Institute students, in contrast to those in the colleges, was preparing to teach in secondary schools. Secondly, while in the ATO there was a constant increase in numbers, year on year, at the Central Institute there were fluctuations, with peak years of 1,451 students in 1958–9 and 1,489 in 1960–1. These fluctuations stemmed from the greater variety of Institute courses, the physical limitations of the building and site, and the need to dedicate some premises and facilities to ATO purposes.

Three major changes may be noted in the initial course of training. In 1950–1 the Ministry announced the ending of the four-year grant system whereby students had to secure acceptance by a UDE prior to embarking on three years of undergraduate study followed by one year of teacher training. In future students would be recruited during the third year of their degree for a one-year postgraduate course.[68] The second was a change of name. Given the rapid growth of advanced diplomas, both general and specific, a new title was sought for the initial qualification. From the start of the session 1950–1 the teacher's diploma was replaced by the postgraduate certificate in education (PGCE).[69] The third change concerned arrangements for school practice. It was a cardinal Institute doctrine that theory and practice must be closely connected. Institute tradition decreed that the best way of achieving this was for students to go into schools on Tuesdays and Thursdays of the first two terms followed by a continuous period of three weeks in the third term. Students and teaching practice schools regularly questioned these arrangements. For example, in 1950 Institute students informed the Visitors that two consecutive days per week in the first term and continuous periods of practice in the second and third terms would be preferable. The Visitors were sufficiently impressed by these arguments to report that 'the staff of the Institute should take into very careful consideration the representations made by the students and the success of continuous periods of practice in other universities'.[70] Four day per week block practices were duly introduced.

Student culture on initial (and other) courses of training in this period was, as always, 'a mixture of camaraderie and irreverence, with strongly held opinions on everything, not least on the teaching staff'.[71] As a teacher's diploma course student in 1949–50, Norman Graves appreciated the 'humanity about the place', and 'an emphasis on educating the whole person'. Relationships between students and staff were 'warm', especially with curriculum tutors. Lectures were the customary method of teaching, 'even in the curriculum departments, there was but one seminar per week'.[72] David Bridges, a PGCE student in 1963–4, discovered 'a feast of intellectual excitement which certainly exceeded my previous experience as a history undergraduate at Oxford'. At the Institute, perhaps as nowhere else at this time, the minds of postgraduate students were being extended by contact with leading thinkers in education. For Bridges the key contributors to this intellectual feast were Bernstein, Hirst, Lauwerys and Peters, together with his curriculum tutor, James Henderson. Nevertheless:

all of these were undoubtedly overshadowed by a wonderful lady ... who combined a lecture on health education with a demonstration of the use of visual aids. This included an explanation of the process of human excretion conducted with the aid of a nylon stocking and an orange (and to the accompaniment of the massed grunting of the Beveridge Hall audience) – a height of hilarity only exceeded when, in a subsequent demonstration of the use of the felt board to teach the human reproductive system, a felt representation of the male member was observed slowly to curl over and drop off the board.[73]

One of the most significant features of this period was the increased popularity of the academic diploma. In 1949–50 the diploma had 13 full-time and 14 part-time students. By 1962–3 these numbers stood at 41 and 182. The course comprised one year of full-time or two years of part-time study and was open to non-graduates as well as graduates. Prior to the introduction of the B.Ed., the diploma served both as a substitute for a first degree in Education and as a qualification for proceeding to a higher degree. The diploma was particularly attractive to non-graduate staff, not only within schools but also among the constituent colleges of the ATO. A further rung in the ladder of qualification was provided in 1963 when the Senate approved regulations whereby candidates for the MA degree would sit examination papers and write a dissertation. A new research degree, the M.Phil., was introduced to replace the former MA by thesis.[74]

An example of the range of courses and possibility of progression available in this period is provided by the career of Norman Graves. In 1946 Graves applied to the Institute under the four-year scheme. Following a B.Sc. (Econ.) at LSE he was a full-time Institute student for the teacher's diploma in the Geography

53. Norman Graves in 1962, student 1949–63 and member of staff 1963–90

Department in 1949–50. Subsequent study was part-time: for the academic diploma, 1952–4; for the MA by thesis, 1954–7; and for the Ph.D. 1958–63. The last two years were as an external student, following his appointment as lecturer in the University of Liverpool Department of Education. In 1963 Graves joined the staff of the Institute as senior lecturer in Geography. He retired in 1990, having become Professor and Pro-Director for Initial Training.

Advanced studies in the ATO comprised courses for the academic diploma, MA and Ph.D. The Department of Advanced Studies included work conducted under the auspices of the Institute and King's. Goldsmiths' and the colleges were excluded. In 1949–50 42 full-time and 166 part-time students were registered at the Institute and one full-timer and 34 part-timers at King's.[75] During this period the Institute's share of advanced work markedly increased. Institute student figures for 1962–3 were 102 full-time and 318 part-time. King's, however, had no full-time students and only 16 part-time.[76] The *Annual Report* of 1959–60, indeed, declared that 'Advanced courses and studies were seen as the main future work of the Institute'.[77] In sharp contrast, the Education Department of King's College, in common with most UDEs, remained small and essentially committed to initial training. Between 1949–50 and 1962–3 initial course numbers at King's rose from 74 to 134.

The creation of the wider Institute was reflected in student organization, and the *Londinian*, which had previously been the magazine of the Institute Union Society, became the student organ for the wider Institute.[78] In 1952–3 Jeffery was elected honorary president of ULIESA, and money was made available to the Union from funds placed at the disposal of the Institute by the Senate. ULIESA provided a programme of conferences, debates, social events and sporting activities, and from 1954–5 names of the student officers were included in the *Annual Reports*. Between 1954–5 and 1959–60 all the presidents of ULIESA were men, and all but one came from Borough Road College. In 1957–8 ULIESA achieved one of its long cherished aims with the provision of accommodation and clerical assistance in the Central Institute.[79] In 1960–1 R. Hayden, President of the Institute's Students' Union in the previous year, became ULIESA President.

The most significant student controversy occurred in 1958. In that year ULIESA undertook a survey of regulations and staff–student relationships in the constituent colleges, published as *U.L.I.E.S.A. Report on TRAINING COLLEGE CONDITIONS*. Some 31 colleges were circularized and responses received from 22 (17 women's, four men's and one mixed). The report highlighted practices in some women's colleges, where students could be fined for such misdemeanours as 'lateness for meals, running along the corridors, and leaving water running in an unattended bath', and were required to 'wash up after at least one meal per day'. They also noted a widely expressed point of view that 'The Principal is very just and reasonable until it comes to the question of dancing and young men'. These findings were juxtaposed with quotations from a House of Commons debate on 14 February 1958. For example, Fred Mulley, for Labour, had argued that 'It is absurd to try to run teacher training colleges on kindergarten lines … training college students should have the facilities and treatment of university students'. Sir Edward Boyle, Conservative Parliamentary Secretary to the Ministry of Education, agreed 'that Training Colleges must be up to date in the way they plan both curriculum and discipline. They must not in any way remain or become glorified boarding schools.'

The report received wide publicity and led to angry reactions from some college principals. Nevertheless, it could not be ignored. In subsequent discussions with representatives of the Committee of Principals, ULIESA argued that the three-year course provided an opportunity for the introduction of university practices. Individual freedom and responsibility should replace the old tradition of *in loco parentis*. Compulsory attendance at lectures, prohibitions on entertainment of members of the opposite sex, late-night and weekend passes, were but some of the restrictions challenged by ULIESA as being inappropriate to student life in the

1960s.[80] A further survey of student conditions and problems experienced in the colleges was produced in 1962–3.

By contrast, the affairs of the Central Institute's Students' Union often seemed less contentious, with a focus on social and sporting activities. In 1960–1, for example, some 50 clubs were active under Union auspices. The President was George Foot, educated at Winchester and Trinity College, Cambridge and a former officer in the Royal Hampshire Regiment. Foot's aims were to promote more friendly relationships between staff and students and to raise the prestige of the Institute, particularly within the University of London. The staff were prevailed upon to appear in full academic dress for the Foundation oration, although the dignity of the occasion was marred by a student chorus of 'The animals came in two by two' as the academics filed into the Beveridge Hall. A motion requiring both staff and students to wear gowns at lectures and on other formal occasions was only narrowly defeated in a general meeting.[81] The following year marked a significant change. Miss J. Walford of Maria Assumpta was President of ULIESA, and a new magazine, *Compass*, first appeared in the spring term. Margaret Maden was President of the Institute's Students' Union, with Miss Y. Ayanbule as Oversea Vice-President, Miss C. Folland as Secretary and Miss J. Hopkins as Treasurer. Contemporaries remarked that 'This all-female leadership was as radical as its predecessors had been traditional'.[82] Although some sporting clubs were short of recruits, 'a Judo club with the slogan "How to avoid a fate worse than

death?" got off to a vigorous start with a large female membership'. The *Annual Report* concluded that: 'The female management of the Union was a definite success'.[83] In 1963, discussion in the Union magazine, *Slate*, exemplified the emergence of a new and more fundamental student agenda. Fred Stephenson argued that students should have 'a real say in the planning of the Institute as a whole'.[84]

In this period training college students within the ATO were typically full-time, straight from school, British and engaged in two- and, from 1960, three-year courses of initial training. The Central Institute's student body was more varied. For example, in 1949–50 the 110 students in the Institute's three hostels came from more than 30 countries, and had 'an average age of thirty rather than twenty'.[85] One expression of this international dimension was *International Education Notes*. This journal was edited by a student and published twice yearly by the

**54.** The front cover of the *Slate* for 18 January 1963 reflects the emergence of a new student culture

Students' Union, with an editorial board chaired by Lauwerys and contributions from staff and students of the Institute and elsewhere. Paul Huygelen from Belgium was the first editor; the first number appeared in June 1949. The publication arose from a memorandum submitted by students to Jeffery in July 1948 which 'set forth a number of recommendations on how international understanding might be furthered among the extraordinary number of national groups represented in the student body of the Institute'.[86] One purpose of *International Education Notes* was to assist in 'the formation of desirable attitudes, which are more fundamental than mere administrative re-organisation or the accumulation of mere knowledge'.[87] Such attitudes were clearly needed, for some overseas students suffered from racial prejudice both inside the Institute and out. For example, Eileen Lake, a diploma student of 1949–50, found it 'impossible ever to forget the bewildering, stinging shrieks of "Whore! Prostitute!" from women of Coram Street when I walked there one tea-time with black fellow students'.[88]

## Buildings

> Accommodation problems dominated every discussion which we had during the Visitation. The present premises were planned to accommodate 350 full-time students and 20 academic staff, in 1948–9 there were 704 full-time students, 344 part-time students, and an academic staff of 68. ...
>
> Most serious of all, perhaps, is the fact that the Institute is unable to offer the central facilities which it should be able to offer to the Constituent Colleges.[89]

So wrote the three Visitors, Allen, Niblett and Thomson, who inspected the Institute in 1950. Their assessment of the situation was just. The work of the Institute had more than doubled in ten years. The creation of the wider Institute had further increased the pressure upon space. Administrative staff numbers had burgeoned to cope with the plethora of meetings, visitations, examinations and other activities of the ATO. A Teachers' Centre was established in 1950, with C. Willis Dixon as Adviser to Teachers, 'available by letter or interview to any teacher in the area who wanted advice on further study', and responsible for organizing 'refresher courses for practising teachers'.[90] In 1953–4 Dixon was appointed Deputy Secretary to Wacey, and David Johnston, senior lecturer in English at Borough Road College, replaced him as Adviser to Teachers. The centre moved into a fourth hut in the quadrangle in the following year.

Accommodation for teaching departments was obtained outside the main building. Two adjoining properties in Woburn Square were converted for use by the Language Division. Further relief was provided by the acquisition of houses in Gordon Square. By 1961 the original site had expanded into numbers 56–58, a separate teaching block, now scheduled for Child Development and research units.[91] In 1957–8 a University grant of £15,224 was received for the conversion of 35 Tavistock Square to house the Music Department.[92] Such acquisitions provided only a temporary respite. The search for yet more teaching space led to a loss of facilities and activities within the main building. The gymnasium was converted into a lecture hall; seminar groups met in the showers.

In spite of transferring some volumes to departments, for example in 1953–4 the entire linguistics collection was moved to the houses in Woburn Square, for most of the 1950s the main Library was in an increasingly 'congested state'. Some collections were housed on landings, and the need for a separate periodicals room was keenly felt.[93] In December 1956 de Montmorency, the Institute's Librarian for 31 years, resigned upon her marriage, to be succeeded in September 1957 by Douglas Foskett. In 1958 the Library moved into a new home. This was a large hut, which had become vacant as a result of the transfer of the University of London Students' Union to substantial new premises in Malet Street. The hut was rather different from the Senate House premises, and far removed from the faded grandeur of Institute houses in neighbouring squares. Built in 1918, originally to house Belgian refugees from the First World War, it nevertheless provided some four to five times as much space as the existing premises.[94] The University supplied a non-recurrent grant of £10,266 to convert the hut for library use, and several immediate benefits were evident. Loans increased by 40 per cent, and the stock of 78,000 books and pamphlets and 660 periodicals was soon augmented by further gifts from institutions and individuals of books and other materials of contemporary and historical interest.[95] Foskett also secured a large collection of educational textbooks, some 12,000 in all. In future a free copy of all newly-published textbooks would be sent to the Institute Library.[96] This rate of acquisition meant that the hut would be outgrown within two or three years.

55. Douglas Foskett, appointed Librarian in 1957

Residential student accommodation remained in short supply. Two houses were acquired in Woburn Square; seven rooms were added to the hostel at 12–15 Bedford Way. A new hostel for 43 women students was provided at 35–37 Bedford Way by the repair and adaptation of Meier's Hotel with the aid of a University grant of some £8,000. Nevertheless, of the 1,032 full-time students of 1959–60, 286 lived at home, 556 were in lodgings and only 190 were accommodated in hostels.[97] The most significant development, by far, was the University's offer in 1960–1 of 19–23 Endsleigh Street as a dedicated hall of residence with accommodation for a resident warden. The offer was accepted and the building was fittingly named John Adams Hall.

The problems of accommodation noted by the Visitors of 1950 led them to two major recommendations. The first was that there should be no increase in student numbers on the existing site. The second, that since substantial expansion of the Senate House itself was impossible, a search should be made for a new site in a central location upon which a separate Institute of Education building could be constructed. In spite of internal conversions and dispersal into houses and huts, a visitation by members of the University Grants Committee on 3 May 1960 came to the same conclusion. By that date the Institute had acquired an increase of 30 per cent in its accommodation over 1938–9, but a 300-per-cent increase in students. Staff, students and a variety of ATO functions were pent up in accommodation of 80,000 square feet. In September 1960 first plans were prepared for a new building in Bedford Way, but the existing situation would continue for several years. Many interests were involved. The Court of the University retained responsibility for overall financial control and negotiations with the UGC. Detailed planning, however, lay with the Institute and in December 1960 the Committee of Management appointed an executive committee to oversee major decisions. The architect was to be Denys Lasdun.[98] The potential for conflict was soon revealed when the University Court pruned the Institute's estimate of a minimum space of 280,000 square feet to 237,055 square feet. This revised schedule was submitted to the UGC in July 1962. In June 1963 the Institute was informed that approval had been given for Schedule I of the work.[99]

## Conclusion

During this period the Institute became more of a multi-purpose institution – characterized by research, advanced studies and overseas work, as well as by initial training. It became unique among UDEs, and also acquired further power and prestige as the central activity of what was by far the largest ATO in the country. Nevertheless, two problems were also apparent. The more immediate and visible of these was a desperate shortage of accommodation. The second concerned the very nature and identity of the Central Institute.

At the start of this period the Institute was known for its unity and sense of purpose – the training and development of good teachers. Its culture was one of care and concern, qualities reinforced by a widespread post-war belief in the power of education to create a better world. The Visitors of 1950 indicated their support for this professional role. They declared that 'a great many of the staff are clearly in close and constant contact with the schools; and we feel certain that every member, from the Professoriate downwards, should be encouraged to maintain this contact and so keep in touch with the problems of teachers in the schools'.[100] Such sentiments would have been shared by those students on PGCE and academic diploma courses who by the 1960s were expressing concerns not only about the content of some of the lectures but also about the quality of much of the teaching. The *Annual Report* for 1962–3 acknowledged that 'There has been dissatisfaction for some time with the teaching arrangements for initial training courses'.[101]

By 1963 the Institute culture had become more academic and intellectual. It was also becoming more departmental. Education was being divided into separate disciplines. Some professors and other staff were appointed not because of their prowess as teachers or standing in the world of education, but for their research skills and reputations in such fields as philosophy, psychology or sociology. These newcomers might look askance at the lack of interest in research, publications and academic qualifications of some Institute staff. Many questions were raised in this process. Was equal status to be given to the Institute's various spheres of activity or should it concentrate upon research and advanced studies? Should the Institute's original identity as an institution for the professional training of intending teachers be abandoned? Was the initial training of teachers to become a low-level and preliminary activity?

Issues such as these were regularly discussed, not only in committees and in the Senior Common Room, but also at the Staff Weekend. The most significant event, however, which provided the opportunity for a new unity and sense of identity, occurred in 1963. Shortly after his appointment in October 1962 Richard Peters informed Elvin that he wished to read a paper at the Staff Weekend '"On some educationally indefensible practices that I have found on joining the Institute of Education". And he did.'[102]

# Chapter 8

# Expansion and stalemate
## 1963–1973

### Introduction

The 'swinging sixties' ushered in a period of considerable social and intellectual ferment. The Beatles and Carnaby Street symbolized the changing worlds of popular music and fashion. Sexual relationships were transformed by the introduction of the contraceptive pill. After 13 years of Conservative governments, Harold Wilson, a former economics don at Oxford and the youngest Cabinet minister since Pitt, was Prime Minister of a Labour administration, 1964–70. Wilson's commitment to modernization and scientific progress was exemplified by the appointment of C.P. Snow, physicist, author and the progenitor of the 'Two Cultures' debate, to a life peerage and to a post at the Ministry of Technology. Students were to the fore in a plethora of protests and demonstrations – for example against American intervention in Vietnam and British policy in Northern Ireland and in favour of nuclear disarmament and a range of feminist causes such as abortion on demand. These protests were part of an international movement. In May 1968 there were violent clashes between students and police in Paris; in May 1970 four students were shot dead during demonstrations at Kent State University in the USA.

Education was a key element in this momentous decade, with major change occurring at all levels. In 1964 the Ministry of Education was transmuted into the Department of Education and Science. Reforms in primary schooling were prompted by the Plowden Report of 1967. Following Circular 10/65 secondary schools were reorganized along comprehensive lines, while in 1972 the school-leaving age was raised to 16. Lionel Elvin was a member of the Robbins Committee whose Report, published in 1963, led to a doubling of higher education numbers over the next ten years, the redesignation of training colleges as colleges of education and the introduction of a Bachelor of Education (B.Ed.) degree.[1] The Robbins Report also proposed that 'The colleges in each university's Institute of Education and the University Department of Education should be formed into a School of Education'. This was advocated as 'the best hope of raising the status and standards of the colleges and securing their full integration into the system of higher education of the future'.[2]

Elvin was convinced that the colleges should be brought fully into the university sector. He was a staunch defender of academic integrity and freedom and deplored the bureaucratic, 'nine to five', mentality of many local authority politicians and administrators. Following the report of the Weaver Committee in 1966, colleges of education were required to establish academic boards, to be responsible for the academic policy and work of the college and for electing staff members, other than the principal, to serve on the governing body. The *Annual Report* of the Institute for 1968–9 'warmly welcomed these moves to secure liberality and independence in the government and administration of colleges'.[3]

University schools of education, however, were not created. As Niblett acknowledged, two genuine concerns existed at central and local authority level. These were a loss of control over teacher supply and 'an undue "academization" of the content of initial teacher training'.[4] Additionally, as in the 1940s over McNair, some universities already fully involved with plans for expansion as an outcome of Robbins were anxious about further problems, including dilution of academic standards, which the integration of the colleges would involve. Although London University was the largest in the country, with 33,635 full-time and 5,994 part-time students in 1970–1, the admission to full membership of some 20,000 or even 30,000 college of education students in a single school of education would swamp the whole institution.[5]

Closer ties between the colleges and the universities were also thrown into doubt by the Labour government's binary policy for higher education. This was announced by Tony Crosland in 1965 in a speech at Woolwich. In the following year some 30 polytechnics were designated. These came under local authority control, their degrees being validated by the Council for National Academic Awards (CNAA). According to Niblett, the main justification for the introduction of the binary system was 'the continuing lack on the part of universities to conceive imaginatively enough what their possible function in an era of rapidly expanding student numbers should be'.[6] During the 1960s the LEAs emerged as serious rivals for the control of teacher training. By 1968 they owned 113 colleges of education as opposed to 53 in the voluntary sector. Five of the new polytechnics, moreover, established departments of education.[7] Though few in number and small in size, these departments provided a new model of integration at a time when it was widely argued that teachers should no longer be trained in the geographical and intellectual isolation of monotechnic institutions.

Further problems were to arise. The James Report of 1972 and the White Paper of the same year, optimistically entitled *Education: A Framework for Expansion*, not only sounded the death knell for the proposed schools of education but also presaged the end both of the ATO system and of monotechnic institutions for teacher education. In consequence the Institute's identity and role would be transformed from being at the centre of the largest organization for teacher education in the land to a position of potential isolation. Expansion in teacher education was swiftly followed by contraction. Balance of payments problems led to successive economic crises, culminating in that triggered by the oil price rise of 1973. A sharp fall in the birth rate led to a steep decline in the numbers of new teachers required. In 1963 the main problem for the colleges was how best to expand; by 1973, diversification, contraction or closure was the order of the day.

## The wider Institute

The later 1950s heralded a new bulge in the birth rate. Expansion of student numbers, therefore, proceeded apace. In 1963–4, at the start of the period under consideration in this chapter, there were 13,202 full-time students in the wider Institute following courses of initial training. Five years later there were 20,933 full-time students, together with a further 566 following part-time courses.[8] Few extra resources were made available for capital expenditure, and colleges were 'urged to apply industrial organization' to their use of buildings.[9] Ever more pressure was placed upon teaching practice places.

Government emphases were initially upon training for infant and junior work, but the progression of the bulge through the system, coupled with plans to raise the school-leaving age to 16 in 1972, also dictated a need for more teachers in secondary schools. There was a general concern to recruit more men into teaching and in 1966–7 the Froebel Institute, Furzedown, Gipsy Hill, Philippa Fawcett and Nonington College of Physical Education admitted their first intakes of male students. Another development was the establishment of day colleges and annexes for mature students. These were particularly welcomed by those LEAs in which they were situated, for it was hoped that mature students already resident in the area would proceed to posts in the authority's schools.[10]

Two developments in the summer of 1967 showed the effect of new universities and polytechnics. Four colleges – Brighton, Eastbourne, Seaford and Chelsea College of Physical Education – departed to the new University of Sussex. The departments of education at Barking Regional College of Technology and at the North-Western Polytechnic, both of which opened in September of that year, were admitted to the ATO. In the following year, the Centre for Science Education at Chelsea College of Science and Technology also became an Institute member. Although student numbers were small – Barking began with 108 students, North-Western with 123, and Chelsea a mere 28 – these institutions were more likely to challenge the nature of the wider Institute and its relationship to the Central College. A subtle change occurred in the presentation of the *Annual Reports*. Whereas in previous years institutions had been grouped into three categories: 'Central Institute', 'Constituent Departments' (King's and Goldsmiths') and

**Appendix C**

## Analysis of Students of the Institute following Initial Courses of Training for Teaching, 1968–69

| | Men | Women | Total |
|---|---|---|---|
| Constituent Departments: | | | |
| Central Institute .. .. .. .. | 197 | 329 | 526 |
| King's College .. .. .. .. | 35 | 86 | 121 |
| Chelsea Centre for Science Education .. | 16 | 12 | 28 |
| Goldsmiths' College .. .. .. | 702 | 1,203 | 1,905 |
| | | | |
| Constituent Colleges: | | | |
| Acton College .. .. .. .. | 50 | 200 | 250 |
| College of All Saints .. .. .. | 50 | 626 | 676 |
| Avery Hill College .. .. .. .. | 429 | 826 | 1,255 |
| Barking Regional College of Technology .. | 42 | 178 | 220 |
| Battersea College .. .. .. .. | 100 | 508 | 608 |
| Borough Road College .. .. .. | 461 | 369 | 830 |
| Cavendish Square College .. .. .. | — | 127 | 127 |
| Christ Church College .. .. .. | 204 | 492 | 696 |
| Coloma College .. .. .. .. | — | 776 | 776 |
| Dartford College .. .. .. .. | 6 | 356 | 362 |
| Digby Stuart College .. .. .. | — | 784 | 784 |
| Froebel Institute .. .. .. .. | 46 | 566 | 612 |
| Furzedown College .. .. .. | 128 | 637 | 765 |
| Garnett College .. .. .. .. | 325 | 112 | 437 |
| Gipsy Hill College .. .. .. | 71 | 660 | 731 |
| Hornsey College of Art .. .. .. | 25 | 24 | 49 |
| Maria Assumpta College .. .. .. | — | 412 | 412 |
| Maria Grey College.. .. .. .. | 66 | 648 | 714 |
| Nonington College of Physical Education .. | 76 | 191 | 267 |
| North-Western Polytechnic .. .. | 77 | 164 | 241 |
| Philippa Fawcett College .. .. .. | 96 | 476 | 572 |
| Rachel McMillan College .. .. .. | — | 452 | 452 |
| St Gabriel's College .. .. .. | — | 380 | 380 |
| College of S Mark and S John .. .. | 568 | 90 | 658 |
| St Mary's College .. .. .. .. | 740 | 481 | 1,221 |
| Shoreditch College.. .. .. .. | 665 | | 665 |
| Sidney Webb College .. .. .. | 112 | 383 | 495 |
| Sittingbourne College .. .. .. | 49 | 204 | 253 |
| Southlands College .. .. .. | 161 | 674 | 835 |
| Stockwell College .. .. .. .. | 205 | 682 | 887 |
| Trent Park College .. .. .. .. | 325 | 577 | 902 |
| Whitelands College .. .. .. .. | 84 | 703 | 787 |
| **Total** | **6,311** | **15,188** | **21,499** |

56. The *Annual Report* for 1968–9 lists the colleges and numbers of students in initial training within the wider Institute

'Constituent Colleges', that for 1968–9 listed the Central College, King's, Chelsea, and Goldsmiths', in that order, as constituent departments. Barking and North-Western continued to be placed alphabetically among the constituent colleges.[11]

Although university schools of education did not materialize, other elements of the Robbins proposals were implemented. In June 1966 an Order in Council permitted the amendment of the statutes of the University of London to provide for the establishment of a Faculty of Education and the award of the degrees of Bachelor and Master of Education.[12] Committees and working parties proliferated at Institute and college levels, and the academic year 1966–7 was characterized by feverish activity. In December 1966 Elvin, the full Committee of Professors (including Beales and Hirst from King's) and Dixon, repaired to the Berystede Hotel, Ascot, where every aspect of the new faculty was discussed.[13] A Joint Planning Committee of 12 members, drawn equally from the Academic Council and the Institute Academic Board, was constituted as an interim body to oversee policy and planning for the B.Ed. degree. Subject working parties drew up syllabuses and examinations. Eminent professors from the several colleges of the University gave of their time and expertise. The proposals of the Joint Planning Committee were duly ratified in July 1967. Lauwerys was subsequently elected the first Dean of the Faculty of Education, and Chairman of the Standing Committee of the Board of Educational Studies which began work in January 1969.

The London B.Ed., a four-year honours degree, was intended to be both of equivalent standing to other well-established first degrees and a professional qualification. Part I was the three-year teacher's certificate, which candidates had to pass at an appropriate level to be admitted to a further year for Part II. Although 1968 would be the first formal year of examination for Part I and 1969 for Part II, retrospective qualification was permitted from 1963 onwards and the teacher's certificate examination of 1967 was used as a trial run for the Part I selection procedure. Results in this examination, however, were not encouraging. Of 3,548 candidates in 1967, while 1,237 (35.8 per cent) reached the qualifying standards in their main (academic) subjects, only 254 (7.3 per cent) did so in Education. Since candidates had to pass in both areas, only 164 students (4.7 per cent) were qualified to proceed to Part II. These figures were the occasion of considerable controversy and some gloom, but they were not unusual. Eligibility lists of students who completed three-year courses in the constituent colleges of the Institute in the years between 1963 and 1967 showed that only about 5 per cent reached the qualifying standard.[14] In the light of these figures examiners, particularly those in Education, were advised to 'award more marks in the upper ranges'.[15] Such advice, coupled no doubt with other factors, had the required effect. Of the 4,278 candidates who completed the three-year course in 1968, 443 (10.4 per cent) were deemed to have qualified for Part II of the degree.[16]

The B.Ed. sparked a variety of developments. Some college staff, now engaged in undergraduate teaching for the first time, themselves registered for higher degrees. Goldsmiths' College, which had previously conferred its own teacher's certificate, placed this award under the aegis of the Institute in order that its students might be qualified to proceed to Part II of the degree. Greater collaboration occurred between subject specialists in the colleges of the Institute and those of the University, both in the framing of syllabuses and in the conduct of examinations. Intercollegiate teaching was organized for Part II of the degree. Further collaboration resulted from the decision of the University of Cambridge not to establish a first degree in Education. Agreement was reached for a period of two years whereby students from the 11 colleges of the Cambridge Institute wishing to proceed to a degree could take the London examinations for Part I and Part II. A total of 400 students, including 54 from the Cambridge Institute, registered for Part II of the degree in 1968–9.[17]

In February 1970 the Institute was faced with a further challenge. Edward Short, Secretary of State for Education and Science, wrote to the heads of ATOs, including Lord Fulton, Chairman of the Council of the Institute, inviting them to 'initiate a major review of the content and structure of your present courses'.[18] The agenda was clear. Short's letter declared that there was 'often little opportunity for a two-way flow of ideas between the profession and those responsible for teacher education in relation to the content of the courses provided and not surprisingly an inadequate consensus of opinion on the objectives of teacher education and the means by which they should be attained'. His list of 'some of the areas of teacher education which recent public discussion has shown to be subjects of concern' included: 'the distribution of time between the various elements'; 'doubts about the relevance of the traditional main academic subject to the education of teachers of young children'; 'the organisation, supervision and assessment of teaching practice, and the role of the practising teacher in this field'; 'the adequacy of the course in relation to practical teaching problems'; 'the content and relevance of courses in the theory of education'.[19]

The Institute's Enquiry was a mammoth undertaking. The co-ordinating committee was chaired by Lord Fulton, who in 1967 had succeeded Adam as chairman of the Council and of the Committee of Management. It concluded that 'the University involvement with the Area Training Organisation through the Institute should be maintained and extended'.[20]

There was no Institute representative on the James Committee, appointed in 1970 to inquire into teacher education and training by Margaret Thatcher, Secretary of State in the Conservative government of Edward Heath.[21] The James Report, published in 1972, was highly critical both of concurrent and consecutive courses of training. 'Much of the theoretical study of education', it concluded, 'is irrelevant to students who have had, as yet, too little practical experience of children or teaching, and the inclusion of this theoretical study is often at the expense of adequate practical preparation for their first teaching assignments'.[22] Lord James later queried 'the desire to give intellectual respectability to a lot of studies that aren't really very profound' and 'studies which have all the aroma of academicism without the real essence of true scholarship'.[23] The solution was to be found in reordering teacher training into three 'cycles'. The first would consist of a two-year diploma in higher education (or three-year degree) taken in a polytechnic or university. The second cycle of two years would include a first year of professional training in a college or department of education followed by a year of practice in a school or further education college with one day per week released to a 'professional centre'. The third cycle consisted of a programme of in-service education. ATOs should be abolished and replaced by 15 Regional Councils for Colleges and Departments of Education, overseen by a National Council for Teacher Education and Training.

Although the in-service proposals received a general welcome, other parts of the James Report were widely condemned. Elvin declared that 'the incoherence of the total course proposed is frightening'.[24] Initial training would be reduced from 60–80 weeks to 42; there was no guarantee that the third cycle would be implemented.[25] The government, however, declined to engage in major reform. *Education: A Framework for Expansion*, the White Paper published in December 1972, affirmed support for the B.Ed. degree but also signalled the end of the ATOs. While universities might continue to validate college awards, the White Paper made it clear that the majority of colleges were expected to merge with the rest of the non-university sector of further and higher education. Elvin described the assertion in the White Paper that such mergers would bring the colleges of education fully 'into the family of higher education' as an 'hypocrisy that was nauseating'.[26]

In March 1973 the wider Institute received yet a further blow. Circular 7/73 drew attention not only to the massive decline in the birth rate, and hence in the need to recruit teachers, but also advocated a more uniform distribution of higher education places across the country. Since London was over-supplied, the Circular indicated that even were teacher training places across the nation to be reduced by less than 30 per cent, from 114,000 in 1971 to 80,000 in 1981, the cut in Greater London, where most of the Institute's colleges were based, would be well over 40 per cent, from 19,400 to 10,900.[27]

Elvin toured the colleges to speak to packed meetings of anxious staff. As ever, his wisdom, urbanity and gentle humour were much appreciated, but his simple message was not. The situation was grave, and in his capacity as Director of the wider Institute he could offer neither reassurance nor solutions.

### Initial training

Throughout the period covered by this chapter the PGCE course was under constant discussion and review.[28] External factors which sharpened the debate about the initial training of teachers included the Central Advisory Council's Report, *Half our Future* (Newsom Report), published in 1963. This focused upon the education of children of average and less than average ability, and reiterated calls for a raising of the school-leaving age to 16. Another important spur was the reorganization of secondary schools along comprehensive lines. What changes in curricula and teaching methods would be required in such schools and how should their teachers be trained? Edward Short's letter of 1970 requiring an ATO enquiry reflected a general concern that the education and training of teachers was becoming too academic and divorced from mainstream schooling.

In contrast, within the Central Institute Richard Peters used the occasion of a Staff Weekend to promote a more academic reformulation of the PGCE. Since 1963 university departments and institutes had seen 'a proliferation of educational theory – and of educational studies'.[29] Philosophy and sociology were the dominant disciplines at this time, with Peters and Bernstein the acknowledged leaders. Peters wished to see the more rigorous approach to educational studies developed for advanced work extended to initial training. He deplored the practice of launching three successive lectures at students in the Beveridge Hall on Friday mornings, and proposed follow-up sessions in seminar groups. Although Peters failed to persuade all members of the Institute's teaching staff to become involved in leading such seminars, sufficient volunteers were found to make the scheme viable. From 1963 students were required to take five three-hour written papers, only one of which was concerned with the principles and methods of teaching. Not only was philosophy of education now compulsory – along with educational psychology and health education, the English educational system and principles and methods – advanced philosophy of education also became an option. The more substantial and efficient teaching of educational theory in turn produced a reaction, led by Lauwerys, who in 1965 expressed concern in the Central Academic Board that foundation disciplines rather than the work of curriculum departments and teaching practice had come to dominate the course.

One response to such concerns was to try to enhance the standing of curriculum departments by the promotion of staff to the level of appointed teacher. Hedley Burston, Head of the History Department, which also assumed responsibility for history of education, was promoted to reader in 1964 and professor in 1972. He was, however, the exception rather than the rule. Nevertheless, some curriculum departments did expand their activities beyond initial training. For example, in 1964–5 the Geography Department had several students at academic diploma level, nine at MA and one Associateship.[30] In 1965–6 James Britton, Head of the English Department, was appointed reader and received a grant of £26,680 from the DES to direct a five-year research project into 'Written language in the secondary school'. In 1970 Britton was appointed to the Goldsmiths' Chair of Education.[31]

One major change was the creation of a Curriculum Studies Department. In 1948 Joan Davis, a former head of a secondary modern school, had been appointed senior lecturer in the curriculum of the secondary modern school. At first her role was uncertain, but Davis was a person of considerable energy and from 1951 it was agreed that she could admit students with general arts degrees who might proceed to posts in secondary modern schools. The General Arts Department, as it became known, also served as a home for students with degrees in the social sciences. When Davis retired in 1967, the General Arts Department was closed. In future all PGCE students would be assigned to curriculum departments. The 35-year-old Dr Denis Lawton was appointed to a senior lectureship in curriculum studies.[32] Quinquennial proposals for 1967–72 included the establishment of not one, but two, chairs in curriculum studies.[33]

Given that the PGCE course amounted to some 30 weeks and comprised educational theory, methods work in two subjects and a variety of optional courses, as well as preliminary and main teaching practices, it was clearly difficult to make sufficient provision for all elements. As Peters acknowledged, some students responded well to the multiplicity of challenges, others were bewildered, while others, and possibly the majority, 'use their judgement about where to concentrate their efforts'.[34] Elvin's long-term solution was a two-year course of initial training that might enable all elements to receive adequate treatment. More immediately, Niblett instituted a useful scheme of visiting tutors whereby practising teachers were assigned to the Institute for half a day a week. They contributed both to training in the Institute and to supervision of teaching practice. By 1967–8 there were 12 visiting tutors, one for each curriculum department. The practice required co-operation with schools and LEAs, the tutors being paid a modest £100 per year for their services. Other attempts to bridge the perceived gap between the Institute and schools were made at department level. For example, the Modern Languages Department held monthly meetings with groups of teachers to discuss common issues in language teaching.

Arrangements for teaching practice remained under constant review. Although many schools preferred a block practice of one term, the Institute adhered to its tradition of integrating theory and practice wherever possible. From 1966–7 there were three periods of teaching practice: four weeks of four days in the autumn term, six of four days in the spring term and three of continuous practice in the summer term. In 1969–70 this was reduced and simplified to five weeks in the autumn term and six in the spring. Those staff and students who feared that even more of the summer term might now be given up to preparation for examinations advocated a greater use of continuous assessment. In addition, the distinction grade both in theory and practice was widely criticized as being of dubious value to students and an unreliable guide to future performance.[35]

Three points may be made in conclusion. In this period student numbers in initial training remained relatively constant. This was partly because of constraints upon space but also reflected a deliberate policy of concentrating growth in the areas of advanced studies and research. The Central Institute did not establish a B.Ed. course of its own. Secondly, while most criticisms of teacher education in this period emphasized the need for more practice and contact with schools, under the leadership of Richard Peters the theoretical dimensions of initial training were strengthened. Some tutorials in educational theory worked well but, given the lack of enforced student attendance and the unease of many tutors, others were desultory and simply collapsed. A third feature was that some tutors recruited to curriculum departments were themselves former Institute PGCE students now in their mid- or late-20s and with very scant school teaching experience. Such appointments, which might seem even less appropriate in the context of a rapid development of comprehensive secondary schools, were justified on grounds of intellectual calibre and an expected growth of higher degree work in the curriculum areas. As Elvin observed, however, 'we are very inbred in this Institute'.[36]

## Advanced studies

Advanced studies in this period fell into two broad groups.

The first of these comprised further courses of advanced training for which there was considerable demand, not least from central government. Thus the Ministry of Education pressed for an increase in recruitment to the Child Development Diploma, the Department of Education and Science supported the institution of a Diploma in Philosophy of Education, while the Home Office funded students on the Diploma in the Educational Rehabilitation of Young People. Specialist diplomas flourished and the *Annual Report* for 1964–5 noted that 'This is the kind of work in which the future of the Institute lies, because we are particularly well equipped in staff and in facilities in the area to cope with the specialised aspects of education'.[37] These diplomas catered for experienced headteachers, teachers, college of education lecturers and others who wished to acquire a specialist qualification. Some returned to their previous posts, but a significant number gained instant promotion. For example, of the 61 home students who took the Child Development course in 1964–5, 12 were immediately appointed to colleges of education, six to headships, two to deputy headships and one as an LEA adviser.[38] Established courses continued and new ones were added: for example, a Diploma in the Education of Deaf and Partially Hearing Children and another in the Education of Physically Handicapped Children began in October 1965. Some co-ordination of specialist diplomas proceeded under the aegis of the Child Development Department, headed by Professor Jack Tizard, whose chair was supported by an endowment from the Spastics Society. Thus in 1965–6 more than 150 diploma students in this department attended a common core lecture programme on Child Development, Relations within the Family, the Physiology of Growth, and Aspects of Special Education. In contrast, one casualty was the externally examined Health Visitors course, organized in association with the LCC and located at the Institute since 1954. This was discontinued in 1966 on the grounds of 'a lack of proper integration with other work in health education at the Institute' and because 'accommodation is no longer available'.[39]

The second group of advanced studies comprised the academic diploma in education, MA, M.Phil. and Ph.D. In sharp contrast to the specialist diplomas, the great majority of students on these courses were part-time. For example, in 1963–4 there were 367 part-time students as opposed to 88 full-time. No fewer than 77 of the full-timers were from overseas.[40] In 1967–8, however, the Department of Education and Science included the academic diploma in its list of specialist advanced courses eligible for funding, thus enabling up to 20 experienced teachers per annum to be released on full salary to attend the course. One outcome of this arrangement was the provision of some elements of the work during the daytime. Hitherto the diploma course had only been provided after 5 p.m.

Part-time student numbers on the academic diploma, which doubled to 258 in the three years to 1964–5, placed a considerable extra burden upon teaching staff. Although the advent of the B.Ed. raised some initial doubts about the continuing need for the academic diploma, recruitment remained strong throughout this period. Many students, ineligible to take the B.Ed., valued the diploma both as an award in its own right and as a qualification for admission to the MA. The cause of the academic diploma students had been taken up in 1961 when Klaus Neuberg, appointed as lecturer in philosophy in 1953, produced a memorandum outlining their plight. Neuberg proclaimed that 'Academic Diploma students are the Cinderellas of the Institute. They get less guidance than any other set of students; there are no tutorial groups and as for individual tutoring the part-timers get none at all and the full-timers get some only.'[41]

Neuberg, who already had a considerable reputation as a friend and mentor to overseas students, was duly appointed Adviser to Academic Diploma students and promoted to senior lecturer. He threw himself wholeheartedly into the role: assigning tutors to full-time students, making himself available most evenings and Saturday mornings to the part-timers, and trying to promote academic and social contacts between them. In a memorandum of 1963, however, Neuberg claimed that academic diploma students were still 'Cinderellas'. Even though about a third of the home students had never attended a university before and the majority had not undertaken any systematic study or writing for years, part-time students taking the academic diploma course still had no tutors and most did little or no written work. Neuberg declared that:

> PGCE students are being positively pampered in comparison; yet a majority of the staff only recently considered the PGCE set up 'not viable' as an example of true education and an embarrassment if not an insult as a provision to have to acknowledge 'in what purports to be an Institute of Education'. How much less viable must be the provision made for the majority of Academic Diploma students.[42]

This memorandum prompted the immediate establishment of a powerful working party, but in 1966 Neuberg resigned to become principal of a new college of speech and drama. Modest progress was made via the provision of some written work and additional seminars and a restriction was placed on part-time student numbers.

One major feature of this period was the success of the M.Phil., which replaced the former MA by thesis. Students for this degree were required to present a thesis based upon research and to defend it in a viva voce examination, but at a less rigorous level than that required for a Ph.D. The new qualification clearly fulfilled a need and numbers grew rapidly. For example, in 1968–9 there were 17 full-time and 110 part-time students registered for M.Phil. as opposed to 25 and 85 for Ph.D. MA/M.Sc. numbers stood at 41 full- and 128 part-time.[43]

Table 10 shows the distribution of students across the three main areas of the Institute's work in the middle years of the period covered by this chapter.

| Table 10  Numbers of students at the Central Institute, 1968–9[44] | | | | | |
|---|---|---|---|---|---|
| | Full-time | | Part-time | | Total |
| | Men | Women | Men | Women | |
| Initial courses of training for teaching | 197 | 329 | – | – | 526 |
| Further courses of training | 166 | 181 | 104 | 71 | 522 |
| Advanced studies | 99 | 46 | 428 | 160 | 733 |
| Totals | 462 | 556 | 532 | 231 | |
| Combined totals | 1,018 | | 763 | | 1,781 |

Three comments may be made upon these figures. The first is that the balance of the work of the Institute had now fundamentally shifted. Numbers engaged in further courses of training, principally for specialist diplomas, now matched those in initial training. The most numerous students, however, were engaged in advanced studies, either for the academic diploma or higher degrees. Secondly, although women students predominated in initial training and numbers were broadly the same in further courses, men were in the majority in advanced studies. Finally, it is clear that while initial training students were full-time and full-timers predominated on further courses, work in advanced studies was principally a part-time activity. Given that initial course students spent considerable time in schools on teaching practices, the Institute building was often more fully used in the evenings than in the daytime. Much teaching and learning took place after 5 p.m.

One effect of this shift in student composition was a decline in participation in the Foundation Week functions. Formal balls and humorous reviews held little attraction for busy mature professionals. This was particularly true for part-timers, whose principal concern was to make their way from school or college through the London traffic in order to arrive in time for an evening lecture. On the other hand, many full-time students, both home and overseas, sought to challenge the traditional culture, values and practices of the Institute, higher education in general and of the world at large. The demise of Foundation Week also reflected a decline in the overall sense of community and the growth of a departmental culture. In 1968–9, as student protests erupted in London and in many other parts of the world, the Students' Union decided to 'recommend to its successors that functions should be reduced in scale with emphasis on activities that are organised departmentally rather than centrally'. One PGCE student of this year, Geoff Whitty, later recalled 'lining up in Malet Street and marching through London and I can certainly remember the night that LSE was occupied and we sat outside the police station where the students had been taken'.[45] A more serious approach to student affairs might even have contributed to the bar in the junior common room making a profit – for the first time on record.[46] The decline in the former sense of community was also reflected among the academic staff. Formal staff dinners at hotels such as the Dorchester came to an end. Although the Committee of Management voted a subsidy of £380 for the Staff Weekend to be held in June 1973, this event had to be 'cancelled for lack of support'.[47]

## Research

In this period growth in advanced studies was matched by growth in research, indeed, the two frequently went hand in hand. Much money still came from American agencies. For example, in 1963–4 the American Association of Aid to Crippled Children gave a grant of $7,000 annually for three years to enable Vernon to conduct research into handicaps to intellectual development. In the following year the Ford Foundation made a grant of $100,000 to the Reading Research Unit. Examples of grants from major bodies closer to home included those from the Nuffield Foundation in support of the Sociological Research Unit, the Leverhulme Trust for a study of the economic effect of higher education on women, and from the Joseph Rowntree Memorial Trust for research into the purpose and function of student residence. Other grants which reflected the broadening of the Institute's educational interests and expertise included those from Dr Barnardo's for work in the field of child care, and the Sembal Trust for a research project on aids for the blind.

Central government and its agencies, however, were the major sources of finance for research. In 1961 the Institute's annual research expenditure amounted to some £16,000. In the financial year to July 1971 research grants totalled £111,118, including £86,610 from government sources.[48] Grants now came not only directly from the DES, Home Office and the Ministry of Health, but also from the Schools Council, established in 1964, and the Social Science Research Council (SSRC) set up in the following year. The Schools Council was particularly concerned with curriculum development. In 1967–8 grants to the Institute included £20,000 to the Sociological Research Unit over three years for a study of 'The Questions Children Ask', and £11,000 over two years for an investigation into 'Social Studies for the Years 8–13'.[49] The SSRC not only provided grants – on topics as varied as student unrest, the occupational requirements and training needs of graduate secondary school teachers and the development of ethnic awareness into adolescence – but also funded a small number of research studentships.[50]

In this period Child Development and Sociology emerged as leading elements in the culture of funded research. Psychology was still a major area, but there were problems of continuity and co-ordination. In 1964, when Vernon was appointed to a research professorship, Brian Foss of Birkbeck College was appointed Professor of Educational Psychology. Foss, whose inaugural lecture was entitled 'Education as Art, Science and Technology: A psychologist's view', was best known for his editorial work – particularly as the general psychology editor for Penguin. Although several grants were obtained, including that from the Sembal Trust for the development of Braille books and one from the DES to inquire into programmed learning,[51] in 1968, the same year in which Vernon left for Calgary, Foss took up an appointment as Professor of Psychology at Bedford College where he remained for 19 years. His successor as Professor and Head of Department, W. Thelma Veness, also recruited from Birkbeck, died unexpectedly in 1971.

Another appointment in 1964 was that of Jack Tizard as the country's first Professor of Child Development. Now the work begun by Isaacs and carried on by Gardner could be placed on a more substantial footing. The Spastics Society provided a large endowment of £600,000 spread over ten years. Tizard, who had taught at universities in New Zealand and Scotland as well as at the LSE, brought large grants in his train. His inaugural lecture, 'Survey and Experiment in Special Education', provided an account of his research to date and stressed its concern with finding solutions to practical problems. By 1967–8 Tizard was overseeing no fewer than five major projects, funded by six different bodies.[52] Such activity, coupled with the large number of students in advanced courses, led Tizard to seek some relief from teaching and administrative duties. This was made possible by the support of the Department for Health and Social Security (DHSS) which in 1970 declared itself 'extremely interested in the consolidation and extension of Professor Tizard's research in areas of mutual interest and is prepared to provide funds for this purpose in advance of consideration of the formation of a research Unit'.[53] Agreement was reached for the establishment of a Child Development Research Unit, funded by the DHSS for seven years. In September 1971 Tizard resigned from his existing chair and the University conferred a new professorial title upon him.

Sociology of Education, headed by Basil Bernstein, who was appointed reader in 1966 and professor in the following year, was another key department for the receipt of external grants for research. For example, in 1967–8 the Sociological Research Unit was funded by grants from the DES, Ford Foundation and Nuffield Foundation. Under the charismatic leadership of Bernstein the Unit's research into the relationships between social class, language, learning and intelligence aroused worldwide interest.

One significant initiative came from members of the University's departments of dentistry, engineering and medicine. With the aid of a grant from the Leverhulme Trust, the Institute established a University Teaching Methods Unit (UTMU). This

Niblett attributed his dissatisfaction with the role of Dean to a number of factors – declining government enthusiasm for ATOs, inadequate financial resources, the scattered nature of the London colleges and the failure to give priority to library provision in the new building. Personal considerations included his belief that:

> I was better at being a leader, able to pioneer and take the initiative fairly freely. As well, I found the permeating humanist climate of the administration in the Institute too cool for comfort and the lack of any sympathy for religion among so many of the brightest and best of the members of its staff – highly intelligent and excellent at their jobs though so many of them were – more inhibiting than I ought to have done.[59]

57. W.D. Wall, appointed Dean in 1968. An accomplished artist, some of his works are displayed in the Newsam Library

Niblett's successor as Dean was W.D. (Bill) Wall, Director of the NFER since 1956. Wall came with an outstanding reputation as a researcher, particularly in the application of psychological research to educational improvement. He also had standing with teachers. The *Times Educational Supplement* recounted the story of how Wall, when asked in a school as to what researchers knew about teaching, 'met the challenge by asking to have the bottom stream of the fourth form last period on a Friday afternoon, and gave a poetry lesson to the satisfaction of staff and pupils'.[60] He enjoyed good relations with Elvin, with whom he had worked at Unesco. Problems of demarcation of roles, however, did not disappear and were exacerbated by the increasing difficulties of the wider Institute. Rightly or wrongly, some in the colleges thought that neither Dean had been sufficiently diligent in safeguarding the colleges and had seen them as objects of, rather than partners in, research. Such views complicated the search for a new Director who would be acceptable both to the wider and Central Institutes, and Elvin was persuaded to continue beyond the retiring age of 67 until September 1973. Wall, who had been expected to succeed Elvin, relinquished the post of Dean and was appointed Professor of Educational Psychology and Head of the Department of Child Development and Educational Psychology.

The transference of both Deans to Institute chairs reflected the considerable power of the professors in this period. This power was exercised individually, at department and divisional levels and through the Committee of Professors. Substantial power resided with this body, which Elvin somewhat disingenuously described as 'an informal committee that met fairly frequently in my room'.[61] For it was in this committee that Elvin tried out the proposals which he previously might have discussed in other even less formal situations, for example at Lord's cricket ground with Sir Ronald Forbes Adam, the Chairman of Council and the Committee of Management, or on the golf course with Richard Peters. One important feature of the Committee of Professors was that it comprised the professors of the wider Institute. For example, in 1968 its membership included A.C.F. Beales and Paul Hirst from King's College and Kevin Keohane from Chelsea. From 1968, however, the Committee's agenda was divided into two. Part A dealt with wider Institute matters and part B with those of the Central Institute.[62]

It was in the Committee of Professors that negotiations took place for the restructuring of the Institute into six divisions. Henceforth restructuring was to become a permanent feature of the Institute's history. The divisions as established for the academic year 1964–5, were:

Psychological Foundations of Education [Professor Foss]
   Educational psychology, child development, handicapped children
Research units: reading, centre for the study of human development
Philosophical Foundations of Education [Professor Peters]
   Philosophy of education
Social Foundations of Education [Acting head pro tem Professor Peters]
   Sociology, administration
   Research units: administration and economics, social studies
Comparative Education [Professor Lauwerys and Professor Lewis]
   Comparative education, education in tropical areas
Humanities [Professor Pattison]
   Languages, history, geography, religious education, general arts, art and
   crafts, music
Natural Sciences [Acting head pro tem Professor Lauwerys]
   Physical and biological sciences, health education, mathematics
Services
   Audio visual aids [Professor Lewis]
Library [The Dean]

Such divisions reflected the desire of the professoriate to bring all elements of the Institute's work under their control, and to relieve Elvin and Niblett of some of their administrative responsibilities. The new structures reflected the considerable power of those professors who headed two divisions, the need to balance responsibilities for the two professorial rivals who belonged to the same division, and the marginalized position of the Dean. The divisions confirmed the redrawing of the Institute's intellectual map consequent upon the growth of advanced work and research. Three divisions, including two that had research units supported by external funding, were concerned with the foundations of education. Comparative Education continued the Institute's longstanding commitment to overseas work, although with two different, at times sharply different, emphases. Humanities and

Natural Sciences were primarily concerned with initial training. The divisional structure, however, neither replaced nor fundamentally blurred the departmental organization. Some members of academic staff saw the divisions as an unnecessary administrative tier.

In previous sections of this chapter, reference has been made to the work of individual professors but three further mentions may be made here. The first is to the role of Doris Lee, the former Institute student and lecturer in mathematics, who was appointed to a readership in 1963. Two years later when Harold Dent retired as Assistant Dean, the college principals called for a professor of education with special responsibility for the work of the constituent colleges. Lee was appointed to the chair and proceeded to devote her formidable personality and energies to the task. Lee could be 'gruff and dismissive' and 'her temper was a sight to behold'. It was she, however, who ensured the production of syllabuses and book lists in good time for the new B.Ed. Above all, from the colleges' point of view, 'she cared, she cared about students, she cared about children and she cared about academic standards'.[63] Doris Lee's death in the summer of 1971, a mere two days after the equally unexpected demise of Thelma Veness, robbed the Institute of its two female professors and the colleges of their staunchest champion.[64] It also prevented what might have been an interesting power struggle, for Lee's ambition was to be the first woman Director of the Institute.[65]

58. Richard Peters, appointed Professor in 1962: 'The activity of Professor Peters in every side of the Institute work was phenomenal'

By 1970, the year of his retirement at the age of 67, few members of the Institute could remember a time when Joseph Lauwerys had not been a member of staff. His final years were as busy and as controversial as ever: as Dean of the Faculty of Education and head of two divisions, as the Institute's champion of the importance of teaching as against research and as the leading campaigner for an established chair in comparative education. If Lauwerys was arguably the most influential professorial figure of the 1950s, there is no doubt that Richard Peters came to occupy that position in the next decade. Peters was everywhere – a philosopher of education of national and international fame, Elvin's most respected adviser, leading the Philosophy Department to a position of primacy in the Central and wider Institutes, sorting out the PGCE and the academic diploma, and on Friday afternoons spending many hours chairing the Higher Degrees Committee's scrutiny of each application for advanced study.[66] As Dixon justly concluded: 'The activity of Professor Peters in every side of the Institute work was phenomenal and tended to put Philosophy of Education into the primacy in general theory of education study previously held by Educational Psychology'.[67] Such application ensured that the analytical philosophy associated with Peters and his colleagues replaced the 'undifferentiated mush' and 'pot-pourri of idealistic up-lift and religious exhortation, with some occasional reference to the "Great Educators" which had gone before'.[68] It also led to the discomfiture and departure of some staff. As Klaus Neuberg, whose interests lay in academic and pastoral responsibilities rather than in research explained: 'Rounding off a lecture on moral education with the Officer Krupke song from West Side Story would have made Louis Arnaud Reid chuckle and Richard Peters frown'.[69]

## Administration and finance

One feature of the new Institute created in 1949 was the growth in administration and the numbers of administrators. This was a far cry from the days when Wacey, who was the Institute's Secretary from 1920 until 1958, was the sole full-time administrative officer. For example, in 1965–6, Dixon, as Secretary, led a team that included Miss K. Egan as deputy secretary, Eric Earle as assistant secretary, Denis Bowyer as accountant, Clare Henry as registrar, an organizing tutor and an examinations officer. Six other staff, including the Director's secretary, Beryl Lesmonde, were graded at assistant level, a further eight as senior executive officers, with 15 executive officers and 28 secretarial assistants. David Johnston was the adviser to teachers and Mary Carr the adviser to overseas students. Similarly, in sharp contrast to the days when Geraldine de Montmorency was the sole Librarian, Douglas Foskett was assisted by a deputy librarian, four assistant librarians and a chief library assistant.

Much of this administrative work was concerned with the ATO function. Egan, indeed, who was in charge of the ATO side and reported directly to Elvin, headed a team within a team, which included two staff at assistant level and two senior executive officers. In 1968 when Egan retired, her devotion to the ATO cause was recognized by the Committee of Principals, who gave a dinner in her honour. The Committee of Management also expressed appreciation of her 'long and energetic service', but declined to extend this beyond the normal retirement age. There was a concern to devolve more responsibilities to College academic boards, to cut down 'on paper-work, rubber stamping, duplication of attendance at committees' and to unify the Institute's administration.[70] Accordingly, the Committee of Management endorsed the decision of its staffing sub-committee that in future 'the action of the Secretariat would ... take place without reference to ATO or Central Institute points of origin'.[71] Earle, a former Institute student whose previous administrative experience had been in Ghana and at the Regent Street Polytechnic, succeeded Egan as deputy secretary. When Dixon retired in 1973 Earle was appointed Secretary.

As Elvin acknowledged, Dixon, who had MA, B.Litt. and Ph.D. degrees, was not only a good administrator 'but also a scholar in his own right, an historian in

59. Three Institute Secretaries: from left to right, Eric Earle, 1973–88, Grace Wacey, 1920–58 and Willis Dixon, 1958–73

the first place, and then a leading authority on education in Scandinavia'.[72] A cutter of administrative short cuts, whose desk was always clear, much of Dixon's considerable ability and energy was devoted to the planning and implementation of the new building, and in the interim to curbing the Institute's burgeoning range of activities. For example, in March 1966 he warned Elvin: 'The basic difficulty is that our existing activities are expanding, that new activities are being proposed which will require extra accommodation, and properties which we now occupy will have to be demolished in the near future'.[73] Two years later his tone was more strident:

An alarming situation is developing in the relationship between our academic and business affairs ... we have no money to meet extra commitments ... we are in desperate troubles about accommodation ... we cannot employ more staff, even if money were available, because there is no room. Instead, as you know, I am trying to cut staff to save money.[74]

In December 1968 some relief was provided when the Library moved to new premises in Ridgmount Street, leased until 1981. Although its floor space was thus doubled at a stroke, the Library was now a short walk away from Senate House. Meanwhile the Art and Crafts Department took over the former Union hut, thus freeing some space in the main building. A further easement occurred in respect of student accommodation when the main hall of residence, which had been scheduled for redevelopment, was reprieved. In 1964–5, of the 984 full-time students, 219 were living in halls of residence, 480 in lodgings and 285 at home.

Delays in the authorization and construction of the new building created mounting problems. The years 1968–9 and 1969–70 saw reductions in government capital expenditure on universities and a standstill in many major building projects. Further problems arose closer to home. Indeed, in 1969 the future of the whole project, and of new buildings for the School of Oriental and African Studies (SOAS), was thrown into doubt. Sir John Summerson, a leading figure in the architectural world, champion of historic buildings and Fellow of University College, led the protest. Much public interest was aroused and on 18 February the Institute, in conjunction with the University and SOAS, took advertising space in *The Times* to present its case. Two days later Summerson's motion that the University should reconsider the demolition of Georgian houses in Woburn Square, essential to the construction of the new buildings, was narrowly defeated at an extraordinary meeting of Convocation by 301 votes to 281. Elvin's role in rallying support from staff and students, both of the Central Institute and of the constituent colleges, was crucial.[75]

Financial problems also came to a head in 1969 when Elvin was informed that the Court of the University was not prepared to approve the Institute's expenditure for 1969–70, which involved a deficit of £39,000. The planned list of economies, drawn up by Elvin, Wall, Dixon and Bowyer, proceeded via the Committee of Professors to the Committee of Management. Savings included the ending of some leases on rented buildings, the discontinuance of the health diploma course and the reduction in the budget for public lectures to £50 per annum – a move which would 'save approximately £600 and much administrative work'.[76] The most significant step, however, was to leave vacant the posts of those members of academic staff who were retiring in the immediate future, while buying in temporary help to cover existing teaching commitments. The most expensive, and by far the most strongly contended, of these posts was the chair in comparative education that Lauwerys would vacate in September 1970. Such economies, coupled with supplementary Court grants of £51,000 for 1970–1 and £53,000 for 1971–2 and the deaths of Veness and Lee, meant that the Institute's immediate financial problems were eased. Deficit, indeed, was replaced by surplus and some deferred appointments were made. These included Colin Hindley as Professor of Child Development and George Parkyn, a former Director of the New Zealand Council for Educational Research, as Professor of Comparative Education.[77]

At this time, as so often in the Institute's history, financial problems appeared to stem from misallocation rather than mismanagement. When compared with other colleges of the University of London, the Institute was demonstrably under-supplied in terms of finance, and hence of staff. For example, the UGC returns for 1962–3 showed that Bedford College, London, which had 965 full-time and 36 part-time students, received a grant of £483,633 from the Court and employed 142 academic staff. In contrast the Institute, which had 939 full-time and 497 part-time students, received a Court grant of only £323,263, of which some £70,000 had to be devoted to ATO purposes. In consequence, the Central Institute could only employ 79 academic staff. Application of the national average of 11 students per member of staff also showed that the Institute should have an academic complement of 140. Quinquennial proposals for 1967–72 accordingly requested the creation of at least 55 new academic posts, together with appropriate levels of administrative, clerical and technical support.[78]

Elvin, Wall and Dixon had meetings with the University's Principal and Clerk of the Court to discuss the situation but to little avail. Supplementary grants were secured, but increased financial support on the desired scale with consequent increases in numbers of staff would not be forthcoming until the Institute moved into its new premises. Delays in the completion of the Bedford Way building, coupled with the reduction in space within it to be allocated to the Institute, produced further frustrations. There was a growing feeling that the only way for the Institute to receive its just deserts in terms of finance and staffing would be to abandon the ATO function and to reduce, or possibly even to eliminate, courses in initial training.

## Conclusion

By 1973, the Institute was unrecognizable in terms of nature, size and function from what it had been before 1949. The work and prestige of such scholars as Peters and Bernstein further enhanced its reputation as the leading centre for advanced studies in education. Nevertheless, of the Institute, as elsewhere, it could be argued that 'as educational studies became more rigorous and inevitably academic, the historic neglect of pedagogy was accentuated'.[79]

Other changes were also noted. In December 1977 de Montmorency, who had just produced a brief history of the Library, wrote to Wacey urging her to provide 'an outline on the background administration and organisation which resulted in a small college growing into a mammoth and international organisation'. 'I imagine', she continued, 'that up to the 1944 Act and ATO Act the Peoples and Bodies would be fewer and less complicated and genuinely concerned with the training of teachers. (Heresy to say that now it's also a lot of individual ego!).'[80]

Professorial, and other, egos do seem to have flourished in this period, a reflection in part, perhaps, of the less directive style of Elvin and of the imperial, and frequently imperious, position of the Central College within the ATO. A more humble and engaging attitude was evident in the advice given by Daltry, senior lecturer in mathematics, to W.A. (Bill) Dodd, who was appointed lecturer in the Education in Tropical Areas Department in 1965. On his first day Dodd was nervously savouring the rather intimidating aura of the Senior Common Room. 'Does it feel like sitting in a first class carriage with a second class ticket?' Daltry enquired. 'Yes sir', came the reply. 'Don't worry' Daltry confided, 'we've all got second class tickets'.[81]

Since 1949, the Institute under the leadership of Jeffery and Elvin had entered a third phase of its existence. Its identity, however, and indeed its very name of Institute of Education, had been ambiguous. The London Institute was by far the largest ATO and one of only five out of a total of 17 Institutes of Education in which university department and colleges were combined in a single organization under one director.[82] Elvin attributed the loss of the university ideal to the attitude of DES officials and to the diversion of a genuine concern about the quality of teacher education into a 'reorganization manoeuvre'.[83] While praising the commitment to the wider Institute of such staff as Lee, Niblett, Peters and Wall, he also indicated that other Central Institute staff and some college principals were not so committed to the cause.[84] In contrast, Hencke argued that 'McNair and Robbins, by seeking compromises, had failed to satisfy either the college aspirations for university status or to encourage real university involvement in college problems'.[85]

The year of 1972, however, not only saw the publication of the James Report and the White Paper, *Education: A Framework for Expansion*, but also the Murray Report on the governance of the University of London. This showed the anomalous and potentially precarious position of the Central Institute in the years of retrenchment and restructuring that lay ahead. The Institute of Education was by far the largest of the University's 14 Institutes. In 1970–1 it had 1,069 full-time students out of a total of 1,890. Yet other institutions with fewer full-time students, including Birkbeck, Queen Elizabeth College, Royal Holloway College, SOAS and Westfield College, had superior status and independence as schools of the University. The Report concluded that government reactions to the James Report might require the University to organize 'a special enquiry into the future role and status of the Institute'. Such an enquiry might raise serious problems. On the other hand, the prospect was raised that were the Institute to continue in its central activity there was 'a good case for it becoming an independent School of the University'.[86]

Chapter 9

# The turbulent years
## 1973–1983

### Introduction

By 1973 the expansion and optimism of the heady days of the early 1960s had long since departed. Strikes and shortages at the end of the year led to the introduction of a three-day working week. The Institute's new building was a major casualty of these discontents and in November 1973 the architect advised that the current delay was 'at the rate of almost one week for each notional month of completion'.[1] In March 1974 the Conservative government of Edward Heath resigned and Labour again took office. Economic problems, however, continued. The oil crisis triggered a run on sterling which in turn led to increased taxation and a demand for substantial cuts in public expenditure. The British economy was in poor shape and in October 1975 unemployment figures exceeded 1 million for the first time since the Second World War.

In October 1976, the year in which he succeeded Harold Wilson as Labour Prime Minister, James Callaghan signalled his personal disquiet about the state of education in a speech at Ruskin College, Oxford. Callaghan expressed concern that in spite of increased expenditure on education, levels of attainment were low and many former pupils and students were ill equipped for employment. Reaction to the speech and the ensuing 'Great Debate' indicated that such perceptions were widely shared. A Green Paper of 1977, *Education in Schools. A Consultative Document*, noted a general concern that:

> Teachers lacked adequate professional skills, and did not know how to discipline children or to instil in them concern for hard work and good manners. … Wherever possible preference should be given to applicants for teacher education courses who have had some employment outside the world of education … more attention should be given in initial teacher training to the national importance of industry and commerce.[2]

The growth of general unemployment cut wastage rates among teachers, and left many of the newly qualified without posts. The birth rate continued to decline. Indeed, for the first time since records had begun in 1837, in 1976 deaths in England and Wales exceeded the number of live births.

In 1979, following a 'winter of discontent', memories of which were to pave the way for four successive Conservative electoral victories, Margaret Thatcher arrived in Downing Street. Thatcher was still smarting from her unhappy period as Secretary of State for Education from 1970 to 1974. She believed that 'the ethos of the DES was self-righteously socialist'[3] as were the teacher education institutions. Her perception that 'increases in public spending had not by and large led to higher standards' and that 'too many teachers were less competent and more ideological than their predecessors'[4] signalled a new culture of governmental intervention.

Political and public hostility, financial stringency, ideological controversies, student militancy, redundancies and low morale among staff characterized the teacher education world of this period. The Institute was not immune from such problems and indeed faced one of the most turbulent periods in its history.

## William (Bill) Taylor

Given the general difficulties of the national situation and the specific problems of the London ATO, it is hardly surprising that the Institute took great care in the appointment of a new Director. Of Adams' four successors three – Nunn, Clarke and Elvin – had been members of the Institute staff at the time of their appointments. Their succession to the post had been little more than a formality. The fourth, Jeffery, a former LDTC student, had been closely involved in the Institute's work from the proximity of University College. In 1972–3, however, there was an open competition with public advertisements. After an exhaustive search and intensive interviews the selection committee chose William (Bill) Taylor, Professor of Education at the University of Bristol. Taylor was young and ambitious. His coming marked the beginning of a new era in the Institute's history. Not only was Taylor the first Director to be appointed in open competition, he was the first and only Director in the Institute's history to see the post as a stepping stone to a more powerful position. His subsequent career included the posts of Principal of the University of London, and Vice-Chancellor of the University of Hull.[5]

In 1952 Taylor had been rejected by the Institute for a PGCE course on the grounds that his LSE degree of B.Sc. (Econ.) in Sociology was inappropriate to secondary school teaching. Nevertheless, Taylor subsequently became a part-time Institute student, completing an academic diploma in 1954 and a Ph.D. in 1960. Though only 43 when he took up his appointment, Taylor already had considerable and varied experience. After a mere three years of school teaching in Kent, complemented by teaching adult education classes in the evenings, at the age of 26 he was appointed deputy head of Slade Green Secondary School. Subsequent

60. William Taylor, whose appointment as Director in 1973 signalled a change in the culture of the Institute

posts were at St Luke's College, Exeter, Bede College, Durham, and the Oxford University Department of Education. Since 1966 he had been Professor of Education at Bristol University. Taylor's national and international roles had included service as a part-time research consultant to the DES, as a member of the UGC Education Committee, and Chairman of the European Committee for Educational Research. His publications included *The Secondary Modern School* (1963), based upon his Ph.D. thesis, and *Society and the Education of Teachers* (1969).

Taylor was a realist. Unlike some contemporary sociologists of education he did not see schools and institutions of teacher education primarily as sites of struggle against capitalist society. If the Institute were to survive it must recognize the employment and financial realities of the 1970s and accept that 'we were part of a global change, demographic and economic, and that impinged heavily upon an institution such as this'.[6] The most important issue for the Central Institute was to ensure its own survival and development. Much attention had to be paid to financial matters; in contrast time-wasting conflicts with radical 'single-interest' groups were to be avoided. In Taylor's judgement development would be promoted by the appointment of more professors with curriculum specialisms, further investment in advanced studies and research and the maintenance and strengthening of the Institute's contribution to national debates on education.[7]

Taylor was a highly efficient administrator and a skilled chair of committees. He had clear objectives, coupled with the sense and sensitivity required to postpone or abandon a project if the opposition was too great. Taylor generally carried the Institute with him, as for example by calling all staff – from porters to professors – to meetings in the Logan Hall to explain the financial problems 'in the world of contraction and reduction of income into which we have moved'.[8] This ability to provide leadership and yet to convince the majority that 'everyone needs to share responsibility for the way an academic institution is to be managed' was crucial.[9]

Taylor frequently faced opposition, for example from some senior members of academic staff who regretted the loss of professorial power and influence and from those who thought that more should be done to oppose government policies. He appealed, however, to the broader Institute community. An accomplished teacher himself, he was aware of the power of knowing names – of everyone from the most senior professor to the most junior attendant or cleaner. Eric Earle noted how in December 1973 Taylor visited all the offices to thank people for their work and to wish them Happy Christmas. The new Director 'was part of a different generation, and in personality he was more friendly and open and outgoing, less formal. I suppose he was of a less formal generation.'[10] David Warren, who in 1977 joined the Institute as Registrar in succession to Clare Henry, noted that Taylor 'knew everybody's name, he … never put on any particular airs or graces or pretences, he was down to earth, he spoke to you straightforwardly … very personable, knew what you were doing, was interested and would help you out'.[11]

## Management and finance

At a time of acute financial retrenchment Taylor saw the overriding need to manage the Institute as efficiently as possible. Following his arrival as Registrar in July 1977, Warren produced a report which led to a major (though by no means the last) restructuring. In future the registry would be responsible for the admission of all students, a function which had become fragmented and duplicated across the registry and the advanced studies and overseas departments. At the same time the accounts department would assume responsibility for dealing with all student fees. In 1982 when the post of deputy secretary was abolished, that of Registrar was upgraded to Administrative Grade IV, the same level as the Secretary and Finance Officer. Such regrading reflected a more specialized management structure. Provision was also made for the appointment of a personnel officer.

Denis Bowyer had been the Institute's accountant since 1950. Meticulous and painstaking, he stressed the importance of maintaining adequate financial reserves, and always ensured that every column of figures was accurate down to the last penny. Bowyer eschewed the use of modern aids, even a biro, and relied upon pen and ink, which he kept in a pot on his desk. In 1977 the post of accountant was renamed as Finance Officer and regraded to Administrative Grade IV. From 1979 his successor as Finance Officer, the 32-year-old Garry Philpott, continued the traditions of prudence and efficiency but also brought financial matters into the public domain by the production from 1981–2 of an *Annual Financial Report and Accounts*. This glossy and extremely informative publication of some 40 pages was widely distributed. The most carefully perused of the many tables and diagrams was that which showed costs per student and staff–student ratios by academic department. This demonstrated wide variations and the potential in smaller departments for considerable fluctuations from year to year. For example, in 1981–2 the cost per full-time equivalent student in the Comparative Education Department was £922, as opposed to £2,463 in Science. Staff–student ratios ranged from 21.28 in Comparative and 18.65 in Health and Welfare to 8.19 in Economics of Education.[12]

At this time the centrality of the work of the Finance Officer and his colleagues to the overall life and work of the Institute was not in doubt. For example, in 1979 the Institute was faced with a projected reduction in grant of 28.6 per cent over a four-year period, from £3,020,000 in 1979–80 to £2,156,000 in 1983–4. This cut compared with a reduction for London University as a whole of 18 per cent and for UK universities overall of 13 per cent.[13] Such projections, compounded by the decision of the new Conservative government to charge full-cost fees for overseas students, led to a wide range of emergency measures. Given that staff costs amounted to about 75 per cent of total expenditure, from 1979 a policy of non-replacement or temporary one-year appointments was adopted in respect of all departing academic staff. In March 1981 the Committee of Management decided that although savings of some £300,000 had already been made as a result of non-replacement of staff and other economies, no further full-time appointments could be made for the immediate future.[14] This decision was prompted by a reduction of more than half a million pounds in the recurrent grant for 1981–2, a cut in real terms of some 12–13 per cent compared with the previous year. In 1978–9 the Institute employed 156 academic staff. By 1982–3 this number had fallen to 142. Over the same period administrative, clerical, technical and ancillary staff numbers were reduced from 268 to 223. Both figures for 1982–3 included much larger percentages of temporary staff than in 1978–9.[15] Over a three-year period no permanent staff appointments were made. In September 1982 a tentative step to reverse this policy was taken when a few three-year appointments were approved. Further reductions in the numbers of support staff, however, were still being considered.[16] Widespread compulsory redundancies among staff were only avoided by the introduction of a national premature retirement compensation scheme and voluntary redundancy arrangements. For example, in 1981–2 seven academic and five administrative staff retired with enhanced pensions under these schemes.[17]

## Deans and Deputy Directors

The impending demise of the ATO led to the abolition of the post of Dean and the creation of a new office of Deputy Director. In November 1973 Dr Ian Michael, former Vice-Chancellor of the University of Malawi, became its first incumbent. Michael's main responsibility was to deputise. For example, in the summer of 1975 he was appointed Acting Director during Taylor's three-month visit to Mauritius, Australia and New Zealand. He also served as Dean of Students from 1974 and spent much time, including evenings and weekends, in dealing with student problems, both individual and group, and in providing genial hospitality for students and staff at his university flat in Tavistock Square. Some indication of the growth in student problems was provided by the decision taken in 1976 to establish a Hardship Committee. By January of the following year the Necessitous Students Fund was overdrawn by £600, and £2,000 had to be transferred from the Student Amenities Fund.[18] Another of Michael's roles, as Chairman of the Charter and Statutes Working Party, did not lead to a successful outcome in this period. By the summer of 1978 when he retired at the age of 62, a fourth draft had been sent to the University.

From January 1977 the post of Deputy Director was complemented by that of Dean of Professional Studies. Dr Terry Davis, formerly Director of the University of Mauritius Institute of Education, was the first incumbent. His task was to provide academic leadership for the PGCE course, to chair the Initial Courses sub-board of the Central Academic Board, and to oversee the expected expansion in the work of the University Centre for Teachers in the aftermath of the ending of the ATO. The broader implications of the Dean's appointment became apparent when the job description was drawn up for Michael's successor. This showed that the new Deputy Director would have an academic rather than a pastoral role. One major responsibility would be to co-ordinate advanced studies and research, 'a role somewhat analogous to that of the Dean of Professional Studies in the area of initial training'.[19]

Denis Lawton, who became Deputy Director from October 1978, retained his conferred title as Professor of Education. Lawton had begun work at the Institute in 1963 as a temporary research assistant. Appointed lecturer in 1965, senior lecturer in 1967, reader in 1972 and professor in 1974, this new post represented a further stage in an impressive career. The Committee of Management clearly expected a great deal of Lawton, noting that in addition to his new responsibilities he should continue to 'have a substantial teaching responsibility in Curriculum Studies and will continue research in that field'.[20] Lawton enjoyed working with Taylor and gained considerable administrative experience. He also managed, as Deputy, to continue with much of his writing and some teaching.[21] Nevertheless, in 1983 when Lawton succeeded Taylor as Director the post of Deputy was abolished. Three Pro-Directors, each with responsibility for a specific area of the Institute's work, were appointed instead.

## Professors

Lawton's appointment as Deputy Director may be seen not only as a reflection of his personal ability and energy, but also of the centrality of the Curriculum Studies Department at this time. Dr Richard Pring, a lecturer in the department who in January 1978 proceeded to a chair at Exeter University, saw the department as an important means of promoting a culture of intellectual and personal co-operation. Pring declared that 'It is a sad feature of the Institute that it has so far failed to grapple with problems of interdisciplinarity in any systematic way'.[22] One outcome of such concerns was the development of centres to co-ordinate and develop research and teaching across subject boundaries. One prominent example was the Centre for Multicultural Education, established jointly by the Institute and the Inner London Education Authority (ILEA) in 1979.

While issues of interdisciplinarity and equal opportunities prompted considerable concern, Taylor saw the main staffing need of this era as the provision of professorial leadership, particularly in the several subjects of the school curriculum. Thus Harold Rosen was promoted to a chair with special reference to the teaching of English, Norman Graves to a chair with special reference to the teaching of geography and Keith Swanwick to a chair in music education. Other professors were recruited from outside. For example, the 36-year-old Roy Macleod came from a readership in the history and social studies of science at the University of Sussex to be Professor of Science Education in 1978. Following his resignation in 1982 to become Professor of Modern History at the University of Sydney, in the next academic year Macleod was succeeded by Jon Ogborn from Chelsea College. Other professorial appointments of this period included the promotion of Brian

61. Hazel Francis, appointed Professor in 1979 and Pro-Director in 1985

Holmes to a chair in comparative education in 1975 and the recruitment of the 38-year-old Harvey Goldstein to a chair in statistical methods in 1977. Two years later, Hazel Francis was appointed to a chair in educational psychology and Klaus Wedell to a chair in psychology with reference to children with special needs.

Some professors with conferred titles might be appointed to established chairs without any board of advisors or interview under the terms of the University's Statute 121. For example, in 1979 Brian Holmes was appointed to the established chair in comparative education, vacant since the retirement of George Parkyn in 1977. In the same year, Basil Bernstein, professor since 1967, was appointed to the established chair in sociology of education vacated by Lester Smith as long ago as 1953. This chair was now named for Karl Mannheim. Another named established chair was the Robert Ogilvie Buchanan Chair in Geography Education. This was a tribute to Buchanan, former Professor of Geography at the LSE, who died in the summer of 1980 at the age of 85 having served on Institute committees since 1955, most recently as Vice-Chairman of the Committee of Management. In 1981 Norman Graves was appointed to this chair.

With the impending retirement of George Baron in 1978, application was made to the University for an established chair in educational administration. This produced another youthful professorial appointment in the 35-year-old Tessa Blackstone. At the time of her appointment Blackstone was on secondment to the Central Policy Review Staff at the Cabinet Office from her post as lecturer in social administration at the LSE. In 1983 Blackstone was appointed Education Officer (Resources) for the ILEA. She subsequently served as Master of Birkbeck College and was created a life peer. In 1997 Blackstone became Minister for Higher Education in the Labour government of Tony Blair.

While some professors retired or resigned, others died in office. One particularly bitter blow was the death of Jack Tizard in August 1979. Tizard had been primarily responsible for the establishment in 1973 of the Thomas Coram Research Unit (TCRU) as a major centre of research funded by the Department of Health and Social Security. Dr Barbara Tizard was appointed to succeed him as head of TCRU. In April 1981 Hedley Burston, Professor of Education with special reference to the teaching of History, died in post. In the following year Dr Peter Gordon of the Curriculum Studies Department was appointed professor by conferred title and subsequently became head of a merged department consisting of History and the Humanities consortium. Dr Malcolm Skilbeck was appointed to the established chair in curriculum studies in 1980. Originally four-fifths of his time would be devoted to work for the Schools Council.[23]

In spite of considerable financial restraints, professorial appointments in this period, both conferred and to established chairs, helped to reshape the intellectual and administrative maps of the Institute. Nevertheless, at the same time as individual parts of the Institute were strengthened by the increased numbers of professors and readers, the power of the Committee of Professors was much reduced by Taylor, who preferred to employ the Policy Advisory Committee as a sounding board. One poignant manifestation of the passing of the former era was that in 1980 Richard Peters gave up his position as Head of the Philosophy Department. He retired in 1982.

## Students and courses

During this period there was a modest overall growth in student numbers, from 2,035 in 1973–4 to 2,581 in 1982–3, of whom 1,239 were full-time. Growth, however, was not continuous; for example in 1981–2 the figure was 2,710.[24] Business studies was introduced as a teaching subject in PGCE from 1975, but given the dramatic decline in the need for new teachers in secondary schools there were few opportunities to respond to the curriculum concerns of comprehensive schools. Indeed, the main concern was to preserve existing subjects and departments, with Classics most at risk from the demise of grammar schools. In 1978 the department assumed a new title and role as Classics and Humanities. This enabled it to recruit students with mixed degrees, including those who had followed courses in classical studies but without Latin or Greek beyond a rudimentary level.[25] Three years later

Classics and Humanities was absorbed into a Humanities consortium, which also comprised Political Education, Religious Education and Social Studies. At the same time the name of the Art Department was changed to that of Art and Design, while English as a Foreign Language became English for Speakers of Other Languages (ESOL).[26]

Substantial reductions in student numbers on initial training occurred as a result of central government directives. For example, in November 1981 the Secretary of State announced a 20-per-cent cut overall.[27] In consequence PGCE numbers for 1982–3 totalled 465 as opposed to 520 the previous year.[28] One means of countering such reductions was the introduction in 1981 of a part-time B.Ed. degree (both Ordinary and Honours). This was designed for non-graduate serving teachers and organized on a course unit structure. Numbers rose from 12 in 1981–2 to 32 in the following year, and to 57, including 14 full-time students, in 1983–4.[29]

The two most significant innovations of this period, however, were the development from 1974 of an Alternative PGCE course and the introduction from 1978 of postgraduate training for teaching in primary schools. The Alternative Course, which began in 1974 as the Experimental Course, was designed to counter the low status of teacher education in many schools, and to produce 'teachers strong enough to take what is going on out there'.[30] Key elements in the course were the concept of partnership between inner-city schools and teachers and the Institute and its tutors, a school-based day throughout the course in addition to the usual teaching practices, and the placement of a large core group of students in each school. Core group seminars in schools and in the Institute were employed as a 'means of developing theory from systematic reflection upon shared practice'.[31] Participation in such seminars was frequently favourably contrasted with those more sparsely attended tutorial meetings which followed the delivery of Friday morning lectures on the main PGCE course.

The Alternative Course developed new methods of organization, pedagogy and assessment. It produced new ways of working and new relationships for both students and staff. The social studies subject method group, under its tutor, Jean Jones, was involved from its inception. These students were typically older than the average PGCE students and brought a wider range of previous work experience. About half were considering teaching in further education. They were less committed to the teaching of a single school subject and tended to see education as part of a process of social change. The Alternative Course was also open to students in the English Department. In 1979 it was extended to mathematics and two years later to students in religious education and humanities.[32]

In this period the Alternative Course catered for a minority of students. It demanded considerable commitment from tutors. Indeed, the Education Sub-Committee of the UGC reported in March 1979 that 'The alternative PGCE course seemed a worthwhile experiment but it was clearly very "labour intensive" and its growth would need to be monitored carefully in relation to available resources and staffing'.[33] Nevertheless, the Alternative Course anticipated the general direction of reform in initial teacher training that took place, albeit under central government direction, in the later 1980s and 1990s.

The primary PGCE also grew from small beginnings into a major course. An increase in the numbers of graduates, coupled with financial exigencies, had led to a major change in the balance of training nationwide. By 1980, 60 per cent of those entering the profession did so by the PGCE route. Although apart from shortage subjects such as maths there were few posts for newly qualified teachers in secondary schools, a modest bulge in pupil numbers would arrive in the primary schools in the later 1980s. The primary course proved to be successful, both in terms of the quality of student recruitment – some applicants had good degrees in subjects such as psychology and sociology which made it difficult for them to secure places on secondary courses of training – and in terms of subsequent placements in schools.

By the end of this period student numbers on diploma courses were giving cause for concern. The academic diploma declined in popularity, both as an award in its own right and as a qualification for proceeding to a higher degree. At the same time teachers found it increasingly difficult to secure secondment in order to take a full-time specialist diploma. Student numbers on the academic diploma course fell from 307 in 1981–2 to 245 in the following year. This was mirrored by a decline in successful completions, from 167 in 1982 to 118 in 1983. Specialist diplomas also saw a reduction in student numbers – from 293 to 257. In consequence, part- and full-time B.Ed. students were integrated into existing diploma programmes.

Student numbers at higher degree levels prompted less immediate concern. Indeed, given the relative success in recruitment at this level there was some danger of over-pressure on accommodation and facilities – a topic raised by higher degree students in their meeting with the UGC visitors in 1979.[34] In 1982–3 there were 797 Master's, 329 M.Phil. and 205 Ph.D. students. Nevertheless two-thirds of higher degree students were part-time and the percentage was increasing.[35]

In contrast with most colleges and departments of education where there was a much smaller proportion of higher degree work, the Institute was relatively well placed to cope with reductions in student numbers on initial training. On the other hand, the announcement in 1979 of the withdrawal of government grants in respect of foreign students was a particular blow to an institution of international standing in which more than a quarter of the full-time students came from overseas.[36] As the Institute, in common with other sectors of higher education, was forced to move to full-cost fees, there was an immediate reduction of 150 overseas students. In 1974–5 overseas student fees were still only £250 a year.[37] Fees for 1981 were fixed at £2,000 a year for new overseas students and £1,505 for those continuing an existing course. In the following year there were further increases, to £2,500 and £1,803 a year respectively. The move from a quota system to one in which universities were free to recruit as many overseas students as they could, provoked a substantial debate both nationally and within the Institute itself. Significant contributions to this debate, particularly in respect of students from developing countries, were made by Professor Peter Williams of the Institute's Department of Education in Developing Countries (EDC) and by Professor Mark Blaug from Economics of Education.[38] There was a general consensus that it was essential to restore and even to increase overseas student numbers. Financial arguments were complemented by a determination to maintain the Institute's character and role as an international community.

In 1979–80 Henry Widdowson, Professor of Education with special reference to the teaching of English as a Foreign Language, and Peter Williams chaired an Institute working party on the recruitment of overseas students. Their report prompted further consultations with the British Council and the Overseas Development Administration. A number of initiatives ensued: special one-term courses for students from developing countries, modularization of the popular Diploma in the teaching of English for Speakers of Other Languages, and introductory orientation courses for overseas students. An external relations office was established within the registry to co-ordinate overseas initiatives. Existing overseas links were strengthened and recruiting teams were sent to Hong Kong, Malaysia, Mexico, Nigeria and the United States. In addition to the recruitment of individuals, package deals for groups of students were negotiated. An Institute of Education Society with a newsletter and programme of events was inaugurated. Nevertheless, in the short term numbers of overseas students, excluding those from the European Economic Community (EEC), continued to fall: from 410 in 1981–2 to 351 in 1982–3 and 345 in 1983–4. In contrast, student numbers from EEC countries rose, from 19 in 1981–2 to 21 and 45 in succeeding years.[39]

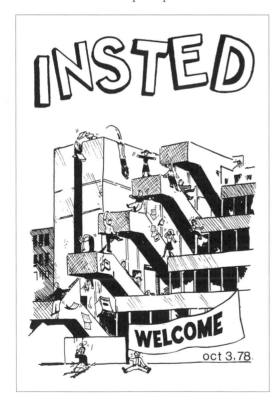

62. *INSTED* welcomes students to the academic year 1978–9 and the opportunities presented by the Bedford Way building

From January 1977 the Institute student body was led by a sabbatical president, supported from Students' Union funds. From 1980 there were two sabbatical co-presidents, one general, the other concerned with welfare and services. This strengthening of student leadership took place at a time when there were many justifiable causes for concern. Fee increases were a perpetual source of discontent and students were keen to encourage resistance to government policies in this area. For example, at a meeting of the Central Academic Board (CAB) in November 1979 it was a student member, Sally Bell, who proposed a resolution condemning the increases in overseas student fees, calling for public opposition and for a guarantee that existing Institute students would be supported to completion of their courses. This resolution, after amendment by Taylor and Williams, was carried with only five against.[40]

One major concern of PGCE students in this period was how, in an era of growing teacher and more general unemployment, to obtain a post at the completion of the year. There was also considerable pressure to reform the existing PGCE year along the lines of the Alternative Course. For example, in January 1976 the student paper, *INSTED,* called for school experience to be placed at the core of the course, with a corresponding reduction in the amount of time spent on educational theory and the production of 'compulsory essays in splendid isolation from real life'.[41] Other longstanding concerns included the facilities and levels of charges in John Adams Hall and the need to make nursery provision for the children of students. The nursery campaign attracted considerable student and staff support, and in 1976 possible premises were identified in the basement of 59 Gordon Square. The Court, however, refused to make a capital grant for the estimated conversion costs of £9,500, and the UGC confirmed that recurrent grants could not be used to subsidize such projects.[42] After much expenditure on conversion and equipment, many delays and some recriminations the nursery began operation in 1979. In its first two years, however, the average number of children attending each session was only 10 and a deficit of more than £8,000 occurred. Carefully constructed policies about ensuring that children of Institute students and staff should have priority were hastily revised, and a search begun for outside funding.

In this period student representation on committees increased. Indeed, from 1981, in anticipation of the implementation of the charter and statutes, there was a student observer at meetings of the Committee of Management.[43] Student concerns were also voiced in the student newspaper, *INSTED,* and there were several instances of direct action. Some of these were personal; for example, pages in Institute Library books written by one member of staff were defaced or ripped out. Others were in support of broadly based campaigns against government cuts in expenditure. In 1976 there was a three-week occupation of the Institute building by some 30 students. This action had support from staff unions, including the Association of University Teachers (AUT). National and Local Government Officers' Association (NALGO) members responded with a go-slow and a one-day strike while National Union of Public Employees (NUPE), the union to which the porters belonged, circulated a

63. Institute students take part in a demonstration against teacher unemployment and cuts in university funding

petition in favour of the students. On 5 May 1979 students occupied the Students' Union premises so that a 'National Revolution Rally could be held there'.[44] Such actions were not necessarily aimed at the Institute, but rather part of a wider campaign based upon the premise that 'Only a united fight by the working class can reverse the cuts and put us on the road towards a properly planned economy'.[45]

The most significant evidence of student power in this period occurred in 1977. The opening ceremony for the new building had been scheduled for March of that year. A resolution passed at a Students' Union General Meeting, however, proposed to open a major campaign of opposition to the cuts in the Institute:

> As a first step, we publicly withdraw our membership of the working party on the Opening Ceremony and therefore withdraw our co-operation with the preparations being made at the Institute. … The Executive is further instructed to investigate the possibility of joint trade union action in the Institute to boycott the Official Opening on March 1st as a means of protest against the cuts.[46]

In consequence, a mere five weeks before the due date the Committee of Management reluctantly decided by 14 votes to 1 to ask the University to postpone the opening.[47] At a subsequent Students' Union meeting the boycott decision was reversed by 66 votes to 37. Preparations began again.[48]

## Changes of culture

Increased student power was one feature of the changing culture of the Institute in this period. Other examples are provided here.

As indicated in the previous chapter, the Senior Common Room in Senate House could be an intimidating place. A club culture prevailed. It was here that the powerful members of the Institute's staff – professors, other heads of departments and senior administrators – held court at lunchtimes and in the early evenings. Confidence oozed from every pore of academic staff whose research and writings were so widely quoted or whose former students now held positions of authority in the countries of the Commonwealth and in the nation's independent and grammar schools. In the later 1960s Eric Earle noted the four 'B' readers – Baron, Bernstein, Blaug and Burston – all of whom were subsequently to achieve chairs. He was also initially intimidated by a quartet of '"formidable ladies": Mrs Hodgson (I don't think I was aware of her Christian name for at least two years), Doris Lee, Winnie Warden, Dorothy Gardner'. Powerful administrators, at a time when the Institute still oversaw the work of some 30 colleges, included 'Beryl Lesmonde, guarding access to the Director, Clare Henry running (sometimes literally) the Registry; Miss McDonald (Mac) ruling the third floor with a rod of iron'.[49]

There was no similar room in the Bedford Way building. Although a succession of small rooms was designated as a senior common room, these tended to be marginal places, characteristically occupied by retired or visiting staff who had time to read the newspapers and who had no rooms of their own. It also became a refuge for smokers, as a no-smoking policy was adopted in other public rooms. In contrast, the main meeting place for staff, both academic and administrative, became the cafeteria on the sixth floor. This room was open to all employees and there were no special tables for senior staff. It was subsequently named the Lawton Room. During the 1990s the whole of the Institute building became a no-smoking area and the Lawton Room bar was removed.[50] Staff who wished to indulge in tobacco and/or alcohol, two of the main characteristics of the Senior Common Room in Senate House, now had to repair to the Students' Union.

Another cultural shift occurred as a result of secondary school reorganization. John Sharwood Smith, a former PGCE student who became head of the Classics Department in 1959, retiring in 1982, noted that in the 1950s and 1960s the Institute's main function was still the initial training of teachers for grammar and independent schools. In such schools the PGCE year was frequently regarded as being at best an amusing irrelevance: 'In consequence, the lecturers in the Institute's subject departments tended to be more or less talented amateurs, eccentric in their antecedents, experience, and educational ideas'.[51] By the 1970s such amateurism and eccentricity were viewed more critically by many PGCE students, as was the discipline-based approach to initial teacher education principally associated with the influence of Richard Peters. As students struggled with the teaching of mixed-ability classes in split-site comprehensives, they were only too aware that some of their tutors could bring little direct experience to bear.

A further cultural change concerned the traditional autonomy of academic staff, autonomy underpinned by the doctrine of academic tenure. Even the Registrar, David Warren, remembered the relatively leisured style that he had enjoyed as an academic assistant in Senate House: 'indeed when I first came over here, I still played cricket on Wednesday afternoons for my first year or so'.[52] It is reputed that when Taylor asked one eminent academic with some 30 years of Institute service what he intended to do on the first Monday afternoon of his retirement he replied: 'I shall go to the cinema. There is no point in breaking the habit of a lifetime.' The prodigious commitment and workloads of some members of the Institute's academic staff left little time for sport, the cinema or other forms of recreation. In contrast, a minority of staff claimed that while the Institute had full claim upon their services for five days a week in term times, weekends and vacations were their own. Such an approach might once have had official blessing. For example, Peter Tregear, the former Director of Education in Sierra Leone, was lecturer in education in tropical areas for 17 years until his retirement in 1972. He recounted his own bemusement when on presenting himself at the Institute on 1 September 1955 to take up his post, Jeffery advised him to go away and come back in October for the start of term.[53] From 1973, financial stringency, coupled with increasing attacks on the doctrine of academic tenure, combined to replace the culture of autonomy with one of accountability.

A series of major, and at times highly public, challenges to the Institute's traditional male culture were brought by Dr Margherita Rendel. Appointed in 1964, Rendel had been held at the efficiency bar on the lecturer's scale in 1973, although permitted to pass the bar from September 1974. In challenging the original decision Rendel received considerable support from the AUT. From 1975 she was given a new title and free-standing role as research lecturer in Human Rights and Education. In this capacity she reported directly to the Deputy Director.[54]

In 1976, at Rendel's instigation the Central Academic Board (CAB) set up a working party 'To investigate the implications of the Sex Discrimination Act 1975 for the Central Institute'. Chaired by Rendel, the working party produced a 20-page report which alleged the existence of sex discrimination at the Institute and urged 'the Institute to take immediate action to remedy the evident grievances, injustices and discrimination'.[55] Copies of the report, which was presented to the CAB on 23 February 1977, were leaked to journalists. The resultant publicity led to Taylor being bombarded with phone calls, not only from the press, but also from an MP, the Equal Opportunities Commission, the National Office of the AUT and from provincial associations.

Professor Harvey Goldstein, who reviewed the report, was highly critical of its analysis and interpretation of the data that had been collected. He concluded that 'This does not of course mean that the basic thesis of sex discrimination is untrue, merely that there is no evidence here to substantiate the claim'.[56] Rendel, however, applied to the Office of Industrial Tribunals, alleging that she had been discriminated against in terms of salary and denied promotion, on the grounds of her sex. She subsequently made further application to the Industrial Tribunal on the grounds of 'victimisation', naming both the Institute and the Director personally as respondents. The hearing began on 6 February 1978 with Rendel, a qualified barrister, defending herself; a report appeared in the *Times Higher Education Supplement* on 10 February. At a subsequent hearing in July, however, Rendel withdrew all her complaints. The Tribunal decided that she had 'acted vexatiously and frivolously' and awarded costs against her, although these were limited to £1,000.[57] The Committee of Management sought Rendel's resignation, but to no avail. As a temporary measure she was made an associate member of the Sociology Department. Promotion followed – to senior lecturer in 1982 and to reader some four years later.

Cultural change and conflict in society at large in terms of such issues as gender, social class and race were not unnaturally reflected in the Institute in this period. Sociology of education was particularly influential and Michael F.D. Young's edited volume, *Knowledge and Control: New directions for the sociology of education*, published in 1971 was widely used, not least as a set book by the Open University. It was frequently argued that for too long teachers had been unwitting agents in the reproduction of the capitalist system, with all its inequalities and injustices. It was now time for schools to become sites of struggle in the overthrow of this system and the creation of a socialist future. One such site was the William Tyndale School in Islington whose Head, Terry Ellis, obtained a Diploma in Primary Education at the Institute by part-time study in 1973.[58] In the 1970s sociologists such as Young and Whitty (a future Director) and teachers like Ellis, argued that radical politics should be brought into education.[59] The 1980s and 1990s, however, would belong not to the radical left, but to the radical right.

## Research and publications

Academic staff were eligible to apply for one term of study leave after five years, providing their work could be covered without cost by their colleagues. This system proved difficult to operate in smaller departments, and was one argument employed in favour of the creation of larger units. There was little internal financial support for research. In 1977, when hundreds of thousands of pounds were annually attracted from funding agencies, the maximum sum available from the Institute's own minor research fund was still only £75.[60] Accordingly a new internal research fund was established in that year. By 1982–3 the Institute's research fund was dispensing some £25,000 a year. This money was used to initiate and sustain projects and to provide bridging funds for funded research staff between the ending of one research contract and the commencement of another.

Although student numbers showed only a modest increase in this period the growth in externally funded research proceeded apace. Research income in 1978–9 totalled £525,000; by 1982–3 it had more than doubled to £1,104,000. This represented an increase as a proportion of total income from 10.4 per cent to 13 per cent. It constituted some 20 per cent of external funding for educational research in the United Kingdom as a whole. By 1982–3 there were more than 50 externally funded research projects. In 1980 the Social Science Research Council designated the Thomas Coram Research Unit, founded some seven years before, as a major research centre. In 1982–3 nearly half a million pounds, some 45 per cent of the Institute's total external research funding, was associated with the 13 projects of TCRU. Five projects funded by the Department of Health and Social Security accounted for the bulk of this income.[61] The Linguistic Minorities Project (LMP), established in 1979, was funded by the Department of Education and Science at a cost of £415,000 over three and a half years. The purpose of this research was to investigate patterns of bilingualism in different parts of England, and to assess the educational implications of linguistic diversity. In 1981 this work was extended when the EEC funded the Language Information Network Co-ordination (LINC) to develop strategies for disseminating the findings of LMP within Europe. In 1982–3 expenditure on this project totalled £119,420.[62] Other substantial grants awarded in 1982–3 included £130,527 from the Department of Education and Science to examine special education policy and practice following the 1981 Education Act. Social Science Research Council grants in this academic year included £110,230 to investigate screening and special educational provision in schools, and £101,270 for research into community languages and education.[63] One major consequence of this increase in funding was an increase in numbers of research staff. During 1982–3 103 staff were employed by the Institute on research projects funded by outside bodies.[64]

One Institute publication, the *London Educational Review*, begun in 1972, foundered in 1975, after a mere 12 issues. Other ventures were more successful. The first volumes in a new monograph series of Studies in Education was published in 1975, and by 1979 11 were in print. Titles included *Language and Literacy in Our Schools*, *Control of the Curriculum* and *Minder, Mother and Child*. These were complemented by a new series of published inaugural lectures launched in 1979 with *The End of the Secret Garden? A study in the politics of the curriculum* by Denis Lawton and *Ivory Towers, The Glass Bead Game and Open Societies: The social functions of comparative education* by Brian Holmes. The most influential of the new publications of this period, however, were the Bedford Way Papers. These were designed speedily to share 'with a wider public, especially teachers and schools, the thinking, discussion and discoveries taking place at the Institute'.[65] The first, authored by Barbara Tizard *et al.* and published in 1981, was a series of discussions on Michael Rutter *et al.*'s best-selling book, *Fifteen Thousand Hours: Secondary schools and their effects on children*, which had appeared some two years before. Subsequent titles included *Issues in Music Education*, *Girls and Mathematics*, *How Many Teachers? Is Teaching a Profession?*, *Secondary School Examinations* and *Education: Time for a new act?* The frequency (some 20 by 1984) and popularity of Bedford Way Papers was such that the Institute was sometimes referred to as 'the place where the Bedford Way Papers come from'. This level of activity led to considerable work for Denis Baylis, the publications officer, and for the publications committee.

## Bedford Way

Throughout the 1960s the Bedford Way building had been seen as the panacea for many of the Institute's ills. In particular, for those staff housed in dirty and dingy temporary accommodation, such as the former hostel at 35–37 Bedford Way, now awaiting demolition prior to the construction of a hotel, occupation of the new building was a matter of great anticipation. Finally, on 29 September 1975, the building was taken over by the Institute, although a further year of fitting out would elapse before it was fully occupied. The new premises, it was believed, would combine the existing advantages of a central university location with the inestimable benefits of modern purpose-built accommodation of generous size and considerable presence. Designed by Sir Denys Lasdun, in 1976 the Institute's third dedicated home was hailed by one commentator as 'the only public monumental building in anything like the style of the seventies'.[66] On 8 December 1977 the new building was formally opened by Her Majesty Queen Elizabeth, The Queen Mother, Chancellor of the University.

The spine of the building occupied the full length of the western side of Bedford Way. Three of the nine floors were at or below ground level. The largest lecture hall, the 900 seat Logan Hall, was named after Sir Douglas Logan, Principal of the University from 1948 until 1975. This facility, indeed, was shared with the University, although its day-to-day management was in Institute hands. The Logan Hall had a well-equipped stage, with scenery dock and dressing rooms, a closed circuit television studio and facilities for simultaneous translation. Other major halls were named after former directors – Nunn, Clarke, Jeffery and Elvin. General lecture, seminar and meeting rooms were complemented by specialist provision, for example for art, drama, media studies, music and science. Some Institute services that had long languished in the wilderness, including the University Centre for Teachers, which had spent the first 26 years of its existence in court-yard huts, were now integrated into the main building. One welcome feature was the number of spacious rooms for tutors. These could accommodate teaching groups of up to a dozen students.

Yet while the benefits of the new building were immediately obvious, so too were its drawbacks. First and foremost the building was to be shared. The Institute of Advanced Legal Studies occupied the southern end of the spine, while the northern end became the province of departments from University College. This was an acceptable feature of the original design, whereby the Institute would have occupied the central portion of the spine and three of the five wings. It was clearly unacceptable given that only one of the five wings was ever built.

Lasdun's design, which echoed his other work, for example the University of East Anglia and the National Theatre, included other elements which were lost – for example covered car parking for 312 vehicles, and an upper level pedestrian walkway to link Russell Square and Gordon Square. His overall vision included both the Institute's new building and that for the School of Oriental and African Studies. One purpose was to create a new pedestrian precinct to be shared by members of the University and general public alike.[67]

This vision never materialized. In spite of the subsequent demolition of Vulliamy's church in preparation for a second wing, and some modest landscaping, the new building and the new precinct would remain incoherent and incomplete. As the architectural writer, J.H. Davies, commented in 1977:

> The present structure does not have the planned accent towards the School of Oriental and African Studies: in fact it has a quite lopsided stress, thrusting out amid the doomed buildings of the square. ... The general impression smacks more of an air raid than of the Groves of Academe.[68]

64. Her Majesty
Queen Elizabeth, The
Queen Mother,
Chancellor of the
University, inspects a
model of the overall
design during her
formal opening of the
Bedford Way building
in December 1977

In December 1977 the Chancellor had inspected a model of the completed project.[69] The cover of Dixon's history also showed a representation of the building as originally envisaged, with five stepped wings providing a ziggurat shape. The expense of these wings, however, which provided ever diminishing amounts of accommodation in each successive storey, was prohibitive. Neither the resourceful Taylor, nor his successor as Director, Denis Lawton, was able to secure even the building of a second wing. In consequence, many of the 'doomed buildings' were reprieved and refurbished.

The most serious effect of the failure to complete the Bedford Way building spine was that the Library, situated in less than half of the space to which the Institute was entitled under UGC norms, remained marooned in Ridgmount Street. By 1980 only two sections – the short loan collection and the National Textbook Reference Library – had been relocated to the main building.[70] With hindsight it is clear that the substantial costs of the Library lease, some £110,000 per annum from 1981, together with associated expenses over a period of many years, might have been better employed in the construction of a new wing.[71] In 1978 Foskett departed to take up the post of Goldsmiths' Librarian to the University of London, and was succeeded as Institute Librarian by Dr Norman Beswick from Loughborough University.[72] Two years later, in an admission of defeat, Taylor noted that 'Meanwhile the site has been tidied up, the sad ruins of Christ Church, Woburn Square have been replaced by a "French park" of gravel and neat lines of saplings, and we wait'.[73] Two lecture rooms on the sixth floor of the Bedford Way building were converted to provide a staff refectory and kitchen, but six departments remained in precinct houses in Gordon and Woburn Squares.

65. Christ Church, Woburn Square, an example of the early Gothic revival, is demolished in preparation for a second wing of the Bedford Way building that was never constructed

Several faults in the new building soon became apparent. The low ceilings, long narrow corridors devoid of natural light and drab internal concrete walls generated an atmosphere of incarceration rather than of education. As Dixon wryly commented, 'We did not want long corridors, in which if you lie on the floor you can detect the curvature of the earth. We wanted alcoves for sitting out on each floor.' Such essential elements were not secured. The new accommodation represented the most that the Court Department and the UGC would allow. Dixon characterized the decision-makers as 'very nice people' who served freshly ground coffee, demanded excessive amounts of information about every proposal and after considerable delay consistently said 'no' with considerable style and charm. Having retired to Northumberland, where he rapidly converted a cottage for his own use, Dixon reflected that:

I was left with an indelible impression of the inadequacy of government departments to conduct what I will call 'commercial business'. ... All the normal tenets of conducting business successfully, such as counting time as money, recurrent costs against capital costs, costs against effectiveness, took second place to correct procedures and precedents.[74]

Apart from the exclusion of the Library, the most serious defect of the new building was the poor provision for teaching. The spine building might well, as Lasdun argued, 'protect the precinct from the noise of traffic in Bedford Way',[75] but lecture rooms were not so protected. A lack of air conditioning and double-glazing meant that in the summer staff and students on the Bedford Way side either roasted in the heat or were overwhelmed by the din and fumes of passing vehicles. Given that similar problems had been so evident and well recorded in respect of the Southampton Row building, it was reprehensible in the extreme that they should have been replicated in the Institute's third home some 70 years later. Outside, the 'attractive "piazza", paved in mauve coloured tiles'[76] which joined the building's fourth floor western entrance to Woburn Square, was traversed by a series of potentially dangerous shallow steps, and water seeped into the roof of the Logan Hall. In due course the tiles were replaced and the steps removed. Thus,

**66. The shallow steps outside the western entrance pose a hazard to children, students and staff releasing balloons in support of the nursery in 1984**

while the new building represented a considerable improvement upon the Institute's accommodation in Senate House, it was a solution that in turn produced a multiplicity of problems. As Dixon commented in 1977, 'I am still not sure whether to be pleased at what we did get or annoyed at the omissions and inordinate delay'.[77]

The Bedford Way building might indeed receive the dubious accolade of representing the architectural style of the seventies. It would also stand in its divided and truncated state as a monument to the economic and demographic downturns of that troubled decade.

## The wider Institute

In March 1973 Circular 7/73, *Development of Higher Education in the Non-University Sector*, set out an administrative framework for the reorganization of teacher education. By 1977 it was clear that 'Circular 7/73 and the abrogation of the Area Training Organizations by the Further Education Regulations of 1975'[78] were leading to the dismemberment of the wider Institute. Several Institute colleges were closed. For example, the last intakes to initial training at Coloma, Maria Assumpta and Sittingbourne colleges took place in 1976, and at Nonington, Stockwell, Thomas Huxley and the newly merged Philippa Fawcett and Furzedown in 1978. Other colleges were absorbed into polytechnics: Gipsy Hill into Kingston, Trent Park into Middlesex, Battersea and the Rachel McMillan annexe into South Bank, Avery Hill and Dartford into Thames. Rachel McMillan and St Gabriel's were incorporated into Goldsmiths' College.

Three Institutes of Higher Education were created. These sought to provide a third way  diversification without incorporation into a polytechnic or university institution. Chelmer Institute was based on the former Brentwood College. The West London Institute was a union of the historic and prestigious colleges of Borough Road and Maria Grey. The Roehampton Institute, also situated in west London, comprised a federation of the colleges of Digby Stuart, Southlands and Whitelands (representing Roman Catholic, Methodist and Anglican traditions respectively) with the Froebel Institute.

While closures and amalgamations provided one threat to the wider Institute, another came from decisions to abandon University of London awards and to seek validation of courses from the Council for National Academic Awards (CNAA). This was a natural step for those institutions that were merging with polytechnics whose degrees were granted by the CNAA. Nevertheless, following the recommendations on diversification in the James Report, the University of London agreed to the introduction of new degree courses from 1975 for colleges wishing to retain an association with the Institute. These degrees were based on a course-unit structure and led to the award of BA, B.Sc., B. Humanities and B.Ed., degrees after three years, with a fourth year of study for the B.Ed. honours degree.

The three-year certificate in education and old B.Ed. were phased out. Regulations were also drawn up for a two-year diploma of higher education.[79] Following the formal ending of the ATO in 1975 the task of administering the new course unit qualifications passed to a reconstituted department known as the Collegiate Division. This was still based at the Central Institute with one of the two deputy secretaries, David Booth, designated as 'Collegiate', the other, Derek Aston, as 'Central'.[80] The overall examination structure was still under the aegis of the University's Faculty of Education. Given the diversification into non-education degrees, however, more members of staff from other faculty boards were involved through a system of joint committees.

Although by the later 1970s there was no longer an ATO, the Institute of Education that existed at that time was a creation of the University of London, approved by Senate in 1948 and formally inaugurated in the following year. The fate of the wider Institute, therefore, would ultimately be determined by the University. In the 1960s and 1970s the University of London was itself facing a series of substantial challenges. The London external degree was threatened by the qualifications of the CNAA, created in 1964, and the Open University established in 1969. Similar challenges appeared overseas where universities in Commonwealth countries acquired powers to award their own degrees. Within the capital itself one of the former colleges of advanced technology joined the University of London as Chelsea College, but two others decamped, to become Brunel University and the University of Surrey. The Northampton College of Technology, which in 1966 acquired a new charter as the City University, broke the University of London's monopoly within the capital.[81] The Royal College of Art also acquired degree-awarding powers.[82] Financial difficulties intensified as the system of quinquennial allocations collapsed in the face of cuts in public expenditure and mounting inflation.

Within the University there was a widespread view that the associated colleges and their courses had become an encumbrance. The wider Institute seemed to be in a perpetual state of flux, and worryingly susceptible to the interventions of central government. Institute staff charged with representing the new degrees at meetings of the University's Academic Council and its sub-committees were sometimes treated with disdain. For example, the chairman of one B.Ed. committee suggested that while marking of arts degrees was normally undertaken using Greek letters and science subjects by percentages, education degrees would no doubt be assessed by a system of little blocks.[83] The several colleges appeared to be forever seeking amendments or exceptions to the new degree regulations. Course units proliferated, so that some university staff were spending considerable time in trying to administer an ever more complex system of examinations in the interests of an ever decreasing number of students. Some of these views were shared within the Central Institute, especially by those whose task it was to argue in university committees for special cases and treatment outside the normal regulations. In

December 1979 the Senate, on the recommendation of the Academic Council, decided that the University should cease to validate courses in colleges associated with the Institute. The final date for entry to full-time courses would be October 1983, with the final examinations in the summer of 1988. The Council of the Institute, which had been formally consulted in November, was not alone in expressing profound regret at the ending of validation. University involvement in college courses and examinations had been in place since 1949, and in some cases since 1928 under the auspices of the Training Colleges Delegacy.

In the *Annual Report* for 1980–1 Taylor confirmed the ending of the ATO era, and the third phase of the Institute's history, in the following terms:

> During 1979 the University carried out reviews of its relationships with the public-sector colleges and the working of the new pattern of awards. After much deliberation it decided that it could no longer undertake validation for the colleges and that the relationship with them should therefore come to an end. The predominating practical consideration which led to the decision was that the Institute, as a single-faculty institution, no longer provided a suitable base for the validation of awards, an increasing proportion of which were in fields other than education.[84]

Some of the remaining colleges turned to the CNAA; others found alternative university validation. In 1982 there were still 25 staff in the Collegiate Division. By 1988 when the final examinations took place there were one and a half.[85] Some Collegiate staff such as Donald Sutherland took early retirement; others, including Wendy Barber and Rita Donaghy, were re-deployed within the Central Institute.

Despite the ending of the old Institute, only slow progress was made towards formal recognition of the new. Early in 1980 the Senate and Court approved the Institute's draft charter and statutes and these were submitted to the Privy Council. Preparations began for a special ceremony at which the Institute would be presented with its long-awaited charter, but to no avail. Difficulties over representation and tenure brought further delays. In March 1982 a letter was received from the Privy Council which stated that Statute 17, which had provided for dismissal 'only for good cause', was unacceptable.[86] Provision must be made 'for the termination of academic appointment on grounds of redundancy or financial exigency'.[87] In consequence a further five years were to pass before the Institute was granted a charter. A second feature of the proposed celebrations of 1982 also failed to materialize. A history of the Institute from 1902 until 1982 was commissioned. The first 30 years were to be written by Richard Goodings, Dean of Education at the University of Durham, a former assistant editor of the *Year Book of Education*, and the latter 50 by the Institute's former Secretary, Willis Dixon. Goodings' work, however, was never completed.[88] Dixon's history, reduced to the years 1932–72, finally appeared in 1986.

## Conclusion

The demise of the wider Institute was the most important event of this period. Events in the worlds of teacher supply and of higher education dictated that Taylor, who had been appointed Director as the person best fitted to safeguard the future of the edifice built by Jeffery and sustained by Elvin, should preside over its downfall. Thus by 1983 the Institute had entered the fourth phase of its existence.[89]

In many respects the new Institute would be leaner and fitter than the old. It was still by far the largest university department of education in the country, and its pre-eminence in such matters as funded research and publications was not in doubt. It had survived successive reductions in government grants, including the introduction of full-cost fees for overseas students, in better shape than most university institutions. Lawton, the new Director, was fully acquainted with the Institute's strengths and weaknesses. He was well known by staff and enjoyed the full confidence of the Chairman of the Committee of Management, Sir Brian Windeyer. As Principal of the University, Taylor was still at hand in Senate House.

Nevertheless, several problems remained. The new building was unfinished and divisive. Progress towards independent status as a school of the University was painfully slow. The government appeared to be making a test case over the Institute's charter and statutes in respect of abolition of academic tenure. The dangers of the Institute's monotechnic status had been underlined by the demise of the colleges of education. The relocation of initial training from universities to schools was now on the political agenda. A Conservative administration that would radically reduce the rights and powers of trade unions and the professions and kill off the Greater London Council and the Inner London Education Authority, might well have the Institute in its sights. In spite, or even because, of the Institute's size and standing, survival would remain the name of the game.

# Chapter 10

# Survival of the fittest
## 1983–1994

## Introduction

During this period the Institute's very survival remained in question. Although the problems associated with the wider Institute had been removed, for Denis Lawton 'crisis management' was still too often the order of the day.[1] His successor, Sir Peter Newsam, judged that 'the political climate was hostile, the educational argument was increasingly unfavourable, so too was the likely financial position of a comparably small, single-purpose Institute – despite its obvious strengths and high reputation'.[2]

The Conservatives remained in power and in June 1983, a year after British forces recaptured the Falkland Islands, Margaret Thatcher was returned to office with an increased majority. Criteria for the approval of initial teacher education courses were issued in April 1984. William Taylor, who was still Principal of the University of London and who became Vice-Chancellor of Hull in the following year, was appointed chairman of the Council for the Accreditation of Teacher Education (CATE). The Council, which first met in September 1984, was empowered to review all existing courses and to assess proposals for new ones.[3] The White Paper, *Better Schools*, published in March 1985, reiterated the government's determination 'to promote a more rigorous approach to initial teacher training'. All PGCE courses should be extended to 36 weeks and should include a substantial element of school experience and teaching practice. No student whose practical classroom work was unsatisfactory should be awarded qualified teacher status. The White Paper also confirmed that 'The staff of training institutions concerned with pedagogy will themselves be expected to have had recent successful experience of school teaching'.[4] In 1986 Kenneth Baker replaced Sir Keith Joseph as Secretary of State for Education. In June of the following year, a further Conservative election victory presaged radical changes in education, changes epitomized by the Education Reform Act of 1988.

67. Denis Lawton, appointed Director in 1983, who sought to introduce 'a period of stability and consolidation'

## Denis Lawton

By 1982 Lawton had decided to leave the Deputy Directorship and return to full-time teaching and research. Following Taylor's resignation, however, he agreed to continue for a further two years to see a new Director into office. Lawton did not apply for the post of Director and was in Canada when the interviews were held. No appointment was made, and upon his return Lawton was invited to lunch at the Athenaeum by the Chairman of the Committee of Management, Sir Brian Windeyer, and advised that 'it was my duty to do the job, whether I wanted to or not. I succumbed.'[5] Following a formal interview by the appointing committee, Lawton agreed to serve as Director for five years.[6]

Lawton brought many strengths to the post of Director. He had an intimate knowledge of the Institute and enjoyed the support of the Committee of Management and of Windeyer. Many Institute staff regarded him not only as a colleague but also as a friend. His personal style was less circumspect than that of his predecessor. Taylor's recreations, as listed in *Who's Who*, were writing and walking. Lawton's entry under this heading was 'walking German Shepherd dogs, photographing bench-ends, sampling real ale'.[7] The new Director's commitment to research and teaching was widely respected. His several publications on social class, language, culture and the curriculum were eminently readable.[8] Indeed, the clarity of his teaching and of his published work was legendary. Basil Bernstein, 'tremendously stimulating and challenging, and a splendid companion when we found time for an off-duty drink at the Marlborough', had supervised Lawton's doctoral studies.[9] Students, however, were sometimes advised that 'if you want to understand Basil Bernstein read Denis Lawton'.

On the other hand, while Lawton was widely respected, both in the Institute and in the University, for his large presence, mellifluous voice and urbane conduct of meetings, he clearly did not have the same interest in administration and in promoting new initiatives as had Taylor. Nor did he have the variety of institutional and political experience of his predecessor, nor indeed of his successor. Lawton was an Institute person, through and through: 'I have never been tempted to go elsewhere'.[10] Some aspects of being Director were enjoyable; 'Others, such as cost-cutting and countless committees, I found less appealing'.[11] Lawton publicly opposed some Government education policies. For example, he described Kenneth Baker's proposals for a national curriculum as being 'fundamentally flawed',[12] while Conservative reforms in education were characterized as signalling a clear message: 'State schools may be good enough for others, but not for our children'.[13] While Taylor, both as Director and subsequently, received honours and appointments from Conservative governments, Lawton did not.

One of Lawton's two major aims, following several years of financial and staffing cutbacks, was to introduce 'a period of stability and consolidation'.[14] 'My intention was to preserve stability for five or six years and then hand over an institution ripe for exciting new developments'.[15] Unfortunately, financial problems continued and difficult choices had to be made – for example, between computers and Classics. Some tutors were made anxious by the requirement to return to the school classroom to demonstrate that their teaching experience was both 'recent and relevant'. A more general insecurity was generated by the government's determination to abolish academic tenure. Much time and effort was devoted to solving the problems of the Library. Other time-consuming, and ultimately fruitless, discussions concerned the possibility of merger – with the Department of Extra Mural Studies, Birkbeck, King's or University College. Within the University of London painful restructuring was the order of the day. Bedford College was amalgamated with Royal Holloway; Chelsea College and Queen Elizabeth College with King's. Subjects were redistributed between colleges. One ominous conclusion was that 'mergers and concentrations ... leave the future of some of the components of the University unsettled, including several of the Senate Institutes'.[16]

Lawton's other main concern was to continue the process of democratization begun by Taylor. For example, he gave up chairing the Committee of Professors, whose power and influence was further reduced. Central initiatives for managerial and administrative reform were complemented by a more transparent structure of committees provided under the Institute's own Statutes and Ordinances. One example of this more democratic approach was the use of secret ballots in the Academic Policy Committee to decide between competing departmental proposals for academic staff. In 1986 there was a major ballot of academic and academic-related staff on the amendments put forward by the Privy Council to the Institute's proposed Statute 17, which dealt with tenure.[17]

Lawton abolished the position of Deputy Director and appointed three Pro-Directors from among the existing staff. Pro-Directors were expected to spend some 75 per cent of their time on these duties and the remaining 25 per cent on teaching and research. Basil Bernstein became Pro-Director (Research) and Brian Holmes, Pro-Director (Academic) with responsibility for in-service education for teachers (INSET) including Master's courses. As Pro-Director (Professional Studies) Norman Graves was in charge of initial training.[18] Peter Mitchell, for the past 11 years Head of Quintin Kynaston School who was currently a visiting professor at

68. Pro-Directors in concert: Basil Bernstein (left) and Brian Holmes

the Institute, was appointed to the post of senior tutor for a period of three years from September 1984 to assist Graves in PGCE work.[19] In 1985 Professor Hazel Francis became Pro-Director (Academic and Staff Development) in succession to Holmes, who had retired. By this time the system of appointing three internal Pro-Directors on a part-time basis in place of a Deputy Director had been adopted as a permanent part of the Institute's management structure. This change, however, was not incorporated into the draft Charter, Statutes and Ordinances. Instead the Council decided that where references were made in such documents to a Deputy Director, the senior Pro-Director should be regarded as fulfilling this role.[20] Though fully sensible of the honour and importance of his position as Director, Lawton had always made it clear that his real interests were academic rather than administrative. His decision to vacate the office of Director at the end of the 1988–9 session and to return to the Curriculum Studies Department was both respected and understood.

## Peter Newsam

The Joint Advisory Committee which conducted the search for a new Director consisted of four members appointed by Council, four by the Senate of the Institute, together with two externals – the one a Chief Education Officer, the other a distinguished academic. Some 18 applications were received as a result of advertisements; other persons were approached directly.

Peter Newsam, who fell into the latter category, was 60 years of age when he took up his five-year appointment as Director. An Oxford graduate, with a distinction in the diploma of education, Newsam had seven years of teaching experience in schools but none in higher education. His recent administrative career had included five years as Chairman and Chief Executive of the Commission for Racial Equality, 1982–7; since 1987 he had been Secretary to the Association of County Councils. His reputation, however, had been made as an educational administrator: in the North and West Ridings of Yorkshire (where he was much influenced by the example of Sir Alec Clegg) in Cumberland and at the Inner London Education Authority. His ten years at ILEA, 1972–82, the first five as Deputy, the last as Education Officer, gave him substantial knowledge of London and of its schools. Newsam's service on major committees and his knighthood, granted in 1987, indicated the respect he enjoyed across the educational and political spectrum. As Director he was at pains to maintain contacts with members of all political parties.

Newsam's aim was to preserve and where possible to strengthen the Institute's leading position in teaching and research. This he sought to do by improvements in structure and infrastructure. Two of Newsam's building projects – the total refurbishment of the Students' Union premises to create first-class catering facilities for the whole Institute, and new provision for a nursery – could not be completed during his five-year term and thus were deliberately left undone.[21] Completions included a new Library, a new Bedford Way entrance, and increases in student numbers and in income generation. Newsam personally took the lead in these reforms. His most tangible achievement was the Library, begun in 1989, opened in 1993 and fittingly renamed 'The Newsam Library' in September 1997.[22] Newsam's appointment and policies, however, also symbolized a renewal of the partnership between the Institute and London. Newsam sought to re-emphasize the Institute's metropolitan connections and responsibilities and to meet the post-ILEA needs of the capital's schools and colleges.

Newsam was aware of the need to make rapid decisions in some areas, and was concerned that the Institute's committee structures and consultative processes might be too cumbersome. Change had become 'a permanent condition' and the Institute had

69. A portrait of Peter Newsam, Director 1989–94, hangs in the entrance to the Library which fittingly bears his name

to 'manage a process' rather than indulge in lengthy deliberation and elaborate plans. As he stated in a report to Council in June 1991: 'the administrative time-scale, whereby the Institute has to respond to outside pressures, is much shorter than the academic one, in which matters of concern need to be fully debated and considered'.[23] Even as Director-designate Newsam took the initiative in creating a new management structure, 'as a reflection of the way I am best able to work'.[24] His paper of June 1989 recommended the appointment of a Deputy Director from January 1990 or as soon as possible thereafter. Newsam's priorities and style of management were in complete contrast to those of his predecessor. Whereas Lawton had sought (often in vain) to allocate some one-third of his time to his own academic work, the new Director expected, at least initially, 'to devote that proportion of my time to issues arising from initial training'.[25] The Deputy would be in charge of research, act for the Director in his absence and 'undertake other functions that from time to time might be agreed between them'.[26] Given the imminent retirement of Bernstein and Graves, the posts of Pro-Director (Research) and Pro-Director (Professional Training) would not be filled. Although Newsam wished to be involved with INSET work, he envisaged that Hazel Francis would continue in her post as Pro-Director (Academic), 'at least over the next two or three years'.[27]

In spite of objections raised at the Joint Planning Committee and in the Council, Newsam's proposals were implemented. The two retiring Pro-Directors took study leave and Francis indicated her wish to relinquish the title of Pro-Director when the Deputy Director assumed office. In September 1990, following a national advertisement and interviews, Peter Mortimore, Professor of Educational Research and Director of the University of Lancaster School of Education since 1988, became Deputy Director. Mortimore had previously worked for ILEA: as Director of Research and Statistics, 1979–85, and as Assistant Education Officer (Secondary), 1985–8. His budget in the latter post had been some £400 million per annum; the total Institute budget for 1989–90 was £15.5 million.

## The Charter

Considerable delays had occurred in securing a charter that would guarantee the Institute's status as an independent school of the University. In 1980 when a joint petition from Institute and University was submitted to the Privy Council, approval was withheld over the issue of academic tenure. In October 1983 Lawton was in direct communication with Sir Keith Joseph, Secretary of State for Education and Science, but to no avail. It appeared that the Institute was being singled out for unfavourable treatment. No similar clause allowing for dismissal other than for 'good cause' had been required either in the new charter for the University of Ulster or as a condition of the private bills for the recent amalgamation of schools of the University of London. In August 1985, however, the Deputy Clerk to the Privy Council informed the Institute's solicitors that the government now intended 'to

impose its policy in this area through legislation, and this means that the focal point of the controversy has, for now, moved away from the Charter giving process'.[28] In January 1987 the Privy Council accepted the restriction of dismissal to 'good cause'.[29] On 10 June 1987 the Queen in Council approved the 'grant of a Charter of Incorporation constituting a University College by the name and style of Institute of Education, University of London'. Alternative names had been considered along the way, and much attention paid to resultant acronyms. For example, a proposal for the London Institute of Educational Studies was firmly rejected and the Institute remained, as it had been since the days of Nunn, the I. of E. The Royal Charter, granted on 30 July 1987, admitted the Institute as a school of the University in the faculties of Education, Science and Economics from 1 August. It was formally presented to the Institute by the University's Chancellor, HRH The Princess Royal, at a ceremony held on Derby Day, 1 June 1988. The Charter declared that:

> The objects of the Institute shall be to promote for the public benefit learn-
> ing and research in all branches of knowledge, especially in Education and
> related fields, and to make available to the public the results of such research
> and to provide instruction, and to organise postgraduate courses of study in
> Education and related fields.

70. Pictured with Her Royal Highness, The Princess Royal, Chancellor of the University, at the Charter presentation ceremony in 1988 are (left to right) Brian Holmes, Garry Philpott (shaking hands), Norman Graves, David Warren and Denis Lawton

71. Wang Cheng-xu and Daphne Gould, who received Honorary Fellowships at the Institute's first presentation ceremony in 1993

The acquisition of a Royal Charter put the seal on the Institute's independence. Lord Flowers, the University's Vice-Chancellor, praised the Institute's contribution to education in the service of society as being 'both international and incalculable'. He also urged the Institute to demonstrate its newly independent status by upholding 'that critical function of a University – to question and test both received wisdom and new propositions – which itself appears to be under threat'.[30] An article in the *Times Educational Supplement* acknowledged that 'people at the Institute have done a lot to set the agenda'.[31] Nevertheless, in the very year of the Education Reform Act the renewed determination of the Conservative government to set the educational agenda of the present and future could not be in doubt.

The Charter produced significant changes in terms of status, finance and management. The Institute now had legal status – it could sue and be sued. It could own buildings, land and investments in its own name. Its former governing body, the Committee of Management, was replaced by a Council, which had final responsibility for all matters of policy and major decisions, although on academic matters its decisions were subject to 'consultations' with the Senate of the Institute. The Council was composed of three ex officio members, nine appointed members (four by the Senate of the University, two apiece by LEAs and teachers' organizations, and one by voluntary providing bodies) ten members elected by the Institute staff from among their number, two students elected by the whole student body and between ten and 12 co-opted persons. In the short term, many members of the Committee of Management, including the Chair and Vice-Chair, Sir John Ellis and E. Dunstan Roberts, continued to serve as members of the Council. Indeed, six of the seven persons immediately co-opted for a three-year period from October

1987, had been members of the former Committee. The one new co-option, Piotr Poloniecki, Managing Director of Midland Montague Asset Management, signalled the Council's increased concern with financial matters, including the direct management of its own investments.[32] Poloniecki was immediately appointed to the Council's new Investment Sub-Committee, falls on the stock market having reduced the value of the Institute's investments by £668,000 in the period between 31 July and 31 October 1987.[33]

Another new power was the right to award honorary fellowships and degrees. For many years Institute graduates had attended the massive and impersonal presentation ceremonies of the University of London held in the Royal Albert Hall. In 1991 the University agreed that schools should be allowed to organize their own ceremonies. The first Institute ceremony, held in the Logan Hall on 25 May 1993, saw 231 graduates presented. Honorary fellowships were conferred upon the former Director, Professor Lionel Elvin, Daphne Gould, former Head of Mulberry School in Tower Hamlets, and Professor Wang Cheng-xu, Director of the Comparative Education Centre at Hangzhou University in China, who had first studied at the Institute in 1938.[34] The Presentation Ceremony, held in subsequent years in March, immediately became the most important event in the Institute's calendar. PGCE students were included for presentation from 1994, and by 2001 numbers were such that it had become necessary to hold two ceremonies per year.

## The Library

In the mid-1980s the Institute Library was faced with a number of problems. The existing building in Ridgmount Street, separated by distance and culture from Bedford Way, was manifestly inadequate.[35] New concerns arose about the use of the Library by outsiders and there were anguished discussions about reciprocal borrowing rights and the necessity of charging fees for lending books 'to persons who are not members of a public body'.[36] In August 1986 the Librarian, Norman Beswick, retired to write books. Following a public advertisement, Gordon Brewer, Head of Learning Services at Bedford College of Higher Education, was appointed Librarian and took up his post in 1987. At this time the University was considering the construction of a joint library for the Institute, Birkbeck and Extra-Mural Studies. A feasibility study carried out for the University in the autumn of 1988, however, revealed that the cost of the Bedford Way wing block would now exceed £11 million.[37] Although the building of the joint library was 'currently the top building priority for the University',[38] in reality there was very little chance that the UGC would approve such a sum.

In memory of
Alan Dale
1914-1960
Biologist, teacher and author
Student at the Institute 1936-37

given by his daughter Dr Susan Dale Tunnicliffe
Student here 1967-68

and his grandson Alan Dale Tunnicliffe
Student here 1994-95
Co-president of the Student's
Union 1995-1996

**72. A desk plaque in the new Library records the names of three generations of Institute students**

Moreover there would be a gap of 36 months between any sanction of the project by the UGC and occupation by the Institute. It could not therefore be completed before the expiry of the lease on the Ridgmount Street building in March 1991.

Newsam was very doubtful about the viability of the University's proposal. Shortly after taking up the post of Director he telephoned the new Universities' Funding Council (UFC) and spoke to a former colleague. The advice he received made it 'immediately clear that they weren't going to fund the new wing for us, and that the University had been putting up schemes on our behalf which were quite impracticable'.[39] Newsam, therefore, decided that the Library project would have to be undertaken by the Institute for the Institute.[40] The wing block was rejected and plans for a more modest three-storey extension on the north-west side, corresponding to levels three, four and five of the Bedford Way building, drawn up. The Ridgmount Street premises were vacated in March 1991 and several areas within the Institute, including the Elvin and Jeffery Halls, adapted to provide temporary library accommodation. Even in this temporary and scattered state, however, it was noticeable that once the Library was in the main building usage increased by 30 per cent. The total cost of the project, some £5 million, was obtained from a variety of sources. These included £1 million from the University, £700,000 from the UFC and £520,000 from the ILEA and London Residuary Body. This last was on account of the transfer of ILEA library collections to the Institute. Other money came from savings from the ending of the Ridgmount Street lease and from the Institute's reserves. In July 1992 the new building was topped out with traditional hard-hatted ceremony. Newsam and the Chairman of Willmott Dixon Symes, the contractors, duly added red wine, salt and corn to the final mix of concrete. The University Chaplain blessed the proceedings.[41]

After some 22 years in the cramped surroundings of Ridgmount Street the new premises provided light and spacious accommodation, 'a comfortable environment for study, to a large extent insulated from the noise of Bedford Way traffic, yet located centrally within the Institute and readily accessible to its users'.[42] There were secure storage areas with temperature and humidity control for archives and special collections, and mobile shelving to maximize their capacity. A new Library and Media Services Department was created prior to the occupation of the new premises. Thus in addition to books, journals and a rapidly increasing range of special collections, the Library building also included workshops, a media suite and training room. The Newsam Library, as it became, was a great success, immediately acknowledged as the best education library in Europe.

## Students and courses

During the first half of this period there was little change in overall student numbers. In 1991–2, however, a dramatic increase occurred to 3,201 from the 2,679 of the previous year. This was achieved across the three main areas of the Institute's work.

Initial teacher education student numbers rose from 572 to 751; B.Ed. and diploma numbers from 669 to 848,[43] and those taking higher degrees from 1,234 to 1,365.[44] Even the 'other' category – which mainly included those on special and short courses – increased from 204 to 237. This upward trend continued in 1992–3 with a total of 3,725 students, of whom 2,184 were part-time. Once again there were large increases at initial and in-service levels: with 945 students on PGCE courses and 1,199 on B.Ed. and diploma. Higher degree numbers showed a more modest rise, to 1,396. Numbers in the 'other' category declined to 185.[45] The following year showed a relatively steady state overall. The similar total of 3,732, however, masked a decline of some 150 students at B.Ed. and diploma and a corresponding increase at higher degree level.[46] These numbers were complemented by a further 3,000–4,000 teachers, and others, who came to the Institute each year for short, non-award-bearing courses. In this period overseas student numbers were usually between 400 and 500, typically from around 80 countries.[47]

Although in the early 1990s there was a substantial growth in student recruitment, not least as a means of increasing income, the main emphasis in this period was on the nature and quality of courses – particularly at the level of initial training. The Institute PGCE course, in common with all others, was now required to meet the criteria laid down by government and administered by CATE. A plethora of documents, for example *Teaching in Schools: The Content of Initial Training*, 1983, the White Paper, *Teaching Quality* of the same year and DES Circular 3/84, *Initial Teacher Training: Approval of Courses*, 1984, indicated the government's determination to exercise much greater control over initial training.

The new secondary PGCE course began in October 1985 with some 540 students. Based upon a partnership between the Institute and London schools, emphasis was placed upon professional practice and the development of professional skills.[48] November 1986 saw visitations both from HMI and from the Education Sub-Committee of the UGC. Reams of documentation were required, particularly for the bevy of 28 HMI. In due course the Institute was informed that the several CATE criteria had been met and that its courses of initial professional training were officially recognized.[49] While both HMI and UGC reports were favourable overall, some concerns were expressed about 'too many small areas of activity', and the organization and staffing of the primary course.[50]

Aided by a grant of £100,000 from the University in acknowledgement of the need for extra resources for the PGCE, a new Child Development and Primary Education Department (CDPE) was established, with Audrey Curtis as its first chairperson. By 1988–9, when the primary PGCE course reached its target of 100 students, there was a core of six permanent and two temporary tutors. Two senior lecturers had special responsibilities for advanced work. Some smaller secondary PGCE courses were phased out.

Following two years of further research and negotiation with schools, a pilot area-based secondary PGCE course in the London borough of Camden was introduced in 1991. By this time, however, the government had moved to a much stronger commitment to school-based training. In November 1989 new CATE criteria were introduced. These laid down additional conditions in respect of such issues as local committees, length of teaching practice, time devoted to subject and professional studies, and use of information technology. CATE itself was reconstituted, although Taylor continued as its chairman. Two initiatives of 1989 were the Licensed Teacher and Articled Teacher schemes. The Licensed scheme enabled LEAs to employ mature people with two years of higher education as teachers and to provide appropriate training. Articled teachers would spend two years of training on a bursary, with four-fifths of the time in schools. The Institute provided an early course for some 20 articled teachers in partnership with the LEAs of Camden, Harrow and Islington.[51]

In January 1992, in a speech to the North of England Education Conference, the Secretary of State for Education, Kenneth Clarke, announced the introduction of yet another set of accreditation criteria and called for all PGCE students to spend four-fifths of their training year in schools. DES Circular 9/92, *Initial Teacher Training (Secondary Phase)*, however, required only two-thirds of the PGCE course to be school-based by 1994–5. Frequent changes in criteria generated a very considerable amount of work, for example the Institute had to establish and then modify partnership arrangements with some 180 schools and colleges.[52] Such changes also had important staffing and financial implications. From September 1992 the area-based secondary course was headed by a professor and senior tutor, with five area co-ordinators, 47 general tutors from the Institute and 26 part-time general tutors from the schools. The Institute agreed to pay each school £8,000 per part-time general tutor and £250 per student. At the same time administrative support for the PGCE office was strengthened both in terms of staffing and enhanced facilities.[53]

Further changes ensued. School-Centred Initial Teacher Training (SCITT), independent of higher education institutions, was introduced, and in September 1994 the Council for Teacher Education was replaced by a new controlling body, the Teacher Training Agency (TTA). This body was directly responsible to the Secretary of State, who had the power to nominate all of its members. The change in title from 'Education' to 'Training' was symbolic and was reflected in the general use of the term, Initial Teacher Training (ITT), in place of Initial Teacher Education (ITE). The new authority, indeed, was charged with securing 'a diversity of high quality and cost-effective initial training'.[54]

Some elements of government control over initial teacher education continued to grow – not least the very frequent inspection of courses by the Office for Standards in Education (Ofsted). By 1994, however, it was apparent that other initiatives had foundered. The 'Mums' Army' of teachers for nursery and infant schools, proposed in June 1993, was laughed out of court. The Licensed Teacher Scheme exhibited many weaknesses, and the Articled Teacher Scheme was brought to an end in 1994 on financial and other grounds.[55] An Ofsted report of 1995 showed that by most measures traditional PGCE training was superior to that carried out under the SCITT schemes.[56]

Nevertheless, by 1994 PGCE courses at the Institute, in common with those elsewhere, were very different from what they had been in 1983. For example, at the beginning of this period the basic secondary course consisted of five elements:

(i) general educational theory;

(ii) principles and methods of teaching a subject or groups of subjects, with some 20 courses on offer;

(iii) one foundation option chosen from comparative education, education in developing countries, health and welfare in schools, history of education, philosophy of education, psychology of education, sociology of education;

(iv) one curriculum option chosen from a list of some 22 which ranged from art in education to women's studies;

(v) practical training in teaching with a minimum of 50 days spent in schools.

Theoretical aspects were emphasized. Thus the prospectus for 1983–4 described principles and methods as 'The theoretical basis of methods of teaching a subject'; the foundation option as 'An opportunity to study to some depth an aspect of educational theory'; the curriculum option as 'The use of educational theory in elucidating a problem of the curriculum'.[57]

The prospectus for 1993–4 demonstrated the radical changes that had occurred. The term 'student' was now complemented by that of 'beginning teacher'. The introduction to the secondary area-based course, as it was now called, made no mention of theory, but much of the five area bases – central, east, north, south and west – 'The area provides the location within which students gain practical experience of schools'.[58] The three elements of the course were:

(i) curriculum subject teaching with some 15 courses definitely on offer. Two new courses in performing arts and design and technology were currently being developed but would be subject to accreditation by the Department for Education;

(ii) a single professional studies course in such topics as how children learn and the local and national provision of education. 'Much of the component is located in the area so that students can contextualize their studies within the variety of schools and broader educational provision in the area-base';[59]

(iii) practical training in teaching. The first two weeks of the course were spent in a primary school; in addition there were block practices in the autumn and spring terms, with at least three days per week in school prior to the teaching practices and during the summer term.

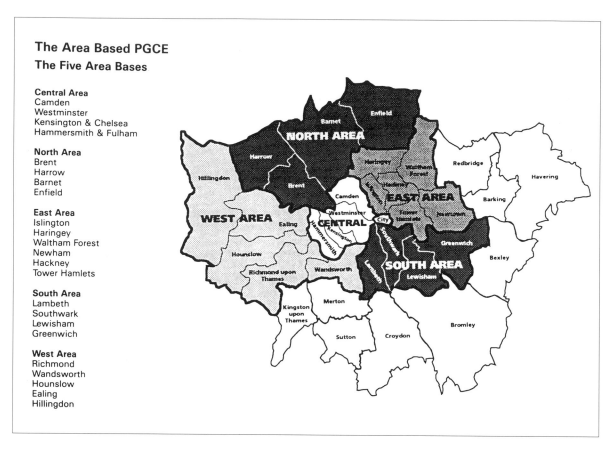

**The Area Based PGCE**
**The Five Area Bases**

**Central Area**
Camden
Westminster
Kensington & Chelsea
Hammersmith & Fulham

**North Area**
Brent
Harrow
Barnet
Enfield

**East Area**
Islington
Haringey
Waltham Forest
Newham
Hackney
Tower Hamlets

**South Area**
Lambeth
Southwark
Lewisham
Greenwich

**West Area**
Richmond
Wandsworth
Hounslow
Ealing
Hillingdon

73. A map of the area-based secondary PGCE course in the prospectus for 1993–4

These changes were shaped by a number of influences: the example of the Alternative Course, the concerns of students, teachers and Institute staff, the greater sense of responsibility for London schools in the aftermath of ILEA's demise, the CATE criteria. Additionally, by the end of this period the Institute had not only consolidated and enlarged its initial training of teachers for primary and secondary schools, it had also moved into the area of further and adult education. In 1993–4 there were 58 full-time students on the post-compulsory PGCE together with a further 30 taking a two-year, part-time course for the Further Education Teacher's Certificate.[60]

The Institute's B.Ed. degree course for serving teachers also underwent significant developments. Begun in 1981, it was assumed that the course would only be taken part-time, and in 1982–3 all 32 students fell into this category. In 1983–4, however, there were 14 full-time students in a total of 57, and 29 out of 69 in the following year. Regulations were amended to permit practising teachers from overseas with an approved teacher's certificate to sit qualifying examinations to gain entry to a two-year, full-time course. This route proved to be popular, not least with primary teachers from Hong Kong. In consequence a Part I course was taught in Hong Kong, with the first students taking their exams in the summer of 1993 and arriving as a group in September of that year to take the Part II at the Institute in 1993–4.[61]

General diploma and specialist diplomas and certificates also underwent considerable changes. In 1983–4 there were 69 full-time and 179 part-time students on the diploma in education course.[62] By 1991–2 there were only 10 full-time and 24 part-time.[63] The diploma suffered from the development of first degrees in education. Full-time recruitment to specialist diplomas also declined. As with the PGCE, in-service work demanded much closer co-operation with LEAs than hitherto and an INSET Advisory Committee with LEA representation was established early in 1987. Courses were created or modified to suit the training needs of LEAs. For example, a special arrangement was made with ILEA to retrain some staff to become teachers of English as a Second Language. Many courses at diploma levels were modularized, and complete modularization of Master's courses in accordance with the Universities Council for the Education of Teachers (UCET) 120 credit transfer scheme was achieved by the beginning of the 1992–3 session. The length of time for completion of courses was extended, and in some cases it was possible to combine periods of full- and part-time study. An INSET Office was established and Institute staff became more involved in advisory and consultancy work in LEAs, their schools and colleges.

Similar forces were at work at higher degree level. Although numbers on Master's and M.Phil. degrees increased, there was a decline in Ph.D. registrations. Some of this decline might be attributed to a greater emphasis upon initial registration at M.Phil. with subsequent transfer to Ph.D., but concerns were increased by the actions of the Economic and Social Research Council (ESRC). In 1985 the ESRC published a list of completion rates by ESRC-funded research students. Institutions in which fewer than 10 per cent of funded students had successfully completed their degrees within four years would be debarred from studentships in 1986 and 1987. According to the ESRC only one of the 15 students who had commenced at the Institute in 1979 and 1980 had completed within four years – a percentage of 6.66. Although the Institute was restored to the list, an error having been made in the calculations, much bad publicity occurred.[64] In a letter of February 1988 (by which date the Institute's four-year completion rate had been raised to 35 per cent) the ESRC advised all institutions of higher education that 'In future only the departments and doctoral programmes specifically recognised by ESRC will be eligible to receive ESRC-funded research students'. This advice highlighted the need to provide greater support for and monitoring of research students across the whole Institute. Students had become the responsibility of supervisors and their departments, and there was considerable variation in provision and practice.

General concerns about the provision for students led to the commissioning of a report by Michael Barber in 1993.[65] One of the major themes of his report was that the facilities of the Students' Union were totally inadequate. Its style and atmosphere were more suited to a provincial undergraduate college than to a metropolitan postgraduate institution, many of whose students, whether from home or overseas, were senior professionals.[66] Some improvements were made in respect of facilities and an adviser to students and an accommodation officer appointed. Student initiatives in this period included confrontations over racist incidents. Pressure on equal opportunities issues led to the appointment of a half-time equal opportunities officer. Statements of commitment to the promotion of anti-racism and of equal opportunities were included in the prospectus, and procedures for dealing with any future incidents drawn up. The nursery remained a focus of concern, and in 1985 1,000 students and staff signed a petition against its closure. In the following year an appeal was launched in the first number of the *Newsletter* of the Institute of Education Society (which by this date had more than 1,000 members) for funds 'to help us to become a Nursery that the Institute can be proud of!'[67]

An article by an American student on a year's sabbatical leave from a junior high school in Enfield, Connecticut in the same *Newsletter* provides an interesting viewpoint on the Institute of this period. Gail Kennedy, who was studying education in multi-cultural urban areas, was assigned to a tutor who offered home-brewed coffee, a reading list of 300 books to dip into, and an injunction to 'live London' and see all the art galleries, museums, exhibitions and theatres. In the first term she analysed theory and together with other full-time students was taken on cultural 'crawls' through the East End by another of their number, a former dock worker. The second term was spent in school visits, organized by Gill Hinson of the School Relations Office: 'a definite plus for the Institute – should be advertised in your brochure'. Other features of Institute life to receive special commendation included 'THIS WEEK, the local Institute gossip sheet published each Thursday … I fill my diary only after reading about the lectures, seminars, films, discussions, art exhibits, concerts and demonstrations listed in THIS WEEK', and the mix of full- and part-time students in evening lectures, which led to more invitations to visit schools and introductions to community workers. Kennedy left the Institute 'wishing I had another year to study. I'd attend more short courses. I'd become involved with the Multicultural Centre … I would make the library more accessible'.[68] Other students took the opportunity of the Charter presentation in 1988 to record their appreciation and gratitude: 'I have found it an extremely stimulating and happy two-and-a-half years', wrote one Ph.D. student. Another declared that 'the moment I walked into the Institute building the intellectual excitement always returned'. A mature primary PGCE student, a solicitor for 12 years, recorded that 'the course was everything I hoped it would be. I had a marvellous tutor and there was a very experienced group organizing it.' Even Kenneth Baker, a Secretary of State for Education and Science with whom the Institute did not always see eye to eye, took 'this opportunity to thank the Institute for all it has achieved in the past and to wish it well for the future'.[69]

## Staff and structures

Academic staff numbers in 1983–4 were recorded as 16 professors, five readers, 32 senior lecturers, 90 lecturers and 50 research staff – a total of 193.[70] In 1993–4 the total of 265 academic staff comprised 20 professors, 11 readers, 44 senior lecturers, 111 lecturers and 79 research staff.[71]

Professorial appointments in 1984 included Celia Hoyles in Mathematics Education and Gareth Williams in Educational Administration. Hoyles soon became a national figure and the *Daily Mirror* reported that her television programme on mathematics, 'Fun and Games', attracted some ten million viewers and had toppled Terry Wogan in the ratings. Hoyles was hailed as being as 'natural in front of a TV camera as she is tangling with tangents and trigonometry'.[72] The same year saw the resignation of Peter Williams from EDC to become Director of the Education programme of the Commonwealth Secretariat, and the retirements from full-time employment of Mark Blaug, Colin Hindley and Harold Rosen.[73] In the following year, 1985–6, Michael Stubbs was appointed Professor of Education with special reference to the teaching of English in succession to Rosen, to be succeeded in turn by Gunther Kress in 1991. Guy Neave succeeded Holmes as Professor of Comparative Education and in 1987 Angela Little was appointed to the vacant chair in Education in Developing Countries. In 1985 Malcolm Skilbeck resigned from his chair in Curriculum Studies to take up the post of Vice-Chancellor of Deakin University in Australia.[74]

One notable retirement of 1986 was that of Tom White, who had been an attendant only since 1976, but was probably the best-known and respected member of Institute staff.[75] His smiling presence and words of encouragement and advice from the reception desk on level four brightened the days of staff and students alike. The inclusion of the notice of his retirement in the *Report of Activities 1981–1986*, and in the first issue of the *Institute of Education Society Newsletter* were indications of the affection and respect in which he was held.

74. Tom White, 'a very special person, giving warmth, friendship and a willing hand to everyone he met'

His retirement was short-lived, but his funeral on 28 October 1987 was a memorable occasion, with family and Institute mourners overflowing the country church at West Kingsdown in Kent. White's picture and obituary notice appeared in the *Institute of Education Society Newsletter* for March 1988 alongside those of two former secretaries of the Institute, Grace Wacey and Willis Dixon, and of Sir Douglas (Jock) Logan, former Principal of the University. It was an appropriate tribute to 'a very special person, giving warmth, friendship and a willing hand to everyone he met'.[76]

Two of the retirements of this period, those of Holmes and Bernstein, typified the achievements (and passing) of an era. Both had made considerable contributions to the development of the Institute – not least as Pro-Directors in their concluding years – and to the very creation of their respective disciplines of education. Holmes, who retired as Professor of Comparative Education in 1985, and died in 1993, was well described as 'a friend of great generosity and kindness … a tough and rough university politician … a brilliant seminar leader and a dedicated supervisor'.[77] His capacity for work was unbounded. A member of 33 committees of the Institute and of the University at the time of his retirement, Holmes's subsequent roles included service as Dean of the College of Preceptors. He joined the Institute of Education Society in 1982, the year after its foundation, succeeded Norman Graves as its third president in 1985 and edited the Society's *Newsletter* from 1986 until his death.

Bernstein, who retired as Karl Mannheim Professor of Sociology in 1990, enjoyed a similar reputation as a supervisor of doctoral students, both home and overseas. By his personal example and in his role as Pro-Director, Bernstein 'more than anyone else helped to transform the Institute's research activities and had a permanent effect on the research culture of the Institute'.[78] Two of his former students, Denis Lawton and Geoff Whitty, became Director. Edited volumes, both about and for Bernstein, indicated the extent of his influence and reputation.[79] For example, Alan Sadovnik argued that for more than three decades Bernstein's work was 'acknowledged internationally as among the finest attempts to construct a systematic theory of school and society', and had 'influenced a generation of sociologists of education and linguists'.[80] Nevertheless Sadovnik also noted that with Bernstein's retirement Sociology of Education had disappeared as a separate department. Bernstein died in 2000. In January 2001 a celebration of his life held at the Institute was attended by scholars from around the world.[81]

Another Pro-Directorial retirement in 1990 was that of Graves, whose national and international reputation in geography education was second to none.[82] There was no professorial replacement and the named chair was left unfilled. In contrast, following the retirement of Professor Barbara Tizard who had been Director of the Thomas Coram Research Unit since 1979, Professor Harry McGurk was appointed in her stead. In this period the TCRU often accounted for between 45 and 50 per cent of the Institute's income for funded research.[83]

New appointments to academic staff indicated continuity, change, and a further strengthening of the London connection. In 1992 Professor Geoff Whitty from Goldsmiths' College succeeded to the post of Karl Mannheim Professor of the Sociology of Education. This chair was now situated within the Department of Policy Studies. In the same year Desmond Nuttall was appointed Professor of Curriculum and Assessment Studies. Nuttall came from a post at the London School of Economics and, like Mortimore, had previously been Director of Research and Statistics at the ILEA. His tragic early death in the following year was a severe blow.[84] Michael Barnett came from Imperial College, London to be the Institute's first Professor of Technology and Education. Two appointments of former inspectors indicated the Institute's increasing concern with quality and external audit. In 1990 Barbara MacGilchrist, Chief Inspector of ILEA, was appointed Head of the Institute's INSET Department. In the following year Eric Bolton, recently retired from the post of Her Majesty's Senior Chief Inspector, was appointed Professor of Teacher Education. In 1994, following Bolton's retirement and the restructuring consequent upon Peter Mortimore's appointment as Director, MacGilchrist was appointed Dean of Initial Teacher Education.

As the figures given at the start of this section demonstrate, a significant number of Institute staff were now employed on funded research work. Some academic and administrative colleagues who daily coped with a multiplicity of tasks and interactions no doubt envied the researchers' role. Concentration upon one project, the opportunity to research, reflect and write, might represent the world they had lost. For many researchers, however, whether members of a large research group such as TCRU or working in a department or centre, there were different problems. First among these were the limited contracts of employment, which depended upon the length of grants. Others included low pay and a sense of isolation and exclusion from many aspects of university life. In 1988 Bernstein chaired a working party on the staff development of funded research staff. The report drew attention to 'the assumption that the funded researcher will be "here today and gone tomorrow or next week"'. Its recommendations provided a basis for 'The integration of the researcher into the general academic and administrative functions of the Institute'.[85] Some progress was made in this direction, for example by the provision of bridging money between grants and entitlement to study leave. From September 1990 four half-time research lectureships were made available to funded research staff.[86] Although in 1998 Professor Ann Oakley, Director of the Social Science Research Unit (SSRU), still described contract research as 'the undervalued bread and butter of knowledge development',[87] by this date the Institute was acknowledged as an example of good practice in its provision for research staff.

Some elements in the academic and administrative restructuring of the Institute in this period – the introduction of Pro-Directors under Lawton, and their replacement by a Deputy Director under Newsam – have been considered in previous sections. Other academic and administrative dimensions are considered here. In this period there was some re-ordering of academic departments and centres. No clear pattern emerged, however, as three potentially contradictory forces were at work. The first was a longstanding concern – previously expressed in the divisional structure – to reduce the number and increase the size of departments. The second was a wish, reflected in the growth of centres, to develop academic groupings that better reflected contemporary professional and academic concerns. The third was a desire to reduce the power of departments and of some of the 'feudal barons' at their heads, and to produce a more homogeneous academic culture across the whole Institute.

By 1993–4 there were 14 academic departments. Two large amalgamations were the Department of Policy Studies and the Department of History, Humanities and Philosophy.[88] Smaller mergers produced the Department of International and Comparative Education and the Department of Economics, Geography and Business Education. One important de-merger took place. The former Department of Child Development and Educational Psychology (CDEP) separated into Child Development and Primary Education (CDPE), led by Professor Kathy Sylva, and Educational Psychology and Special Needs (EPSEN) headed by Professor Klaus Wedell.

Although the number of departments was reduced, centres and units continued to multiply. The Post 16 Education Centre was established in 1984 with a remit to develop the Institute's activities in the field of 16–19 education. Co-ordination across the Institute and grants from the Department of Employment were soon accompanied by a teaching role. An MA in Vocational Education and Training was launched in 1989, a Further Education Teacher's Certificate in 1991 and a PGCE course in 1993.[89] Academic initiatives grants from the University of London were used to establish the Centre for Higher Education Studies (CHES) in 1987[90] and the Centre for Educational Evaluation in 1989. The latter's role was to provide independent evaluation of national curriculum and assessment initiatives. This centre was based in the Curriculum Studies Department but was complemented by the International Centre for Research on Assessment (ICRA) which had a cross-departmental character. The Education Management Unit (EMU) was formed in 1985 to design and deliver management development programmes for LEAs and schools and to provide courses and consultancy services.[91]

Whatever their origins, most centres and units, old and new, soon found themselves involved both in research and teaching. In contrast the SSRU, established in October 1990 and directed from 1991 by Professor Ann Oakley, concentrated upon research. While providing some consultancy, research training and seminars, SSRU's primary concern was to undertake funded research in the fields of education and health. In 1993 Mortimore identified SSRU and TCRU as the Institute's 'two specialist research units'.[92] Oakley, who had been Deputy Director of TCRU since 1985, gained an outstanding reputation for her research and writing in respect of the position of women, gender differences, the family and health. Oakley's doctoral research into contemporary attitudes towards housework, the history of the housewife's role in industrial society and the ideologies framed to support it led to major publications, including *Housewife*, first published in 1974,[93] and some notoriety.[94] Other volumes, for example *Man and Wife*, a memoir of her parents, Kay and Richard Titmuss, novels, including *The Men's Room*, which became the basis for a television series, and *Overheads*, extended her reputation into an even wider world.[95]

In October 1988 Eric Earle took early retirement from his post as Secretary. Over a period of 24 years at the Institute, he had seen 'the whole business of university administration become vastly more complex' while in recent years 'resources have been regularly reduced'.[96] Earle would continue to have strong links with the Institute, working initially for two days a week on such matters as fund-raising, the development of an alumni organization and external relations. Nevertheless, the post of Secretary was abolished, with net savings of £30,000 per annum, and administrative departments and sections were grouped in two broad divisions. One was headed by David Warren, with the title of Secretary and Registrar; the other by Garry Philpott as Financial Secretary. Warren's role and status were much enhanced. His responsibilities included the administration of academic matters and of the material facilities provided by the Institute for its staff and students.[97] His was the senior post, even though at this time the Registry had some six members of staff; the Finance Department, 15. The work of the latter was divided into three broad areas: financial management, accounting and payments. The cosmopolitan composition of the Finance Department was frequently noted: four of its members had been born in the United Kingdom, four in Africa, two each in Eire and Pakistan, and one apiece in Australia, India and Mauritius.[98] Two new posts were established. The first, for research administration, reflected the Institute's growing dependence upon external research funding and the importance of the research selectivity exercises. The second, for planning and information, was in recognition of the need to provide data for a variety of purposes, both for external audit and for internal use. Jane Perry was appointed to the research post and Michael McGarvie to that of planning.

From 1994, when the post of Deputy Director was abolished, Warren frequently deputised for Mortimore, for example, by chairing meetings of heads of groups, and most notably when the Director took study leave in the summer term of 1999. In 1993 an external review of the Registry led to its re-constitution as the Student Programmes Office. In January 1994 Dr Loreto Loughran was appointed as head of this office; she reported directly to Warren. The illogicality of having a Secretary and Registrar but no Registry led to further changes in Warren's title – first to that of Secretary and Head of Academic Services and then simply to that of Secretary. In May 1999 the Student Programmes Office absorbed the International Development Unit and reverted to its former title of Registry. Loughran assumed the title of Academic Registrar.

## Quality audit

This period saw the extension of the term and practice of 'audit' from financial matters to the whole Institute enterprise. Academic staff were appraised in terms of their research, publications and teaching; courses were subject to accreditation; the performance of administrative departments was regularly reviewed.

Financial constraints continued. In 1985 the UGC asked all universities to plan for possible cuts in grant of 2 per cent per annum for the rest of the decade.[99] The Institute continued its programme of economies: encouraging academic and academic-related administrative staff to take early retirement or voluntary redundancy, cutting the allocation of secretarial staff and reducing departmental grants by 25 per cent. In 1986–7 the UGC grant allocation was scheduled to increase: as a result of more money for PGCE, a recognition of the part-time and postgraduate nature of the majority of Institute students and of the Institute's 'outstanding' rating in the research assessment exercise of the previous year. Application of various 'safety nets' and 'ceilings', however, meant that in real terms the grant remained at about the level of the previous year. The 1987–8 grant of £5,301,000 represented an increase of 10 per cent, the maximum permitted, over the previous year, with substantial increases of 19.7 and 16.1 per cent indicated for the next two years.[100] These hopes were to be dashed. The Court subjected the grants for 1988–9 and 1990–1 to a 'ceiling' of 8.5 per cent in order to ensure that no school of the University received a reduction in grant. Central funding mechanisms were in a perpetual state of flux. The UGC was replaced, first by the UFC and then from 1993, with the abolition of the binary line between universities and polytechnics, by the Higher Education Funding Council for England (HEFCE).

During this period the Institute's leading position in educational research was confirmed in three separate research exercises. In 1986 it was rated as outstanding in its research work and received a top grade on a four-point scale. In 1989 the Institute achieved the top grade on a five-point scale. This showed that the majority of Institute departments carried out research of international distinction and that the research of all departments was of national significance. The rating also reflected the level of funded research, which had risen from £0.7 million in 1983–4 to £2.1 million in 1987–8, and an increase in Ph.D. completion rates over the same period by 44 per cent.[101] In 1992 the Institute was again awarded the top grade of 5A with no fewer than 97.5 per cent of its staff designated as research active. In consequence HEFCE forecast that the research element in the Institute's grant for 1993–4 would show an increase of £1.5 million over the previous year. Nevertheless, in spite of this forecast and unofficial encouragement for the Institute to maintain rather than increase its student numbers and concentrate upon research, even the research element in the grant was reduced by more than £570,000.

| Table 11 Funding Council Research Allocation[102] | | |
|---|---|---|
| 1992–93 | 1993–94 | |
| Actual | HEFCE Forecast | Actual |
| £4,453K | £5,801K | £3,878K |

Details of the HEFCE grant for 1993–4 were received on 25 February 1993. On the same day the Institute also received a copy of a letter from HEFCE to Professor Stewart Sutherland, the Vice-Chancellor. This expressed concern 'that the impact upon the Institute of Education will be serious' and requested a meeting to discuss how 'to maintain the financial viability of the Institute'![103] The reduction in the Institute's research grant, in spite of its top rating, had occurred because former polytechnics and colleges were included in this third exercise and funds were being distributed more widely.

In addition to the various inspections of the PGCE course which occurred throughout this period, in May 1993 the Institute also received a visit from the Higher Education Quality Audit team, led by its Director, Peter Williams. The report, 'one of the most complimentary yet issued by the Quality Audit Team',[104] congratulated the Institute on its quality audit structures. Amongst other features particular mention was made of the high degree of commitment and leadership, the standard of the PGCE, and the responsiveness of the INSET Department. On the other hand, it was suggested that the Institute might also wish to consider, among other elements, 'reviewing the apparently great variability in services and facilities available to students of different departments' and 'establishing an effective institutional focus, both academic and social, for the body of research students'. These comments reinforced other suggestions for further reform of the departmental structure and better provision for higher degree students, particularly those from overseas.[105]

Some elements in the quality of education at the Institute at this time, elements of culture and of service, were less susceptible to external audit, but continued to flourish and to provide a breadth of experiences for students and staff alike. For example, the Arts Centre, which played a prominent role in the life of the Institute at this time, encouraged all members of the Institute community to organize and participate in cultural ventures, including art, dance, drama, film, music and theatre arts. Lunchtime concerts took place in the Logan Hall, while the two Bloomsbury Galleries at the Bedford Way entrance, and the Dixon Gallery on the Woburn Square side, provided ample space for visual display.[106] Thus in 1985–6 two important exhibitions from overseas were mounted. The first was a collection of contemporary Czech glass in architecture; the second, an exhibition of Norwegian drawings, opened by Crown Princess Sonja. In October 1990 one particularly moving exhibition of photographs and paintings demonstrated the work of Child to-Child, the movement jointly founded in 1978 by the Institute of Education and the Institute of Child Health to promote health education amongst children in developing countries.[107] Another fundraising event was a picture fair held in November 1986 in aid of the Southern African Scholarship Fund. More than one hundred works, donated free, were exhibited in the Dixon Gallery. Participants purchased a ticket, price £50, and in return chose a work of art according to the order in which the ticket numbers came up in the draw. Star attractions included a Goya etching and a watercolour by Sir Hugh Casson. Nearly 90 tickets were sold and some £4,500 raised for the Fund.[108] A second fair was held in May 1990. The Art Department, as represented by Bill Newland and Alfred Harris, was naturally to the fore in these artistic ventures.

## Conclusion

Survival was the paramount concern of this period and Lawton and Newsam showed great skill in steering the Institute through a series of political and financial minefields. Both adopted a cautious and constructive approach in responding to press articles, even when faced with extreme provocation. For example, in 1991 an article in the *Daily Telegraph* by John Clare referred to Taylor as 'an apologist for wishy-washy teaching', Lawton as 'the chief peddler of "progressive" theories' and 'the pervasive influence of the Institute of Education as the most pernicious of all'.[109] Nevertheless Newsam's main complaint was neither against the press nor central government, but against its funding agencies. For example, in 1993 the Institute received 46 circulars from HEFCE, was asked to respond to nine consultative documents and to digest three reports.[110] Yet HEFCE's advice to concentrate upon research and the Institute's success in the third research exercise were followed by a substantial reduction in research funding in 1993–4. Not only were government-directed changes in initial training generally under-resourced, the Institute regularly received some £500 less for each PGCE student than any other institution in the London area.[111]

While survival was the main priority, notable advances were also achieved in this period. In 1988, after many years of delay, the Institute's status and independence were enhanced by the grant of a Royal Charter. Five years later it acquired the equally long-awaited Library. Ties with London, which had gradually weakened since 1932, were strengthened by new partnership arrangements with LEAs and schools. Such partnerships were prompted by reforms in the initial and in-service education and training of teachers that proceeded from both Institute and government initiatives. The process was facilitated by the recruitment to key positions of former ILEA staff such as Newsam, Mortimore and MacGilchrist. These staff, whose previous professional experience had been spent largely or even wholly outside the realms of higher education, brought new and important perspectives to bear on the changing relationship between autonomy and accountability.

In March 1991 these changes were well summarized by Newsam in a report to Council when he maintained that 'We have to achieve a cultural shift within the Institute'.[112] As he argued, although in the future the Institute would still be responsible for admitting, examining and passing judgements on students, increasingly those students, and outside bodies, including government and its funding agencies, would be passing judgement on the Institute. In a highly competitive situation neither the Institute, nor any other higher education institution, could afford to rely upon its former reputation. The position of the Institute could not be taken for granted; 'it has constantly to be re-earned'.[113] In this period that position was regularly re-earned: as demonstrated on the one hand by the Royal Charter, the renewed partnership with London and improved facilities, most notably the Library, and on the other by outstanding research ratings and increases in student numbers.

Chapter 11

# Into a new century
## 1994–2002

### Introduction

In May 1997, after 18 years of Conservative rule, a Labour government headed by Tony Blair came to power. David Blunkett replaced Gillian Shephard as Secretary of State for Education and Employment. One former and one current member of the Institute's staff were appointed to office. Tessa Blackstone, Professor of Educational Administration, 1978–83, became Minister of State for Higher and Further Education. Michael Barber, Dean of New Initiatives since 1995, was seconded to the Department for Education and Employment (DfEE) as head of the Standards and Effectiveness Unit.[1] Many things were expected of the new government, including, not unnaturally, a closer working relationship with the Institute. Some Conservative policies, for example grant maintained status for schools that had opted out of LEA control and assisted places in fee-paying schools, were rescinded. New Labour initiatives included increasing emphasis upon raising standards of attainment in schools, a commitment to life-long learning and the establishment of a General Teaching Council. There were also continuities with former policies. The spate of central directives on education increased; Chris Woodhead, the highly controversial Chief Inspector, remained in post.

Central direction of teacher training had been strengthened in September 1994 when the Council for the Accreditation of Teacher Education (CATE) was replaced by the Teacher Training Agency (TTA). The TTA moved to establish a national curriculum for initial teacher training. At a time of economic prosperity and low unemployment, however, recruitment of students to courses of initial training became increasingly problematic. The *Times Educational Supplement* was swollen to unmanageable size by countless pages of job vacancies, including headteacher posts. TTA campaigns led to some imaginative advertisements, but few new recruits. Desperate situations resulted in desperate measures, and from September 2000 every student on a PGCE course was guaranteed a £6,000 training 'salary'.

75. Tessa Blackstone, former Professor of Educational Administration, who was appointed Minister of State for Higher and Further Education in 1997

Those training for shortage subjects – design and technology, information technology, mathematics, modern foreign languages or science – would receive a further £4,000 'Golden Hello' on commencing their second year of teaching. Shortage of recruits was accompanied by a massive wastage rate. For example, national statistics showed that a third of those who qualified to teach in secondary schools in 1998 and a quarter of primary trainees were not in teaching posts by the end of the school year in 1999.[2] The introduction of performance-related pay from September 2000, designed in part to counter such wastage, provoked industrial action and legal challenges from the teacher unions.

## Peter Mortimore

In 1994 Peter Mortimore succeeded Newsam as Director. Mortimore brought a wide variety of experiences to the post. A teacher's certificate at St Mary's College, London in 1964 had been followed by nine years of music teaching in ILEA schools in Brixton and Camberwell. He also acquired three University of London degrees in psychology – a B.Sc. from Birkbeck, an M.Sc. from the Institute of Education and a Ph.D. from the Institute of Psychiatry, where his supervisors were Michael Rutter and the Institute of Education's Jack Tizard. After three years as a research officer at the Institute of Psychiatry, Mortimore served for a year as a member of HMI, 1978–9. For the next six years he was Director of Research and Statistics at the ILEA, followed by a further three as Assistant Education Officer (Secondary). During the two years prior to 1990 he was Professor of Educational Research and Director of the School of Education at the University of Lancaster.

Mortimore enjoyed an international reputation as a researcher and author, particularly in the area of school effectiveness and school improvement.[3] Two of his most important books were co-authored with his wife, Jo Mortimore.[4] He was a high profile, hands-on director. A year after his appointment an article in the *Times Educational Supplement* described him as 'cutting an intellectual dash ... and a sartorial one too', and as 'ambitious in all senses of the word. He wants to improve himself, improve his Institute, improve education in Britain.'[5] Mortimore led by example, as when giving an inaugural lecture in February 1995. He tried to preserve two days each week – Thursdays and Sundays – to engage in his own research and writing. He promoted a culture of excellence, and members of academic staff without a Ph.D. were encouraged to acquire one. In the six years of his directorship some 25 people were appointed to established or conferred chairs within the Institute and a further 11 to readerships. In addition, nine Institute staff (eight of them women) were appointed to chairs in other universities. Mortimore also fostered the Institute's sense of community. He knew everyone by name and one of his prime functions in the Lawton Room, which he regularly visited, was to introduce staff, some of them with many years' service, to each other. Mortimore's University standing was indicated by his appointment as Pro-Vice-Chancellor; his position in the education research community by service as president of the British Educational Research Association (BERA).

Mortimore's intimate knowledge of London and of its schools – as parent, teacher and administrator – enabled him to continue that rapprochement between the capital and the Institute begun under his predecessor. In common with Newsam, Mortimore also sought at first to steer a cautious political course. In 1993 he was awarded an OBE, and established good relationships with Gillian Shephard. Nevertheless, Mortimore warmly welcomed the Labour election victory of 1997, sanctioned Barber's secondment to the DfEE and looked forward to a more sensitive approach to educational reform based upon research. Initial signs were promising. In the 1998 New Year's Honours list Patricia Collarbone, Director of the London Leadership Centre, and Tamsyn Imison, Head of Hampstead School and a member of the Institute's Council, were created dame. Rita Donaghy, the Permanent Officer of the Students' Union, was awarded an OBE.

Those hopes were not to be realised. In the later years of his Directorship Mortimore became increasingly involved in public controversy. Mortimore's opposition to the use of school league tables which took little or no account of pupil intake, and to the policy of 'naming and shaming', won support from many teachers, but was less popular with politicians and civil servants. Mortimore was the leading British advocate of the theme that schools matter. In 1998 he published a major volume, a compilation of the fruits of more than 20 years of research entitled *The Road to Improvement: Reflections on school effectiveness*. While repeating his message that schools could make a difference, however, Mortimore warned policy makers to 'desist from claiming that school improvement – by itself and in the absence of extra resources – can solve all the problems. While this might be true in "advantaged" schools, it is certainly not true in disadvantaged situations.'[6] The book was criticized by columnists such as Melanie Phillips, who accused

76. Peter Mortimore (seated centre) and Caroline Gipps (seated left) with a group of M.Phil. and Ph.D. graduates, including Jo Mortimore (standing far left) at the presentation ceremony in 1998

Mortimore of failing to accept the significance of his own research and also took the opportunity of launching a general attack upon the Institute.[7]

Mortimore was also involved in disputes with the Chief Inspector, Chris Woodhead, over the quality of research conducted by the Office for Standards in Education and over the nature and frequency of inspections in schools and departments of education. For example, an Ofsted report on reading in three London boroughs, published in 1996, was cited by Woodhead as evidence 'that much teaching is "mediocre and weak"'. In reply Mortimore and Goldstein argued that none of the report's conclusions was supported by the evidence, and that 'Using the data underpinning this report to blame teachers ... is quite unjustified'.[8] Mortimore's most public confrontation, however, was with the Secretary of State. On the evening of 26 January 1999 a debate took place in the Logan Hall between Blunkett and Mortimore on the issue of the government's Green Paper, *Teachers: Meeting the Challenge of Change*.[9] David Blunkett commended his proposals for performance related pay. There would be extra money for the best teachers in order to retain them in the classroom. Peter Mortimore emphasized the collegial nature of good schools and the need to provide adequate pay for all teachers. The Director's comments and replies to questions were received with applause by an audience which included teachers, governors, trade unionists and parents, in addition to members of the Institute. The Secretary of State was subjected to some hostility and abuse. The event did little for the promotion of harmonious relationships between the DfEE and the Institute.[10]

In 1999 Peter Mortimore's appointment for a further five-year term as Director was confirmed. On 15 December, however, he announced to the Council his intention to retire from the post of Director in the summer of 2000. In a letter to all staff and to the co-presidents of the Students' Union Mortimore adduced a recent 'serious health scare' and his wife's health problems as one explanation for this decision. Others included a wish after 10 years of service to the Institute to make way for new blood, and to devote more time to other activities.[11]

## The matrix

In the previous chapter attention was drawn to the growth of quality audit procedures and to changes in the nature and numbers of departments and centres. Newsam had argued that the position of the Institute had constantly to be re-earned. This prompted the question – how should the Institute best be organized to enable this process to take place? The question was sharpened by successive reductions in funding for higher education over 15 years; a process euphemistically described as 'making efficiency gains'. Restructuring became the order of the day.

Mortimore took the lead in this process. In 1988 on moving from ILEA to Lancaster University he had been struck by the emphasis in academic life on the individual as opposed to the team. On taking up the post of Deputy Director in 1990 he noted the great variety and variability of cultures within the Institute, not least in respect of research, his own particular area of expertise and responsibility. During the academic year 1993–4 a working party, established by the Institute's Academic Board and chaired by Mortimore, met on 18 occasions. Its tasks were to clarify the Institute's mission statement; to consider and evaluate alternative structures; to consult widely and to make proposals for reform. Following nine open meetings and eight informal workshops, a matrix structure was adopted. The post of Deputy Director was abolished, as were the existing departments, Senate boards and resource mechanisms.

The new structure had four Institute-wide programmes on one side of the matrix. These were designed to cover the Institute's major activities: initial teacher education; professional courses, including non-award bearing courses, certificates, diplomas, Associateship, B.Ed. and Master's degrees; research, both personal and funded, research training and supervision; new initiatives both at home and overseas. Each programme area would be a major cost centre and would be led by a Dean who would have overall responsibility for the programme area. The Dean would also chair the programme board and report to Senate. Deans would be appointed by a committee comprising Senate and Council members and chaired by the Director. They would serve for four-year periods and receive an additional salary of £7,000 per annum. They would be expected to devote some 60 per cent of their time to the role of Dean.

The other axis would consist of academic groups; the term 'department' having been proscribed. These groups would provide a home base for academic and research staff. Groups would be accounting, but not cost centres, and heads of group would receive no additional remuneration. Heads of group, who would be appointed for three years with the possibility of renewal, would have overall responsibility for the work and pastoral care of those in the group. A Planning and Resources Committee (PRC) would provide overall management and co-ordination. The PRC, chaired by the Director, comprised the four Deans, three heads of academic groups elected by Senate, the Secretary and Registrar and the Financial Secretary. Its terms of reference were to advise the Director on a range of issues, including the allocation of resources, academic developments and income generation, and responses to requests from external bodies. A new resource allocation model (RAM) would be devised.[12]

The matrix structure was implemented during 1994–5. In the summer of 1994 two Deans were appointed: Dr Barbara MacGilchrist for initial teacher education and Professor Caroline Gipps for research. Acting Deans were chosen for the other two areas: Dr Ronald Barnett for professional development and James Porter for new initiatives. Barnett's post was confirmed in 1995.[13] Following Porter's retirement in the summer of that year Michael Barber, formerly head of the education and equal opportunities department of the National Union of Teachers (NUT), and Professor of Education at Keele University from 1993, became Dean of New Initiatives. Original guidance on the size of group was liberally interpreted. By the year 2000 there were 20 academic groups.[14]

These groups were broadly as formed in 1995. Nevertheless, movement by individuals and sections between groups did occur and new centres were established. One major change in 1995–6 was the merger between English for Speakers of Other Languages and Modern Foreign Languages to form Languages in Education. In 1995 the largest academic group was Policy Studies. Four years later, staff in the Post 16 Education Centre and the Centre for Higher Education Studies seceded from Policy Studies to form a new group, Lifelong Learning. The London Leadership Centre, directed by Patricia Collarbone, was established in January 1997 as the result of a joint initiative by the Institute, the Government Office for London and the business community. Its purpose was to promote the leadership skills, intellectual growth and overall effectiveness of headteachers and school governors. In addition to providing a programme of conferences, seminars and workshops, the Centre was also home to the London Regional Community Assessment Centre for the National Professional Qualification for Headship (NPQH).[15] One significant arrival was that of the Centre for Longitudinal Studies (CLS) in October 1998. Headed by Professor John Bynner, and previously located at the City University, the CLS was responsible for the National Child Development Study (1958 cohort) and for the 1970 British Cohort Study.

The final element in restructuring was the academic staffing resource allocation model (RAM). The purpose of the RAM was to ensure that resources were used in the most effective way and that work should be distributed equitably among staff, while reflecting individuals' differing responsibilities and levels of experience.[16] In the first model each full-time member of staff was given a target of 450 units of resource (URs) to accumulate during the year. URs could be earned by teaching, research, administration and publication. From 1996 a new academic information management system (AIMS) replaced the RAM. This provided a tariff of URs for each activity and notional totals of URs to be earned by staff in each grade. Thus a professor would be expected to generate considerably more URs than a lecturer. Although some concerns remained, the system provided an Institute-wide basis for measuring the relative output of individuals and of groups, and for making decisions about the allocation of staffing and other resources.

The matrix system did lead to more uniformity in terms of provision and practice. The system of URs made it possible to identify those members of staff whose commitment and output were insufficient or misplaced. Some academic and research staff found more opportunities for collaboration and success than under the previous departmental system. Each of the three major areas of the Institute – initial teacher education, professional studies and research – now had a champion and leader in the shape of a Dean. One Dean had specific responsibility for innovation, for ensuring that the Institute was at the forefront in educational developments. Unlike their predecessors, the Pro-Directors, the Deans had a more clearly defined role within the Institute, with membership of the PRC and budgetary responsibility for their programme areas. In contrast to the Pro-Directors, moreover, the first Deans were not usually appointed from the group of senior professors approaching retirement age. The post of Dean became a stepping stone to further advancement.[17]

Nevertheless there were problems. The new structure did not necessarily present a coherent picture either to students or to the outside world. The loss of the term, 'department', so widely used and understood in the academic world, was regretted. Heads of groups complained that they had little power and spent too much time in collecting and relaying information for management purposes. In spite of the increase in professorial appointments, the majority of heads of groups were not professors. This had significant effects upon the composition of Senate and of the PRC. In 2000–1 not one of the three heads of group on the PRC was of professorial rank. The AIMS system introduced a competitive element between individuals and groups and acted as a disincentive to collaboration. There was a perception that the matrix was increasingly becoming a pyramid, as more academic and administrative staff were appointed to the programme areas. By 2000 there were two Assistant Deans for initial teacher education, three for professional development and three for research.[18]

## Initial teacher education

In the first decade of its existence the majority of students of the London Day Training College had followed a course determined in large part by the Board of Education and inspected by HMI. By the middle of the twentieth century the control of courses and decisions about their content had passed to the Institute and to the University. By 2002, there had been a further change whereby the government now prescribed elements of a national curriculum for teacher training to complement the national curriculum in schools. Thus beginning teachers on the Institute's primary and secondary courses followed the national curriculum for teacher training in English, mathematics, science and information and communication technology. The measurement of the quality of these courses and of the progress of students was no longer left to the determination of the Institute and of the University. The Office for Standards in Education regularly sent teams of HMI to carry out detailed inspections. Subjects in the secondary course were inspected on a three-year cycle while the primary course was subjected to no fewer than three inspections in a space of five years.

The primary PGCE course, inspected by HMI in the autumn and summer terms of 1995–6, was awarded top grades in all four elements of the assessment. One member of the inspection team commented informally that the Institute's primary course was the best in the country. In consequence, the Chief Inspector's announcement in July 1996 that the Institute's primary course would be one of 20 to be re-inspected with specific reference to the teaching of reading and number work was greeted with anger and dismay. Characteristically, Mortimore led the campaign against this Primary Follow Up Survey (PFUS). The Institute's solicitors were instructed to ask the TTA whether the Chief Inspector was acting unreasonably in re-inspecting the primary PGCE.[19] Accountability was one thing; annual inspections for the purpose of finding fault and which served to divert time and resources from the preparation of beginning teachers were another. Although the TTA decided that it was not unreasonable to re-inspect successful courses in successive years, the Institute's action meant that the re-inspection scheduled for 1996–7 was postponed to the following year.

The sheer size of the secondary course cohort meant that inspections by Ofsted were undertaken on a subject basis. For example, in 1996–7 five subjects – English, geography, history, mathematics and modern languages – were inspected.[20] Under the new Framework for the Assessment of Quality and Standards in Initial Teacher Training 1996–7, inspection took place in three phases and covered six areas. In the 1996–7 inspection no fewer than 28 of the 30 areas were awarded very good or good grades. By 1998 all secondary courses except social studies, where the HMI post was vacant, and the information technology course, which only began in 1997, had been inspected. These two courses were inspected in 1998–9.

By this date the system of competence based assessment introduced under Circulars 9/92 and 14/93, had been replaced by a new set of 'standards' outlined in Circular 10/97.[21] In consequence all course documentation had to be re-written. The national curriculum for primary teacher training was redrawn. New requirements in respect of school practice necessitated a reorganization of contracts with all secondary partnership schools. A further requirement from 1998 was that all beginning teachers had to be able to demonstrate a working knowledge of information technology (IT) to a standard equivalent to level 8 in the national curriculum for pupils, and an understanding of the contribution IT made to their specialist subject. The new Circular necessitated a rapid in-service training programme for all Institute staff and school tutors engaged in PGCE.

While the DfEE, TTA and Ofsted concentrated their efforts upon ever more detailed prescription and assessment of ITT courses, students began to vote with their feet. Recruitment fell nationwide. In October 1998, although the Institute's primary and post-compulsory courses were full, there was a shortfall of 155 on the target of 778 secondary places. Some relief was provided by a new part-time primary PGCE over 18 months, which began with 51 students in April 1999.[22] Secondary PGCE recruitment improved in the following year, but in October 1999 there still was a shortfall of 59.[23]

One TTA initiative of 1999 focused upon increasing the recruitment to ITT courses of members of ethnic minorities, and males from any background. The Institute was set a target of 2-per-cent increases in applications and acceptances. Progress would be monitored by the TTA and Ofsted, and might have consequences for funding levels. Primary and secondary PGCE applications and acceptances for 1997 were consistent at 64 per cent female and 36 per cent male. Male acceptances for primary, however, constituted only 15 per cent of the total as opposed to 40 per cent for secondary. These figures differed little from the national picture. In 1998, the recruitment of males at primary level was still 15 per cent but the figure for secondary had fallen to 34 per cent. Statistics of ethnic origin were less reliable. Nine categories of ethnic origin were identified by the TTA, but the ethnic origins of 363 of the applicants and 164 of the acceptances of the Institute's 1997 entry were not given or unknown, with a further 110 and 28 respectively simply recorded as 'other'.[24] Percentages of 'white/other' for 1997 were recorded as 66/34 for applications and 71/29 for acceptances. Comparable percentages for 1998 were 61/39 and 68/32.[25]

Thus, in this period government and its agencies, principally the TTA and Ofsted, rather than higher education institutions, increasingly determined the nature of initial training and who should obtain qualified teacher status (QTS). As Geoffrey Partington observed, 'The TTA made fulfilment of QTS standards, which it controlled, central to entry to teaching, rather than the achievement of awards by HEIs'.[26] Nevertheless, the growing control of central government and its agencies over initial training was not uncontested, and at times the Institute took the lead in opposing policies that were deemed to be unreasonable and counterproductive.

## Professional development

In 1994–5 there were 570 full-time and 1,652 part-time students engaged in professional courses.[27] In 1995 more than 400 students gained a Master's degree and a further 150 an advanced diploma.[28] The continuation of such numbers, however, could not be taken for granted. For example, in 1996 new full-time registrations for Master's courses fell by nearly 20 per cent in comparison with the previous year.[29] In consequence, the various planning statements of this period envisaged at best a very modest growth. Indeed, in June 2000, while part-time numbers had increased to 2,125, full-time numbers only stood at 361.[30] At this date the average age of students on advanced taught courses was 35. More than 70 per cent were women. Some 85 per cent of students were part-time, with approximately 55 per cent of the full-time students drawn from countries outside the UK.[31] The rapid expansion of higher education meant that teachers and others engaged in courses of professional development now had a much wider choice of institutions and courses than hitherto. Student debts from undergraduate days, low school and academic salaries, the intensification and lengthening of teachers' working hours, a generally buoyant employment market and the high cost of living in London provided the context for recruitment at this level.

The Institute's rich variety of advanced taught courses included the Associateship, B.Ed. for serving teachers, a Graduate Certificate in English for Academic Purposes with Educational Studies, and a Certificate in Primary Health Care Education and Development. Two general diplomas – the Advanced Diploma in Education and the Advanced Diploma in Professional Studies – furnished links with the academic diploma of former years. Specialist diplomas continued to provide the opportunity to concentrate upon a particular area of professional expertise. Pre-sessional courses, which focused on academic skills in relation to the study of education, were provided for some overseas students and specialist short courses for others. By far the largest group of courses, however, was at MA level. Of the 63 advanced taught courses examined under the Quality Assurance Agency's (QAA) subject review of January 2001, no fewer than 52 were at Master's level.[32]

Continuing education in the form of award- and non-award-bearing INSET constituted a further group of professional courses. Collaboration with LEAs and partnership schools in connection with initial training proved to be of considerable benefit in developing courses and programmes of study for serving teachers. In consequence TTA-funded INSET courses were transferred from the professional development programme to that of initial teacher education. Another justification for this relocation was provided by the Teaching and Higher Education Act 1998, whereby Ofsted assumed responsibility for inspecting INSET courses funded by the TTA.[33] The two-year inspection programme began in 1999. A geography course for newly qualified teachers (NQTs) and a special educational needs course for special educational needs co-ordinators (SENCOs) were among the first to be inspected. Finally, there were the courses provided by the London Leadership Centre, whose first cohort of NPQH candidates began the training and development phase of their programme in September 1997.

Ron Barnett, the first Dean of Professional Development, and the Professional Development Programme Board were faced with four main tasks. The first was to rationalize courses, particularly at Master's level. This required the elimination of areas of overlap, the appointment and induction of course leaders and the provision of a coherent overall framework in terms of credit accumulation and transfer. The second task was to ensure that the Institute's courses were sensitive to the demands of the market. There was no future in continuing with tried and tested programmes, albeit of high quality, which attracted few students. The third was to establish a system of regular and systematic course review. This would not only indicate courses that had outlived their usefulness and appeal, but would also identify areas for possible growth, both at home and overseas. One development was a school-based MA in Curriculum Studies in association with Hampstead School.[34] Another was split-site courses for overseas students, taught partly in the home country and partly at the Institute. Examples included an MA in Teacher Education designed for Hong Kong and another in Teaching English to Speakers of Other Languages developed for Mexico. Annual course review was also essential for the purpose of enhancing and demonstrating the quality of teaching and learning in professional courses at the Institute. Finally, just as the Institute's courses of initial teacher training had come under the inspection of Ofsted, and its research output had been judged in a series of research assessment exercises, now the quality of its professional courses would also be subject to stringent formal assessment by an external body. In 2001 the QAA examined all of the Institute's 63 advanced taught courses under six headings with a maximum of four points for each. These were curriculum design, content and organization; teaching, learning and assessment; student progression and achievement; student support and guidance; learning resources; quality management and enhancement.[35]

## Research

Ofsted inspections and QAA reviews reinforced concerns with teaching and learning and led to a revival of the longstanding debate about the relative places and worth of teaching and research within the Institute.[36] Nevertheless, research was the first of the four themes listed in the Institute's mission statement, while, prior to their appointments, both Mortimore and Whitty, the two Directors of this period, had borne overall responsibility for the Institute's research. Mortimore, himself, frequently referred to the Institute as 'a research-led institution'.

Professor Caroline Gipps was the first Dean of Research. A former part-time Ph.D. student of the Institute, Gipps had considerable experience of supervising research students and of securing research funding. In September 1998, Professor Geoff Whitty was appointed Dean in succession to Gipps, who took up the post of Deputy Vice-Chancellor of Kingston University from January 1999. In the summer of 2000, following Whitty's appointment as Director, Professor Keith Swanwick became Dean of Research.[37] His most important task was to oversee the final stages of the RAE submission for 2001.

Research student numbers in 1994–5 were 154 full-time and 402 part-time with one completion at M.Phil. level and 35 at Ph.D. There were only 29 home students among the full-timers. Twenty-eight came from other countries in the European Union (EU) and a further 97 were classified as overseas. While this continuing recruitment from outside the UK was encouraging, the numbers of British students, both full- and part-time, were a source of concern. The situation was complex. On the one hand it was not financially advantageous for the Institute to exceed its HEFCE target numbers for research students. On the other, it was clear that for the Institute to be a truly 'research-led institution', reliance upon scholarship and publications as reflected in success in the RAE and upon the attraction of research funding from outside, was not enough. A true research culture required an increase in the numbers and proportion of research students from the existing 15 per cent of the total student body. Accordingly a target of 20 per cent was set for the year 2000. Numbers of M.Phil./Ph.D. students, however, did not markedly increase and recruitment fairs and open evenings for research students were mounted both at home and overseas. Improvements in completion rates – for example 46 students were awarded Ph.D. degrees in 1996–7 – while welcome, only served to exacerbate the problem.[38]

Numbers of research students and the research culture were, however, strengthened by the introduction of the degree of Doctor in Education (Ed.D.). M.Phil. and Ph.D. studies had a long and established history at the Institute. The degree of Doctor in Educational Psychology (D.Ed.Psy.), introduced in January 2000, was a specialist qualification for experienced educational psychologists and intended for a modest number of students. In contrast the Ed.D. was an entirely new degree, designed for a wide range of educational professionals. Launched in January 1996 with a pilot group of 15, a further cohort of 41 students was recruited in the same year. Another group of 39 began in January 1997. The three elements in the Ed.D. programme comprised four taught courses, an institution-focused study usually undertaken by students with reference to their own institutions, and a thesis. In spite of some teething problems there can be no doubt that the Ed.D. supplied a long-felt need for a professional doctorate. As John Durrant, an education officer with Essex County Council who began the course in 1997, remarked, 'Its great strength is that practice and study are welded together: there's a dynamic inter-relationship between my role in an LEA and my role as a student, and I've already seen the positive impact of my studies on my work within Essex'.[39]

While the Ed.D. was the major innovation of this period, significant changes also took place in the provision for M.Phil./Ph.D. students. The situation at the Institute was complicated by the widely differing needs and expectations of research students. Overseas students might expect a full programme of doctoral courses and training on the American model. Part-time students on the other hand, might wish to devote all of their precious spare time to researching the chosen topic. Several reforms were introduced to promote a stronger sense of a research community among students and a Centre for Doctoral Studies in the fifth floor of the wing block was officially opened in October 1995. Two lecturers in research methods were appointed to lead the Institute-wide doctoral studies training programme for students and to provide support for staff seeking to enhance their own research and publications. Additional facilities and resources for research students were made available at group level, and students were encouraged to form networks and support groups. Indeed, many key initiatives, including the extension of library opening hours, came from the Research Students' Society. In 1996 new Institute-wide procedures for the supervision of research students were drawn up. These included criteria for the appointment, induction and training of supervisors, the monitoring of supervisory performance, an enhanced definition of the role of the group research tutor, annual progress reports on students and Institute-wide procedures for upgrading from M.Phil. to Ph.D.[40] In 1999 a Doctoral School, designed to develop a more enhanced research community and research culture, replaced the Centre for Doctoral Studies. The Doctoral School organized the Institute-wide research training programme and provided a range of other activities, including winter and summer conferences. By this date, in addition to the Dean of Research and Assistant Deans, there were three doctoral tutors. By the following year, not only had the Institute-wide programme received full recognition by ESRC both for full- and part-time studentships, but the Institute itself was also offering 12 new scholarships with half-fee remission.

Funded research was the second main area in the Institute's research programme. Some indication of the centrality of this work was provided by a return of February 1999. This showed that there were 106 research staff at the Institute as compared to 183 members of lecturing staff. Marked gender differences were apparent. Whereas 96 of the lecturers were women and 87 men, all but 20 of the researchers were women.[41] Under the matrix system further attention was paid to the career prospects of researchers. Rolling contracts for research staff, introduced during 1993–4, were complemented by research lectureships funded by the Institute and by HEFCE funded contracts whereby researchers could teach for 0.1 or 0.2 of their time on courses related to their expertise. Some 80 new research contracts were begun in 1993–4[42] and by 1995–6 some 43 per cent of HEFCE funded staff were grant holders.[43] A further 82 new research contracts were begun in 1995–6, including a grant of £1.5 million from the DfEE to undertake research over a five-year period into the effective provision of pre-school education. In 1997–8 research funding totalled £4 million. Major grants at this time included the Department of Health's £522,070 to Professor A. Oakley and Dr S. Oliver for 'Field Co-ordination in Health Promotion' and £424,939 from the European Commission to Professor R. Noss and Professor C. Hoyles for 'Playground – Animated Playground for Learning'.[44] In 1999 the Institute, together with partner institutions, was successful in bids for three centres established by the DfEE. These were a Centre for Research on the Economics of Education, a Centre for Research on the

Wider Benefits of Learning and a Review Centre for Evidence-based Policy and Practice in Education.[45] The latter two were based at the Institute.

Scholarship and publications constituted the third main area of research and the Institute's overall record of scholarship and research was confirmed in the 1996 RAE exercise. Once again it was awarded a top rating. Over the four-year period, 1992–6, there was an increase in annual research income from £2.5 million to £3.6 million, a rise in funded research applications from 132 to 160 per annum with a constant success rate of 40 per cent. Publications averaged some five per year for every FTE member of HEFCE funded lecturing and research staff, with a total output of all categories of research-related output of 1,178 items in 1996 in comparison with 703 in 1992. Over the same period the average completion time for Ph.D.s was reduced from 4.2 to 3.8 years for full-time students and from 9.3 to 6.6 years for part-time.[46] Nevertheless, in contrast to 1992 when 97.5 per cent of the Institute staff had been returned as 'research active', the figure in 1996 was only 83 per cent. This was the result of two factors. The first was a change in the format for 1996; the second that reductions in funding since 1992 had resulted in a reduction in the number of full-time academic staff and a corresponding growth in the numbers of those working on a part-time or fee-paid basis, and on short-term contracts. Many of these staff were employed only for PGCE work and devoted their time solely to teaching. Although, as in 1992, financial rewards for the 5* rating were disappointing, the Institute had now achieved the top ranking in all four assessment exercises.

## New Initiatives

The fourth programme area, that of New Initiatives, was the most contentious and the least understood. Initial teacher education, professional development and research were widely recognized and appreciated. New (presumably as opposed to old or existing) initiatives would be constantly needed in each of these areas and indeed in every part of the matrix and of the Institute's activities. Would the new Dean have responsibility for them all? Was the Institute failing to keep abreast of change? Was the post essentially concerned with seeking new sources of funding, or with public relations? These, and other, questions were answered in different ways by the three Deans of New Initiatives: James Porter, Professor Michael Barber and Toni Griffiths, together with the New Initiatives Board. Nevertheless, in 1998 when Griffiths left the Institute to take up the new post of Director of Education and Professional Development at University College, London, she was not replaced.[47]

At the time of his appointment to the post of acting Dean of New Initiatives, James Porter was Head of the Institute's International Development Office (IDO).[48] As Dean, Porter continued to focus upon international initiatives. In 1994 he had drawn attention to the need to expand the Institute's world-wide role by taking courses to students in other countries, offering split-site degrees in conjunction with other universities, supplying course materials, and by engaging in advisory and consultancy work. Porter also emphasized the potential role of the Institute of Education Society, with 'probably well over 4,000 ex-students in over 100 countries who have had full-time postgraduate experience of the Institute'.[49] Following a review of the Society and its activities by Robert Thornbury, a new Alumni Association was set up in 1996. One of the best known and widely admired members of Institute staff, Rajee Rajagopalan, was appointed to the post of Alumni Officer. The first *Bulletin* of the new Association appeared in the early summer of 1997; on 19 June the new Alumni Association of the Institute of Education was formally launched by one of the Institute's honorary fellows, the Secretary General of the Commonwealth, His Excellency Chief Emeka Anyaoku.[50]

Michael Barber, who became Dean in 1995, brought a different set of experiences and ambitions to the role. Barber had a high political profile and strong media connections. In addition to his experience at the NUT and at Keele, Barber had been a councillor in the London Borough of Hackney and chair of its education committee. A Labour parliamentary candidate in the general election of 1987, he had been an educational adviser to Tony Blair. Barber's book, *The Learning Game,* published in 1996 bore the subtitle 'arguments for an education revolution' and proclaimed the need to create a 'learning society'. Barber's first major report to the Institute's Senate, in March 1996, referred to a number of initiatives already in train. These included the establishment of the London Leadership Centre and a new publications agreement with Cassell. Initiatives from across the Institute would be encouraged. A new policy on consultancy was being produced, while the work of IDU was under review with particular reference to strengthening initiatives within the frameworks of the European Union.[51] Consultancy was a key issue in 1995–6 and new funding arrangements, consistent with those for INSET, academic conferences and other services rendered, were introduced in August 1996. The main objective of the new policy was 'To generate income for the Institute which, in the short term, would contribute to covering its deficit and, in the medium and long term would generate revenue which would help the Institute fulfil its overall mission and enable it to determine its own priorities'.[52]

77. Rajee Rajagopalan, appointed Alumni Officer in 1996

One means of raising the Institute's profile, and of improving its finances, was to adopt a more creative use of the Logan Hall and other venues within the Bedford Way building. Thus in 1994–5 lectures on the educational policies of the Labour

78. His Excellency,
Chief Emeka
Anyaoku, who
launched the Alumni
Association in June
1997

and Liberal Democrat parties were given by Tony Blair and Paddy Ashdown, and in March 1996 by Gillian Shephard, Secretary of State for Education and Employment. Other notable lectures in 1995–6, jointly sponsored by the Institute and the *Times Educational Supplement*, were given by James Callaghan on the Ruskin Speech of 1976 and Kenneth Baker on the Education Reform Act of 1988. Collaboration with the *Guardian* newspaper led to a series of high-profile debates about current education policies. The first of these took place in November 1996 between Roy Hattersley MP and Will Hutton, editor of the *Observer*. On the day of the debate the views of the opposing speakers were printed in the *Guardian*. Live (and sometimes very lively) debate took place in the evening in the Logan Hall. The debate was simultaneously transmitted on the *Guardian*'s website; thus allowing e-mail comments and questions to be interspersed with those from the audience in the Logan Hall. The series continued. Speakers in 1997–8 included Stephen Byers, the Minister for School Standards, who defended 'Naming and Shaming', and Baroness Blackstone, the Minister for Higher and Further Education, who justified 'The Government's policy on student funding'. Chief HMI, Chris Woodhead, proposed that 'Schools rely too much on LEAs', while Michael Barber, in his role as Head of the DfEE Standards and Effectiveness Unit, denied that 'The attempt to improve education from the centre by relentless pressure is bound to fail'. Their respective opponents, who invariably won the audience's vote, if not always the argument, were: David Hart of the National Association of Head Teachers, Stephen Dorrell, the Conservative shadow Education and Employment Secretary, Tim Brighouse, Chief Education Officer, Birmingham, and Professor Richard Pring of the University of Oxford.

Toni Griffiths, appointed originally to develop links with European agencies and to serve as the Institute's press officer,[53] succeeded Barber as Dean in 1997. By this stage, however, the scope for further initiatives was becoming less clear. The Institute already had enough on its plate. Griffiths' departure in 1998 led to the ending of New Initiatives as a separate programme area. Responsibilities were redistributed, with consultancy and publications coming under the aegis of the Dean of Research. One of the major disappointments of the New Initiatives programme, and one which involved Griffiths in much time and effort, was the failure to implement a project, initially described as the Classroom of the Future, and subsequently as the Future Learning Centre.[54]

Two other features of this period may be noted here. The first was the increased turnover of staff. For example, during the academic year 1998–9 113 members of staff from all grades (one-third of the total complement) departed the Institute.[55] The second was the more intensive use of the Bedford Way and other Institute buildings. As had happened on at least two previous occasions, the Institute had outgrown its accommodation. Moreover the building was show-ing considerable signs of wear and tear. An audit of the use of space carried out in 1999 concluded that some academic and research staff were principally work-ing from home because the Institute was unable to provide them with adequate facilities. Although more PGCE work was now conducted in schools, numbers of research and part-time staff had increased. New commitments had been made to visiting fellows and research students, so that each academic group should provide a separate room for this constituency. Accordingly, the space audit panel recommended open-plan offices for administrative departments, and the location of resources in Information Services rather than in academic groups or centres. While professors and heads of groups might continue to occupy full-size, three-bay rooms, the conversion of other three-bay rooms into two-bay rooms, thus providing an extra 20 rooms, was recommended. Part-time and research staff should normally share rooms. These recommendations were steadily, if at times acrimoniously, implemented.

Other alterations to the main Institute building included the establishment of a bookshop on level three by the Bedford Way entrance, in space previously occupied by the Bloomsbury Art Gallery. It soon became a central feature of Institute life, a location for launching books written by members of staff and a showcase for Institute publications. In 1998 the Centre for Longitudinal Studies moved into space vacated by Computing Services, which were relocated on level three of the east wing of the library. Improvements in the catering and other facilities were made in the Students' Union premises. A major refurbishment of the level three entrance, main stairway and crush hall on level one took place in 2000, aided by a grant of £250,000 from the Wolfson Trustees. Lord Wolfson took a personal interest in this project and was appointed an honorary fellow of the Institute in 2001. Improvements in teaching accommodation, particularly on the Bedford Way side of the building, were also implemented. From 2001, however, the Bedford Way complex was declared a listed building, thus restricting scope for further alterations and improvements.

## Geoff Whitty

In the spring of 2000 the national and international search for a new Director was conducted with great thoroughness. Sir Clive Whitmore, the Chair of Council, led a Joint Appointing Committee of representatives from the Institute's Council and Senate, together with one external member. Views were canvassed from staff and students. In addition, a firm of 'head-hunters', Saxton Bampfylde Hever, was retained. As so often in the Institute's history, however, the choice fell upon an internal candidate, Professor Geoff Whitty, the Dean of Research. Whitty, who was 53 years of age at the time of his appointment, came from a family of teachers.

80. Barbara
MacGilchrist,
appointed Deputy
Director in 2001

assume a key responsibility for the management, assurance and enhancement of quality across all aspects of the Institute's work, to prepare for QAA audit in spring 2003, to develop the Learning and Teaching Strategy and to oversee academic partnerships with other institutions. One very welcome piece of news contained in the Director's second update on progress with the reform programme announced in September 2000 was that HEFCE had granted £1.6 million to assist in the restructuring process. Another was the confirmation of a grant of £3.7 million from the Science Research Investment Fund, to be pooled with similar funds from Birkbeck College, to create a joint facility to house an education archive and a knowledge laboratory.[65]

The reform programme announced in September 2000 also included 'a major Strategic Review of the Institute, involving both internal and external stakeholders entitled "The Institute of Education: Preparing for the Next Hundred Years"'. In this exercise no options should be ruled out. These might 'include the very name of the Institute, as well as the scale and nature of its market, activities and image, and its relationship to other institutions within the University and the outside world'.[66]

## Conclusion

Three major themes may be identified from the period covered in this chapter. The first was the growth of academic accountability, which affected all aspects of the Institute's work. In consequence many resources, both human and financial, had to be devoted to preparations for a series of external assessments. The second feature was internal restructuring. The matrix system of 1994 was designed to reduce the power of departmental heads and the variety of departmental practices and to produce a more uniform Institute-wide culture under the leadership of the Director and Deans. The introduction of schools from 2002 was intended to strengthen the departmental side of the matrix and to secure a greater involvement of members of the professoriate in the Institute's academic and administrative leadership. Finally, it is clear that in this period both Directors were fully committed to the Institute's research role and to the importance of recruiting as many leading scholars as possible. A return of March 2001 showed a staff profile fully commensurate with that of a postgraduate institution of international calibre. By that date there were 48 professors, 16 readers, 40 senior lecturers, 75 lecturers and 101 research officers.[67]

There can be little doubt that by its centenary year of 2002 the Institute of Education had fulfilled, and indeed exceeded, many of the expectations of its founders. In common with other specialist colleges of the University of London, such as the London School of Economics and the Imperial College of Science, Technology and Medicine, it had become, as Sidney Webb had envisaged, one of the foremost post-graduate centres of the intellectual world. Within the United Kingdom in the field of education it had no peer. From 1932 the Institute's international reputation steadily grew and in due course bore comparison with the institution which Adams and Nunn had seen as its role model, Teachers College, Columbia. The very name of Institute of Education indicated its specialist nature. It existed as a separate entity focused upon education, rather than as one of several departments within another higher education institution. In education circles, 'The Institute' could only mean the Institute of Education of the University of London. The Institute's size made it possible for the broad area of knowledge that is education to receive substantial coverage. Other advantages included the Institute's London location, at the heart of a great city, the capital both of a nation state and of an empire. Thus it was close to the centre of government, and for the first 88 years of its existence was also sustained by a close relationship with the largest local authority for education in the country. It also benefited from the general support and federal nature of the University of London.

Some of the Institute's success was attributable to sheer size. Continuous growth, however, from the initial group of 58 students, also brought problems, for example the provision of sufficient premises, and throughout the first hundred years much time and effort was spent upon the management of change. In the early decades all members of staff would have been known to each other and to the students. Some members of staff, indeed, might have known all of the students. In spite of the lack of residential accommodation, the London Day Training College, and the fledgling Institute of Education were close-knit communities. The early sense of community, of shared values both professional and academic, was well represented in the leadership, teaching, publications and reputations of Adams and Nunn. Clarke continued to embody these several roles, albeit in the more diversified and reduced circumstances of war. From Jeffery onwards, however, and particularly during the ATO period, the Institute acquired a dual, even a multiple identity. The latter years saw a greater range of courses and of students and the development of a more varied set of cultures, with distinct departments and specialist research units. For example, some individual staff and departmental reputations were based principally upon experience in the field, whether in the schools of London or in those of the Empire and Commonwealth; others depended mainly upon substantial research grants and influential publications.

In spite of its pre-eminence, steady growth and the ability to adapt to changing circumstances, however, the Institute also exhibited weaknesses which curtailed its work and influence. Two are identified here. First, neither the Institute nor the

University of London was, as Webb had hoped, financially well endowed. The LCC kept the LDTC on a tight financial rein, while from 1932 the Institute often seemed to be treated as a poor relation within the University. The capacity for fund-raising on its own account was severely limited by the prior commitments of its students to their undergraduate institutions and by the modest salaries received by its alumni when they became teachers. In contrast to the initial training year, there were few funds to enable students to engage in full-time higher degree work in education. In consequence much of the Institute's advanced work took place in the evenings, with part-time home students who were paying their own fees. A second less tangible but strongly related factor was that in England the subject of education was seen neither as a discipline in its own right nor as a high prestige area of knowledge. Tight governmental controls over student numbers in initial training and over the content and organization of their courses meant that universities often regarded their education departments as a drain on resources and a threat to academic freedom and academic standards.

Nevertheless, in spite of such difficulties, throughout its history the Institute of Education attracted leading scholars and students. It gained and sustained a reputation as a place of academic and professional leadership in the field of education. Although the ten directors were men, much of that leadership was

provided by women – as a list which includes Clotilde von Wyss, Susan Isaacs, Marion Richardson, Margaret Read, Doris Lee, Barbara Tizard and Ann Oakley amply demonstrates.[68] From the beginning women students predominated at the initial training level. Moreover, in spite of changes in function and the substantial growth of advanced and international work, the Institute continued to fulfil the original purpose of the LDTC. Each year it sent a cohort of newly qualified teachers, many of them from the London region and including many London graduates, into posts in London schools.

Change and continuity are the essentials of history. In the first century of its existence the Institute experienced four different identities – as LDTC, Senate Institute, ATO and College of the University. While further major changes will doubtless occur during the next 100 years, it is impossible to predict their nature and extent. What is clear, however, is that in the future, as in the past, the Institute's ability successfully to respond to change and to continue to provide academic and professional leadership in education will depend principally upon the quality and commitment of its staff and students.

# Notes

## 1: Foundation

1. University of London Institute of Education, 1952, *Studies and Impressions, 1902–1952*, London: Evans Brothers, 10 (hereafter referred to as *Studies and Impressions*). In contrast Sir Peter Newsam, Director 1989–94, identified the need for a centenary history in good time.
2. University of London Institute of Education, 1952, *Jubilee Lectures*, London: Evans Brothers (hereafter referred to as *Jubilee Lectures*). The lectures were delivered in the Beveridge Hall in the Senate House in the Spring term of that year. General Sir Ronald Forbes Adam, Chairman of the Institute's Council and Committee of Management, spoke on 'From Day Training College to the Institute of Education'; I.J. Hayward, Leader of the London County Council, on 'The London County Council and the training of teachers, 1902–1952'; R.A. Butler, Chancellor of the Exchequer, on 'The 1944 Act seen against the pattern of the times'; Sir Christopher Cox, Educational Adviser to the Secretary of State to the Colonies, on 'The development of the Institute in relation to the colonies'; G.B. Jeffery on 'The Institute of Education and oversea students'; W.F. Russell, President of Teachers College, Columbia University, on 'The challenge to educational leadership in the United States'.
3. *Studies and Impressions* was compiled by an editorial board consisting of A.S. Harrison, Senior Lecturer in Education in Tropical Areas, A.V. Judges, Professor of the History of Education, King's College, J.A. Lauwerys, Professor of Comparative Education, and Sophia Weitzman, Senior Lecturer in History, with Shirley Gordon, Lecturer in History, as the editorial secretary.
4. C.W. Dixon, 1986, *The Institute: A personal account of the history of the University of London Institute of Education, 1932–1972*, London: Institute of Education. A projected history of the LDTC years, 1902–32, by Richard Goodings was never completed. Goodings did, however, publish a continuing article on the LDTC beginning in the *Education Libraries Bulletin*, 1958, 2, 2–8.
5. See, for example, D.E.M. Gardner, 1969, *Susan Isaacs*, London: Methuen Educational and F.W. Mitchell, 1967, *Sir Fred Clarke: Master-teacher 1880–1952*, London: Longmans.
6. Under the terms of the reconstitution of the University of London in 1900 several London colleges, including the first foundations, University College and King's College, were designated as schools of the University and their students as internal.
7. Terminologies change and the Institute is now one of the University's 17 colleges. Most of the University's former institutes are currently designated as schools of advanced study, but three, the British Institute in Paris, the Centre for Defence Studies and the Courtauld Institute of Art, are still known as institutes.
8. Or approximately 34 million square kilometres and 270 hectares.
9. For an excellent account see A.S. Williams, P. Ivin and C. Morse, 2001, *The Children of London: Attendance and welfare at school 1870–1990*, London: Institute of Education.
10. Quoted in E.J.T. Brennan, 1972, 'Educational engineering with the Webbs', *History of Education*, 1, 2, 179.
11. N. Harte, 1986, *The University of London, 1836–1986: An illustrated history*, London: Athlone Press, 159.
12. Quoted in S. Maclure, 1970, *One Hundred Years of London Education, 1870–1970*, London: Allen Lane, 15.

13. *Jubilee Lectures*, 25. The pupil-teacher scheme was introduced in 1846. Pupil teachers served a five-year apprenticeship from the age of 13, teaching in school during the day and receiving instruction from the master or mistress after school hours. By 1902 the scheme had been modified and some pupil teachers received their out-of-class instruction in pupil-teacher centres. For an overview of the history of teacher education see R. Aldrich, 1990, 'The evolution of teacher education', in N. Graves (ed.), *Initial Teacher Education: Policies and progress*, London: Kogan Page, 12–24. Key works include: H.C. Dent, 1977, *The Training of Teachers in England and Wales, 1800–1975*, Sevenoaks: Hodder and Stoughton; L.G.E. Jones, 1924, *The Training of Teachers in England and Wales: A critical survey*, Oxford: Oxford University Press; D.E. Lomax (ed.), 1973, *The Education of Teachers in Britain*, London: John Wiley; J.B. Thomas (ed.), 1990, *British Universities and Teacher Education: A century of change*, Lewes: Falmer Press. For an overview of education in the twentieth century see R. Aldrich (ed.), 2002, *A Century of Education*, London: RoutledgeFalmer.
14. *Jubilee Lectures*, 24–6.
15. Brennan, 1972, 183–4.
16. E.J.T. Brennan, 1962, 'Sidney Webb and the London Technical Education Board: IV: The London Education Act of 1903', *Vocational Aspect*, XIV, 28, 56.
17. Maclure, 1970, 69.
18. Former demonstrator at the Cavendish Laboratory at Cambridge, and Professor and Principal respectively at University College, Nottingham and Durham College of Science, Newcastle upon Tyne.
19. Harte, 1986; F.M.L. Thompson (ed.), 1990, *The University of London and the World of Learning, 1836–1986*, London: Hambledon Press; F.M.G. Willson, 1995, *Our Minerva: The men and politics of the University of London, 1836–1858*, London: Athlone Press.
20. Quoted in Harte, 1986, 120.
21. W. Taylor, 'Education', in Thompson, 1990, 229–30. For the College of Preceptors see J.V. Chapman, 1985, *Professional Roots: The College of Preceptors in British society*, Epping: Theydon Bois Publications and R. Aldrich, 1995, *School and Society in Victorian Britain: Joseph Payne and the new world of education*, New York: Garland.
22. Taylor, 1990, 234.
23. Women were admitted from 1925.
24. M.J. Tuke, 1939, *A History of Bedford College for Women, 1849–1937*, London: Oxford University Press; Taylor, 1990, 231–2; *Studies and Impressions*, 191–3.
25. University of London Archives (hereafter ULA) CF/1/2/297, Garnett to Dr Frank Heath, 3 July 1901.
26. Brennan, 1972, 179.
27. Quoted in A.V. Judges, 1961, 'The educational influence of the Webbs', *British Journal of Educational Studies*, X, 1, 33.
28. Judges, 1961, 46.
29. E.J.T. Brennan (ed.), 1975, *Education for National Efficiency: The contribution of Sidney and Beatrice Webb*, London: Athlone Press, 143–7.
30. ULA ST/2/2/18, Senate minute 720, 18 December 1901.
31. ULA ST/2/2/18, Senate minute 720, 18 December 1901.
32. ULA ST/2/2/18, Senate minute 721, 18 December 1901.
33. ULA ST/2/2/18, Senate minute 723, 18 December 1901.
34. ULA CF/1/2/84, Webb to Rücker, 9 November 1901.
35. Graham Wallas shared many of Webb's interests. A Fabian and founder of the LSE, he also served on the LSB, the LCC and the TEB. See R. Aldrich and P. Gordon, 1989, *Dictionary of British Educationists*, London: Woburn Press, 252–3.
36. These scholarships, established in 1846, enabled the best pupil teachers to proceed to training colleges.
37. ULA CF/1/2/50, Pooley to Rücker, 31 July 1902.
38. ULA ST/2/2/18, Senate minute 2197, 25 June 1902.
39. ULA CF/1/2/50, Pooley to Rücker, 31 July 1902.

## 2: From Clare Market to Southampton Row 1902–1907

1. P. Gordon (ed.), 1980, *The Study of Education: A collection of inaugural lectures, Vol. I: early and modern*, London: Woburn Press, 48. I am most grateful to Anna Towlson, archivist at the LSE, for information about the LDTC at the LSE. See also, R. Dahrendorf, 1995, *LSE: A history of the London School of Economics and Political Science 1895–1995*, Oxford: Oxford University Press.
2. *Jubilee Lectures*, 27–8; *Studies and Impressions*, 208, 229.

3. *Studies and Impressions*, 23.
4. These chairs were originally endowed with money left in the trust funds of Dr Andrew Bell, one of the pioneers of the monitorial system. For Laurie and Meiklejohn see Aldrich and Gordon, 1989, 146 and 171. For Joseph Payne, the first British non-university professor of education, see Aldrich, 1995, 127–59.
5. For details of Adams' career see Institute of Education Archives (hereafter IE), Staff register 1912, and R. Rusk, 1961, 'Sir John Adams, 1857–1934', *British Journal of Educational Studies*, X, 1, 49–57.
6. Rusk, 1961, 54.
7. Quoted in Rusk, 1961, 54.
8. Rusk, 1961, 51.
9. TEB minutes, 30 July 1902.
10. Rusk, 1961, 53.
11. *Studies and Impressions*, 63–4.
12. IE, Jubilee lectures 1952 correspondence.
13. TEB minutes, 21 July 1902; IE, Staff register 1912.
14. See, G. Collins (ed.), 1996, *Education Matters: Excerpts from the Saffron Walden College magazines, 1899–1995*, London: Carlyon Print. I am most grateful to Dr Gillian Collins for information about Margaret Punnett's early career.
15. TEB minutes, 21 July 1902.
16. These terms and those of master and mistress of method appear to have been used interchangeably.
17. TEB minutes, 12 May 1902.
18. For Bryant, see North London Collegiate School, 1922, *Sophie Bryant, D.Sc., Litt.D. 1850–1922*, London: North London Collegiate School, especially a contribution from Adams, entitled 'Work for the training of teachers in London', 45–9. See also a pamphlet, *c.* 1914, entitled *Training of Teachers for Secondary Schools*, which explains the co-operation of the Frances Mary Buss Schools with the LDTC in a special scheme to train graduate or equivalent students to teach in secondary schools. I am most grateful to Karen Morgan, Senior Librarian and Archivist at the North London Collegiate School for this and other references. See also, P.H.J.H. Gosden, 1972, *The Evolution of a Profession: A study of the contribution of teachers' associations to the development of school teaching as a professional occupation*, Oxford: Basil Blackwell, 228.
19. *Studies and Impressions*, 15.
20. Dixon, 1986, 10.
21. IE, J. Fairgrieve, 'In memory of Miss Margaret Punnett', *Londinian*, 1946.
22. J. Rose, 1992, *Marie Stopes and the Sexual Revolution*, London: Faber and Faber, 23. I am grateful to Dr Kevin Brehony for this reference.
23. Quoted in R. Hall, 1977, *Marie Stopes: A biography*, London: Andrew Deutsch, 38–9.
24. TEB minutes, 16 February 1903; IE, Staff register 1912.
25. Dixon, 1986, 11.
26. *Studies and Impressions*, 46.
27. J.W. Tibble, 1961, 'Sir Percy Nunn, 1870–1944', *British Journal of Educational Studies*, X, 1, 58.
28. TEB minutes, 21 December 1903; IE, Staff register 1912.
29. *Studies and Impressions*, 65, 61.
30. *Studies and Impressions*, 14.
31. Tibble, 1961, 63.
32. TEB minutes, 6 July 1903, 7 December 1903.
33. IE, Staff register 1912.
34. IE, London Day Training College Local Committee (hereafter LDTCLC) minutes, 17 October 1904.
35. IE, LDTCLC minutes, 17 October 1904.
36. TEB minutes, 26 October 1903.
37. TEB minutes, 26 October 1903; IE, LDTCLC minutes, 2 March 1904.
38. IE, LDTCLC minutes, 27 November 1905.
39. TEB minutes, 19 December 1902.
40. TEB minutes, 19 December 1902. For a defence of the pupil-teacher centres see W. Robinson, 1999, 'In search of a "plain tale": rediscovering the champions of the pupil-teacher centres 1900–10', *History of Education*, 28, 1, 53–71.
41. IE, Record of students, women, 1902–1909.
42. TEB minutes, 19 December 1902. Criticism lessons were given by students and critiqued by the tutor and other students; demonstration lessons were given by the staff.
43. IE, LDTCLC minutes, 17 October 1904.
44. IE, M. Punnett, 'Ancient History', *Londinian,* Lent Term 1915.
45. IE, LDTCLC minutes, 2 March 1904.
46. IE, LDTCLC minutes, 24 February 1904.
47. IE, LDTCLC minutes, 24 February 1904.
48. *Studies and Impressions*, 27.
49. *Studies and Impressions*, 57–8.
50. *Studies and Impressions*, 59; IE, Jubilee lectures 1952, reminiscences 1902–1918, letter from L.S. Suggate.
51. IE, LDTCLC minutes, 28 November 1904.
52. *Studies and Impressions*, 61–2.
53. TEB minutes, 24 November 1902.
54. Chapman, 1985, 117.
55. IE, LDTCLC minutes, 20 January 1904.

56. *Studies and Impressions*, 67.
57. IE, Staff register 1912.
58. *Studies and Impressions*, 67.
59. *Studies and Impressions*, 61.
60. *Studies and Impressions*, 24.
61. Chapman, 1985, 122.
62. IE, LDTCLC minutes, 28 November 1904.
63. The whole building is now occupied by the Central St Martins College of Art and Design. I am most grateful to Sylvia Backemeyer, Head of the College's Museum and Study Collection, for information about the LDTC at Southampton Row.
64. *Daily Graphic*, 2 November 1907.
65. *Studies and Impressions*, 97.
66. Quoted in *Studies and Impressions*, 99.
67. IE, LDTCLC minutes, 28 January 1907.
68. IE, LDTCLC minutes, 25 October 1909.
69. *Studies and Impressions*, 98. The first Wembley final was in 1923.
70. P.B. Ballard, 1935, 'Sir John Adams', *British Journal of Educational Psychology*, V, 8.
71. *Daily Graphic*, 2 November 1907.
72. See D. Shorney, 1989, *Teachers in Training 1906–1985: A history of Avery Hill College*, London: Thames Polytechnic. Yet another model in south-east London was provided by Goldsmiths' College at New Cross. See A.E. Firth, 1991, *Goldsmiths' College: A centenary account*, London: Athlone Press.
73. I.G. Gibbon and R.W. Bell, 1939, *History of the London County Council 1889–1939*, London: Macmillan, 479.

## 3: A clash of cultures 1907–1922

1. D.W. Thoms, 1980, *Policy-Making in Education: Robert Blair and the London County Council, 1904–1924*, Leeds: University of Leeds, 14.
2. Thoms, 1980, 8.
3. Thoms, 1980, 2.
4. IE, LDTCLC minutes, 28 January 1907.
5. Quoted in Thoms, 1980, 14.
6. London Metropolitan Archives (hereafter LMA) EO/TRA/2/23, P.J. Hartog to H.J. Mordaunt, 24 July 1908. I am most grateful to Rhys Griffith, Senior Archivist at the LMA, for his generous assistance.
7. LMA EO/TRA/2/23, Higher Education Sub-Committee minutes, 16 July 1909.
8. LMA EO/TRA/2/23, LCC minutes, 26 October 1909.
9. IE, London Day Training College Council (hereafter LDTCC) minutes, 22 November 1909.
10. LMA EO/TRA/2/23, memorandum by Adams, 14 October 1913; report by E.E. Constance James and H. Bompas Smith, 26 June 1914.
11. IE, Extract book 1916–1918, report on the LDTC dated 1 July 1914. Extract books contain miscellaneous collections of materials.
12. IE, LDTCC agenda papers, 26 October 1914, 8 February 1915.
13. IE, LDTCC agenda papers, 18 March and 20 May 1912.
14. IE, LDTCC agenda papers, 2 November 1920, 8 March 1921.
15. Harte, 1986, 192–4.
16. IE, LDTCC agenda papers, 27 April 1914.
17. IE, LDTCC minutes, 24 January 1910. These hours included time spent in demonstration and practising schools.
18. IE, LDTCC agenda papers, 5 December 1910.
19. IE, LDTCC agenda papers, 25 November 1912.
20. IE, LDTCC agenda papers, 18 March 1912.
21. IE, LDTCLC minutes, 25 October 1909.
22. IE, LDTCC agenda papers, 24 October 1910.
23. IE, LDTCC agenda papers, 27 November 1911.
24. IE, LDTCC agenda papers, 27 November 1911.
25. IE, LDTCC agenda papers, 26 October 1914.
26. IE, LDTCC agenda papers, 5 December 1910.
27. IE, LDTCLC minutes, 25 October 1909.
28. IE, LDTCC, agenda papers, 26 October 1914.
29. *Studies and Impressions*, 67.
30. IE, LDTCC agenda papers, 24 October 1910.
31. IE, LDTCLC minutes, 15 May 1908.
32. IE, LDTCLC minutes, 25 October 1909.
33. IE, LDTCC agenda papers, 20 May 1913.
34. IE, LDTCC agenda papers, 20 May 1913.
35. IE, LDTCC agenda papers, 20 May 1913.
36. IE, Register of students, men, 1902–1915.
37. IE, Extract book 1907–1913.
38. IE, Extract book 1916–1918, report on the LDTC dated 1 July 1914.
39. IE, *Londinian*, Summer term 1911, Lent term 1912, Lent term 1914. In 1909 admission as a school of the University gave LDTC teams entry to University sports competitions.
40. IE, LDTCC agenda papers, 23 January 1911.
41. IE, LDTCC minutes, 22 February 1909.
42. IE, LDTCC agenda papers, 12 July 1911.
43. IE, LDTCC agenda papers, 27 October 1913.

44. IE, Record of students, women, 1909–1917.
45. ULA ST/2/2/38 Senate minutes 1534–1535, 25 January 1922, HMI report on the LDTC forwarded to the LCC, 22 April 1921.
46. IE, LDTCC agenda papers, 24 January 1910.
47. IE, Extract book 1916–1918.
48. Information kindly supplied by Reginald Penfold's daughter, Mrs Marjorie Dodd; IE, Extract book 1913–1916; LDTCC agenda papers, 26 January 1914, 26 October 1914; Record of students, men, 1910–1915.
49. IE, Extract book 1913–1916.
50. IE, LDTCC agenda papers, 20 November 1916.
51. *Studies and Impressions*, 152.
52. *Studies and Impressions*, 68.
53. IE, Record of students, women, 1919–1921.
54. IE, LDTCLC minutes, 12 July 1907.
55. IE, LDTCLC minutes, 15 May 1908.
56. IE, LDTCC agenda papers, 28 February 1910.
57. IE, LDTCC agenda papers, 26 February 1912.
58. IE, LDTCC agenda papers, 28 February 1910.
59. IE, LDTCC agenda papers, 26 January 1914.
60. IE, LDTCC agenda papers, 20 November 1916.
61. IE, Extract book 1916–1918, memorandum entitled 'The Case against taking over the London Day Training College Buildings for War Offices', 8 June 1917.
62. IE, LDTCC agenda papers, 25 October 1915.
63. For Adamson see H.C. Barnard, 1961, 'J.W. Adamson, 1857–1947', *British Journal of Educational Studies*, X, 1, 19–32 and J.B. Thomas, 1979, 'The curriculum of a day training college. The logbooks of J.W. Adamson', *Journal of Educational Administration and History*, 11, 2, 29–34.
64. IE, Extract book, 1916–1918, memorandum entitled 'The Case against taking over the London Day Training College Buildings for War Offices', 8 June 1917.
65. IE, Record of students, women, 1909–1917.
66. IE, LDTCC minutes, 3 February 1919.
67. IE, LDTCC agenda papers, 31 May 1921.
68. *Studies and Impressions*, 69.
69. IE, LDTCC agenda papers, 2 June 1919; *Londinian*, Easter 1919.
70. IE, LDTCC minutes, 3 March 1922. At this meeting the Council formally approved the appointment of Nunn as the next Principal.
71. IE, Principal's letter book, 6 December 1918–21 January 1919, Adams to Partington, 11 December 1918.
72. IE, Principal's letter book, 7 December 1918–6 October 1919, Nunn to B.M. Allen, 4 February 1919.
73. Leeds University Archives, Leeds University Committee minutes XII, 1 and 8 July 1919; P.H.J.H. Gosden (ed.), 1991, *The University of Leeds School of Education 1891–1991*, Leeds: University of Leeds, 24. I am most grateful to Professor Peter Gosden for his assistance in consulting the Leeds University Archives.
74. Although even in 1922 some of the weaker students still sat for a Board of Education certificate examination conducted by the college.
75. Ballard, 1935, 4.
76. Quoted in R. Goodings, 1959, 'The London Day Training College: staff and students in the early years', *Education Libraries Bulletin*, 4, 22.
77. In 1942, a doctoral thesis by Morford Riddick of the University of Southern California provided an 'Appreciation of Sir John Adams and his contribution to modern education', while in 1953 Theodore Yukas of the University of California at Los Angeles wrote an Ed.D. dissertation entitled the 'Educational work of Sir John Adams in the United States'. See also Rusk, 1961, 49–57.

## 4: From Day Training College to University Institute 1922–1932

1. B. Simon, 1974, *The Politics of Educational Reform 1920–1940*, London: Lawrence and Wishart, 294.
2. Simon, 1974, 363–72. Although this increase was mainly caused by more children staying on at school. Annual intake rose only from 90,601 in 1922 to 98,820 in 1938.
3. IE, Jubilee lectures 1952 correspondence, reminiscences 1919–1930.
4. *Studies and Impressions*, 46.
5. A.B. Robertson, 1990, *A Century of Change: The study of education in the University of Manchester*, Manchester: Manchester University Press, 27.
6. Quoted in H.R. Hamley, 1945, 'Sir Percy Nunn', *British Journal of Educational Psychology*, XV, 4.
7. *Studies and Impressions*, 34.
8. R.J.W. Selleck, 1972, *English Primary Education and the Progressives, 1914–1939*, London: Routledge and Kegan Paul, 46. See also P. Gordon and J. White, 1979, *Philosophers as Educational Reformers: The influ-*

*ence of idealism on British educational thought and practice*, London: Routledge and Kegan Paul, 207–16.

9. The following quotations are taken from the second revised edition of 1930.

10. Quoted in Selleck, 1972, 47.

11. For a recent criticism of Nunn see M. Phillips, 1998, *All Must Have Prizes,* London: Warner Books, 203.

12. IE, Jubilee lectures 1952 correspondence, 1919–1930, letter from A.R. Moon.

13. IE, Board of Education Consultative Committee papers, February–May 1930.

14. G. McCulloch, 1998, *Failing the Ordinary Child? The theory and practice of working-class secondary education*, Buckingham: Open University Press, 34–6.

15. G. Howson, 1982, *A History of Mathematics Education in England*, Cambridge: Cambridge University Press, 157.

16. Other LDTC and Institute staff who played important roles in the New Education Fellowship included Susan Isaacs and Joseph Lauwerys.

17. IE, Nunn papers, International Institute Examinations Enquiry, 1929–1936; A. Wooldridge, 1994, *Measuring the Mind: Education and psychology in England c.1860–c.1990*, Cambridge: Cambridge University Press, 64–5.

18. *Studies and Impressions*, 88.

19. IE, Record of students, women, 1914–1918.

20. *Studies and Impressions*, 152–5; Dixon, 1986, 28.

21. *Studies and Impressions*, 171–2.

22. L.S. Hearnshaw, 1979, *Cyril Burt, Psychologist,* London: Hodder and Stoughton, 339–41.

23. Hearnshaw, 1979, 42.

24. IE, Principal's letter book 82, 11-6-1919–24-7-1919, Nunn to Burt, 12 June 1919. In the summer of 1922 the LCC argued that the retirement of Adams would permit a deduction of £800 from the annual grant to the University, LMA EO/TRA/2/27, memorandum dated 15 June 1922.

25. ULA ST/2/2/39, Senate minutes, 24 January 1923.

26. Quoted in Wooldridge, 1994, 64.

27. F.J.C. Hearnshaw, 1929, *The Centenary History of King's College London, 1828–1928,* London: George G. Harrap, 483–4. For a more positive assessment of Dover Wilson's influence, particularly upon future members of staff of the Institute's English Department including James Britton and Margaret Spencer, see I. Reid, 2002, 'Wordsworth institutionalized: the shaping of an educational ideology', *History of Education*, 31, 1, 28.

28. IE, Jubilee lectures 1952 correspondence, reminiscences 1919–1930, letter from Dorothy Wakeford.

29. IE, Directorate correspondence, 1902–39, correspondence T.P. Nunn 1926–30, letters relating to J.A. Thornley.

30. *Studies and Impressions*, 73.

31. IE, Jubilee lectures 1952 correspondence, reminiscences 1919–1930, letter from Brian Stanley. Eventually Burt became engaged to a student, Joyce Woods; they were married in 1932, Hearnshaw, 1979, 43.

32. Claudia Clarke Papers, file 41, Nunn to Clarke, 5 March and 4 June 1932. I am most grateful to Dr Clarke for her many kindnesses in allowing me to consult her father's papers.

33. IE, Staff register 1912; *Studies and Impressions*, 147–8; Dixon, 1986, 25–6.

34. The 'Statement of Policy', drawn up by Nunn, was approved as the 'University of London, Institute of Education, Statement of Policy', by the Provisional Delegacy at its meeting on 21 June 1932.

35. Howson, 1982, 169–204.

36. Aldrich and Gordon, 1989, 219–20.

37. IE, Jubilee lectures 1952 correspondence, reminiscences 1902–1918, letter from Elizabeth Jeffery.

38. IE, LDTCC agenda papers, 19 May 1925, University of London 'Report of Inspectors of Research, Training and Equipment' by J.J. Findlay, T. Raymont and H.M. Wodehouse.

39. Howson, 1982, 157.

40. IE, Jubilee lectures 1952 correspondence, reminiscences 1919–1930, letter from G.T. Daltry.

41. IE, Staff register 1912.

42. The account which follows is taken from that source, *Studies and Impressions*, 28–37.

43. *Studies and Impressions*, 29.

44. *Studies and Impressions*, 30.

45. IE, LDTCC correspondence and memoranda, October–November 1924, Bell to Nunn, 3 November 1924.

46. *Studies and Impressions*, 75.

47. IE, Jubilee lectures 1952 correspondence, reminiscences 1902–1918, letter from L.S. Suggate.

48. IE, *Londinian*, Summer term 1925.

49. Dixon, 1986, 19–20.

50. *Studies and Impressions*, 75.

51. Claudia Clarke Papers, file 41, Nunn to Clarke, 4 June 1932.

52. Dixon, 1986, 2.

53. P. Gordon and R. Aldrich, 1997, *Biographical Dictionary of North American and European Educationists*, London: Woburn Press, 87–8.

54. IE, Jubilee lectures 1952 correspondence, reminiscences 1919–1930, letter from H.C. Whaite.
55. *Studies and Impressions*, 77.
56. For example, it was widely used in British colonies in Africa. See W.A. Dodd, 1988, 'Marion Richardson: a world influence', *Institute of Education Society Newsletter*, 3, 2, 7 and A. Spencer, 1992, 'Marion Richardson', *Institute of Education Society Newsletter*, 7, 1, 5.
57. The letter 'e' in the current Institute logo is based upon her calligraphy.
58. Selleck, 1972, 156.
59. Dixon, 1986, 19.
60. 'Colonial' in the sense of students who were prepared for posts in the colonies.
61. *Studies and Impressions*, 49.
62. B. Simon, 1998, *A Life in Education*, London: Lawrence and Wishart, 18.
63. IE, Staff register 1912.
64. IE, Staff register 1912.
65. *Jubilee Lectures*, 96–7.
66. *Jubilee Lectures*, 93.
67. *Jubilee Lectures*, 93.
68. IE, Record of students, women, 1914–1918.
69. IE, Record of students, women, 1919–1921.
70. IE, Jubilee papers 1952, 'Numbers of Oversea Students, 1902–1952'. The term 'oversea' was frequently used in place of 'overseas'.
71. Gordon and Aldrich, 1997, 520–1. In 1939 Margaret Wrong shared a house in North London with Margaret Read. See J. Read, 1991, 'Professor Margaret Read, known to our family as Auntie M.', *Institute of Education Society Newsletter*, 6, 2, 13.
72. For the background see F.J. Clatworthy, 1971, *The Formulation of British Colonial Education Policy, 1923–1948*, Ann Arbor: University of Michigan School of Education; Sir Christopher Cox, 'The development of the Institute in relation to the colonies', in *Jubilee Lectures*, 57–89 and C. Whitehead, 1988, '"Not wanted on the voyage": a study of the Colonial Department, ULIE 1927–1956', in *DICE Occasional Papers*, 11, London: Institute of Education, 1–20. I am most grateful to John Cameron, Bill Dodd and Clive Whitehead for their comments on the work of the Colonial Department.
73. Clatworthy, 1971, 88–105.
74. IE, Nunn papers, Colonial Office 1926–1928, Vischer to Nunn, 4 December 1928.
75. IE, Nunn papers, Colonial Office 1926–1928, Keating to Nunn, 14 March 1927, Nunn to Keatinge, 15 March 1927.
76. IE, Nunn papers, Colonial Office 1926–1928, memorandum on the course.
77. *Studies and Impressions*, 131.
78. *Studies and Impressions*, 132.
79. IE, Nunn papers, Colonial Office 1929–1930, reports by Nunn dated 9 June 1929 and 23 July 1930.
80. IE, Nunn papers, Colonial Office 1931–1935, Anthony Bevir to Nunn, 9 March 1932 enclosing a despatch from the Governor of Northern Rhodesia. See also Public Record Office (PRO) CO 323/1133/2, London Day Training College, Report of the Probationers Sub-Committee of the Education Advisory Committee, 1931.
81. IE, Jubilee lectures 1952 correspondence, reminiscences 1919–1930.
82. IE, Jubilee lectures 1952 correspondence, reminiscences 1919–1930.
83. IE, Nunn papers, Colonial Office 1931–1935, Nunn to Richards, 30 March 1933.
84. *Studies and Impressions*, 116.
85. IE, 'University of London, Institute of Education, Statement of Policy', 1932, appendix C.
86. IE, 'The University Department of Education', memorandum by Nunn, 22 February 1930.
87. IE, 'The University Department of Education', memorandum by Nunn, 22 February 1930.
88. The correspondence also suggests that Clarke was already identified as a possible successor to Nunn.
89. Claudia Clarke Papers, file 41, Nunn to Clarke, 12 September 1930. Clarke's memorandum, 'Proposed Imperial Institute of Education in London', is reprinted as Appendix B in Mitchell, 1967.
90. IE, 'University of London, Institute of Education, Statement of Policy', 1932.
91. IE, Miscellaneous correspondence, Tuke to Adams, 27 January 1920.
92. Tuke, 1939, 259.
93. IE, LDTCC minutes, 20 February 1931; Provisional Delegacy minutes, 15 December 1931.
94. This was the last year in which the Board of Education examined students, although the Board was still responsible for probationary teachers and thus for full certification. P. Gordon, R. Aldrich and D. Dean, 1991, *Education and Policy in England in the Twentieth Century*, London: Woburn Press, 253.
95. IE, 'The University Department of Education', memorandum by Nunn, 22 February 1930.
96. IE, 'The University Department of Edu-

cation', memorandum by Nunn, 22 February 1930.

97. Dixon, 1986, 4.
98. IE, Provisional Delegacy agenda papers, 11 March 1932. See also PRO ED24/2016, Transfer of the London Day Training College to the University to take the rank of Institute of Education papers, 1928–1932.
99. IE, Nunn papers, LCC transfer to University, LCC Education Committee minutes, 9 March 1932.
100. Claudia Clarke Papers, file 41, Nunn to Clarke, 5 March 1932.
101. Claudia Clarke Papers, file 41, Nunn to Clarke, 4 June 1932.
102. Quoted in Dixon, 1986, 4. The transfer would place additional financial burdens on central government.

## 5: New directions 1932–1939

1. Harte, 1986, 223–5.
2. *Studies and Impressions*, 89.
3. IE, Delegacy agenda papers and minutes, 23 November 1932, memorandum by Nunn.
4. IE, Annual report 1933–4.
5. Dixon, 1986, 143.
6. I am most grateful to John Grant for providing me with a copy of the *Diario do Noticias* for 13 December 1944 and for his assistance in locating the grave.
7. IE, Delegacy agenda papers and minutes, 1 February 1934.
8. Clarke was also required to continue in his role as Adviser to Oversea Students. See the later section of this chapter headed 'Fred Clarke and the Oversea Division'.
9. Mitchell, 1967, 13.
10. Three-page typescript tribute to Clarke kindly provided by Roy Niblett and in the possession of the author.
11. *Studies and Impressions*, 52.
12. Harte, 1986, 224.
13. *Studies and Impressions*, 91.
14. Claudia and Anna Clarke interviewed by Richard Aldrich, 14 August 1997.
15. Dixon, 1986, 37. In 1930 appointed teachers counted for 40 per cent of the full-time staff. By 1937 they had been reduced to 13 per cent.
16. Dixon, 1986, 36.
17. IE, Jubilee lectures 1952 correspondence, reminiscences 1930–1940. The following quotations are also from this source.
18. IE, Annual reports.
19. IE, Jubilee lectures 1952 correspondence, reminiscences 1930–1940. The following quotations are also from this source.
20. Simon, 1998, 16. The following account is taken from this source, 15–29. I am most grateful to Professor Simon for letting me see an earlier draft of this autobiography. For his later career see Simon, 1998 and D. Jones, 2001, *School of Education 1946–1996*, Leicester: University of Leicester.
21. A.C.F. Beales, the author's PGCE tutor and research supervisor, was widely known as 'Rudolf' or 'Rudolph', supposedly on account of his resemblance to the Italian-born, American film star, Rudolph Valentino.
22. For a more favourable view of Young see M. Richardson, 2000, 'A search for genius in Weimar Germany: the Abraham Lincoln Stiftung and American philanthropy', *Bulletin of the German Historical Institute*, 26, 44–109. I am most grateful to Malcolm Richardson for sending me a copy of this article.
23. IE, Jubilee lectures 1952 correspondence, reminiscences 1930–1940, letter from M. Burton.
24. Simon, 1998, 16.
25. Simon, 1974, 215 noted, for example, that in England and Wales 1,100 newly qualified teachers were still unemployed at the end of 1932.
26. Jubilee lectures 1952 correspondence, reminiscences 1930–1940, letter from M. Burton.
27. Dixon, 1986, 19.
28. IE, Annual report 1938–9.
29. *Studies and Impressions*, 147.
30. Annual reports. A similar breakdown into MA and Ph.D. is not provided for 1938–9 but the total for that year was 77, of whom 12 were full- and 65 part-time.
31. *Studies and Impressions*, 155–73.
32. One of these was by Clarke's biographer, Frank Wyndham Mitchell, an Australian, who wrote on 'The nature of mathematical thinking'.
33. *Studies and Impressions*, 155–73; Dixon, 1986, 28.
34. IE, Annual report 1933–4.
35. Dixon, 1986, 46.
36. M. White, 1999, *Thomas Logan Robertson, 1901–1969, A biographical study*, Perth: Curtin University of Technology, 50.
37. White, 1999, 45.
38. I am most grateful to Jennifer Haynes, Malcolm Richardson, Brian Simon and Clive Whitehead for their assistance in unravelling this complex story.
39. G. Shairer and E. Jameson, 1938, *Heroes of British Lifeboats*, London: George G. Harrap. The copy in the library of the Royal National Lifeboat Institution is similarly

signed 'Gerda Shairer' (not 'Schairer'). I am most grateful to Barry Cox, the honorary librarian of the RNLI, for supplying me with this information and for a copy of the review of the book in *The Life-boat*, December 1938, 618.

40. IE, Young to Clarke, 20 December 1940 enclosing a memorandum on Schairer dated 16 December 1940; Young to Clarke, 3 January 1941.

41. IE, Clarke to Dr Frank Aydelotte, Director of the Institute for Advanced Study in Princeton, 15 January 1941.

42. Malcolm Richardson to Richard Aldrich, 28 August 2000. Once in the USA, the Schairers came under the surveillance of the FBI 'and were indeed suspected – of being Communist sympathizers!' Malcolm Richardson to Richard Aldrich, 28 December 2001.

43. Wooldridge, 1994, 111. See also Gardner, 1969, and L.A.H. Smith, 1985, *To Understand and to Help: The life and work of Susan Isaacs (1885–1948)*, London: Associated University Presses.

44. Isaacs initially refused Nunn's invitation, on account of her reluctance to give up her work in psychoanalysis with its daily contact with patients and her several contributions to the *Nursery World*, including the weekly column written over the pseudonym, Ursula Wise. The correspondence, Isaacs to Nunn, 28 December 1932, Nunn to Isaacs, 6 January 1933, Nunn to Isaacs, 8 January 1933, is reproduced in Gardner, 1969, 80–5.

45. Gardner, 1969, 89.

46. *Studies and Impressions*, 179.

47. Gardner, 1969, 91.

48. Dixon, 1986, 23; *Studies and Impressions*, 93.

49. Report by Isaacs to Clarke on the Department of Child Development, February 1939, reproduced in Gardner, 1969, 179–84. Figures given in the annual report for 1938–9 were 16 full-time, 5 part-time, 37 occasional and 53 intercollegiate.

50. Smith, 1985, 90–9 provides examples of these cards.

51. 'Statement of Policy', quoted in *Jubilee Lectures*, 100.

52. *Studies and Impressions*, 136.

53. Whitehead, 1988, 4.

54. Dixon, 1986, 31.

55. Mayhew's contributions were informed not only by his experiences as an inspector and director of education in India, but also by editorship of the important journal, *Oversea Education*. See C. Whitehead, 1997, 'The Nestor of British colonial education: a por-

trait of Arthur Mayhew CIE, CMG (1878–1948)', *Journal of Educational Administration and History*, 29, 1, 51–76, and *Education Research and Perspectives*, 25, 1, 1998, which contains articles on Mayhew and Vischer

56. Dixon, 1986, 31.

57. IE, Annual reports.

58. IE, Annual report 1937–8.

59. IE, Annual report 1937–8.

60. Claudia Clarke Papers file 41, correspondence between Clarke and Nunn; IE, Nunn papers: the crucial cablegrams authorizing the Carnegie grants were dated 24 May and 8 June 1934. See also R. Glotzer, 1995, 'Sir Fred Clarke, South Africa and Canada: Carnegie Corporation philanthropy and the transition from Empire to Commonwealth', *Education Research and Perspectives*, 22, 1, 1–21.

61. Clarke's previous posts in Cape Town and Montreal had already given him substantial experience of education in South Africa and eastern Canada. See also P. Kallaway, 1996, 'Fred Clarke and the politics of vocational education in South Africa, 1911–1929', *History of Education*, 25, 4, 353–62.

62. IE, 'Report on a tour through certain British Dominions by Fred Clarke', undated.

63. IE, Clarke to Deller, 12 November 1935.

64. IE, Keppel to Clarke, 1 December 1936.

65. IE, Clarke to Keppel, 9 December 1936.

66. IE, Keppel to Clarke, 13 May 1937.

67. IE, Clarke to Keppel, 13 July 1937. During Clarke's absence from his post the Carnegie Corporation paid him an honorarium. IE, Hamley to Keppel, 30 April 1938.

68. IE, Turner and Curry to Hamley, 7 April 1938.

69. IE, Hamley to Taylor, 30 June 1938.

70. *Studies and Impressions*, 120.

71. *Studies and Impressions*, 122.

72. *Studies and Impressions*, 124.

73. Robertson's thesis, 'The special place examination: an investigation into the (London) Junior County Scholarship Examination', was approved in 1942. *Studies and Impressions*, 173–4.

74. *Studies and Impressions*, 126.

75. *Studies and Impressions*, 125.

76. IE, Annual report 1938–9.

77. IE, Taylor to Hamley, 29 June 1938.

78. *The Year Book of Education 1935*, 1935, London: Evans Brothers in association with the University of London Institute of Education, 11.

79. IE, Annual report 1938–9.

80. IE, Delegacy agenda and minutes, 28 June and 23 October 1934.
81. Harte, 1986, 220, 225–6.
82 IE, Delegacy minutes, 29 November 1934.
83. *Studies and Impressions*, 111–12.
84. IE, Annual report 1938–9.
85. IE, Jubilee lectures 1952 correspondence, reminiscences 1930–1940, letter from Eleanor M. Hiscock.
86. Dixon, 1986, 39.
87. Dixon, 1986, 35 attributes the financial problems of the Institute at this time in part to an inappropriate funding bid for the new quinquennium which began in 1935, and suggests that 'the quinquennial submission came too early in the life of the Institute for a proper financial estimate of future needs'. In 1934 the Institute's income was £49,130. 2s. 2d. Information kindly supplied by Marcus McDonald.

## 6: War and reconstruction 1939–1949

1. IE, Annual report 1939–40.
2. C. Whitehead, 'Social anthropologist and colonial educator: a profile of Professor Margaret Read, 1889–1991', unpublished paper kindly supplied by Clive Whitehead. See also Read, 1991, 13–14.
3. Printed student figures for all courses in the Annual report 1939–40 have been crossed out and replaced by handwritten figures as printed in the Annual report 1940–1. This might have been to confuse the enemy but it also raises problems for the historian!
4. IE, Annual report 1939–40. A.C. Wood, 1953, *A History of the University College Nottingham, 1881–1948*, Oxford: B.H. Blackwell, 133–4. I am most grateful to Elizabeth Tebbutt of the Department of Manuscripts and Special Collections of the University of Nottingham for her assistance in locating materials relating to this period. *Studies and Impressions*, 1952, 92.
5. IE, Jubilee lectures 1952 correspondence, reminiscences 1930–1940, letter from Peter Little.
6. IE, Report on History, attached to the Annual report 1940–1.
7. IE, Jubilee lectures 1952 correspondence, reminiscences 1930–1940, letter from Peter Little.
8. IE, Report on Art, attached to the Annual report 1940–1.
9. *Studies and Impressions*, 104–5.
10. Iris Forrester interviewed by Richard Aldrich, 9 December 1996. The author was most fortunate to be her MA and research tutor. There is no doubt as to who benefited the more from this experience.
11. Prior to 1934 Forrester lectured at the Municipal College in Portsmouth and at St George's College in London. Between 1934 and 1937 she was Assistant General Secretary to the Student Christian Movement, followed by two years as Travelling Secretary for the Christian Auxiliary Movement. See the obituary in the *History of Education Society Bulletin*, 67, 2001, 9.
12. IE, Subject reports, attached to the Annual report 1939–40.
13. IE, Delegacy minutes, 23 May and 14 June 1940. A memorandum from Clarke dated 8 May 1940 set out the case for return.
14. IE, Report on Higher Degrees and Research, attached to the Annual report 1940–1.
15. IE, Report on the Colonial Department, attached to the Annual report 1940–1.
16. IE, Jubilee lectures 1952 correspondence, reminiscences 1940–1949, letter from Vera Smith (née Netherway).
17. See W. Taylor, 1996, 'Education and the Moot', in R. Aldrich (ed.), *In History and in Education: Essays presented to Peter Gordon*, London: Woburn Press, 159–86.
18. IE, Report on History, attached to Annual report 1942–3.
19. IE, Delegacy minutes 14 June 1940. See the report of the finance sub-committee meeting of 6 March 1940 and a letter from Grace Mumford to Clarke, 5 December 1939, in which she withdrew the guarantee of £1,000 for five years given in her husband's letter to Hamley, 23 June 1938.
20. *Studies and Impressions*, 105.
21. IE, Report on Art, attached to the Annual report 1943–4.
22. IE, Report on Geography, attached to the Annual report 1943–4.
23. *Times Educational Supplement*, 3 June 1944.
24. *Studies and Impressions*, 105.
25. IE, Report on History, attached to the Annual report 1943–4.
26. *Studies and Impressions*, 106. 'Down the stairs in the midst of the mêlée tripped a young man nonchalantly carrying a neat little unexploded bomb on his outstretched palms. He had found it lying about upstairs and was told, peremptorily, as to a child, "put that *down*".'
27. IE, Jubilee lectures 1952 correspondence, reminiscences 1940–1949, 'Some reflections on the Teachers' Diploma Course, Institute of Education, 1943–44' by Doris Lee.
28. IE, Report on Child Development, attached to the Annual report 1943–4.
29. IE, Report on Higher Degrees and Research attached to the Annual report 1943–4.

30. IE, Delegacy finance sub-committee minutes, 11 November 1942, memorandum by Clarke dated 22 October 1942.

31. K. Mannheim, 1940, *Man and Society in an Age of Reconstruction*, London: Routledge and Kegan Paul, 3.

32. F. Clarke, 1948, *Freedom in the Educative Society*, London: University of London Press, 18.

33. F. Clarke, 'Karl Mannheim at the Institute of Education', in Mitchell, 1967, 165–9.

34. IE, Annual report 1946–7. For Mannheim's ideas on the relationship between education and social planning see his several writings, especially (1936) *Ideology and Utopia: An introduction to the sociology of knowledge*, London: Routledge and Kegan Paul; (1940) *Man and Society in an Age of Reconstruction*, London: Routledge and Kegan Paul; (1943) *Diagnosis of Our Time: Wartime essays of a sociologist*, London: Routledge and Kegan Paul. See also studies by W.A.C. Stewart, 1967, *Karl Mannheim on Education and Social Thought*, London: George G. Harrap; G. Remmling, 1975, *The Sociology of Karl Mannheim*, London: Routledge and Kegan Paul; C. Loader, 1985, *The Intellectual Development of Karl Mannheim: Culture, politics and planning*, Cambridge: Cambridge University Press; G. Whitty, 1997, *Social Theory and Education Policy: The legacy of Karl Mannheim*, London: Institute of Education.

35. Quoted in Dixon, 1986, 49.

36. IE, Delegacy minutes, 14 June 1940; Hartog to Clarke, 18 June 1940 offering the sum of £2,000.

37. IE, Annual report 1946–7.

38. Jeff Griffiths to Richard Aldrich, 21 August 1997.

39. I am most grateful to Jeff Griffiths for his comments on this section and for allowing me to see a draft of his history of the NFER. See also A. Yates, 1972, *The First Twenty-Five Years: A review of the NFER 1946–71*, Slough: NFER.

40. Quoted in Mitchell, 1967, 117.

41. Clarke was among those considered for the chairmanship of the Committee. For the McNair Report see D. Crook, 1995, 'Universities, teacher training and the legacy of McNair, 1944–94', *History of Education*, 24, 3, 231–45 and W.R. Niblett, D.W. Humphreys and J.R. Fairhurst, 1975, *The University Connection*, Slough: NFER.

42. All students entering the four-year course had been required to sign the 'pledge', an undertaking to pursue a career in teaching. The pledge was abolished in 1951.

43. See 'Relations with the Ministry', Wood's contribution to *Studies and Impressions*, 226–37.

44. Joint Boards had been set up from 1925. They were composed of representatives from the universities, training colleges and LEAs and were empowered to set standards of courses and conduct examinations for teachers. See Gordon, Aldrich and Dean, 1991, 253 and P. Gordon and D. Lawton, 1987, *HMI*, London: Routledge and Kegan Paul, 76–7.

45. This is usually referred to as the Hetherington Scheme, after Sir Hector Hetherington, Vice-Chancellor of Glasgow University and Chairman of the Committee of Vice-Chancellors and Principals, but David Crook has shown that McNair rather than Hetherington was the author of Scheme C, Crook, 1995, 239–40. I am most grateful to my colleague, David Crook, for his comments on this section.

46. *Studies and Impressions*, 223.

47. Quoted in Niblett *et al.*, 1975, 111.

48. Niblett *et al.*, 1975, 63.

49. Quoted in Niblett *et al.*, 1975, 75.

50. For Goldsmiths' College see Firth, 1991.

51. Quoted in Crook, 1995, 238.

52. Quoted in Dixon, 1986, 91–2.

53. *Studies and Impressions*, 13. Jeffery was awarded an MA in 1914 and a D.Sc. in 1921.

54. *Studies and Impressions*, 13.

55. *Studies and Impressions*, 17. Sir Harold Claughton was Clerk of the Court from 1929 and Principal of the University, 1941–8; Sir Graham Savage was the LCC's Chief Education Officer 1940–51, having previously been Senior Chief Inspector at the Board of Education.

56. *Studies and Impressions*, 18. Details of the Draft and Final Schemes are given in Dixon, 1986, 122–34.

57. IE, McNair negotiations, Jeffery to the Principals of Training Colleges and Departments in the London area, December 1944.

58. Harte, 1986, 244.

59. Geoffrey Barnard (student 1948–9, staff 1951–65) to Richard Aldrich, 23 February 2001. For example Jeffery took part in the Foundation Week Rag Revue. I am most grateful to Dr Barnard for his information about Jeffery.

60. *Jubilee Lectures*, 91; Mitchell, 1967, 134.

61. Quoted in Mitchell, 1967, 134.

62. Shorney, 1989, 167.

63. Geoffrey Barnard to Richard Aldrich, 23 February 2001.

64. Dixon, 1986, 120.
65. *Studies and Impressions*, 107.
66. IE, Institute of Education Development Policy, Quinquennium 1947–52. Memorandum by the Delegacy, 28 November 1946.
67. *Studies and Impressions*, 1952, 115.
68. IE, Institute of Education Development Policy, Quinquennium 1947–52. Memorandum by the Delegacy, 28 November 1946.
69. IE, University of London Visitation under Statute 114. Information furnished by the Authorities of the Institute, 1950, included with the Annual report 1948–9.
70. Quoted in Dixon, 1986, 141.
71. IE, Jubilee lectures 1952 correspondence, reminiscences 1940–1949, letter from J.M. Ritchie.
72. IE, Annual report 1947–8.
73. IE, Institute of Education Development Policy, Quinquennium 1947–52. Memorandum by the Delegacy, 28 November 1946.
74. IE, Annual report 1948–9.
75. IE, Annual report 1946–7.
76. IE, Institute of Education Development Policy, Quinquennium 1947–52. Memorandum by the Delegacy, 28 November 1946. While the increase in staff numbers was to be welcomed it creates a problem for the historian who hereafter can neither include the names of all leading members of staff nor the activities of all departments. One of the many strengths of Dixon's history is that he does provide names and details of so many staff, including a list of some 89 academic and 62 administrative members of the Central Institute, 1965–6. For examples of the contributions of Institute departments and staff to school curricula see A. Kent (ed.), 2000, *School Subject Teaching: The history and future of the curriculum*, London: Kogan Page.
77. Dixon, 1986, 73.
78. See Thomas, 1990, 197–9 for a list of LDTC and Institute professorial appointments 1902–87.
79. Jeffery to Hamley, 20 August 1947, quoted in Dixon, 1986, 80.
80. Burt to Jeffery, 25 November 1948, quoted in Dixon, 1986, 81.
81. The first Oxford professor, Richard Pring, was a former member of staff of the Institute. See Thomas, 1990, 193–204 and R. Aldrich and D. Crook, 1998, 'Education as a university subject in England: an historical interpretation', in P. Drewek and C. Lüth (eds), *History of Educational Studies*, Gent: C.S.H.P., 121–38.
82. For a different emphasis, which indicates that Wilkinson supported Scheme A but felt that she was being undermined and misrepresented by her officials, see D. Crook, 1997, 'The reconstruction of teacher education and training, 1941–54, with particular reference to the McNair Committee', unpublished Ph.D. thesis, University of Wales, Swansea, 195–200.
83. Quoted in Niblett *et al.*, 1975, 143.
84. Quoted in Dixon, 1986, 99.
85. For the role of HMI in teacher education and training see Gordon and Lawton, 1987 and J.E. Dunford, 1998, *Her Majesty's Inspectorate of Schools Since 1944: Standard bearers or turbulent priests?*, London: Woburn Press.
86. IE, Undated (1944?) memorandum by Clarke entitled 'The Institute in relation to the proposed University School of Education'.
87. Quoted in Niblett *et al.*, 1975, 182.
88. Dixon, 1986, 105.
89. Niblett *et al.*, 1975, 183.

## 7: New identities 1949–1963

1. The term Area Training Organization (ATO) was devised by the Ministry of Education and was generally disliked both in universities and colleges.
2. Chapter three is entitled 'Wider Responsibilities: a new kind of Institute, 1944–52'; chapter four, 'Forward March at the Central Institute, 1949–62'; chapter five, 'Climb to Maturity: the wider Institute, 1952–70'; chapter six, 'Consolidation and Expansion: the Central Institute, 1962–72.
3. J. Cameron, 1996, 'Days of hope: at the Institute in the 1940s', *Institute of Education Society Newsletter*, 11, 1, 22.
4. E. Round (née Lake), 1983, 'Way back to Bedford Way', *Institute of Education Society Newsletter*, 2, 17.
5. Cameron, 1996, 22.
6. IE, Provisional Council minutes, 7 July 1948.
7. IE, Provisional Council minutes, 11 February 1949.
8. IE, *Annual Report 1958–59*, 4. During the ATO period annual reports were published and widely circulated.
9. IE, Provisional Council minutes, 29 October 1948.
10. Dixon, 1986, 103.
11. On the same day the Committee of Management assumed responsibility from the Delegacy.
12. Dixon, 1986, 194.
13. Roy Niblett to Richard Aldrich, 14 October 1997.

14. The London ATO grant for 1951–2 was £20,500, Dixon, 1986, 119.
15. IE, Elvin to College Principals, 10 October 1958.
16. L. Elvin, 1987, *Encounters with Education*, London: Institute of Education, 161. (Jordans, a village in Buckinghamshire, is home to the most famous meeting house and burial ground of the Society of Friends.)
17. IE, Committee of Management minutes, 5 May 1955.
18. IE, *Annual Report 1957–58*, 15.
19. Dixon, 1986, 162.
20. *Studies and Impressions*, 95.
21. Dixon, 1986, 66, 120.
22. Epstein, however, died in 1959 and the commission passed to Peter McWilliam, Elvin, 1987, 161. The bust was unveiled by R.A. Butler in February 1961, *Annual Report 1960–61*, 9.
23. Dixon, 1987, 162. See Elvin, 1987, 171–2 for an explanation of his management philosophy.
24. Elvin, 1987, 161.
25. Quoted in Gordon, Aldrich and Dean, 1991, 217. Elvin's initial salary at Ruskin was half of what he had received at Cambridge. His main rival for the post was Richard Crossman.
26. While Director of the Institute Elvin served for eight years as Chairman of the Commonwealth Education Liaison Committee, and between 1964 and 1966 was a member of the Government of India Commission on Education.
27. The title was a device to avoid the word 'Colonial' and was later changed to Education in Developing Countries.
28. L. Elvin, 1956, *Education and the End of Empire*, London: Evans Brothers, 3, 14–15.
29. Private information.
30. Indeed, Lauwerys, who had been honoured by a D.Sc. from the University of Ghent in 1946, was awarded a D.Lit. by the University of London in 1958. See M. McLean (ed.), 1981, *Joseph A. Lauwerys: A festschrift*, London: University of London Institute of Education Library, especially the contribution by Brian Holmes entitled 'Joseph Lauwerys at the London Institute'.
31. Elvin, 1987, 169.
32. Elvin, 1987, 169.
33. P. Hirst, 1998, 'Philosophy of education: the evolution of a discipline', in G. Haydon (ed.), *50 Years of Philosophy of Education: Progress and prospects*, London: Institute of Education, 4.
34. Hirst, 1998, 4.
35. L.A. Reid, 1965, *Philosophy and the Theory and Practice of Education*, London: Evans Brothers, 5.
36. Elvin, 1987, 170.
37. Dixon, 1986, 81, 238, 252, refers to Vernon's inaudability in lectures, absences overseas and departure in 1968.
38. P. Vernon, 1955, 'The assessment of children. Recent trends in mental measurement and statistical analysis', in *The Bearings of Recent Advances in Psychology on Educational Problems*, London: Evans Brothers, 215. This collection provides full texts of the seven lectures in the series.
39. P. Vernon, 1960, *Intelligence and Attainment Tests*, London: University of London Press, 188. For Vernon's significance see Wooldridge, 1994, 285–9.
40. J.E. Floud (ed.), A.H. Halsey and F.M. Martin, 1956, *Social Class and Educational Opportunity*, London: Heinemann, 149.
41. IE, *Annual Report 1962–63*, 11.
42. The terms, 'disciplines of education', 'educational foundations' and 'foundation disciplines' are variously used and interpreted. In the 1960s reference was frequently made to the 'four disciplines' of history, philosophy, psychology and sociology of education. Comparative education, however, often had the status of a discipline at the Institute.
43. Dr Nicholas Hans of King's College, London was the other.
44. R. Cowen, 'The Year Book of Education', in McLean, 1981, 10, 15.
45. IE, *Annual Report 1960–61*, 16.
46. See her contribution to McLean, 1981, 21–6.
47. *Studies and Impressions*, 186.
48. IE, *Annual Report 1949–50*, 11.
49. Dixon, 1986, 170.
50. IE, *Annual Report 1962–63*, 11.
51. J. Vaizey, 1958, *The Costs of Education*, London: George Allen and Unwin, 23.
52. Dixon, 1986, 171.
53. IE, *Annual Report 1962–63*, 13.
54. Bristow recorded that some Indian and Pakistani students 'objected to their books being placed "under" the other' on the Comparative Education library shelves, McLean, 1981, 22.
55. See B. Pattison, 1984, *Special Relations: The University of London and new universities overseas, 1947–1970*, London: University of London.
56. In 1956 the Gold Coast achieved independence as Ghana.
57. The change took place in 1952, IE, *Annual Report 1951–52*, 13.
58. Lewis used the terms 'New Nations or the Emergent Nations'. L.J. Lewis, 1959,

*Partnership in Oversea Education*, London: Evans Brothers, 1.

59. H. Hawes, 2000, 'Making common sense academically respectable. A profile of Emeritus Professor John Lewis CMG', *Institute of Education Alumni Association Bulletin*, 4, 39.
60. IE, *Annual Reports*.
61. IE, *Annual Report 1957–58*, 11.
62. Precise comparisons are not always possible, given inconsistencies in the format of the *Annual Reports* over such matters as the inclusion of occasional students.
63. IE, *Annual Report 1949–50*, 6.
64. IE, *Annual Report 1962–63*, 1–2.
65. IE, *Annual Reports*.
66. IE, *Annual Report 1949–50*, 7.
67. IE, *Annual Report 1962–63*, 29. There was no separate category of 'occasional student' recorded from 1959–60 onwards.
68. IE, *Annual Report 1950–51*, 8.
69. IE, *Annual Report 1949–50*, 9.
70. IE, Inspectors' report on the visitation of the Institute, 1950.
71. Cameron, 1996, 23.
72. Norman Graves to Richard Aldrich, 30 October 1996.
73. D. Bridges, 1998, 'Educational research: re-establishing the philosophical terrain', in Haydon, 59–60.
74. Dixon, 1986, 236.
75. IE, *Annual Report 1949–50*, 5.
76. IE, *Annual Report 1962–63*, 21.
77. IE, *Annual Report 1959–60*, 16.
78. IE, *Annual Report 1949–50*, 5.
79. IE, *Annual Report 1957–58*, 6.
80. IE, *Annual Report 1959–60*, 4.
81. IE, *Annual Report 1960–61*, 17; Dixon, 1986, 175.
82. Dixon, 1986, 176.
83. IE, *Annual Report 1961–62*, 15.
84. IE, *Slate*, 18 January 1963, quoted in *Annual Report 1962–63*, 14.
85. Round, 1983, 16. I am most grateful to Eileen Round, E. Dunstan Roberts and Joan Clemow-Jones for information about academic arrangements and student experiences in the years covered by chapters seven and eight.
86. *International Education Notes*, 1, 2, January 1950, 2. I am most grateful to Dr Huygelen for sending me information about this initiative. Paul Huygelen to Richard Aldrich, 9 November 1998.
87. *International Education Notes*, 1, 2, January 1950, 1.
88. Round, 1983, 17.
89. IE, Visitation report 1950.
90. Dixon, 1986, 117.
91. Dixon, 1986, 174.
92. IE, *Annual Report 1958–59*, 3.
93. IE, *Annual Report 1953–54*, 19.
94. Dixon, 1986, 160.
95. Contributors included the University Library, the American Library and R.H. Tawney, IE, *Annual Report 1958–59*, 14.
96. Dixon, 1986, 174.
97. IE, *Annual Report 1959–60*, 9. The Bedford Way building would, however, result in the loss of some hostel accommodation.
98. IE, *Annual Report 1959–60*, 9; Dixon, 1986, 175.
99. IE, *Annual Report 1962–63*, 9.
100. IE, Visitation report 1950.
101. IE, *Annual Report 1962–63*, 9.
102. Elvin, 1987, 176.

## 8: Expansion and stalemate 1963–1973

1. For his account of the Committee's proceedings see Elvin, 1987, 179–85.
2. *Higher Education. Report of the Committee appointed by the Prime Minister under the Chairmanship of Lord Robbins 1961–63* (Robbins Report), 1963, London: HMSO, 270, 279.
3. IE, *Annual Report 1968–69*, 6.
4. W.R. Niblett, 1972, 'The place of teacher education in the structure of higher education', *London Educational Review*, 1, 1, 7.
5. *Final Report into the Committee of Enquiry into the Governance of the University of London* (Murray Report), 1972, London: University of London, 117. At that date there were also 33,359 external students and 23,581 extramural students.
6. Niblett, 1972, 8.
7. D. Hencke, 1978, *Colleges in Crisis: The reorganization of teacher training 1971–7*, Harmondsworth: Penguin, 31.
8. IE, *Annual Reports, 1963–64, 1968–69*.
9. IE, *Annual Report 1965–66*, 1.
10. IE, *Annual Report 1966–67*, 1.
11. IE, *Annual Reports, 1967–68, 1968–69*. Chelsea had become a school of the University and thus was given precedence over Goldsmiths' which was not.
12. IE, *Annual Report 1966–67*, 5. The faculty colour was eau-de-nil.
13. IE, Committee of Professors, 1964–71. The group comprised Elvin, Niblett, Beales, Foss, Hirst, Lauwerys, Lee, Lewis, Pattison, Peters, Tizard and Dixon.

14. IE, *Annual Report 1967–68*, 10.
15. IE, *Annual Report 1967–68*, 10.
16. IE, *Annual Report 1968–69*, 10.
17. IE, *Annual Report 1968–69*, 10.
18. University of London Institute of Education, 1971, *An Enquiry into the Education and Training of Teachers in the Area of the Institute 1970/1: An interim report, April 1971*, London: University of London Institute of Education, 83.
19. University of London Institute of Education, 1971, 83–4.
20. University of London Institute of Education, 1971, 76.
21. Lord James, a former headmaster of Manchester Grammar School, headed a committee of seven. The report was published as Department of Education and Science, 1972, *Teacher Education and Training. A Report by a Committee of Inquiry appointed by the Secretary of State for Education and Science, under the Chairmanship of Lord James of Rusholme* (James Report), London: HMSO.
22. James Report, 1972, 67.
23. H. Silver, 1975, 'Since James: interviews with Lord James, Roger Webster and James Porter', *British Journal of Teacher Education*, 1, 1, 12.
24. Quoted in Hencke, 1978, 37.
25. H.L.E., W.D.W., N.H. (Lionel Elvin, William Wall, Norman Haycocks), 1972, 'The James Report: some questions', *London Educational Review*, 1, 1, i–iv.
26. Elvin, 1987, 187.
27. Hencke, 1978, 54. Elsewhere in the Circular an overall reduction to 60–70,000 was mentioned.
28. This included a change in name (which proved only to be temporary) to Graduate Certificate in Education, *Annual Report 1967–68*, 6.
29. B. Simon, 1990, 'The study of education as a university subject', in J.B. Thomas (ed.), *British Universities and Teacher Education: A century of change*, Lewes: Falmer, 135.
30. IE, *Annual Report 1964–65*, 11.
31. IE, Committee of Management minutes, 5 November 1970.
32. IE, Committee of Management minutes, 19 January and 23 February 1967.
33. IE, Institute of Education, *Quinquennium 1967–72, Development Policy*.
34. IE, *Annual Report 1966–67*, 15.
35. IE, *Annual Report 1968–69*, 22. Accordingly, the Central Academic Board asked the Faculty of Education to undertake a review of the whole structure of assessment for what was then called the Graduate Certificate in Education.

36. IE, Elvin to the Institute branch of the Association of University Teachers, 15 February 1963.
37. IE, *Annual Report 1964–65*, 12.
38. IE, *Annual Report 1964–65*, 12.
39. IE, *Annual Report 1965–66*, 12–13.
40. IE, *Annual Report 1963–64*, 27–8.
41. IE, Secretariat, Committee of Professors, June 1959–July 1967, memorandum by Neuberg dated 12 January 1961.
42. IE, Secretariat, Committee of Professors, June 1959–July 1967, memorandum by Neuberg dated September 1963.
43. IE, *Annual Report 1968–69*, 42. Although some students who initially registered for M.Phil. might subsequently transfer to Ph.D.
44. IE, *Annual Report 1968–69*, 41–2.
45. Geoff Whitty interviewed by Richard Aldrich, 20 October 2000. For an account of the British student revolt see C. Crouch, 1970, *The Student Revolt*, London: The Bodley Head.
46. IE, *Annual Report 1968–69*, 25.
47. IE, Committee of Management minutes, 18 January 1973. The Staff Weekend was held in 1974, however, when William Taylor, the new Director, outlined his vision for the future.
48. Dixon, 1986, 253.
49. IE, *Annual Report 1967–68*, 21.
50. IE, *Annual Report 1968–69*, 23.
51. Dixon, 1986, 239.
52. IE, *Annual Report 1967–68*, 42.
53. IE, Committee of Management minutes, 5 November 1970.
54. IE, Committee of Management minutes, 4 December 1969.
55. IE, Committee of Professors 1964–71, undated memorandum by Hindley and Moore with attached note from Niblett to Elvin.
56. J.A. Downing, 1964, *The i.t.a. Reading Experiment: Three lectures on the research in infant schools with Sir James Pitman's initial teaching alphabet*, London: Evans Brothers.
57. IE, *Annual Report 1968–69*, 24.
58. IE, Committee of Professors 1964–71, Peters to Elvin, 21 January 1965. His comment was occasioned by the retirement of Harold Dent, former headmaster, Editor of the *Times Educational Supplement* and Professor of Education and Director of the University of Sheffield Institute of Education, who had been acting as Assistant Dean.
59. W.R. Niblett, 2001, *Life, Education, Discovery: A memoir and selected essays*, Bristol: Pomegranate Books, 111–12.
60. 'Our New Dean', *University of London*

*Institute of Education Bulletin*, 15, Summer 1968, 41.

61. Elvin, 1987, 171.
62. IE, Deputy Director's Office, Committee of Professors 1968–1975, notes on the meeting of 24 April 1968. Professors from other colleges could leave after part A if they wished.
63. Iris Forrester interviewed by Richard Aldrich, 9 December 1996.
64. *The Times*, 1 October 1971, carried the two obituaries side by side.
65. Denis Lawton, 1996, 'President's column', *Institute of Education Society Newsletter*, 11, 1, Spring, 6.
66. David Warren interviewed by Richard Aldrich, 16 October 1997.
67. Dixon, 1986, 238.
68. Information kindly supplied by Terry Moore, who was tutor to the Diploma in Philosophy course.
69. Klaus Neuberg to Richard Aldrich, 2 April 2000.
70. IE, Committee of Management minutes, 18 January and 20 June 1968.
71. Quoted in Dixon, 1986, 255.
72. Elvin, 1987, 163. Dixon's *Society, Schools and Progress in Scandinavia* was reviewed in the *Times Educational Supplement*, 21 January 1966.
73. IE, Committee of Professors, 1964–71, Dixon to Elvin, 16 March 1966.
74. IE, Committee of Professors agenda, March 1968–July 1978, Dixon to Elvin, 19 November 1968.
75. IE, *Annual Report 1968–69*, 19–20.
76. IE, Committee of Management minutes, 4 December 1969.
77. Dixon, 1986, 246, 251.
78. IE, Institute of Education, *Quinquennium 1967–72, Development Policy*.
79. Simon, 1990, 137. Simon defined pedagogy as 'the theory and practice of teaching'.
80. IE, Grace Wacey collection, de Montmorency to Wacey, 3 December 1977.
81. Private information from Bill Dodd.
82. Robbins Report, 1963, 28.
83. Elvin, 1987, 186.
84. Elvin, 1987, 189.
85. Hencke, 1978, 32.
86. Murray Report, 1972, 62, 216.

## 9: The turbulent years 1973–1983

1. IE, Committee of Management minutes, 6 December 1973.
2. *Education in Schools. A Consultative Document*, 1977, London: HMSO, 2, 43.
3. M. Thatcher, 1995, *The Path to Power*, London: HarperCollins, 166, quoted in G. Partington, 1999, *Teacher Education in England and Wales*, London: Institute of Economic Affairs Education and Training Unit, 64.
4. M. Thatcher, 1993, *The Downing Street Years*, London: HarperCollins, 590, quoted in Partington, 1999, 64.
5. After retirement from Hull Taylor also served as Vice-Chancellor of two 'new' universities – Huddersfield and Thames Valley.
6. William Taylor interviewed by Richard Aldrich, 30 July 1997.
7. William Taylor interviewed by Richard Aldrich, 30 July 1997.
8. IE, *Annual Report 1980–81*, 5.
9. IE, *Annual Report 1980–81*, 7.
10. Eric Earle interviewed by Richard Aldrich, 28 July 1998.
11. David Warren interviewed by Richard Aldrich, 16 October 1997.
12. IE, *Annual Financial Report and Accounts 1981–82*, 14.
13. IE, *INSTED*, 7 December 1979.
14. IE, *Annual Report 1980–81*, 7; Committee of Management minutes, 29 October 1981.
15. IE, *Annual Report 1980–81*, 39.
16. IE, Committee of Management minutes, 28 January 1982.
17. IE, *Annual Financial Report and Accounts 1981–82*, 40.
18. IE, Committee of Management minutes, 27 January 1977.
19. IE, Committee of Management minutes, 26 January 1978.
20. IE, Committee of Management minutes, 26 January 1978.
21. Denis Lawton interviewed by Richard Aldrich, 20 October 1997.
22. R. Pring, 1977, 'What is an Institute of Education for?', in University of London Institute of Education, *Seventy Fifth Anniversary*, 12.
23. From 1 May 1983 this was reduced to two-fifths. IE, Committee of Management minutes, 23 June 1983.
24. IE, Institute of Education, University of London, *Report of Activities 1981–1986*, 27. This printed report of 186 pages published in 1987 compensated for the lack of *Annual Reports* in these years.
25. IE, Committee of Management minutes, 26 January 1978. For two years until his retirement in 1982 the head of the department, John Sharwood Smith, worked on a part-time basis as this was seen as the only way of ensuring the continued existence of Classics.
26. IE, Committee of Management minutes, 12

March 1981, reporting decisions from the Policy Advisory Committee meeting of 27 February 1981.

27. IE, *Annual Report 1980–81*, 8.
28. Numbers on the separate Art and Music Teacher's certificate courses (merged into the PGCE in 1985) fell from 22 to 19 and 46 to 36 respectively. IE, *Report of Activities 1981–1986*, 27.
29. IE, *Report of Activities 1981–1986*, 27.
30. J. Jones, 1985, 'Towards Partnership in Teacher Education: the development of structure and process in a postgraduate initial teacher training course', unpublished Ph.D. thesis, University of London Institute of Education, 95.
31. Jones, 1985, 92.
32. Jones, 1985, 90.
33. IE, Committee of Management minutes, 15 March 1979.
34. IE, Committee of Management minutes, 15 March 1979.
35. IE, *Report of Activities 1981–1986*, 27.
36. For example, in 1979–80 27 per cent of the Institute's full-time students were from overseas. IE, *Annual Report 1980–81*, 6.
37. IE, Committee of Management minutes, 20 March 1975.
38. IE, *Annual Report 1980–81*, 14.
39. IE, *Report of Activities 1981–1986*, 60.
40. IE, *INSTED*, 7 December 1979.
41. IE, *INSTED*, 9 January 1976.
42. IE, Committee of Management minutes, 17 June 1976.
43. IE, Committee of Management minutes, 11 December 1980.
44. IE, Committee of Management minutes, 10 May 1979.
45. IE, *INSTED*, 5 October 1976.
46. IE, Committee of Management minutes, 27 January 1977.
47. IE, Committee of Management minutes, 27 January 1977.
48. IE, Committee of Management minutes, 10 March 1977.
49. E. Earle, 1998, 'Continuity and change: the Institute then (1964) and now (1988)', *Institute of Education Society Newsletter*, 3, 2, 2–4.
50. Popularly, if erroneously, attributed to a conjunction of two forces – the policies of a teetotal director, Peter Mortimore, and the final retirement of the convivial Bill Dodd.
51. J. Sharwood Smith, 1995, 'Barbara Hodge', *Institute of Education Society Newsletter*, 10, 1, 17.
52. David Warren interviewed by Richard Aldrich, 16 October 1997.
53. Obituary notice, 1999, *Institute of Educa-*

*tion Alumni Association Bulletin*, 3, 35.
54. IE, Secretariat Annual (Departmental) Reports, Rendel to Michael, 18 October 1976.
55. IE, Committee of Management minutes, 10 March 1977.
56. IE, Committee of Management minutes, 10 March 1977.
57. Costs were rarely awarded in such cases. The Institute's direct legal costs were in excess of £8,000.
58. The starting point for any consideration of this controversy is the *Auld Report* published by ILEA in July 1976.
59. See G. Whitty and M. Young (eds), 1976 *Explorations in the Politics of School Knowledge*, Driffield: Nafferton Books, 5.
60. IE, Committee of Management minutes, 12 May 1977.
61. IE, *Annual Financial Report and Accounts 1982–83*, 30–4. The levels of income and expenditure in respect of funded research were roughly equal in 1982–3 at £1.1 million, although some projects ran for several years.
62. IE, *Annual Financial Report and Accounts 1982–83*, 30.
63. IE, *Report of Activities 1981–1986*, 48.
64. This figure comprised 74 research officers and 29 administrative and clerical staff. IE, *Annual Financial Report and Accounts 1982–83*, 31. Discrepancies between numbers of staff in different sources may be attributed principally to differences between numbers of staff in place at a particular time and totals of staff employed at any time during an academic year.
65. IE, *Report of Activities 1981–1986*, 16.
66. Reyner Banham in an article in *New Society*, 18 March 1976, quoted in *University of London Institute of Education Calendar 1977–78*, 112.
67. Sir Denys Lasdun, 'The new Institute as part of the University precinct', in University of London Institute of Education, 1977, 7.
68. J.H.V. Davies, 'Subtlety, interest and power ... but it needs to be finished', in University of London Institute of Education, 1977, 8.
69. *University of London Institute of Education Calendar 1979–80*, 44–5.
70. IE, *Annual Report 1980–81*, 13–14.
71. IE, *Report of Activities 1981–1986*, 13–14.
72. IE, Committee of Management minutes, 11 May and 2 November 1978.
73. IE, *Annual Report 1980–81*, 13.
74. C.W. Dixon, 'Building a building', in University of London Institute of Education, 1977, 10.
75. Sir Denys Lasdun, 'The new Institute as part

of the University precinct', in University of London Institute of Education, 1977, 7.

76. *University of London Institute of Education Calendar 1977–78*, 112.

77. C.W. Dixon, 'Building a building', in University of London Institute of Education, 1977, 10.

78. *University of London Institute of Education Calendar 1977–78*, 14.

79. *University of London Institute of Education Calendar 1977–78*, 14–15.

80. IE, *Annual Report 1980–81*, 4.

81. For the opposition of the University of London to the inclusion of the word 'London' in the title of the City University see S.J. Teague, 1980, *The City University: A history*, London: City University, 126–7, 132–4.

82. Harte, 1986, 270.

83. Denis Lawton interviewed by Richard Aldrich, 20 October 1997.

84. IE, *Annual Report 1980–81*, 19.

85. D. Sutherland, 1988, 'The decline and fall of an empire', *Institute of Education Society Newsletter*, 3, 2, 9.

86. 'Good cause' had hitherto been defined as incapacity to fulfil duties either as a consequence of an offence, unacceptable conduct or physical or mental incapacity.

87. IE, Committee of Management minutes, 27 January 1983.

88. He died in 1992.

89. The first three being LDTC from 1902, University Institute from 1932 and ATO from 1949.

## 10: Survival of the fittest 1983–1994

1. IE, Committee of Management minutes, 11 December 1986.

2. Peter Newsam to Richard Aldrich, 20 July 1997. Even more worryingly, Newsam noted that all of the educational authorities in which he had previously worked had been abolished!

3. For CATE see G. Macintyre, 1991, *Accreditation of Teacher Education: The story of CATE 1984–1989*, London: Falmer Press.

4. *Better Schools*, 1985, London: HMSO, 50.

5. D. Lawton, 1996, 'President's column', *Institute of Education Society Newsletter*, 11, 1, 7.

6. Denis Lawton interviewed by Richard Aldrich, 20 October 1997.

7. *Who's Who 1986*.

8. See, for example: (1968), *Social Class, Language and Education*, London: Routledge and Kegan Paul; (1975), *Class, Culture and the Curriculum*, London: Routledge and Kegan Paul; (1980), *The Politics of the School Curriculum*, London: Routledge and Kegan Paul.

9. Lawton, 1996, 6.

10. Lawton, 1996, 7.

11. Lawton, 1996, 7.

12. *Times Educational Supplement*, 18 September 1987.

13. D. Lawton and C. Chitty (eds), 1988, *The National Curriculum*, London: Institute of Education, 19. This publication, Bedford Way Paper 33, did not improve relationships with the government.

14. Denis Lawton interviewed by Richard Aldrich, 20 October 1997.

15. D. Lawton, 1989, 'The eighties ...', *Institute of Education Society Newsletter*, 4, 1, 3.

16. Harte, 1986, 284.

17. IE, Committee of Management minutes, 6 March 1986.

18. Terry Davis retired in 1984 to become Acting Vice-Chancellor of the University of Botswana.

19. In 1986 Mitchell resigned to become Chief Adviser to the Leicestershire Education Committee.

20. IE, Committee of Management minutes, 7 March 1985.

21. Although Newsam looked to the future in a number of ways, not least in identifying the need for a centenary history.

22. The ceremony was performed by Baroness Blackstone.

23. IE, Council minutes, 25 June 1991.

24. IE, Council minutes, 29 June 1989.

25. IE, Council minutes, 29 June 1989. Newsam became chair of the Institute's Initial Courses Board.

26. IE, Council minutes, 29 June 1989.

27. IE, Council minutes, 29 June 1989.

28. IE, Committee of Management minutes, 24 October 1985.

29. Five years later, however, the University Commissioners amended Statute 17 under the terms of the Education Reform Act of 1988. IE, Council minutes, 10 December 1992.

30. Institute of Education University of London, 1988, *Charter 1988*, 3.

31. B. Lodge, 1988, 'Upsetting the agenda', *Times Educational Supplement*, 3 June.

32. Investments had previously been managed by the Court of the University.

33. IE, Council minutes, 10 December 1987.

34. D. Warren, 1993, 'Institute Presentation Ceremony', *Institute of Education Society Newsletter*, 8, 2, 9. Richard Aldrich was appointed Public Orator.

35. IE, Committee of Management minutes, 11 December 1986.

36. IE, Committee of Management minutes, 5 December 1985.
37. IE, Council minutes, 15 December 1988.
38. IE, Council minutes, 16 March 1989.
39. 'Interview with Sir Peter Newsam', *Institute of Education Newsletter*, 9, 2, 1994, 7.
40. This show of independence did not damage Newsam's standing within the University. Indeed, he was elected Deputy Vice-Chancellor for the period September 1992 to August 1994.
41. S.D. Tunnicliffe, 1993, 'Topping out the library', *Institute of Education Society Newsletter*, 8, 1, 12. The move into the new library began in February 1993; on 9 November of that year it was officially opened by The Princess Royal.
42. G. Brewer, 1993, 'A new library for the Institute', *Institute of Education Society Newsletter*, 8, 2, 4.
43. The great majority of students in this category were enrolled on specialist diploma/certificate courses.
44. These comprised MA, M.Sc., M.Phil. and Ph.D.
45. IE, *Prospectus 1994–95*, A10.
46. IE, *Prospectus 1995–96*, A10.
47. For example, 414 in 1983–4 and 449 in 1990–1, IE, Council minutes, 28 March 1991.
48. N. Graves, 1986, 'The new PGCE', *Institute of Education Society Newsletter*, 1, 1, 2.
49. N. Graves, 1990, 'News from initial teacher training', *Institute of Education Society Newsletter*, 5, 1, 6.
50. IE, Committee of Management minutes, 5 March 1987.
51. N. Graves, 1991, 'Recent trends in teacher education', *Institute of Education Society Newsletter*, 6, 2, 7.
52. IE, Council minutes, 10 December 1992.
53. IE, Council minutes, 2 July and 10 December 1992.
54. DFE *News*, 215/94.
55. In some cases it became a refuge for those who could not gain admission to a PGCE course.
56. See the Ofsted Reports: *The Articled Teacher Scheme, September 1990–July 1992*, 1993; *The Licensed Teacher Scheme, September 1990–July 1992*, 1993; *School-centred Initial Teacher Training, 1993–4*, 1995.
57. IE, *Prospectus 1983–84*, 63–70.
58. IE, *Prospectus 1993–94*, B9.
59. IE, *Prospectus 1993–94*, B14.
60. IE, *Prospectus 1995–96*, A10.
61. D. Lawton, 1994, 'The B.Ed. Centre', *Institute of Education Society Newsletter*, 9, 1, 12.
62. IE, *Prospectus 1985–86*, 13. Formerly called the academic diploma in education and subsequently the advanced diploma in education.
63. IE, *Prospectus 1993–94*, A4.
64. IE, Committee of Management minutes, 5 December 1985.
65. Michael Barber's Institute and subsequent careers are considered in the next chapter.
66. IE, Council minutes, 1 July 1993.
67. *Institute of Education Society Newsletter*, 1, 1, 1986, 8.
68. G. Kennedy, 1986, 'A U.S. student's viewpoint', *Institute of Education Society Newsletter*, 1, 1, 6–7.
69. Institute of Education University of London, 1988, *Charter 1988*.
70. IE, *Prospectus 1985–86*, 14. Apparent discrepancies between research staff numbers as given in the *Prospectuses* and in the *Annual Financial Report and Accounts* may be attributed to differences in calculation: between those in post on a particular day in the year and the total number employed during a year, and upon the inclusion or exclusion of administrative and secretarial staff.
71. IE, *Prospectus 1995–96*, A10.
72. 'A star is born, the team that toppled Wogan', *Institute of Education Society Newsletter*, 3, 1, 1988, 1.
73. IE, *Report of Activities 1981–1986*, 179–81.
74. IE, *Report of Activities 1981–1986*, 182–4.
75. This was the official designation for staff who were still generally known as porters.
76. *Institute of Education Society Newsletter*, 3, 1, 1988, 4.
77. 'Professor Brian Holmes 1920–1993', *Institute of Education Society Newsletter*, 8, 2, 1993, 6–7.
78. D. Lawton, 1991, 'Professor Basil Bernstein', *Institute of Education Society Newsletter*, 6, 1, 4.
79. See, for example: A. Sadovnik (ed.), 1995, *Knowledge and Pedagogy: The sociology of Basil Bernstein*, Norwood, New Jersey: Ablex Publishing Corporation; P. Atkinson, B. Davies and S. Delamont (eds), 1995, *Discourse and Reproduction: Essays in honor of Basil Bernstein*, Cresskill, New Jersey: Hampton Press.
80. Sadovnik, 1995, vii.
81. See S. Power, P. Aggleton, J. Brannen, A. Brown, L. Chisholm and J. Mace (eds), 2001, *A Tribute to Basil Bernstein 1924–2000*, London: Institute of Education
82. M. Naish, 1991, 'Professor Norman Graves', *Institute of Education Society Newsletter*, 6, 1, 4–5.

83. B. Bernstein, 1991, 'Professor Barbara Tizard', *Institute of Education Society Newsletter*, 6, 1, 5.

84. P. Mortimore, 1994, 'Professor Desmond Nuttall', *Institute of Education Society Newsletter*, 9, 1, 15.

85. IE, Council minutes, 3 March 1988.

86. B. Bernstein, 1990, 'Why the Institute is so good', *Institute of Education Society Newsletter*, 5, 1, 4.

87. D. Baylis, 1998, 'Professor Ann Oakley', *Institute of Education Alumni Association Bulletin*, 2, 19.

88. Policy Studies comprised Economics of Education, Educational Administration, Human Rights and Education and Sociology of Education. History, Humanities and Philosophy incorporated History in Education, History of Education, Humanities, Political Education, Philosophy of Education, Religious Education and Social Studies.

89. M. Young, 1990, 'The Post 16 Education Centre', *Institute of Education Society Newsletter*, 5, 1, 8; M. Young, 1993, 'The Post 16 Education Centre', *Institute of Education Society Newsletter*, 8, 2, 10–11.

90. G. Williams, 1990, 'Centre for Higher Education Studies', *Institute of Education Society Newsletter*, 5, 1, 9; C. Loder, 1993, 'The Centre for Higher Education Studies', *Institute of Education Society Newsletter*, 8, 2, 11.

91. J. Sayer, 1990, 'The Education Management Unit', *Institute of Education Society Newsletter*, 5, 1, 9.

92. IE, *Prospectus 1993–94*, A29.

93. *Housewife*, 1976, Harmondsworth: Penguin.

94. The winner of a limerick competition in the *New Statesman* in 1989 wrote:
    A jaded young housewife from Wapping
    Said her life was all cleaning and shopping
    Her husband said jokily
    Try reading Ann Oakley
    So she did and left home without stopping
    (Baylis, 1998, 19)

95. (1989), *The Men's Room*, London: Flamingo; (1996), *Man and Wife*, London: HarperCollins; (1999), *Overheads*, London: Flamingo. See Baylis, 1998, 18–20.

96. E. Earle, 1988, 'Continuity and change: the Institute then (1964) and now (1988)', *Institute of Education Society Newsletter*, 3, 2, 2–4.

97. 'The Registry Department', *Institute of Education Society Newsletter*, 5, 1, 1990, 16.

98. P. Westley, 1991, 'Finance Department', *Institute of Education Society Newsletter*, 6, 2, 18.

99. UGC Circular 12/85; IE, *Annual Financial Report and Accounts 1984–85*, 5.

100. IE, Committee of Management minutes, 18 June 1987.

101. Bernstein, 1990, 4.

102. IE, Council minutes, 1 July 1993, Newsam to Professor Graeme Davies of the HEFCE, 7 May 1993.

103. IE, Council minutes, 18 March 1993, Paul Hubbard to Stewart Sutherland, 24 February 1993.

104. IE, Council minutes, 16 December 1993.

105. IE, Council minutes, 16 December 1993, Higher Education Quality Council, *The Institute of Education, University of London, Quality Audit Report, November 1993*.

106. The Dixon Gallery was later used to house the National Library for the Handicapped Child and subsequently made way for the Library.

107. 'Child-to-Child at the Institute', *Institute of Education Society Newsletter*, 6, 1, 1991, 8.

108. *Institute of Education Society Newsletter*, 2, 1, 1987, 4–5.

109. John Clare, 1991, 'Who was he talking about?', *Daily Telegraph*, 24 April.

110. IE, Council minutes, 16 December 1993.

111. For example, in 1994–5 the Institute received HEFCE funding of £2,154 for each primary student as compared to £2,951 per student at Goldsmiths' and an average across all institutions of £2,848. Council funding for a secondary maths student at the Institute was £2,151 as compared to £2,626 at King's College, £2,729 at Goldsmiths' and £3,861 at the Roehampton Institute of Higher Education. IE, Senate minutes, 29 November 1995. This issue of underfunding was raised with the chief executive officer of the TTA, Anthea Millett, when she visited the Institute in March 1995. IE, Council minutes, 23 March 1995. Revised funding for PGCE courses was introduced from 1997–8.

112. IE, Council minutes, 21 March 1991.

113. IE, Council minutes, 1 July 1993.

## 11: Into a new century 1994–2002

1. The DfEE was created in 1995. See R. Aldrich, D. Crook and D. Watson, 2000, *Education and Employment: The DfEE and its place in history*, London: Institute of Education.

2. *The Times*, 9 September 1999.

3. His several publications included co-authorship of the highly influential *Fifteen*

*Thousand Hours: Secondary schools and their effects on children*, 1979, London: Open Books, and of *School Matters: The junior years*, 1988, London: Open Books.

4. (1991), *The Primary Head: Roles, responsibilities and reflections*, London: Paul Chapman, and (1991) *The Secondary Head: Roles, responsibilities and reflections*, London: Paul Chapman. Jo Mortimore, a former primary school teacher, was also an Institute person, having worked as a researcher in the Thomas Coram Unit and with Tessa Blackstone. In 1997 she completed a Ph.D. under the supervision of Denis Lawton.

5. L. Hodges, 1995, 'Cut above the rest', *Times Educational Supplement*, 17 November.

6. P. Mortimore, 1998, *The Road to Improvement: Reflections on school effectiveness*, Lisse, The Netherlands: Swets and Zeitlinger B.V., 336.

7. M. Phillips, 1998, 'Spare the teachers and spoil the child', *Sunday Times*, 18 October. See Mortimore's letter of response, *Sunday Times*, 25 October 1998.

8. For an excellent summary of this controversy see Dunford, 1998, 223–5 from which these quotations are taken.

9. This was one in a series of education debates jointly sponsored by the Institute and the *Guardian* newspaper.

10. H. Green, 1999, 'Underrated and underpaid', *Alumni Association Bulletin*, 3, 25.

11. IE, Peter Mortimore to All Staff and Co-Presidents of the Students' Union, 15 December 1999.

12. P. Mortimore and M. McGarvie, 1994, 'All change, for matrix rule', *Times Higher Educational Supplement*, 8 July.

13. He was appointed Professor in the same year and re-appointed Dean for a further term in 1999.

14. IE, *Prospectus 2000–2001*, 106. Some groups had fewer than 10 members of academic staff.

15. *Alumni Association Bulletin*, 1, 1997, 24.

16. IE, Council minutes, 29 June 1995, 'Academic Staffing Resource Allocation Model', C/35.

17. As in the cases of Barber, Gipps, Griffiths, MacGilchrist and Whitty.

18. By this date the post of Dean of New Initiatives had been discontinued.

19. IE, Senate minutes, 26 November 1997.

20. IE, Senate minutes, 27 November 1996.

21. This in turn was overtaken by Circular 4/98 which advised, among other amendments, that introduction of the new primary curriculum in science and the new secondary curriculum in English, mathematics and science could be delayed until September 1999.

22. IE, Senate minutes, 3 March 1999. The Open University had withdrawn its primary PGCE course for two years and top rated institutions, including the Institute, were invited to bid for the 600 places released by this withdrawal.

23. IE, Strategic Planning Document for Academic Board and Senate, October 1999.

24. The nine categories were: White, Black-Caribbean, Black-African, Black-Other, Asian-Indian, Asian-Pakistani, Asian-Bangladeshi, Asian-Chinese, Asian-Other.

25. IE, Senate minutes, 9 June 1999. For statistics on the 1999 and 2000 entries which also showed a higher rate of rejection of students from ethnic minorities see IE, Senate minutes, 6 June 2001.

26. Partington, 1999, 77.

27. IE, Institute of Education, *Corporate Plan, 1995/96–1998/99*, 10.

28. IE, Senate minutes, 29 November 1995.

29. IE, Senate minutes, 26 February 1997. This pattern reflected national trends. IE, Report of Foresight Group on the Changing Student Population, 10 April 2001, 2–6.

30. IE, Institute of Education, University of London, *Self-Assessment Document. Quality Assurance Agency Subject Review. Review of Education January 2001*, 5.

31. Including those of the EU. IE, Institute of Education, University of London, *Self-Assessment Document. Quality Assurance Agency Subject Review. Review of Education January 2001*, 6.

32. IE, Institute of Education, University of London, *Self-Assessment Document. Quality Assurance Agency Subject Review. Review of Education January 2001*, Section C, Annex 2.

33. IE, Senate minutes, 25 November 1998.

34. See R. Heilbronn and C. Jones (eds), 1997, *New Teachers in an Urban Comprehensive School: Learning in partnership*, Stoke on Trent: Trentham.

35. The Institute was awarded 22 points out of 24 in this assessment.

36. One important initiative of this period was *Learning Matters*, re-launched in March 2001 as an on-line journal, discussion forum and archive for pedagogic issues.

37. Swanwick had some experience in the role, having assumed responsibility for student-related research matters between June and November 1996 when Gipps was serving on the Education Panel of the RAE.

38. IE, Senate minutes, 26 November 1997.

39. IE, *Doctoral School Prospectus 2000–2001*, 15. The first completion, by Patrick Finucane, took place in March 2001.

40. Annually updated booklets included: *Procedures and Guidelines for Research Students and their Supervisors, Doctoral Studies Programme: A guide for research students*, and a *Research Tutors' Handbook*.

41. IE, Senate minutes, 9 June 1999.

42. IE, Council minutes, 15 December 1994.

43. IE, Institute of Education, *Corporate Plan 1997/98 to 2000/01*, 5.

44. 'Research news', *Alumni Association Bulletin*, 3, 1999, 4.

45. IE, Senate minutes, 20 October 1999.

46. IE, Senate minutes, 10 June 1998.

47. IE, Senate minutes, 10 June 1998.

48. John Breakell subsequently became head of the IDO which was renamed the International Development Unit (IDU). Following Breakell's retirement in 1999, IDU was merged with the Student Programmes Office, which reverted to the title of Registry.

49. J. Porter, 1994, 'The Institute and the world: issues in international education', *Institute of Education Society Newsletter*, 9, 1, 5.

50. *Alumni Association Bulletin*, 1, 1997, 1.

51. IE, Senate minutes, 6 March 1996.

52. IE, Senate minutes, 12 June 1996.

53. The importance of these two activities was shown by their subsequent conversion into full-time posts.

54. See, however, the later reference in this chapter to the joint project with Birkbeck College to build a knowledge laboratory and education archive.

55. There were 107 replacements.

56. Geoff Whitty interviewed by Richard Aldrich, 20 October 2000.

57. His publications included *Sociology and School Knowledge*, 1985, London: Methuen, and co-authored volumes: *The State and Private Education*, 1989, London: Falmer; *Devolution and Choice in Education*, 1998, Buckingham: Open University Press and *Teacher Education in Transition*, 2000, Buckingham: Open University Press.

58. C.A. Torres, 1998, *Education, Power, and Personal Biography: Dialogues with critical educators*, London: Routledge, 253. Whitty had been a local councillor in Bath in the 1970s and early 1980s.

59. The others were: Nunn 14, Clarke nine, Jeffery 12, Elvin 15, Taylor 10, Lawton six, Mortimore six. There was a gap, 1957–8, between the death of Jeffery and the appointment of Elvin.

60. Newsam was a pupil at Clifton College.

61. 'Interview with Sir Peter Newsam', *Institute of Education Society Newsletter*, 9, 2, 1994, 6.

62. Nunn, Jeffery, Taylor, Lawton and Mortimore. Adams graduated from Glasgow, Clarke and Newsam from Oxford and Elvin and Whitty from Cambridge.

63. Although all were well travelled and had first-hand experience of education in other countries, while Elvin had spent six years in Paris as Director of the Unesco department of education immediately before coming to the Institute in 1956.

64. IE, Director's address to staff, Logan Hall, 18 September 2000. The following quotations are also from this source.

65. IE, Second update on action following the Director's address to staff on 18 September 2000.

66. IE, Director's address to staff, Logan Hall, 18 September 2000

67. IE, Senate minutes, 6 June 2001. The percentages of women in each category, beginning with professors, were 42, 44, 55, 52, and 80.

68. A survey of UK university staff in 1999–2000 placed the Institute first in its percentages of women in senior lecturing and research posts (54 per cent as opposed to 24 per cent nationally) and fourth in its percentage of female professors (38 per cent compared with 12 per cent nationally). *Times Higher Education Supplement*, 26 October 2001.

# Select bibliography

Adams, J. (1897), *The Herbartian Psychology Applied to Education*, London: Isbister and Heath.

—— (1902), *The Protestant School System in the Province of Quebec*, London: Longmans Green.

—— (1909), *Exposition and Illustration in Teaching*, London: Macmillan.

—— (1912), *The Evolution of Educational Theory*, London: Macmillan.

—— (1922), 'Work for the training of teachers in London', in North London Collegiate School, *Sophie Bryant, D.Sc., Litt.D. 1850–1922*, London: North London Collegiate School.

Aldrich, R. (1990), 'The evolution of teacher education', in N. Graves (ed.), *Initial Teacher Education: Policies and progress*, London: Kogan Page.

—— (1995), *School and Society in Victorian Britain: Joseph Payne and the new world of education*, New York: Garland.

—— (ed.) (2002), *A Century of Education*, London: RoutledgeFalmer.

Aldrich, R. and Crook, D. (1998), 'Education as a university subject in England: an historical interpretation', in P. Drewek and C. Lüth (eds), *History of Educational Studies*, Gent: C.S.H.P.

Aldrich, R. and Gordon, P. (1989), *Dictionary of British Educationists*, London: Woburn Press.

Aldrich, R., Crook, D. and Watson, D. (2000), *Education and Employment: The DfEE and its place in history*, London: Institute of Education.

Atkinson, P., Davies, B. and Delamont, S. (1995), *Discourse and Reproduction: Essays in honor of Basil Bernstein*, Creskill, New Jersey: Hampton Press.

Ballard, P.B. (1935), 'Sir John Adams', *British Journal of Educational Psychology*, V.

Barber, M. (1996), *The Learning Game: Arguments for a learning revolution*, London: Victor Gollancz.

Barnard, H.C. (1961), 'J.W. Adamson, 1857–1947', *British Journal of Educational Studies*, X, 1.

Baylis, D. (1998), 'Professor Ann Oakley', *Alumni Association Bulletin*, 2.

Bernstein, B. (1990), 'Why the Institute is so good', *Institute of Education Society Newsletter*, 5, 1.

—— (1991), 'Professor Barbara Tizard', *Institute of Education Society Newsletter*, 6, 1.

Black, M. (1933), *The Nature of Mathematics: A critical survey*, London: Kegan Paul, Trench, Trubner and Co.

Brennan, E.J.T. (1962), 'Sidney Webb and the London Technical Education Board: IV the London Education Act of 1903', *Vocational Aspect*, XIV, 28.

—— (1972), 'Educational engineering with the Webbs', *History of Education*, 1, 2.

—— (ed.) (1975), *Education for National Efficiency: The contribution of Sidney and Beatrice Webb*, London: Athlone Press.

Brewer, G. (1993), 'A new library for the Institute', *Institute of Education Society Newsletter*, 8, 2.

Bridges, D. (1998), 'Educational research: re-establishing the philosophical terrain', in G. Haydon (ed.), *50 Years of Philosophy of Education: Progress and prospects*, London: Institute of Education.

Burt, C. (1920), *The Backward Child*, London: University of London Press.

—— (1921), *Mental and Scholastic Tests*, London: P.S. King.

—— (1925), *The Young Delinquent*, London: University of London Press.

Cameron, J. (1996), 'Days of hope: at the Institute in the 1940s', *Institute of Education Society Newsletter*, 11, 1.

Chapman, J.V. (1985), *Professional Roots: The College of Preceptors in British society*, Epping: Theydon Bois Publications.

Clarke, F. (1940), *Education and Social Change*, London: Sheldon Press.

—— (1948), *Freedom in the Educative Society*, London: University of London Press.

Clatworthy, F.J. (1971), *The Formulation of British Colonial Education Policy, 1923–1948*, Ann Arbor: University of Michigan School of Education.

Collins, G. (ed.) (1996), *Education Matters: Excerpts from the Saffron Walden College magazines, 1899–1995*, London: Carlyon Print.

Cowen, R. (1981), 'The Year Book of Education', in M. McLean (ed.), *Joseph A. Lauwerys: A festschrift*, London: University of London Institute of Education Library.

Crook, D. (1995), 'Universities, teacher training and the legacy of McNair, 1944–94', *History of Education*, 24, 3.

—— (1997), 'The reconstruction of teacher education and training, 1941–54, with particular reference to the McNair Committee', unpublished Ph.D. thesis, University of Wales, Swansea.

Crouch, C. (1970), *The Student Revolt*, London: The Bodley Head.

Dahrendorf, R. (1995), *LSE: A history of the London School of Economics and Political Science 1895–1995*, Oxford: Oxford University Press.

Dent, H.C. (1977), *The Training of Teachers in England and Wales, 1800–1975*, Sevenoaks: Hodder and Stoughton.

Dixon, C.W. (1986), *The Institute: A personal account of the history of the University of London Institute of Education, 1932–1972*, London: Institute of Education.

Dodd, W.A. (1988) 'Marion Richardson: a world influence', *Institute of Education Society Newsletter*, 3, 2.

Downing, J.A. (1964), *The i.t.a. Reading Experiment: Three lectures on the research in infant schools with Sir James Pitman's initial teaching alphabet*, London: Evans Brothers.

Dunford, J.E. (1998), *Her Majesty's Inspectorate of Schools Since 1944: Standard bearers or turbulent priests?* London: Woburn Press.

Earle, E. (1998), 'Continuity and change: the Institute then (1964) and now (1988)', *Institute of Education Society Newsletter*, 3, 2.

Elvin, L. (1956), *Education and the End of Empire*, London: Evans Brothers.

—— (1987), *Encounters with Education*, London: Institute of Education.

Elvin, L., Wall, W. and Haycocks, N. (1972), 'The James Report: some questions', *London Educational Review*, 1, 1.

Fairgrieve, J. (1946), 'In memory of Miss Margaret Punnett', *Londinian*.

Firth, A.E. (1991), *Goldsmiths' College: A centenary account*, London: Athlone Press.

Fleming, C. (1958), *Teaching: A psychological analysis*, London: Methuen.

Floud, J.E. (ed.), Halsey, A.H. and Martin, F.M. (1956), *Social Class and Educational Opportunity*, London: Heinemann.

Gardner, D.E.M. (1969), *Susan Isaacs*, London: Methuen.

Gibbon, I.G. and Bell, R.W. (1939), *History of the London County Council 1889–1939*, London: Macmillan.

Glotzer, R. (1995), 'Sir Fred Clarke, South Africa and Canada: Carnegie Corporation philanthropy and the transition from Empire to Commonwealth', *Education Research and Perspectives*, 22, 1.

Goodings, R. (1958 and 1959), 'The London Day Training College', *Education Libraries Bulletin*, 2, 3 and 4.

Gordon, P. (ed.) (1980), *The Study of Education: A collection of inaugural lectures, Vol.1: early and modern*, London: Woburn Press.

Gordon, P. and Aldrich, R. (1997), *Biographical Dictionary of North American and European Educationists*, London: Woburn Press.

Gordon, P. and Lawton, D. (1987), *HMI*, London: Routledge and Kegan Paul.

Gordon, P. and White, J. (1979), *Philosophers as Educational Reformers: The influence of idealism on British educational thought and practice*, London: Routledge and Kegan Paul.

Gordon, P., Aldrich, R. and Dean, D. (1991), *Education and Policy in England in the Twentieth Century*, London: Woburn Press.

Gosden, P.H.J.H. (1972), *The Evolution of a Profession: A study of the contribution of teachers' associations to the development of school teaching as a professional occupation*, Oxford: Basil Blackwell.

—— (ed.) (1991), *The University of Leeds School of Education 1891–1991*, Leeds: University of Leeds.

Graves, N. (1986), 'The new PGCE', *Institute of Education Society Newsletter*, 1, 1.

—— (1990), 'News from initial teacher training', *Institute of Education Society Newsletter*, 5, 1.

—— (1991), 'Recent trends in teacher education', *Institute of Education Society Newsletter*, 6, 2.

Green, H. (1999), 'Underrated and underpaid', *Alumni Association Bulletin*, 3.

Hall, R. (1977), *Marie Stopes: A biography*, London: Andrew Deutsch.

Hamley, H.R. (1945), 'Sir Percy Nunn', *British Journal of Educational Psychology*, XV.

Harte, N. (1986), *The University of London, 1836–1986: An illustrated history*, London: Athlone Press.

Hawes, H. (2000), 'Making common sense academically respectable. A profile of Emeritus Professor John Lewis CMG', *Institute of Education Alumni Association Bulletin*, 4.

Hearnshaw, F.J.C. (1929), *The Centenary History of King's College London, 1828–1928*, London: George G. Harrap.

Hearnshaw, L.S. (1979), *Cyril Burt, Psychologist*, London: Hodder and Stoughton.

Heilbronn, R. and Jones, C. (eds) (1997), *New Teachers in an Urban Comprehensive School: Learning in partnership*, Stoke on Trent: Trentham.

Hencke, D. (1978), *Colleges in Crisis: The reorganization of teacher training 1971–7*, Harmondsworth: Penguin.

Hirst, P. (1998), 'Philosophy of education: the evolution of a discipline', in G. Haydon (ed.), *50 Years of Philosophy of Education: Progress and prospects*, London: Institute of Education.

Howson, G. (1982), *A History of Mathematics Education in England*, Cambridge: Cambridge University Press.

Humby, M. (1993), 'The Institute of Education centenary history project', *Education Libraries Bulletin*, 36, 1.

Isaacs, S. (1929), *The Nursery Years*, London: Routledge.

—— (1930), *Intellectual Growth in Young Children*, London: Routledge and Kegan Paul.

—— (1932), *The Children We Teach*, London: University of London Press.

—— (1933), *Social Development in Young Children*, London: Routledge and Kegan Paul.

Jones, D. (2001), *School of Education 1946–1996*, Leicester: University of Leicester.

Jones, J. (1985), 'Towards partnership in teacher education: the development of structure and process in a postgraduate initial teacher training course', unpublished Ph.D. thesis, University of London Institute of Education.

Jones, L.G.E. (1924), *The Training of Teachers in England and Wales: A critical survey*, Oxford: Oxford University Press.

Judges, A.V. (1961), 'The educational influence of the Webbs', *British Journal of Educational Studies*, X, 1.

Kallaway, P. (1996), 'Fred Clarke and the politics of vocational education in South Africa, 1911–1929', *History of Education*, 25, 4.

Kennedy, G. (1986), 'A U.S. student's viewpoint', *Institute of Education Society Newsletter*, 11, 1.

Kent, A. (ed.) (2000), *School Subject Teaching: The history and future of the curriculum*, London: Kogan Page.

Lawton, D. (1989), 'The eighties …', *Institute of Education Society Newsletter*, 4, 1.

—— (1991), 'Professor Basil Bernstein', *Institute of Education Society Newsletter*, 6, 1.

—— (1994), 'The B.Ed. Centre', *Institute of Education Society Newsletter*, 9, 1.

—— (1996), 'President's column', *Institute of Education Society Newsletter*, 11, 1.

Lawton, D. and Chitty, C. (eds) (1988), *The National Curriculum*, London: Institute of Education.

Lewis, L.J. (1959), *Partnership in Oversea Education*, London: Evans Brothers.

Loader, C. (1985), *The Intellectual Development of Karl Mannheim: Culture, politics and planning*, Cambridge: Cambridge University Press.

Loder, C. (1993), 'The Centre for Higher Education Studies', *Institute of Education Society Newsletter*, 5, 1.

Lomax, D.E. (ed.) (1973), *The Education of Teachers in Britain*, London: John Wiley.

Lowndes, G.A.N. (1937), *The Silent Social Revolution: An account of the expansion of public education in England and Wales, 1895–1935*, London: Oxford University Press.

Macintyre, G. (1991), *Accreditation of Teacher Education: The story of CATE 1984–1989*, London: Falmer Press.

McLean, M. (ed.) (1981), *Joseph A. Lauwerys: A festschrift*, London: University of London Institute of Education Library.

Maclure, S. (1970), *One Hundred Years of London Education, 1870–1970*, London: Allen Lane.

McCulloch, G. (1998), *Failing the Ordinary Child? The theory and practice of working-class secondary education*, Buckingham: Open University Press.

Mannheim, K. (1940), *Man and Society in an Age of Reconstruction*, London: Routledge and Kegan Paul.

Mitchell, F.W. (1967), *Sir Fred Clarke. Master-teacher 1880–1952*, London: Longmans.

Mortimore, P. (1994), 'Professor Desmond Nuttall', *Institute of Education Society Newsletter*, 9, 1.

—— (1998), *The Road to Improvement: Reflections on school effectiveness*, Lisse, The Netherlands: Swets and Zeitlinger B.V.

Naish, M. (1991), 'Professor Norman Graves', *Institute of Education Society Newsletter*, 6, 1.

Niblett, W.R. (1972), 'The place of teacher education in the structure of higher education', *London Educational Review*, 1, 1.

—— (2001), *Life, Education, Discovery: A memoir and selected essays*, Bristol: Pomegranate Books.

Niblett, W.R., Humphreys, D.W. and Fairhurst, J.R. (1975), *The University Connection*, Slough: NFER.

North London Collegiate School (1922), *Sophie Bryant, D.Sc., Litt.D. 1850–1922*, London: North London Collegiate School.

Nunn, T.P. (1920), *Education: Its data and first principles*, London: Edward Arnold.

—— (1923), *Relativity and Gravitation: An elementary treatise upon Einstein's theory*, London: University of London Press.

Partington, G. (1999), *Teacher Education in England and Wales*, London: Institute of Economic Affairs Education and Training Unit.

Pattison, B. (1984), *Special Relations: The University of London and new universities overseas, 1947–1970*, London: University of London.

Phillips, M. (1998), *All Must Have Prizes*, London: Warner Books.

Porter, J. (1994), 'The Institute and the world: issues in international education', *Institute of Education Society Newsletter*, 9, 1.

Power, S., Aggleton, P., Brannen, J., Brown, A., Chisholm, L. and Mace, J. (eds) (2001), *A Tribute to Basil Bernstein 1924–2000*, London: Institute of Education.

Punnett, M. (1915), 'Ancient History', *Londinian*.

Read, J. (1991), 'Professor Margaret Read, known to our family as Auntie M.', *Institute of Education Society Newsletter*, 6, 2.

Reid, I. (2002), 'Wordsworth institutionalized: the shaping of an educational ideology', *History of Education*, 31, 1.

Reid, L.A. (1965), *Philosophy and the Theory and Practice of Education*, London: Evans Brothers.

Remmling, G. (1975), *The Sociology of Karl Mannheim*, London: Routledge and Kegan Paul.

Richardson, Malcolm (2000), 'A search for genius in Weimar Germany: the Abraham Lincoln Stiftung and American philanthropy', *Bulletin of the German Historical Institute*, 26.

Richardson, Marion (1935), *Writing and Writing Patterns*, London: University of London Press.

—— (1948), *Art and the Child*, London: University of London Press.

Robertson, A.B. (1990), *A Century of Change: The study of education in the University of Manchester*, Manchester: Manchester University Press.

Robinson, W. (1999), 'In search of a "plain tale": rediscovering the champions of the pupil-teacher centres 1900–1910', *History of Education*, 28, 1.

Rose, J. (1992), *Marie Stopes and the Sexual Revolution*, London: Faber and Faber.

Round, E. (1983), 'Way back to Bedford Way', *Institute of Education Society Newsletter*, 2.

Rusk, R. (1961), 'Sir John Adams, 1857–1934', *British Journal of Educational Studies*, X, 1.

Sadler, M. (1935), *John Adams: A lecture in his memory*, London: Oxford University Press.

Sadovnik, A. (ed.) (1995), *Knowledge and Pedagogy: The sociology of Basil Bernstein*, Norwood, New Jersey: Ablex Publishing Corporation.

Sayer, J. (1990), 'The Education Management Unit', *Institute of Education Society Newsletter*, 5, 1.

Selleck, R.J.W. (1972), *English Primary Education and the Progressives, 1914–1939*, London: Routledge and Kegan Paul.

Shairer, G. and Jameson, E. (1938), *Heroes of British Lifeboats*, London: George G. Harrap.

Shorney, D. (1989), *Teachers in Training 1906–1985: A history of Avery Hill College*, London: Thames Polytechnic.

Silver, H. (1975), 'Since James: interviews with Lord James, Roger Webster and James Porter', *British Journal of Teacher Education*, 1, 1.

Simon, B. (1974), *The Politics of Educational Reform 1920–1940*, London: Lawrence and Wishart.

—— (1990), 'The study of education as a university subject', in J.B. Thomas (ed.), *British Universities and Teacher Education: A century of change*, Lewes: Falmer Press.

—— (1998), *A Life in Education*, London: Lawrence and Wishart.

Smith, J. Sharwood (1995), 'Barbara Hodge', *Institute of Education Society Newsletter*, 10, 1.

Smith, L.A.H. (1985), *To Understand and to Help: The life and work of Susan Isaacs (1885–1948)*, London: Associated University Presses.

Spencer, A. (1992), 'Marion Richardson', *Institute of Education Society Newsletter*, 7, 1.

Stewart, W.A.C. (1967), *Karl Mannheim on Education and Social Thought*, London: Harrap.

Sutherland, D. (1988), 'The decline and fall of an empire', *Institute of Education Society Newsletter*, 3, 2.

Taylor, W. (1963), *The Secondary Modern School*, London: Faber and Faber.

—— (1969), *Society and the Education of Teachers*, London: Faber and Faber.

—— (1990), 'Education', in F.M.L. Thompson (ed.), *The University of London and the World of Learning, 1836–1986*, London: Hambledon Press.

—— (1996), 'Education and the Moot', in R. Aldrich (ed.), *In History and in Education: Essays presented to Peter Gordon*, London: Woburn Press.

Teague, S.J. (1980), *The City University: A history*, London: City University.

Thomas, J.B. (1979), 'The curriculum of a day training college. The logbooks of J.W. Adamson', *Journal of Educational Administration and History*, 11, 2.

—— (ed.) (1990), *British Universities and Teacher Education: A century of change*, Lewes: Falmer Press.

Thompson, F.M.L. (ed.) (1990), *The University of London and the World of Learning, 1836–1986*, London: Hambledon Press.

Thoms, D.W. (1980), *Policy-Making in Education: Robert Blair and the London County Council, 1904–1924*, Leeds: University of Leeds.

Tibble, J.W. (1961), 'Sir Percy Nunn, 1870–1944', *British Journal of Educational Studies*, X, 1.

Torres, C.A. (1998), *Education, Power and Personal Biography: Dialogues with critical educators*, London: Routledge.

Tunnicliffe, S.D. (1993), 'Topping out the library', *Institute of Education Society Newsletter*, 8, 1.

Tuke, M.J. (1939), *A History of Bedford College for Women, 1849–1937*, London: Oxford University Press.

University of London Institute of Education (1952), *Jubilee Lectures*, London: Evans Brothers.

—— (1952), *Studies and Impressions, 1902–1952*, London: Evans Brothers.

—— (1971), *An Enquiry into the Education and Training of Teachers in the Area of the Institute 1970/1: An interim report, April 1971*, London: University of London Institute of Education.

—— (1977), *Seventy Fifth Anniversary*, London: Institute of Education.

Vaizey, J. (1958), *The Costs of Education*, London: George Allen and Unwin.

Vernon, P. (1955), 'The assessment of children. Recent trends in mental measurement and statistical analysis', in University of London Institute of Education, *The Bearings of Recent Advances in Psychology on Educational Problems*, London: Evans Brothers.

—— (1960), *Intelligence and Attainment Tests*, London: University of London Press.

Warren, D. (1993), 'Institute Presentation Ceremony', *Institute of Education Society Newsletter*, 8, 2.

Webb, S. (1904), *London Education*, London, Longmans, Green and Co.

Westley, P. (1991), 'Finance Department', *Institute of Education Society Newsletter*, 6, 2.

White, M. (1999), *Thomas Logan Robertson: A biographical study*, Perth: Curtin University of Technology.

Whitehead, C. (1988), '"Not wanted on the voyage": a study of the Colonial Department ULIE 1927–1956', in *DICE Occasional Papers*, 11, London: Institute of Education.

—— (1997), 'The Nestor of British colonial education: a portrait of Arthur Mayhew CIE, CMG (1878–1948)', *Journal of Educational Administration and History*, 29, 1.

Whitty, G. (1997), *Social Theory and Education Policy: The legacy of Karl Mannheim*, London: Institute of Education.

Whitty, G. and Young, M. (eds) (1976), *Explorations in the Politics of School Knowledge*, Driffield: Nafferton Books.

Williams, A.S., Ivin, P. and Morse, C. (2001), *The Children of London: Attendance and welfare at school 1870–1990*, London: Institute of Education.

Williams, G. (1990), 'Centre for Higher Education Studies', *Institute of Education Society Newsletter*, 5, 1.

Willson, F.M.G. (1995), *Our Minerva: The men and politics of the University of London, 1836–1858*, London: Athlone Press.

Wood, A.C. (1953), *A History of the University College Nottingham, 1881–1948*, Oxford: B.H. Blackwell.

Wooldridge, A. (1994), *Measuring the Mind: Education and psychology in England c.1860–c.1990*, Cambridge: Cambridge University Press.

Yates, A. (1972), *The First Twenty-Five Years: A review of the NFER 1946–71*, Slough: NFER.

Young, M. (ed.) (1971), *Knowledge and Control: New directions for the sociology of education*, London: Collier-Macmillan.

—— (1990), 'The Post 16 Education Centre', *Institute of Education Society Newsletter*, 5, 1.

—— (1993), 'The Post 16 Education Centre', *Institute of Education Society Newsletter*, 8, 2.

# Illustrations: sources and acknowledgements

Every effort has been made to trace and acknowledge the origins and copyright owners of the illustrative material used in this book.

Front cover. By courtesy of *The Architectural Review* – photo by Donald Mill.

1. Institute archives.
2. By courtesy of the Passfield Papers, London School of Economics.
3. Institute archives.
4. Institute archives.
5. Institute archives.
6. By courtesy of the North London Collegiate School.
7. By courtesy of the North London Collegiate School.
8. Institute archives.
9. By courtesy of the Museum and Study Collection of the Central Saint Martins College of Art and Design.
10. Institute archives.
11. By courtesy of the London Metropolitan Archives.
12. By courtesy of Associated Newspapers.
13. By courtesy of the London Metropolitan Archives.
14. Institute archives. A copy of the original coloured cartoon is at William Ellis School.
15. Institute archives.
16. By courtesy of Marjorie Dodd.
17. By courtesy of the London Metropolitan Archives.
18. By courtesy of the London Metropolitan Archives.
19. By courtesy of the London Metropolitan Archives.
20. Institute archives.
21. Institute archives
22. Institute archives.
23. Institute archives – photo by Reginald Haines.
24. Institute archives.
25. Institute archives – photo by Sally and Richard Greenhill.
26. Institute archives.
27. By courtesy of the London Metropolitan Archives.
28. Newsam Library.
29. By courtesy of the London Metropolitan Archives.
30. By courtesy of the Archives, Royal Holloway, University of London.
31. By courtesy of Claudia Clarke.
32. Institute archives.
33. By courtesy of the Royal National Lifeboat Institution.
34. Institute archives.
35. Institute archives.
36. Institute archives – photo by Sally and Richard Greenhill.
37. Institute archives.
38. By courtesy of the University of Nottingham Department of Manuscripts and Special Collections, ref. ACC 253/1/39.
39. By courtesy of the London Metropolitan Archives.
40. By courtesy of the London Metropolitan Archives.
41. Institute archives.
42. Institute archives – photo by Frank G. Logan.
43. Institute archives.
44. Institute archives.
45. Institute archives.
46. From a pencil drawing by Michael Noakes, 1974, in the Newsam Library.
47. Institute archives.
48. Institute archives.
49. Institute archives.

50. By courtesy of Marion Waller.
51. By courtesy of Marion Waller.
52. Institute archives – photo by Larkin Bros.
53. By courtesy of Norman Graves.
54. Institute archives.
55. Institute archives – photo by Sally and Richard Greenhill.
56. Institute archives.
57. Institute archives – photo by Sally and Richard Greenhill.
58. Institute archives – photo by Sally and Richard Greenhill.
59. Institute archives – photo by Format Photographers.
60. Institute archives – photo by Mike Tomlinson.
61. Institute archives – photo by Caroline Rees.
62. Institute archives.
63. Institute archives.
64. Institute archives – photo by Sally and Richard Greenhill.
65. Institute archives.
66. Institute archives – photo by Sally and Richard Greenhill.
67. Institute archives.
68. Institute archives – photo by Sally and Richard Greenhill.
69. From the portrait by Ying S. Yang, 1997, in the Newsam Library.
70. Institute archives – photo by Sally and Richard Greenhill.
71. Institute archives – photo by Success Photography.
72. From a desk in the Newsam Library.
73. Institute archives.
74. Institute archives.
75. Institute archives – photo by Sally and Richard Greenhill.
76. Institute archives – photo by Success Photography.
77. Institute archives – photo by Sally and Richard Greenhill.
78. Institute archives – photo by Success Photography.
79. Institute archives – photo by Success Photography.
80. Institute archives.
81. Institute archives – photo by Success Photography.

# Index